Sasha Graham

365 TAROT SPREADS

About the Author

Sasha Graham teaches tarot classes and produces tarot events at New York City's premier cultural institutions, including the Metropolitan Museum of Art. She has shared her love of tarot on film, television, radio, and print. She resides in New York City. Visit her online at sashagraham.com.

Sasha Graham

365 TAROT SPREADS

REVEALING THE MAGIC IN EACH DAY

Llewellyn Publications
WOODBURY, MINNESOTA

SEVENTH PRINTING, 2019
First Edition

Author photo by Karl Giant
Book design and edit by Rebecca Zins
Cover design by Kevin R. Brown
Cover and interior images: *Universal Tarot* by R. De Angelis © Lo Scarabeo;
iStock.com/6524824/Chapman and Smith

LIBRARY OF CONGRESS CATALOGING-IN-PUBLICATION DATA
Graham, Sasha.
365 tarot spreads : revealing the magic in each day / Sasha Graham.—First Edition.
pages cm
ISBN 978-0-7387-4038-6
1. Tarot. 2. History—Miscellanea. I. Title. II. Title: Three hundred sixty-five tarot spreads. III. Title: Three hundred and sixty-five tarot spreads.
BF1879.T2G6565 2014
133.3'2424—dc23

2013046321

Llewellyn Publications
A Division of Llewellyn Worldwide Ltd.
2143 Wooddale Drive
Woodbury MN 55125-2989
www.llewellyn.com
Printed in the United States of America

THIS IS FOR
Isabella, Mackenzie, and Skylar.
Never stop questioning.

Contents

The important thing is
not to stop questioning.
Curiosity has its own reason
for existing. One cannot
help but be in awe when he
contemplates the mysteries
of eternity, of life, of the
marvelous structure of reality.
It is enough if one tries
merely to comprehend a little
of this mystery every day.
Never lose a holy curiosity.

~ Albert Einstein

Introduction

Sometimes an author chooses the subject; other times the subject chooses the author. *365 Tarot Spreads* was a case of the latter; this book chose me.

You'll discover, as I did, a plethora of 365 books if you look for them. Daily books of spells, goddesses, simple advice, daily living, sexual positions, creativity guides, meditations, journaling suggestions, recipes, happiness boosters, motivations, and ideas *ad infinitum* for each day of the year.

I was pleasantly surprised to discover no tarot book for each day of the year existed, especially since for many cartomancers (a fancy name for tarot lovers), tarot is a hallowed daily practice. Pulling daily cards is not only an excellent tarot learning tool but a ritual for what I'd imagine are hundreds of thousands of readers.

Even my sister, director of a large drug addiction rehabilitation facility in the healing airs of Malibu, California, pulls a card from her mermaid deck for guidance and inspiration before important meetings. She wouldn't describe herself as a tarotist, but she understands the importance of a clear, concise message or theme when one is needed and the usefulness of a card as a focal point when focus is called for.

This is the sublime nature of tarot: tarot pulls focus. It gives your attention a resting point. The dialogue a reader has with their cards is a rapid-fire, emotion-filled experience leading to informed decision-making and change. Why? Because we tend to live in our heads and in the experience of our brains. Tarot brings us out of ourselves. It moves our perception outwards and onto the cards before us. Rather than living with the possibility imagined in our mind's eye, the possibility is spread on the table before us. This small bit of space—this foot or two of distance between reader and cards—allows us perspective. Like the value of age and wisdom, tarot spreads allow us to step back, reevaluate, and consider motives, actions, and outcomes from a different vantage point. In this space intuition leaps to life and we actively listen for guidance.

For many of us, this is done on a daily basis. So why not create a tarot spread for each and every day of the year?

On Questioning

The root of a question is a quest—a journey, act, or instance of seeking or pursuing something. A tarot reading is a search, a journey, a quest for truth. Tarot decks lie in wait for your questions: "What do I want to know, see, meditate on—?" The first thing a tarot reader asks the client is, "What do you want to know?" To come to tarot is to come with a curious mind. A tarot spread can alter the course of your life—or not; it is entirely up to you. Will you sit on the information gathered or will you act on it?

At some point in the process of writing this book, it occurred to me that there must be a set number of questions someone could ask about themselves and their life. While each individual's journey is infinite, the language surrounding the journey, the articulation of those questions, must have a set limit. The questions wouldn't include the likes of "What makes volcanoes erupt?" though you can ask tarot anything you want. This book is concerned with questions in regard to one's life: "Does he love me? Am I making the right choice? What should I do?" There are small differences in how questions are phrased, but the essential quest, search, desire, and intended or hoped for outcome is essentially a set number. This is why most tarot readings come down to the same few subjects: love, money, career, and life path.

Interestingly, the relatively small number of questions one could ask doesn't make the experience of life feel small; it's quite the opposite. Magic and uniqueness occur in the way we color our existence. We are far from robots operating in a factory line of mindless repetition. A simple description of the human body states two arms, two legs, one heart, one brain. On the surface, this appears simple, set, and staid. But the way we inhabit our bodies is unique. Therein lies infinity. And if you don't believe me, look at the bodies ambling down Forty-Second Street in New York City. Gaze at ballet dancers leaping across the stage. Watch toddlers move. Infinity exists amidst essentials.

Small, finite sets of human existence are apparent everywhere. The twelve signs of the zodiac cover the fundamental qualities indicative of the human psyche, thus millions of people look at the same horoscope and say, "Yes. This is me!" Shakespeare's thirty-seven plays comprise the essential dramatic narrative of human existence. He's told all of our stories. The Hero's Journey is apparent in cross-cultural mythology. Its narrative arc is rife through the major arcana and resonates with every person on earth. All religious dogma boils down to a handful of essential truths. Our life ultimately contains a few vital themes, issues, and problems. We find ourselves continually working out these same issues over and over again. Even sacred geometry tells us nature is made of repetitive patterns. The tiny spiral of a black snail in morning sunlight is the same shape of spiral galaxies light years away in outer space. Everything repeats.

With repetitiveness comes opportunity—a chance to do something again, to cultivate newness, to reach higher, to love deeper, to become smarter. And if we are lucky—if we work hard, if we question well amidst the repetition—something Charles Darwin referred to as "saltation" occurs: *the pattern changes.*

On Being Human

The Epic of Gilgamesh is one of humanity's earliest surviving works of literature and the subject of a college lecture I think of often. "Why do we care?" asks Ron Long, professor of religion at Hunter College. "Why bother to read this ancient story? Why does it matter?" Great question. Why consider an old story like *Gilgamesh*? Why study a 4,000-year-old adventure about two best friends?

"It matters," Long explains, "because it is what makes us human." The second half of the epic focuses on Gilgamesh's heartbreak and distress when his best friend is killed. Gilgamesh's sorrow is excruciating and sends him off on a quest for immortality. Long's point is that the sudden loss of a best friend for a person living 4,000 years ago is as heartfelt, as tragic, as it is for us today. Four thousand years later we remain the same delicate, fragile, and emotional creatures we have always been. External circumstances may be different—we may fly in airplanes rather than ride camels to traverse deserts—but at our core, we are the same. We are human.

Approaching *365 Tarot Spreads*, I encountered, once again, that not much separates us from our ancestors or our neighbors. The challenge was writing a book where anyone, anywhere, could discover a set of questions applicable to their current situation, desires, and needs—to make it possible for anyone, in any situation, to find articulation for their quest.

It is the same goal a professional tarot reader faces: to offer insight and information to the people who come to them. People from all walks of life cross the path of the professional reader: young, old, wealthy, poor, bored, excited, depressed, enthused. The professional tarot reader becomes an inadvertent sociologist. Within the intimate framework of a reading, be it a five- or fifty-minute session, as complete strangers bare their hearts and souls, a delicate lesson is learned and relearned. We are the same. *We are human.*

From Superbowl athletes to Little League coaches, from movie starlets to housekeepers, from the wealthy to the poor, it doesn't matter; each person yearns for love and validation as much as you do. People's questions are the same. No matter class, color, or creed, everyone wants love, security, and acceptance from their peers. Everyone desires a sense of belonging and purpose. Our essential needs and desires remain the same.

I get the feeling that if any of us sat in ancient Babylon in the corner of a bar, reading tarot for those Babylonians, the questions asked would be the same questions people ask today because we are all human. We all feel scared, we all feel rejection, we are all uncertain, we all have highs and lows. At our core we are all the same.

Why does any of this matter? *Because it means we are not alone.*

On Time

Writing a book for each day of the year, one begins to consider with greater interest the nature of a calendar. What is it and why? Calendars exist to mark the passage of time. Ancient people crawled out of caves, and as summer days grew longer, they knew more sunlight meant greater safety from the hungry beasts lurking in darkness. Our first calendars were the glittering constellations, our night sky. In agricultural societies, calendars let us know when to plant and harvest. Calendar knowledge equaled survival. The Industrial Revolution brought calendars and clocks telling factory workers when to get up and go to work. We are not much different than our farming or factory-working forebears. We use time to coordinate busy lives, careers, schedules, knowing when and where to be. At the movies, we calculate with precision the time it takes to get our popcorn before the previews begin.

But time offers us something more on a profound level: security. Life's true nature is terrifying; it is random. On a deep level we intellectually realize Earth is literally spinning beneath our feet, hurtling through space. We know, on the other side of the world, people are literally upside down from us but feel right-side up to themselves. We know from the painful lessons of tragedy that life can change in the blink of an eye. But time is something we can depend upon. Humanity's agreement of time is regulated. If you buy a ticket to see Bruno Mars next Saturday at 8 PM, 25,000 other people will show up right alongside you to hear the Mars man sing. The dependability and agreeability of time makes it a comforting thing, so calendars prevail and a year is sliced into 365 sunrises and sunsets.

But time is a slippery subject. None of us know how much time we have. When we find out our time is up, it will be too late. Why, when we were ten years old, did a summer last forever but fly in the blink of an eye at age thirty? Maybe because children live in terms of possibility, while adults tend to live in relation to the past. We all fall prey to living in relation to the past. But tarot intercedes. Tarot contains a gift. Tarot, like childhood, presents us with the possible. Each time we flip a card, we sense the possibility. This is why no matter how many years you've worked with tarot, every time you pull a card feels like the first time you've ever done so; it's why tarot never loses its excitement. Tarot makes virgins of all of us.

Author Jeanette Winterson says time stops everything from happening at once. She says there are two times: that time belonging to the outer world—to the calendar, Earth's revolutions around the sun—and time in our personal inner world, our inner landscape. Inside ourselves, we experience events as if time were happening simultaneously. To challenge linear time, realize that events separated by years lie side by side imaginatively and emotionally inside of you. She suggests an attempt to live in total time. While abiding by the time on my computer, I simultaneously feel the warmth of my first real kiss, the thrill running down my spine, the smell of his skin, the song playing in the background. I am fourteen and I am forty-two, in two places at once. Can you do this? Of course you can. You are a supernatural creature. You too can live in total time.

It is the province of the tarot reader to move backwards, forwards, even sideways in time. It is what we do best. Readers, our cards—our imaginations—lie outside of calendar time. These are the highways, landscapes, and environments visited by shamans, artists, seers, and mystics—the world of the imagination. Story, essence, truth, gods, eternity, and symbols exist here. This is why tarot is a gateway to worlds of esoteric study, why tarot is an entrance to the occult. Because what is hidden can only be revealed by experience. Archetypes are experiential. Tarot is experiential.

This is what Greece's ancient mystery schools offered. Their lessons could not be taught, explained, or orated. The lessons had to be experienced. You can't know the mystery until you experience the mystery. A boy in a New Guinea tribe cannot be lectured on his initiatory experience. He is given tools for survival for his three-day initiation in the woods. He is equipped and taught to fend off wild beasts, but his experience occurs alone. He quests for himself. He comes through the process changed. This is exactly what the Fool does. This is what tarot does.

It is what you will do if you allow it. This quest occurs outside of calendar time. It is entirely internal. And *365 Tarot Spreads* is here for you on the outside, provoking you with questions and ideas when you need them.

I hope you enjoy this book—hope it aids you, no matter your quest. May the roads you choose be filled with magic and wonder, with galaxies of possibility and oceans of love. Hopefully you'll never have to use the Heartbreak Spread, the Rejection Spread, or the Lawsuit Spread. But life is full of bumps and bruises just as it is full of soft baby kisses and snuggles, so the spreads are there in case you need them.

I hope you find your truth and that when you do, you stand in the middle of it strong, beautiful, and nimble like the World dancer. Because when the Fool followed her own path and trusted herself, she found herself in the World. And by the time she did, she was so high on the music—so enraptured by the dancing, so lost in the beauty, so in tune with herself, and so filled with magic—she didn't even realize that she'd arrived at her destination.

Sasha Graham
NEW YORK CITY, 2013

January • 1

Vision Board Spread

Julius Caesar established January 1 as the first day of the year in 46 BCE. This was partly to honor the god Janus, for whom January is named.

The Hermit shuts himself from the world to cultivate wisdom. This equates with the meditative state one enters when going through the process of selecting images. When the Hermit emerges, he shines his vision from his lamp, a six-pointed star. It lights the path of enlightenment for those who would follow.

On This Day

Welcome to the first day of the year! New Year's resolutions have been made; many will be broken. Now is the perfect time to create a vision board to usher the bold and beautiful into your life. Rather than merely contemplating resolutions, a vision board helps you spring toward action.

Summation of Spread

A vision board is a collection of images placed where you can see it clearly. You select and assemble images to bring change, manifestation, and direction into your life. Use the Vision Board Spread whenever you begin construction on a new vision board.

Cast Your Cards

This spread lays out like a vision board. Use this spread for inspiration while creating your dreams in visual form. Nine questions are proposed because nine is the number of wish fulfillment. Cast your cards well—and happy visioning!

1. What is the overriding theme of my vision board?
2. What are my wildest dreams?
3. What types of images resonate with me?
4. Can I let go emotionally and mentally in my selection process?
5. Where do I want to travel?
6. How do I want to make a difference?
7. What do I want to attract into my life?
8. What tiny adjustment can I make to manifest this vision board?
9. What happens when I take action on my dreams?

Speak with Ancestors Spread

On This Day

Ancestors' Day (*Jour des Aieux*) occurs today on the tropical island of Haiti. The celebration rings in the new year while honoring the past. Haitians remember those who have died within the previous twelve months and pay homage to those who perished fighting for Haitian independence in the early nineteenth century.

Summation of Spread

Would you like to speak to your ancestors? Communicate with the spirit world using tarot. Conversations with guides, angels, and ancestors will spring forth between cards and candle. Use this spread to converse with souls of family members who have gone before you.

Cast Your Cards

Family magic and wisdom is collected by casting your cards in the shape of a family tree.

1. Who am I speaking with?
2. What talent thrives in our family?
3. What is the overlying challenge or lesson of our family?
4. What is the legacy I hold?
5. What are your hopes for me?
6. How do I make the most with what I have inherited?
7. What must I do?

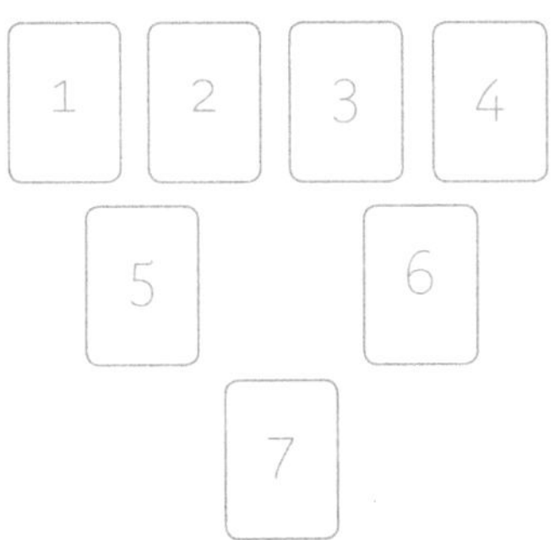

How do you know you are really communicating with an ancestor? Tarot teacher Ruth Ann Amberstone explains, "Simply trust yourself. You will know when they are speaking. You will know when they have left."

The Ten of Pentacles represents pedigree, bloodlines, and the family tree. Complete, strong, and resistant to the ravages of time, it is the card of evolution and kindred connection. Drawing this card is a reminder we play but a small role in the tapestry of a larger generational story.

Protection Spread

Everyone reacts to subtle energies, whether we realize it or not. People, events, animals, and the natural world all affect how we feel.

On This Day

The feast of Saint Genevieve, patron saint of Paris, is celebrated today. Genevieve reported frequent visions of heavenly saints and angels from a young age. Graced with clairvoyance and miracle working, it is said her prayers and fasting saved Paris from a harrowing attack from Attila the Hun in 451 CE. Legend also states when her relics (pieces of her body kept as objects of reverence) were carried through the streets during the Parisian plague in 1129, she miraculously intervened to stop the spread of the plague as the death toll plummeted.

Summation of Spread

Channel St. Genevieve's good graces when you feel the need for extra strength and protection. The questions ponder from whom, how, and why you might need extra security and care.

Cast Your Cards

Witches often raise cones of energy (recall the symbolism of a witch's hat) when needing kinetic protection. Imagine a cone of protective white light around you while casting your cards.

1. Am I open to the influence of others?
2. What energy surrounds me?
3. Is there energy I must be aware of?
4. Who aids me?
5. What protection can I count on?
6. How can I ground myself?
7. What should I do to protect myself?

1

2 3

4 5

6 7

The Queen of Wands maintains the strongest energetic field in the deck because she commands the element of fire, passion, and spirituality. If you plan on reading tarot for others, energetic protection and grounding is important. It is possible to unintentionally absorb the querent's energies, both positive and negative.

Big Purchase Spread

On This Day

Industrialist Cornelius Vanderbilt, one of the wealthiest men of American history, died on this day in 1877. Leaving most of his fortune to his son Henry, who doubled it, this patriarch is ancestor to Gloria Vanderbilt and Anderson Cooper. The Vanderbilts created luxurious residences, many of which are open today for public touring, and left a legacy of philanthropy including Vanderbilt University and the Medical School at Columbia University.

Cornelius Vanderbilt embodied the American dream. Quitting school at age eleven, he started a ferry business shuttling passengers between Manhattan and Staten Island. On his deathbed, he'd amassed a 100-million-dollar fortune in shipping and railroads.

Summation of Spread

Are you about to make a large purchase? The Big Purchase Spread uses captains of finance for inspiration when contemplating financial decisions. Summon a Vanderbilt with your cards and invest wisely.

The Ace of Pentacles represents the revitalization of finance, new forms of income, and the manifestation of a goal. The fertile garden indicates that growth is essential. Money spent is returned twofold, and often it represents a financial windfall or inheritance.

Cast Your Cards

Is the item in question worth the money you are about to spend? Cast the cards to discover your answer.

1. Can I borrow it?
2. What will I do with it?
3. How often will I use it?
4. Do I really even want it?
5. Can I really afford it?

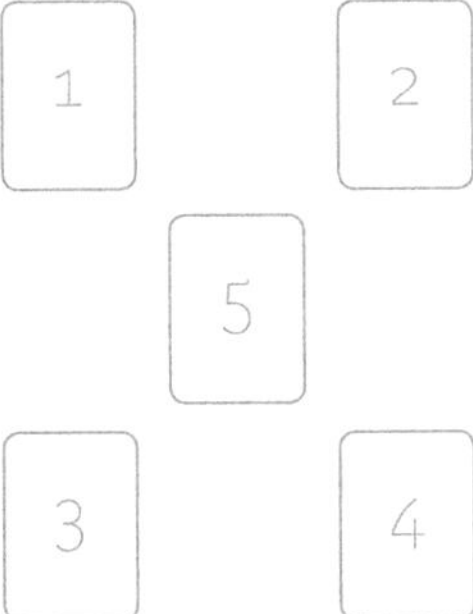

Bird's-Eye View Spread

Birds are often seen as messengers, heralds of change, or spirits of the deceased. Their singing wakes us with the spirit of instinct, inner voice, and the beginning and end to our days.

The Nine of Pentacles holds a fierce falcon on her delicately gloved hand. This falcon represents loyalty. Bird images in tarot represent the highest aspects of our being taking flight and the ability to reach beyond our normal perceptions and boundaries.

On This Day

National Bird Day is observed today. Dedicated to the admiration and preservation of birds, it also raises people's awareness for birds held in captivity. Unbound by human laws of nature, birds often represent a link between conscious and subconscious, heaven and earth, groundedness and possibility. Birds are universally understood as a symbol for soul, anima, freedom, or the world soul hidden in matter.

Summation of Spread

Muddled by decisions? Confused about your path? Taking a bird's-eye view offers a unique way to evaluate your life and choices. This helpful strategy asks you to float up and look at your life from a bird's perspective. This wide angle renders small things as they truly are—insignificant—and focuses on what is truly important in the grand scheme of life.

Cast Your Cards

Shuffle your cards while thinking about the question at hand. Eyes closed, start throwing cards on the table in front of you. Look down like a god from above to discover which cards land upright and face you. Read these cards left to right to answer the Bird's-Eye View Spread's questions.

1. What is my situation?
2. What didn't I see before?
3. How do I best see the overall view?
4. What becomes apparent when looking down from above?
5. Where am I heading?
6. What is truly important?
7. What should I remember?
8. What is my message?

Kick a Bad Habit Spread

Every habit starts with a psychological pattern called a "habit loop." This three-part process begins with a trigger, is followed by a routine, and ends with behavior. Understanding cue, routine, and reward, simply change the routine to something healthy and positive.

On This Day

Today, the twelfth day after Christmas, or Twelfth Night, is known as Little Christmas in Ireland. Older calendars that use the Julian calendar mark today as the traditional Christmas celebration. Modern practices dictate today as the traditional end of the holiday season, when trimmings are removed and festoons are swept away till next year.

Summation of Spread

Why not rid a bad habit as you clean? Remove decorations and make this task a magical metaphor. Decide a bad habit will be removed right along with holiday frill. This spread helps you identify and remove pesky habits, and it's best done before decoration removal.

Cast Your Cards

In your mind's eye, picture yourself free of the habit. Imagine yourself as you'd like to be. In a calm and focused manner, cast the cards in the shape of the holiday garland soon to be removed.

1. My habit.
2. Why do I have this habit?
3. Why does it need to go?
4. What helps end the habit?
5. What happens when it is gone?
6. What challenges me?
7. What supports me?
8. What can I keep in mind when struggling?
9. What is my result?

Swords are the wickedly sharp suit of elimination. Swords can feel frightful because they represent thoughts, calculation, and change. Embrace the fierceness of a sword when slicing away a habit.

Excellent Eating Habits Spread

Fannie Farmer suffered a stroke at age sixteen. Unable to walk, she took up cooking, giving her mother's boarding house a reputation for amazing meals. Publishing cookbooks and opening a cooking school, her story reminds us that our greatest tragedies often define who we are.

The Three of Pentacles depicts three figures in discussion about the building of a sacred space. Often representing collaboration, you can also understand this card as growing in healthy ways and the sacred space being your body.

On This Day

The Fannie Farmer Cookbook, a gastronomic classic, was published this day in 1896. Its emphasis on good foods, fresh flavor, and variety is why it remains a favorite to this day.

Summation of Spread

The consumption and preparation of food is a connection to the life force itself—an opportunity to indulge in pleasure and health simultaneously. If you plan to change eating habits, emphasize the positive rather than dwell on the negative. This spread focuses on cultivating excellent eating habits.

Cast Your Cards

Notice bright sunlight dappling your kitchen, feel the health radiating from a juicy apple, and cast your cards.

1. What role does food play in my life?
2. Do I ever abuse myself with food?
3. How can I nurture myself with food?
4. How does food tie in to my emotional state?
5. When do I eat most unhealthily?
6. What habitual eating pattern is most important to change?
7. What encourages me to eat natural, unprocessed foods?
8. What helps me plan ahead for better eating?
9. What is a small step I can take right now?

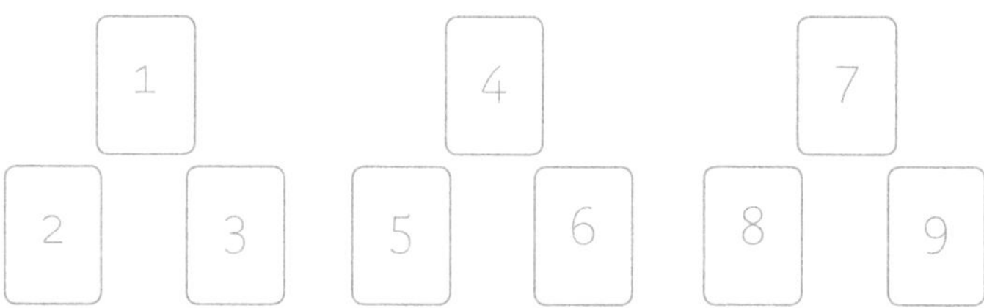

Get Out of Debt Spread

On This Day

In 1835, President Andrew Jackson rose to make an announcement few presidents have had the honor of making: "Gentlemen, the national debt is PAID." It was the first time the nation was debt-free, and it lasted for one year.

Summation of Spread

Being debt-free releases anxiety, allows you to save, and gives you the freedom to choose what you spend money on. Today's spread uses this auspicious day to begin a dialogue with yourself about your debt situation.

Cast Your Cards

Imagine yourself debt-free. Take a breath. Know that you build confidence and stability with each card you cast.

1. What is a core reason I got into debt?
2. How much debt do I really have?
3. Do I use my credit card to pay for basics?
4. Do I buy things I do not have cash for?
5. Do I lie to others about what I spend money on?
6. Do I borrow money from friends and family?
7. Can I stop going over the amount I have budgeted for myself?
8. Can I honestly start tracking my spending?
9. Can I create a financial approach that will work?
10. What is the result of implementing my plan?

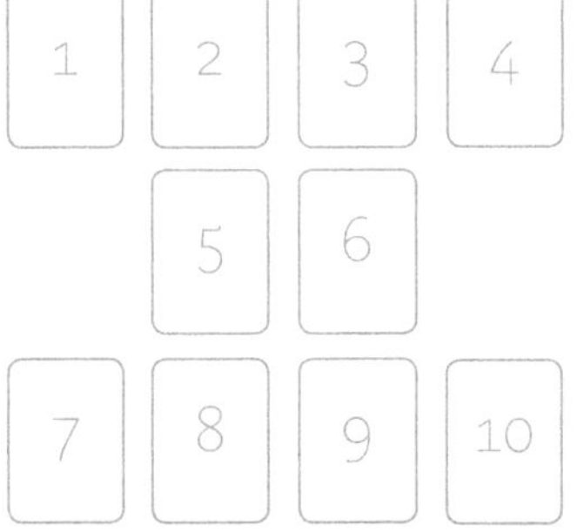

Not all debt is bad. Borrowing for a home or education makes financial sense if you do not over-borrow and can afford the monthly payments.

The King of Pentacles is associated with great wealth. He excels in business, real estate, and practical matters, and he is serious about his financial situation. His scepter represents power and he sits in the very kingdom he has created. He is generous, reliable, and patient.

Mermaid Magic Spread

Mermaid skin is known to be hard as diamonds, protecting the creature from the cold watery depths. It is often said a mermaid caress upon human skin leaves a shimmering mark like fairy dust.

The Queen of Cups connects to mermaid magic as she rules from her throne at the sea. Speaking the language of whales and dolphins, her elusive watery emotional qualities make for empathy whose depths know no bounds.

On This Day

Christopher Columbus, sailing near the Dominican Republic, spotted three mermaids on this day in 1493. He reported them to be "not half as beautiful as they are painted." In truth, Columbus was looking at manatees, slow-moving aquatic mammals with gentle eyes and large, long bodies.

Summation of Spread

Mermaid legends have existed in seafaring cultures since ancient Greece. Some folklore states they can take human form and marry men. Sensual, elusive, and undeniably female, mermaid symbolism inspires questions designed to unleash mermaid magic in your life.

Cast Your Cards

Toss your long locks, bask in the sun, smell salty sea air, and cast your cards.

1. Elusiveness: How can I remain mysterious to the one I love?
2. Mystery: What mystery am I unraveling?
3. Allure: Which of my personal qualities is most alluring?
4. Privacy: What must be kept under wraps?
5. Sensuality: How should I indulge my sensuality?
6. Love: What do I love more than anything?
7. Untamed: What do I cling to that must run free in my life?
8. Tidal Waters: Where is the tide of my life bringing me?
9. Movement: Am I fighting the tide or moving with it?

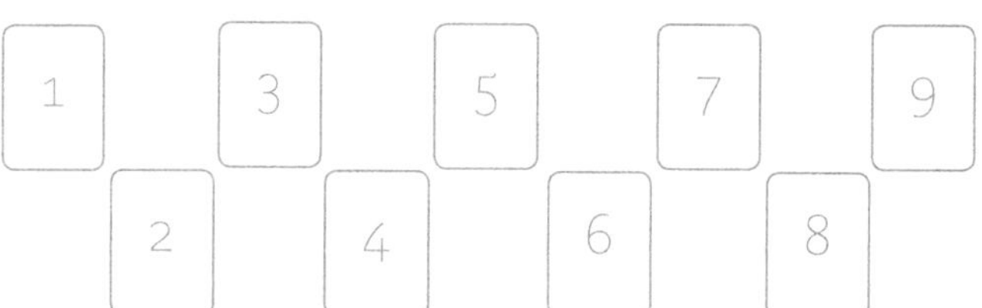

Georgia O'Keeffe's Activate the Muse Spread

On This Day

Artist Georgia O'Keeffe was awarded the Presidential Medal of Freedom by President Ford today in 1977. Famous for her large-scale flower paintings and rock-and-bone New Mexico subjects, O'Keeffe is one of the great artists of the twentieth century.

Summation of Spread

In addition to her own work, Georgia O'Keeffe acted as primary muse to her husband, photographer Alfred Stieglitz. His early nudes of O'Keeffe caused a huge sensation. By retirement, he'd made over 350 portraits of her. This spread uses the couple's creative process to help you invoke your muse.

Cast Your Cards

Muses derive from Greek mythology. Modern usage refers to them as something or someone with the ability to excite innovative passions and call forth fertile creative ideas and illuminations. This spread seeks your muse to aid in any project. To find her, clear the decks and cast your cards.

1. Where is my muse?
2. How can I bring her close to me?
3. When will I know she is here?
4. What does she like?
5. What does she want me to create?
6. How does she help me?
7. What can we achieve together?

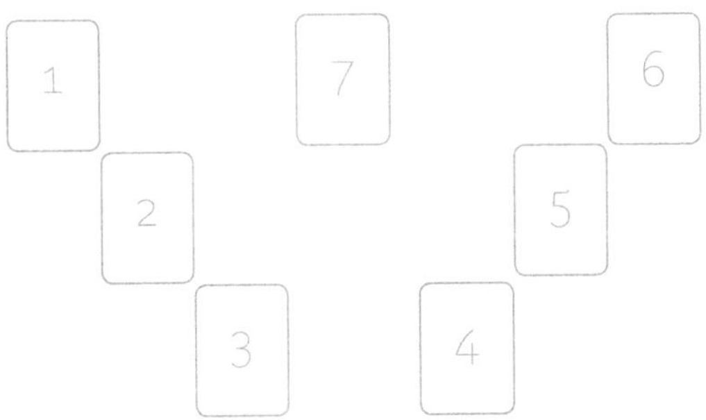

Ancient Greeks held Muses as the inspiration for literature, science, and the arts. Nine muses inspired specific subjects: Epic Poetry, History, Love Poetry, Song, Tragedy, Hymns, Dance, Comedy, and Astronomy.

The Queen of Swords is associated with novelists and writers of all sorts due to her keen finesse with words and articulation. Note the Queen of Swords' hand gesture. Her extended hand represents an invitation and activation of the muse.

Gratitude Spread

Scientific studies show gratitude improves health and the immune system. A gratitude practice can be created in just two minutes a day. Commit to setting a regular time of day to write down why, what, and who you are thankful for.

The Ace of Cups represents the healthy expression of emotions. The Ace of Cups suggests inner attunement and spiritual dynamism. You can trust what your feelings are telling you and it is safe to be emotionally honest. The chalice itself is representative of a ceremonial vessel indicating its intrinsic value.

On This Day

Today is International Thank You Day, dedicated to spreading joy and offering gratefulness to anyone who brightens our day and enriches our lives.

Summation of Spread

Gratitude brings an emotional shift almost instantly. Some studies even claim it can increase happiness by 25 percent. This spread focuses on what, why, and how you can feel grateful.

Cast Your Cards

Take a moment to consider the blessings of life. Cast the cards in the shape of a smiling face.

1. Why should I be thankful for my health?
2. Why am I good at the work I do?
3. To whom do I owe gratitude?
4. Do I thank people enough?
5. How can I practice gratitude every day?
6. How can I find the time for a gratitude practice?
7. How can I be thankful even when I don't feel it?

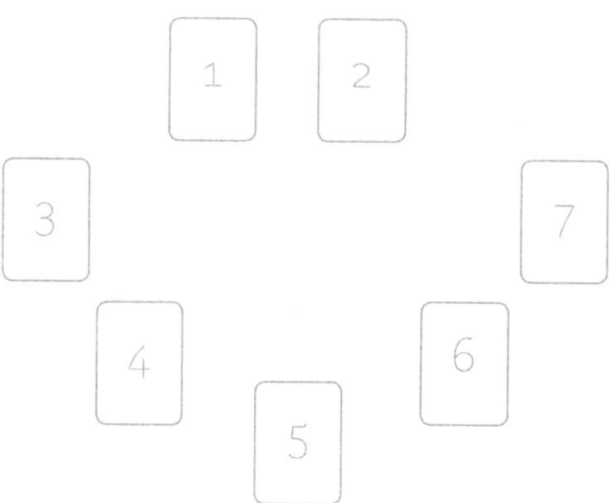

X-ray Vision Spread

On This Day

Three students at Davidson College, North Carolina, illegally produced some of the first x-ray images ever seen on this night in 1896. Bribing a janitor for use of the campus medical lab, they x-rayed a variety of objects, including a human finger they had sliced from a cadaver with a pocketknife.

Summation of Spread

Who wouldn't love the ability to see through items, people, and walls? X-ray vision is a popular superpower for heroes like Superman. Luckily, tarot can take an x-ray survey of any situation you encounter.

Cast Your Cards

Using your powers of perception wisely, cast the cards of the X-ray Vision Spread in the shape of an X to mark the spot.

1. How does the situation appear from the outside?
2. What is the unseen truth on the inside?
3. What unseen elements are at play that I am ignorant of?
4. What element is in my favor?
5. What action should I take now that I see the truth?

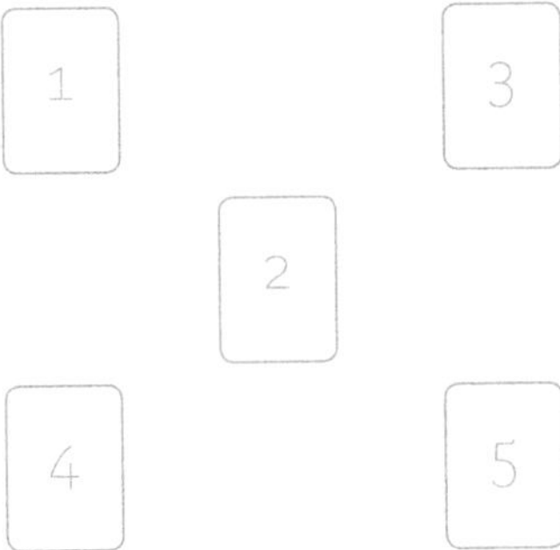

The x-ray uses an X because when German physicist Wilhelm Roentgen discovered a new form of radiation by accident in 1895, he did not know what it was. Therefore, he called it an x-ray.

The Page, or Knave, of Swords, often described as the Nancy Drew of the tarot deck, possesses x-ray vision that he projects at will. His searching eyes and rapid-fire brain see through any deception, straight to the heart of the matter, and discover the truth to any situation.

January • 13

Knights Templar Spread

Friday the thirteenth is considered an inauspicious day because the Grand Master of the Knights Templar, Jacques de Molay, along with hundreds of Templars, was arrested and imprisoned on Friday, October 13, 1307.

On This Day

The Knights Templar were sanctioned by Pope Honorius today in 1128. The Templars grew in size and popularity, gaining so much wealth and influence that by 1307, King Philip of France and Pope Clement V conspired to bring them down. Tortured into false confessions and convicted of heresy, sacrilege, and satanism, many burned at the stake.

Summation of Spread

Knights swear with oaths, vows, and codes of conduct, and these pledges color future actions. The questions in this spread are based on the core tenets of knighthood.

Cast Your Cards

The Knights Templar wore distinctive white mantles with a red cross. Cast your cards in the form of their familiar cross.

1. Why should I release material concerns?
2. How can I correct injustice?
3. What tyranny in my life goes unchecked?
4. What does it mean to live honorably?
5. What does it mean to be noble?
6. Why is it important to be courteous of others?
7. How can I be more honest with myself?
8. What secret do the Templars bestow to me?

Tarot knights are often messengers bearing news. Read the energy of your situation by paying close attention to the speed of the knight's horses. A fast horse equals a speedy resolution, while a slow horse means more time will elapse.

Make Up for Wrongdoing Spread

On This Day

The colony of Salem, Massachusetts, officially regretted the horror and injustice of the Salem witch hunt with a day of fasting on this day in 1697.

Summation of Spread

Though one day of fasting hardly makes up for the inhumane deaths of over a dozen people, making amends for wrongdoing is important. If you've ever found yourself in the wrong, this spread will help you make it right.

Cast Your Cards

This spread surveys the situation, creating a ladder moving upwards toward healing. Consider your actions and cast your cards.

1. What did I do?
2. Why did I do it?
3. Why was it wrong?
4. Can I accept responsibility for my actions?
5. Why do I need to make amends?
6. How can I make it right?
7. How can I best prepare to make it right?
8. Final outcome.

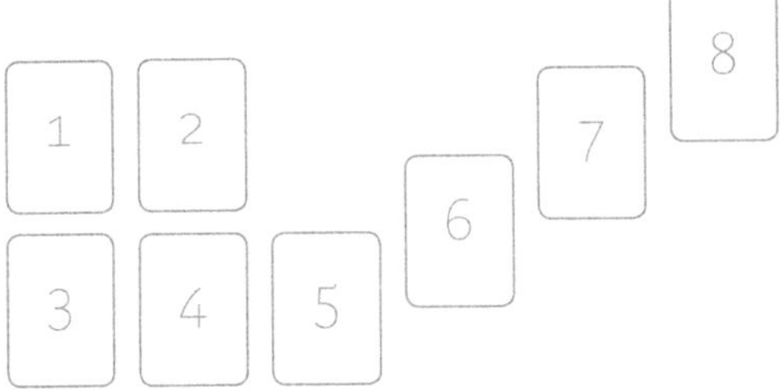

Witch hunts in Europe and North America between 1480 and 1750 resulted in an estimated 40,000 to 60,000 executions. Sadly, witch hysteria is not an isolated incident, having been recorded in classical antiquity and even in contemporary Papua New Guinea.

The Ace of Cups suggests acts of love, empathy, and compassion as a way of healing any situation, both toward yourself and the wounded party. The dove represents peace, the water indicates the subconscious mind, and the water lilies symbolize eternal life.

Carmenta's Divination Spread

Carmenta is derived from the Latin carmen, meaning a magic spell, oracle, or song. It is also the root of the English word charm.

On This Day

Today is the feast day of Carmenta, the powerful Italian goddess of divination and childbirth. Chiefly observed by women, this feast celebrated Carmenta and her powers of prophecy. She protected mothers and acted as patron saint of midwives. Pregnant women offered Carmenta rice for a safe delivery, while those desiring fruitfulness ate raspberries to internalize her fertility.

Summation of Spread

Are you ready to invoke the powers of a goddess? Access Carmenta's divination and ultimate feminine graces with this special spread, excellent for personal empowerment on every level.

Like Carmenta, the Empress represents fertility and pregnancy. The Empress, numbered three, corresponds to creativity, spiritual growth, and gratitude. The Mother archetype reminds you to connect with your imagination, earth energies, and the natural world to cultivate grounding and peace.

Cast Your Cards

Imagine you stand before the sacred steps of Carmenta's temple. Offering herbs, stones, and fruit, cast your cards in a circle while asking for her wisdom.

1. How can I use my divinatory skills to their best potential?
2. What magic do I possess?
3. What do I bring to this world?
4. What new beginning should I embark on?
5. How can I embrace my feminine side?
6. What is ready to bloom within me?
7. Why might I settle for less than I'm worth?
8. How do I fix this?
9. What empowering belief does Carmenta want me to incorporate?
10. What is Carmenta's personal message to me?

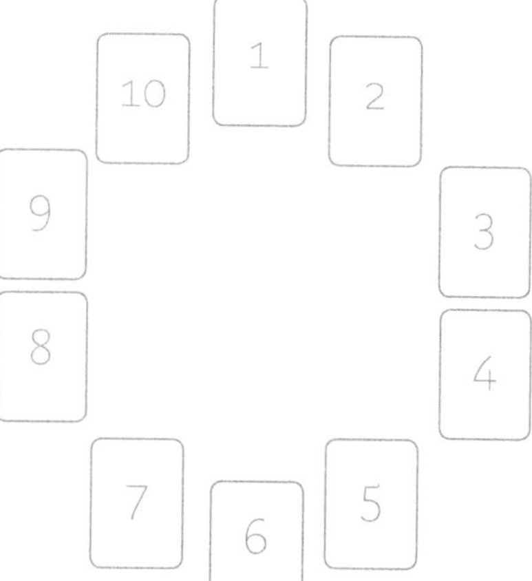

Weight Loss/Gain Spread

On This Day

National Weight Loss Day occurs today in the United States. Focusing on portion control, it aims to help curb appetites and alleviate health issues.

Losing two to three pounds per week is a key number for long range, sustainable weight loss.

Summation of Spread

This spread has been designed to provoke positive, healthy thoughts about weight balance. Reflecting on present behavior is the first step of improvement. The questions are applicable to both weight loss or weight gain.

Cast Your Cards

The cards are cast in the shape of a heart to remind you to love yourself throughout your process of change.

1. How would I feel if I were at my ideal weight?
2. What type of exercise do I enjoy?
3. What does food represent to me?
4. What emotions do I connect with food?
5. Do I eat mindfully?
6. Can I modify my diet myself or do I need help?
7. Do I believe in my ability to change?
8. How do I release old habits and behavior?
9. Have I found the proper strategy to become healthier?
10. What will happen when my body reaches its ideal weight?

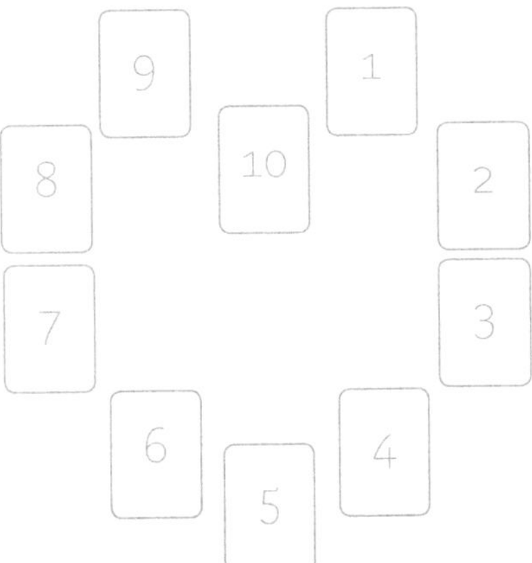

The Temperance card connects to balance and healing and is an excellent card relating to a healthy lifestyle because she blends opposites and avoids extremes. The angel of alchemy mixes and matches for equilibrium. The key to this card is flow, control, and dedication. The healing waters beneath her feet offer renewal akin to a baptismal fountain.

Hidden Desire Spread

Have you ever noticed the word devil *is "lived" spelled backwards?*

On This Day

Majorca, a hot, hedonistic island off the coast of Spain, celebrates the Feast of St. Antoni Festival today. Revelers literally dance with the Devil. Participants dress as devils, dancing from bonfire to bonfire, in honor of a saint who survived a series of horrific demons in a Majorcan cave and lived to tell.

Summation of Spread

The Devil archetype connects to repressed natural urges, and this spread examines of the darker side of our nature. It will guide you to a healthy expression of your deepest, most instinctive desires.

Cast Your Cards

Cast the cards for this spread in the shape of the Dark One's pitchfork.

1. What do I desire but can't express?
2. What does my devilish secret world look like?
3. What hidden desire or theme recurs in my dreams?
4. What relationship do I have to my natural urges such as sex or eating?
5. What pleasure do I seek?
6. What pain do I wish to avoid?
7. Do I desire power over another?
8. Do I desire another to have power over me?
9. Do my secret urges and needs express themselves in unhealthy ways?
10. How can I express my hidden needs in a manner serving my highest good?

1 5
3
2 4 6
7
8
9
10

The Golden Dawn assigned the Devil card the esoteric title of "Laughter," expressing the amount of fun the Devil card contains. The Devil card wants to satisfy all material desires, love, fame, sex, money, pleasure, thirst, and hunger. Where do you draw the line?

Tantric Kundalini Spread

In Sanskrit, kundal *means "coiled."*

On This Day

Sir John George Woodroffe, the man responsible for popularizing Tantric philosophy in the West, passed away on this day in 1936. His hallmark book *The Serpent Power: The Secrets of Tantric and Shaktic Yoga* is the source of many modern Western adaptations of the Kundalini yoga practice.

Summation of Spread

Let your inner serpent rise. Kundalini is described as a dormant force coiled at the base of the spine. Through practice, it rises through the chakras and into the head, producing a profound mystical experience. The Tantric Kundalini Spread is inspired by the notion of your energetic serpent rising through your chakras, lighting you up as it goes.

The Ace of Wands represents the power of Kundalini fire. A symbol of strength, vitality, and energy, this ace provides the transformation of our world through desire.

Cast Your Cards

Imagine the energy at the base of your spine. Feel it moving upwards. For a fun twist, perform this spread on your lover. Have them lie naked on their stomach, and cast the cards along their spine.

1. Root: What can I have?
2. Spleen: What can I feel?
3. Belly: How should I act?
4. Heart: How can I love?
5. Throat: How can I communicate?
6. Third Eye: How can I see truth?
7. Head: How can I best connect?

7
6
5
4
3
2
1

Katharine Hepburn & Spencer Tracy's Soulmate Spread

Many psychics and mediums consider soulmates to be people who have lived and shared various relationships with you in multiple lives as married couples, siblings, and friends. This means we can have more than one soulmate with us in this lifetime.

The Lovers card brings up issues of sex, duality, and choice, while the Two of Cups represents the reflection of oneself in another—the perfect soulmate card. A deep friendship, new romance, or partnership has begun; a kindred spirit has been discovered.

On This Day

Legendary lovers Katharine Hepburn and Spencer Tracy met on the film *Woman of the Year*, released this day in 1942. Their affair would last nearly thirty years, though they never married nor publicly acknowledged their love due to Spencer's marriage.

Summation of Spread

Is your sweetheart your soulmate? Discover the answer with the Soulmate Spread and find out if the relationship is built to last.

Cast Your Cards

Light pink candles for love a few days before the full moon, then cast your cards.

1. Is my sweetheart basically a happy person?
2. Do we want the same type of relationship?
3. Would I want to spend time with this person even if I wasn't attracted to them?
4. Is he or she funny?
5. Is he or she consistent in his or her actions?
6. How well does he or she listen to me?
7. Am I afraid to disagree with him or her?
8. How do we manage conflict together?
9. Do we have similar life priorities?
10. Are we truly soulmates?

Qualities of Aquarius Spread

On This Day

Today marks the first day of the astrological sign of Aquarius, the water bearer.

Summation of Spread

The spread is based on the essential qualities of Aquarius: independent, original, lively, friendly, unpredictable, inventive, and farsighted.

Cast Your Cards

The cards are cast in the form of rippling water, the top half of the symbol, or glyph, of Aquarius.

1. What ties must be cut free?
2. What is my most original quality?
3. What brings me to life?
4. Why are relationships so important?
5. Why is unpredictability a good thing?
6. How does my inventiveness serve me?
7. What is my vision for the future?

Aquarius is ruled by the planet Uranus, its primary color is turquoise, Wednesday is its lucky day, and large cities are their best places for success. Aquarius rules the eleventh house of the zodiac, governing direction.

Like Aquarius, the Star card is about inspiration, optimism, and renewal. Referring to the waters from which we are born, like Aquarius, it refreshes and enlivens us. The Star shines as a beacon of hope, the elixir of peace following the Devil and Tower cards; it's a breakthrough and an opportunity to shine with a higher point of consciousness.

Hug Spread

Human contact and hugging have proven health benefits. Hugging or ten minutes of handholding with a romantic partner can reduce stress and its negative side effects.

Ten of Cups, the "happily ever after" card, depicts physical affection as both couple and children hold each other. Interestingly, the Lovers card relates to sexual intimacy even though no physical contact is displayed.

On This Day

Today is National Hug Day—a chance to show family, friends, or perhaps a special someone how much they mean to you with a warm embrace and a snuggle.

Summation of Spread

Hugs for family and friends are welcome and well received, but the Hug Spread takes a peek at who you want to embrace romantically. Do you dare throw your arms around your special someone?

Cast Your Cards

Get hugging—but before you do, cast your cards.

1. Who do I want to hug?
2. Who wants to hug me?
3. How do I get them in my arms?
4. Will this hug lead to something more?
5. What does this person mean to me?
6. Are we more than friends?
7. Should I pursue this relationship?
8. What should I know that I don't know?

Cleopatra's Needle Spread

On This Day

Cleopatra's Needle, an Egyptian obelisk, was erected in Central Park, NYC, on this day in 1881. Still standing today behind the Metropolitan Museum of Art, it is a reminder of the mystery and magic of ancient Egypt.

Summation of Spread

The Egyptian Book of the Dead explains the complex Egyptian concept of a human soul's life after death. Grave robbing was considered a horrible crime in ancient Egypt. To do so robbed the departed's chance to live in the afterlife. The Cleopatra's Needle Spread uses Egyptian concepts of the afterlife to inform its questions.

Cast Your Cards

Cast the cards in the shape of Cleopatra's obelisk.

1. Ha (physicality): What is the state of my health?
2. Ab (consciousness/heart): What is my intention today?
3. Ka (vital force leaving the body): What makes me feel alive?
4. Sheut (the shadow): What lurks in my darkness?
5. Ren (name): What am I here to do?
6. Akh (transfigured spirit): What lives forever?
7. Ba (soul): Who am I?

1

2

3

4

5

6

7

Cleopatra's Needle has no real connection with the queen of Egypt. The needle's inscriptions by Ramesses II that commemorated his military victories were already over a thousand years old before Cleopatra's lifetime. The needle was moved to one of her temples years after its creation.

The Egyptians describe a profound journey for the soul in the afterlife, just as the major arcana describes a metaphorical journey from the Fool to the World. Some interpretations claim the Fool's pouch contains the four tarot symbols, which he must learn to use during his journey.

Environmental Action Spread

The amount of sunlight that falls on the earth's surface in one minute is sufficient to meet the world's energy demand for one year.

On This Day

Sweden became the first county to ban aerosol sprays on this day in 1978. Doing so because aerosol contains ozone-destroying qualities, they become the first country to lead in environmental action.

Summation of Spread

Earthquakes, tsunamis, and droughts remind us that we live at the mercy of Mother Nature. Damaging the earth, we could well have a hand in our own extinction. Our delicate blue planet's life-sustaining atmosphere is a small bubble of air in an otherwise dark and empty universe. Caring for the earth, we care for ourselves, as we are part of the planet, not separate from it.

The World card connects to the earth from title to meaning. Along with celebration, success, and achievement, the World card represents man's essential symbol, the circle. In its most perfect state, the World card is the path to true liberation.

Cast Your Cards

Cast your cards in the infinite shape of a circle.

1. Why is it important for me to take action?
2. What can I do to protect the environment?
3. How can I reduce my carbon footprint?
4. What does the earth need from me?
5. How do I give back?
6. What can I eliminate?
7. How can I set a good example for others?
8. How can I spend more time outside?

Release Obsessive Thoughts Spread

On This Day

Arctic explorer Ernest Shackleton's ship *Endurance* becomes stuck in ice on this day in 1915. Frozen in packed ice for ten months, the pressure would eventually crush the ship, causing it to sink.

Summation of Spread

Have you ever had thoughts stick in your head like a ship lodged in ice? This is especially frustrating when grappling with tough or painful situations. The trick is to free your mind before tormenting thoughts drive you mad. This spread was created to help you break free when an obsessive thought lodges in your mind.

Cast Your Cards

Free your mind and the rest will follow.

1. Is this a legitimate concern?
2. Will this happen whether I worry about it or not?
3. Are there steps I can take to prepare for the perceived outcome?
4. Am I dwelling too much on the past?
5. Am I doing this to avoid present problems?
6. Is this issue worth the amount of time I'm spending worrying about it?
7. Are there more important issues I should focus on?
8. Can I turn this problem into a hidden opportunity?
9. Is there anyone I can ask for help?
10. What will make it stop?

Buddha described the mind as a drunken monkey's jumping, screeching, and chattering endlessly. Fear, he claimed, was an especially loud monkey that could be tamed by meditation.

The Nine of Swords portrays the pain of obsessive thinking, guilt, and an overworked mind. Her quilt, covered with astrological symbols, represents the need to uncover your eyes and look to the wisdom available.

Evil Villain Spread

A person experiencing bullying often asks, "Why is this person doing this to me? Why is this happening to me?" Most bullying stems from the bully's own issues, not the characteristics of the victim. Usually the bully is the problem, not you.

The court cards represent personality traits. Bully or nemesis behavior can be reflected in card reversals (an upside-down tarot card). Reversals allow you to interpret and examine any number of personality traits as blocked, inverted, or negative.

On This Day

The film *101 Dalmatians* was released on this day in 1961, becoming one of the most popular films of the decade. The film's evil antagonist is Cruella de Vil, who sets out to kidnap a litter of Dalmatian puppies to make a coat from their fur.

Summation of Spread

Is someone being mean to you? The Evil Villain Spread uses the idea of the ultimate antagonist, Cruella, to pose questions on how to deal when you encounter a person displaying cruel behavior.

Cast Your Cards

The Evil Villain Spread's cards are cast in two sections: one representing you and the other representing your nemesis.

1. You
2. The villain
3. Why have they chosen to isolate you?
4. Is there a way to avoid this person?
5. Can I brush off their slings and arrows?
6. How do I nip their behavior in the bud?
7. Why is this person being so cruel?
8. What is their internal struggle?
9. What might make them stop?
10. Who does this person remind you of?
11. What is the ultimate outcome?
12. What is the ultimate lesson of this challenge?

26 • January

Climb Every Mountain Spread

On This Day

Maria von Trapp, inspiration for the film and stage play *The Sound of Music*, was born in Austria on this day in 1905.

Summation of Spread

The Sound of Music's circuitous theme is about facing your fears. Maria—frightened of becoming the nanny, hesitant to fall in love—displays the ultimate act of bravery when she and her family escape the Nazis. Through the story, she rises to meet every obstacle thrown in her path. This spread, inspired by the beloved film, helps face fears and usher a breakthrough.

Cast Your Cards

Toss apprehension aside, plunge ahead, and cast your cards.

1. What is my goal?
2. What is my attitude?
3. When should I begin?
4. What is my challenge?
5. How shall I meet this challenge?
6. What will happen if I give up?
7. What happens if I persevere?
8. Who offers me help?
9. What will I discover?
10. What is my reward?

Real life was far different from the film and stage version. Maria von Trapp admits, "I really and truly was not in love. I liked him but didn't love him. However, I loved the children, so in a way I really married the children…I learned to love him more than I have ever loved before or after."

The Fool climbs every mountain because he doesn't know he shouldn't. The Fool is a constant reminder that life is about the journey, not the destination. He faces northwest, toward the direction of the unknown and untraveled.

Alice in Wonderland Spread

One afternoon Carroll was boating with a few children. Spinning the tale of a bored little girl who sought a very big adventure, the real Alice requested he write it down for her. Obliging her, this became the manuscript for his great novel.

Carroll's Queen of Hearts translates to the Queen of Cups. The traditional card suit of Hearts translates to Cups, Spades to Swords, Clubs to Wands, and Diamonds to Pentacles.

On This Day

Lewis Carroll, author of *Alice's Adventures in Wonderland* and its sequel *Through the Looking-Glass*, was born on this day in 1832.

Summation of Spread

Alice in Wonderland altered the landscape of children's books, pop culture, and fantasy fiction forever. This spread uses Carroll's themes and characters to shed light on your personal life.

Cast Your Cards

Fall down the rabbit hole as you cast your cards.

1. The Rabbit Hole: What adventure is calling me?
2. Pool of Tears: What is making me sad?
3. White Rabbit: What message must I receive?
4. Alice's Size Change: What is changing in my life?
5. Games Afoot: What new rules am I learning?
6. Cheshire Cat: Who is my spirit guide?
7. Mad Hatter: What insanity must I rid from my life?
8. Queen of Hearts: How do I bully myself?
9. Alice's Sister: What is my greatest source of comfort?
10. Wonderland: How can I make my life extraordinary?

End a Family Feud Spread

On This Day

Henry VII was born this day in 1457. Henry Tudor was the last English king to seize the throne on the battlefield. His marriage to Elizabeth of York ended the War of the Roses—a series of bloody civil wars where families fought for control over the English crown—and he was father to the infamous Henry VIII.

The War of the Roses was named for the heraldic symbols of each warring family line, the Lancasters' red rose vs. the Yorks' white rose.

Summation of Spread

Royals aren't the only families apt to feud; no family is immune. Personality conflicts, power and control issues, mental illness, addiction, and any number of reasons cause contention. This spread aims to soothe tensions if you should find yourself in a familial dispute, and it sheds light on proactive ways to end a family disagreement.

The Five of Swords is evocative of a typical family feud involving multiple participants. The suit of Swords deals with communication, calculation, and evaluation. It is a stark reminder to use your words with caution.

Cast Your Cards

As you cast your cards, know the opportunity for peaceful resolution exists.

1. The situation as it stands.
2. Does a middle ground exist?
3. What role do I play in this feud?
4. Is there a personal action I can take to heal?
5. Do I have the strength to truly forgive?
6. Can I be the bigger person and place my feelings aside?
7. What is unsaid?
8. What must be communicated?
9. Would a third party help?
10. Ultimate outcome.

Comfortable bedtime rituals such as warm showers, reading a book, or listening to soothing music all induce a good night's sleep, giving your body subtle clues it is time to wind down and relax.

Sleeping Beauty's Peaceful Night's Sleep Spread

On This Day

The film *Sleeping Beauty* was released on this day in 1959.

Summation of Spread

Ever have trouble sleeping? When a good night's sleep becomes elusive, Sleeping Beauty's image feels painfully out of reach. Using Beauty's slumber as the ultimate goal, this spread examines what you can do to encourage restorative sleep.

Cast Your Cards

Brew a pot of chamomile with extra honey and twists of lemon before casting your cards as the Sandman dances across the Milky Way.

1. What issue is keeping me awake?
2. How can I stick to a regular bedtime schedule?
3. How can I wake at the same time every morning?
4. Are there distractions I can remove?
5. What can I do to make my sleeping space more comfortable?
6. What is the best way to calm my body before sleep?
7. How can I become an outside observer of my mind?
8. How do I help myself back into the habit of a good night's sleep?

The Nine of Swords represents a person struggling for sleep and peace of mind due to thoughts rattling unstoppably through her mind. Swords represent mental images and ideas. In the case of the Nine of Swords, disruptive thoughts keep peaceful slumber at bay.

Walk Away or Try Harder Spread

On This Day

Winston Churchill's state funeral was held on this day in 1965. Churchill is regarded as one of the greatest political leaders of the twentieth century for sticking to his convictions and guiding the UK through the cataclysmic events of World Wars I and II.

Summation of Spread

Churchill failed sixth grade and was defeated in every election for public office until becoming prime minister at age sixty-two. He encouraged others to never, ever give up. His bright spirit informs this spread, created to examine whether you should walk away from a challenge or try harder.

Cast Your Cards

Explore personal conviction and perseverance while casting your cards.

1. What is my calling and what I must do?
2. What happens if I walk away?
3. What happens if I stay and work at it?
4. The biggest challenge as it stands.
5. How can I soothe any stress?
6. What different approach can I use?
7. Who is my support system?
8. Am I truthful about the perceived outcome?
9. How do I improve my knowledge and skills?
10. Am I enjoying the journey?

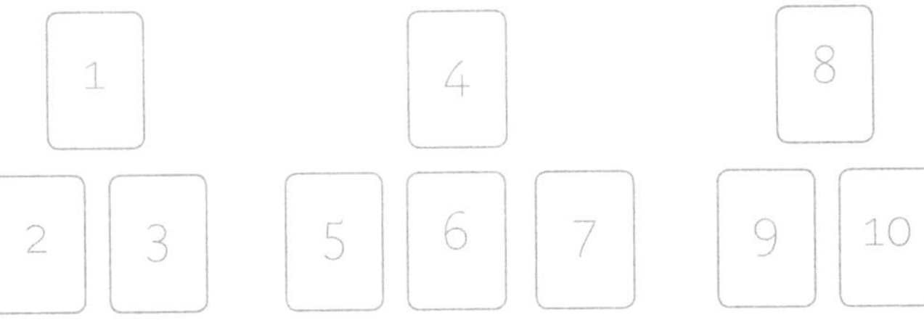

In addition to political prowess, Winston Churchill was a prolific painter. Discovering his passion for oil painting after the age of forty, he would produce almost 600 works in his life.

The King of Wands represents the personality traits of statesmanship. A visionary filled with certainty and charisma, he perseveres, never satisfied until his goals are met. Carrying his authority naturally, others become inspired by this king's bold actions and broad sex appeal.

Saraswati's Creative Flow Spread

Flow is one of the main reasons people play video games. Intrinsic motivation is aroused; skill and challenge utilize the player's brain. Their attention is engaged and motivation is high while the goals of the game are clearly set. All sense of time disappears.

The World card personifies the concept of flow. The World dancer moves in a state of ecstasy, tuning in and perfectly centered in the moment. The consciousness has finally merged with the subconscious, and the result is a superconscious state of transcendence.

On This Day

Saraswati, Hindu goddess of music, arts, science, and knowledge, is honored today in Eastern India. Her symbols include a book (divine knowledge), a crystal (power of meditation and spirituality), sacred water (creativity and purification), and a musical instrument (perfection of arts and sciences, the rhythm of music, emotions and feelings).

Summation of Spread

Saras, "flow," and *wati*, "she who has," mean "she who has flow." Flow describes the mental state of a person performing an activity who is fully involved, has energized focus, and feels intense enjoyment. The questions of this spread are posed to promote flow in the creative activity of your choice.

Cast Your Cards

While a sense of flow can happen spontaneously, you can create favorable circumstances for it and find activities that promote it by casting your cards.

1. What enjoyable task am I challenged by?
2. How do I give my full commitment?
3. How do I create an environment where I can concentrate?
4. Do I have clear goals set for this project?
5. How can I track my progress?
6. What blooms as a result?
7. What unexpected surprise occurs as a result of doing this?

Tarot School's Double-Edged Sword Spread

On This Day

The Tarot School opened its doors in New York City on this day in 1995. Creators Wald and Ruth Ann Amberstone continue to share their love of tarot with eager students worldwide through Readers Studio tarot conferences and correspondence courses.

Summation of Spread

Making a tough choice? The clarity and discrimination needed for decision making comes with the suit of Swords. Wald and Ruth Ann created the Double-Edged Sword Spread for use with any challenging question. From relationships to job offers to moving to career paths, you can examine the ramifications of each choice.

Cast Your Cards

Shuffle the cards and cut your deck into two piles. Assign one pile for choice #1 and the other pile for choice #2. From the first pile, draw five cards and place in a vertical line. Draw five more cards, placing in second vertical line, representing the alternative choice.

While the layout is simple, the interpretation is subtle. There are no specific positions assigned to these cards. Each row reads as a multifaceted picture of energies and outcome. Sometimes the answer is obvious; other times both choices contain pros and cons. Compare and notice the strengths and trouble spots of each side. The responses will aid when making your final decision.

Wald and Ruth Ann Amberstone were married in 2002 at their New York Tarot Festival. Lon Milo DuQuette and Mary Greer officiated, and the ceremony was full of tarot symbolism and personal spiritual references.

Swords always represent thoughts and communication. Ambition, power, and conflict are typical themes emerging in a spread that has multiple Sword cards. Choose wisely before action is taken.

Candlemas Candle Magic Spread

In Scotland, the boy or girl bringing in the most money is declared the Candlemas King or Queen. They "rule" for six weeks and have the power to make one whole afternoon playtime.

On This Day

Candlemas is an ancient British festival marking the midpoint of winter. Before the advent of electricity, dark interiors were illuminated with candlelight and fires. On this particular day, all the year's candles were brought to the church, and blessings were made over them. It was known as a festival day or the mass of the candles, thus creating Candlemas. Scottish children contributed candles to school on Candlemas so the classrooms remained bright. When gas lighting was installed, children brought money to the teacher for sweets and cakes instead.

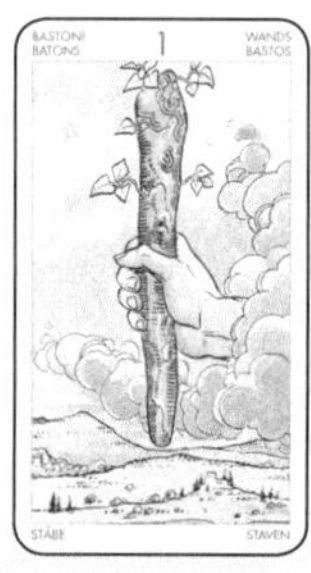

The Ace of Wands represents the energy of candle magic and a spark of something new. See the sprouting leaves on the wand? This indicates future growth and manifestation.

Summation of Spread

Candle magic is accomplished via simple or complex rituals. This is based on the essential elements of candle magic. Use this spread when planning a ritual or simply examining a goal.

Cast Your Cards

Set an intention, light a flame, and cast your cards.

1. Your Altar: What supports me?
2. Incense: What message am I sending?
3. Personal Preparation: What is the best way to cleanse my energy?
4. Candle: What is the best color/intention for my candle?
5. Inscribing: What symbols support my intention?
6. Dressing the Candle: What do I want to attract/repel?
7. Glitter: How does my magic sparkle and multiply?
8. Feed the Candle: What actions can I take to support my magic?
9. Lighting: How do I best ignite my passion?

9
8
7
6
5
4
3
2
1

3 • February

Change Your Situation Spread

On This Day

Ranulf Flambard, the Bishop of Durham, became the first prisoner to escape the Tower of London on this day in 1101. A rope was smuggled to him inside a wine jug. Inviting the guards to join him for a Candlemas celebration, he escaped after they got drunk and passed out.

Flambard tied his rope to a column and escaped out a window. Friends and horses waited below, and off he rode to freedom.

Summation of Spread

Are you being held captive by a situation, person, or thought? This spread aims to help you break free.

Cast Your Cards

The Change Your Situation Spread explores options for change and prepares you for making a great escape.

1. Card representing the oppressive situation.
2. Have I given this serious thought?
3. What belief has led me here?
4. What is my motivation to change?
5. Am I determined enough to change?
6. Am I ready to take action?
7. What can I do to be sure I don't fall back to same situation?
8. Outcome

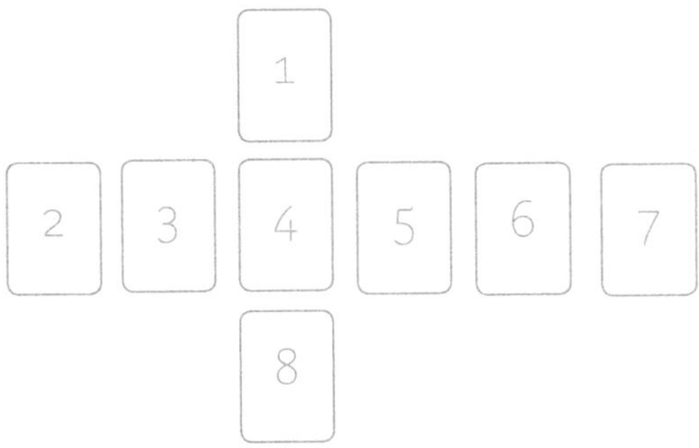

The Devil card is often literal in its interpretation of what holds us captive. The couple could simply slip the shackles off over their heads. We are often held captive by something we have the power to change—a subtle yet powerful reminder of the personal responsibility we bear in improving, leaving, and altering an undesirable situation.

Snow White Spread

The Grimm Brothers's tale Snow White and Rose Red *features another character named Snow White who bears no relation to* Snow White and the Seven Dwarfs.

On This Day

Snow White was released on this day in 1938. This German fairy tale of the girl pursued by a jealous queen, fed a poison apple, and kissed by a handsome prince earned a standing ovation from a glittering, star-studded crowd.

Summation of Spread

The questions of this spread are inspired by the themes and symbols of this iconic fairy tale.

Cast Your Cards

Whistle while you work and cast your cards with a light touch in the shape of a ruby red apple.

1. Miraculous Birth of Snow White: What is possible?
2. Death of Her Mother: What feminine wisdom has been lost?
3. Evil Stepmother: What is my greatest challenge?
4. Murder of Her Father: What masculine wisdom has been lost?
5. Imprisonment of Snow White: What holds me captive?
6. Expulsion of Snow White: What makes me feel like an outsider?
7. Hiding in the Woods: Where do I run for safety?
8. Meeting the Dwarfs: Who are my allies?
9. Poisoned Apple: What lie do I believe as truth?
10. Kiss: What does love teach me about life?

Snow White's apple, a powerful symbol of temptation and a reference to the sensual fall of Adam and Eve, is found in the Lovers card.

Peter Pan Spread

On This Day

Peter Pan, the animated feature based on J. M. Barrie's book, was released on this day in 1953. The story of Wendy and her brothers whisked to Neverland by Peter Pan was the highest-grossing film of the year.

Summation of Spread

Peter Pan's theme is the conflict between the innocence of childhood versus the responsibility of adulthood. This tug of war is a universal experience. This spread lets Peter Pan, Wendy, Tinker Bell, and Captain Hook rekindle the child inside. Accessing your inner child, former dreams, and discarded desires, you can cultivate more magic in everyday adult life.

Cast Your Cards

Believe in fairies, clap your hands, and cast the cards as follows:

1. Me as a child.
2. Me as an adult.
3. Biggest challenge as a child.
4. Biggest challenge as an adult.
5. Favorite game as a child.
6. Favorite game as an adult.
7. What was lost when I grew up?
8. What was gained when I grew up?
9. What magic remains constant?

J. M. Barrie sometimes had Sherlock Holmes and Arthur Conan Doyle revise his work, Robert Louis Stevenson was a pen pal, George Bernard Shaw was his neighbor, and he was friendly with science fiction writer H.G. Wells. Wells, Doyle, and Barrie played together on the same cricket team.

Tarot's four Pages, or Knaves, represent the optimism of youth. Pages contain a sense of childlike wonder, endless enthusiasm, and the ability to be enraptured in the beauty and magic of the world.

Aphrodite's Bombshell Spread

Aphrodite is associated with the sea, dolphins, doves, swans, pomegranates, scepters, apples, myrtle, rose trees, lime trees, clams, scallop shells, and pearls.

On This Day

Today is the sacred day of Aphrodite, Greek goddess of love, beauty, pleasure, and procreation. Known as Venus to the Romans, she is the epitome of sensuality, sexuality, and beauty, and she has many lovers. Risen from seafoam in perfect adult form, innately desirable, she is often depicted in a scallop shell.

Summation of Spread

Do you have your eye on a special someone? This lusty spread will help you seduce the one you love.

Cast Your Cards

Aphrodite's Bombshell Spread's cards are cast in the shape of the delicate, fragile human organ, the heart.

1. How do I know love exists?
2. Whom do I love?
3. Will they love me back?
4. Do they find me attractive?
5. Which of my qualities do they enjoy best?
6. How can I please them?
7. How can I honor the goddess within?
8. How can I make expressions of love deeper and more eloquent?

The Empress card connects to Aphrodite's femininity, passion, and loveliness. While the Empress is not a literal interpretation of Aphrodite, the Empress is the embodiment of female sensuality, physicality, fleshiness, and physical beauty.

Pinocchio's Truthfulness Spread

On This Day

Pinocchio, a timeless tale of mischief, heart, and adventure, was released this day in 1940. Pinocchio is a youth finding his way toward self-worth and self-esteem. When circumstances grow beyond Pinocchio's control, his lies and rationalization result in the famous growing nose.

Summation of Spread

Are you honest with others and with yourself? Pinocchio's Truthfulness Spread plays upon elements of truth as a central theme. The questions posed regard all areas of truthfulness in our lives.

Cast Your Cards

1. Is someone I know lying to me?
2. Am I lying to myself?
3. What is my biggest rationalization for something I failed to do?
4. Why is truth important?
5. How do I get to the truth of my situation?
6. What action do I need to take?

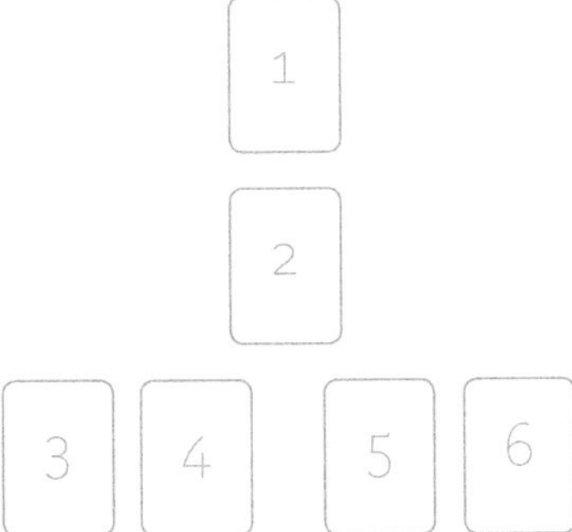

Nose twitching, mouth covering, fidgeting, and tense lips are signs a person might be lying. Other signs include micro-expressions, quick flashes of emotion the liar is attempting to cover up.

The King of Cups is connected to lying, fabrication, and tall tales. While the King of Cups is not inherently deceitful, he is the tarot personality with the broadest imagination. The rolling sea and cresting waves he sits upon are reminders of extraordinary ingenuity and imaginative capacity.

Tree of Life Spread

Levi influenced the work of the Golden Dawn and all of twentieth-century magic by committing his life to metaphysical study and magical practice.

On This Day

Eliphas Levi was born on this day in 1810. Levi changed tarot usage forever by placing it at the center of all occult sciences. He felt tarot was the common ground where various philosophies intermingled.

Summation of Spread

Levi associated tarot with the Kabbalah (Jewish mysticism) by linking the twenty-two letters of the Hebrew alphabet to twenty-two corresponding trump cards. The Tree of Life is a mystical way of understanding the creation of the universe and our connection to divinity. This spread is inspired by the Sephiroth (places on the Tree of Life) to inform its questions.

Cast Your Cards

Cast the cards in the shape of the Tree of Life.

1. Crown: What do I display to the world?
2. Wisdom: What is the deepest truth I know?
3. Understanding: What do I accept about my limitations?
4. Mercy: How do I express kindness?
5. Severity: How am I hard on myself?
6. Beauty: How can I find beauty today?
7. Victory: What is an upcoming success?
8. Splendor: When do I shine?
9. Foundation: What keeps me grounded?
10. Kingdom: How can I enjoy the material world without being deluded by it?

The Magician card connects to Levi as a magician. Tarot's four suits are displayed upon his table. Levi connected the four suits (elements) with the four letters of the Tetragrammaton, which is considered the proper name of God in the Hebrew bible.

Collision of the Elements Spread

On This Day

The US Weather Service was established on this day in 1870, providing forecasts, warnings, safety, and general information for the public.

Summation of Spread

This tempestuous spread uses weather events to inform questions about the winds of change operating in your life.

Cast Your Cards

Look skyward and feel Earth, Air, Fire, and Water collide to make the weather as you cast your cards like pollen in the wind.

1. Flash Fire: Where is passion about to ignite?
2. Earthquake: What should I destroy and rebuild?
3. Tornado: What negative thinking should I sweep away?
4. Tidal Wave: What emotion do I need to experience?
5. Lightning: What is a good idea I should take action on?
6. Snow Storm: What cultivates a sense of peace and stillness within me?

The National Weather Service, a governmental agency, was originally placed under the Department of War when it was formed. Congress felt "military discipline would probably secure the greatest promptness, regularity, and accuracy in the required observations."

The World card represents the manifestation of the elements in your life. Note the creatures in each corner: lion (Fire), bull (Earth), eagle (Air), and cherub (Water). These elements are also representative of the four fixed signs of the zodiac: Leo, Taurus, Aquarius, and Scorpio. They point to the four seasons, the four compass points, and the four corners of the universe.

Snake Bite Spread

Snakes are a widespread mythological symbol in many cultures. Dualistic in nature, they are symbolic of both good and evil, life and death.

On This Day

Today is the Feast of St. Paul on the island nation of Malta. Legend states that St. Paul was a prisoner aboard a ship to Rome when a storm drove it aground in Malta. Paul escaped and was warmly welcomed by the island's people, but a snake bit him on the hand. Suffering no harm, he became the patron saint of snake-bite victims. The feast is celebrated with processions, drinking, tossing confetti, and family gatherings.

Summation of Spread

What do snakes symbolize for you? The questions of this spread are inspired by snakes and snake bites because subconsciously they represent confronting undesirable or uncontrollable situations and the loss of power or control over yourself or circumstances.

Rider-Waite-Smith (RWS) cards make full use of snake symbolism. The Magician's belt is an ouroboros, an ancient symbol of a snake devouring itself, representing eternal return. The Lovers card features a snake whispering to the female. The Wheel of Fortune contains a serpent, while in the Seven of Cups a snake slithers out of the top righthand cup.

Cast Your Cards

Cast your cards in the shape of a slithering snake.

1. What is my greatest fear?
2. What is the most poisonous aspect of my life?
3. How do I remove the poison?
4. What knowledge is needed?
5. Can I relinquish control?
6. What is the greatest challenge to my beliefs?
7. What belief do I need to let go of?
8. What will happen when I lose myself to the unknowable?
9. What is my transformation?
10. How does this affect my life?

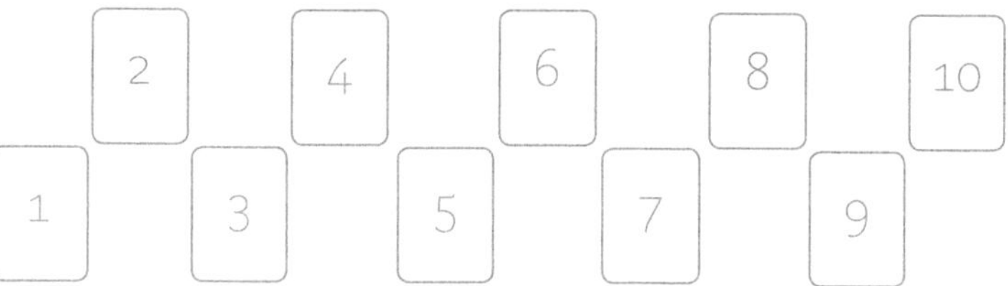

Salome's Dance of Seven Veils Spread

On This Day

Oscar Wilde's play *Salome,* based on the biblical story, premiered on the Paris stage while he sat in prison on this day in 1896. Salome performs the sensual dance of seven veils in exchange for the severed head of John the Baptist. The dance of seven veils is thought to originate with Babylonian fertility goddess Ishtar.

When Ishtar, goddess of sexuality and warfare, approached the underworld, the gatekeeper allowed her to pass through seven gates, one at a time. At each gate she had to shed an article of clothing until she entered the underworld naked.

Summation of Spread

This spread encourages you to examine your inner desires and discover how you might fulfill your heart's wish.

Cast Your Cards

1. What do I desire more than anything?
2. What I am I willing to do to get it?
3. What is my great challenge in receiving it?
4. What will aid me in overcoming the challenge?
5. What lies at the base of my desire?
6. Is there someone who can help me get it?
7. How will my world be changed as a result?

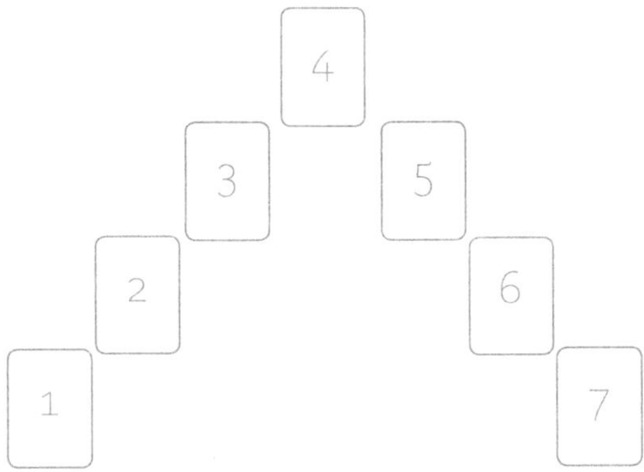

The Nine of Wands represents passage via passion. The seven veils dance is done in order to obtain something, as Ishtar's passage does. The Nine of Wands is a formidable character who forges new ground as a result of bravery, strength, and being a breaker of barriers.

Imbolc Stirring Within You Spread

In Ireland, tradition states you should place a loaf of bread on the windowsill for Brigid and an ear of corn for the white cow with red ears who is her traveling companion.

On This Day

Today marks the ancient calendar date for Imbolc, a fire festival celebrating new life. The most ancient of Celtic pastoral holidays, Imbolc's literal translation is "in the belly," marking the first stirrings and flutterings of life in earth's soil after a long winter.

Summation of Spread

Brigid (both Pagan deity and Catholic saint) is celebrated on this day. She is the spirit of healing, poetry, and music, and she is the patron of artists, poets, craftspeople, and livestock. This spread uses Brigid's fiery, regenerative qualities to inform questions of what stirs inside you.

The Queen of Wands shares a profound connection with Brigid. Brigid connects with fire, manifesting as a pillar of fire or with flames shooting from her head. This is an apt description of the Queen of Wands, who uses passion and power to help or hinder those around her.

Cast Your Cards

Brigid's crosses woven from wheat protected the home from fire and lightning. Cast your cards in the shape of a Brigid's cross.

1. What am I dreaming of?
2. What is it possible?
3. How do I start?
4. Why must I do this now?
5. Why is the journey essential?
6. What is my secret weapon?
7. What gift does Brigid offer me?
8. How can I honor and thank her?
9. What is Brigid's message to me?

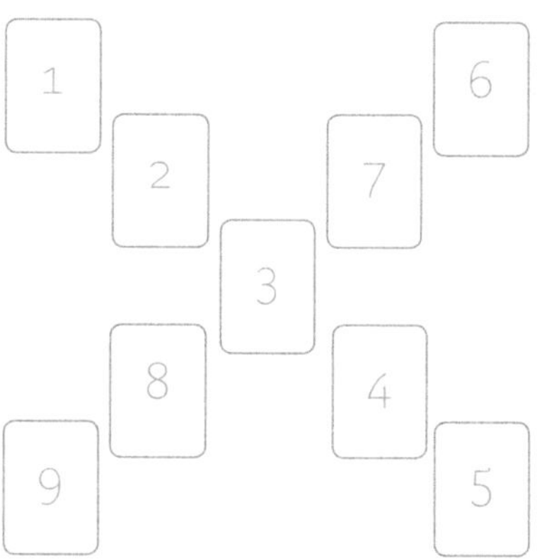

Fertility Spread

On This Day

Today is Lupercalia, the most ancient of Roman fertility festivals. Roman god Lupercus's Greek equivalent is Pan. Goats and young dogs, revered for their strong sexual instincts, were sacrificed at a cave by the foot of Palatine, where the wolf Lupa gave birth to Romulus and Remus.

Summation of Spread

This spread looks at fertility for someone wishing to become pregnant. Keep in mind that tarot is never a substitute for examining medical issues with a professional. The cards can be used in holistic ways to provoke insight, ideas, and opinions.

Cast Your Cards

Cast the Fertility Spread's cards in an egglike circle:

1. What is the state of my health?
2. What helps to improve my health?
3. How can I encourage my partner to be healthy?
4. How can I maintain a healthy diet?
5. How can I keep my stress level at a minimum?
6. Should I stop drinking alcohol?
7. How do I make the fertility process enjoyable?
8. What is the likely outcome?

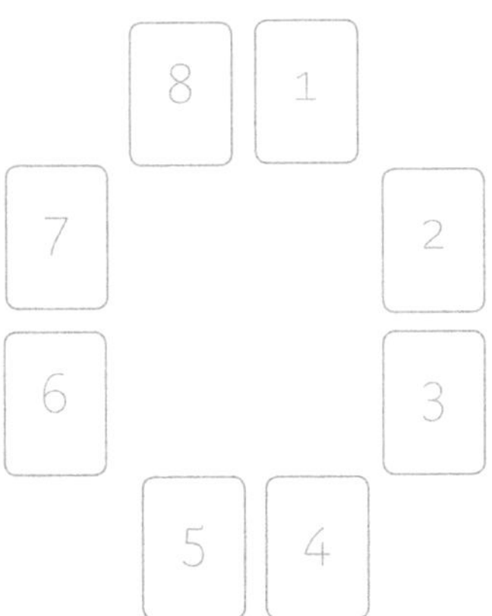

Acts of fertility magic included smearing the foreheads of two youths of noble birth with sacrificial blood. These Luperci ran naked except for the skins of sacrificial goats. They struck women with goatskin thongs. Women eagerly stood forward, as the Luperci touch was thought to make them fertile.

The Queen of Pentacles, the homemaker and master of the material world, sits with a bunny at her feet. This bunny represents the fertility of all domestic things.

The world's greatest lover, Casanova, ate chocolate to keep him virile. More than 35 million heart-shaped boxes of chocolate will be purchased this Valentine's Day.

The searing Ace of Wands contains intensity, attraction, spiritual fire, and love at first sight. Aces are like seeds containing minute qualities of each particular suit. You can see each ace bloom as you move through their numbers.

Valentine's Day Courtly Love Spread

On This Day

Saint Valentine, the namesake of Valentine's Day, was a third-century Roman saint who is widely associated with the tradition of courtly love. Courtly love was a unique medieval concept of the noble, chivalrous expression of love and admiration.

Summation of Spread

Fallen hard for someone? Courtly love was practiced in secret among nobility. Exalting the female in the highest form of worship, it was generally not practiced between husband and wife. Merging eroticism with a spiritual quest, making romantic obsession like a god and not truly obtainable, it leaves unquenched desire in its wake. Sensual desire is explored in this spread, whose questions are based on the seven stages of courtly love, adapted from Barbara Tuchman.

Cast Your Cards

Savor the agony of passion and invoke pleasure while casting:

1. Attraction: Who am I attracted to?
2. Worship from Afar: Why are they so delicious?
3. Declaration of Passion: Should I tell them my feelings?
4. Virtuous Rejection: How will I feel if rejected?
5. Renewed Wooing and Determination: Why can't I give up?
6. Lovesickness: How do they feel when near me?
7. Heroic Deed: What should I do?
8. Consummation of Secret Love: How will we consummate?
9. Endless Adventure and Subterfuge to Avoid Detection: What is our fate?

1 4 5
2 3
6 7 8
9

15 • February

Problem-Solving Spread

On This Day

Galileo Galilei—mathematician, philosopher, physicist, and the father of modern astronomy—was born in Pisa, Italy, on this day in 1564. Galileo led the Scientific Revolution by defending heliocentrism, stating the earth revolves around the sun.

Summation of Spread

The nature of Galileo's innate curiosity led to his many inventions and discoveries. Summoning Galileo for inspiration, this spread helps us think creatively to solve any issue we may be grappling with.

Cast Your Cards

The answers and possibilities you seek are as infinite as the universe itself.

1. What do I want to happen?
2. What don't I want to happen?
3. What's the worst thing that could happen?
4. What's the best thing that could happen?
5. How many possible ways can I approach this problem or project?
6. If I had endless resources, how would I solve this problem?
7. If I had all the time in the world, how would I solve this problem?
8. What is the answer I seek?

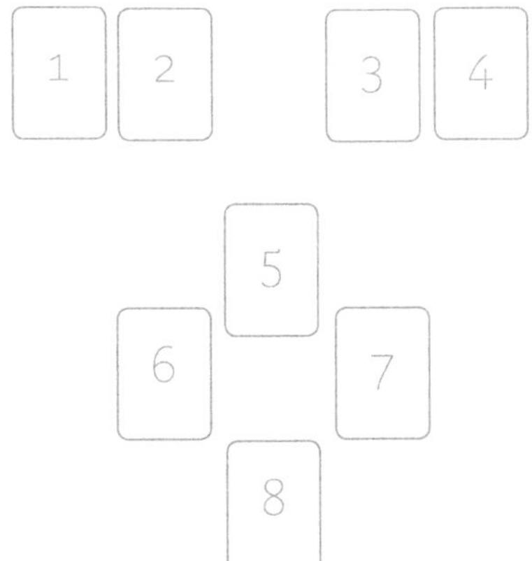

At odds with the church's conviction of an earth-centered universe, Galileo was brought before the Inquisition, charged with heresy, and placed under house arrest in 1633, where he remained until his death.

The Hierophant, like Galileo, shares knowledge. The Hierophant's purpose is purveying education, belief systems, studying, and learning. Originally named the Pope, the Hierophant connects to the rigidity of religion and belief systems—ironically, the very belief systems that imprisoned Galileo.

Synesthesia *stems from the Greek words* syn *("together") and* aisthesis *("perception"). The word literally means "joined perception."*

Pamela Colman Smith's Synesthesia Experiment Spread

On This Day

Pamela Colman Smith was born this day in 1878. Smith paved the way for intuitive tarot reading when she illustrated the minor arcana for the first time since the fifteenth century's Sola Busca deck.

Summation of Spread

Smith had a high degree of synesthesia, a condition where one sense, like sight, is perceived with an additional sense, like hearing. For instance, hearing a Beethoven concerto, you also taste chocolate. Upon hearing the concerto, you would always experience the taste of chocolate. In fact, Smith created artwork by listening to Beethoven's Piano Sonata no. 11 and other pieces of music. This spread is an experiment to discover whether you have these qualities and explore your connection to your senses.

Synesthesia, common among artists, connects to the Empress card, who embodies the imagination. From the possible pregnancy she displays under her flowing garments to the number 3 signifying two forces combined to create a third, the Empress is the essence of creation.

Cast Your Cards

Ask yourself each question; answer with a yes or a no. If the answer is yes, you have synesthesia. If the answer is no, take the question a bit further by answering the second question (in italics) in correlation with a flip of the card.

1. Do numbers or letters cause a color experience to me?
   What color is the number 9?
2. Do calendar days and months have a specific taste to me?
   What does October taste like?
3. Do sounds produce colors in my head?
   What color is a honking car horn?
4. Do certain words ever trigger a taste in my mouth?
   What does the word authority taste like?
5. Does touching objects produce a smell?
   When I feel soft silk, what does it smell like?

Kindness Spread

On This Day

Today is Random Act of Kindness Day. While it's not a national holiday, it is a day where people are encouraged to do something kind for a friend or a stranger.

Summation of Spread

Kindness is a virtue and a value in many cultures and religions. True and heartfelt kindness is worth exploring on a deep level. The Kindness Spread helps you to do this. Use it for inspiration to commit blatant random acts of kindness.

Cast Your Cards

The Kindness Spread's cards are cast in the shape of a ladder reaching upwards. Upon reaching the top of the stairs, you will be ready to perform a random act of kindness.

1. When has the kindness of another touched me?
2. Who is the kindest person I know?
3. What helps me to release negativity toward others?
4. How can I be present for others?
5. How can I better listen to those around me?
6. What do I have in common with all humans?
7. How can I practice kindness toward myself?
8. What random act of kindness can I perform today?

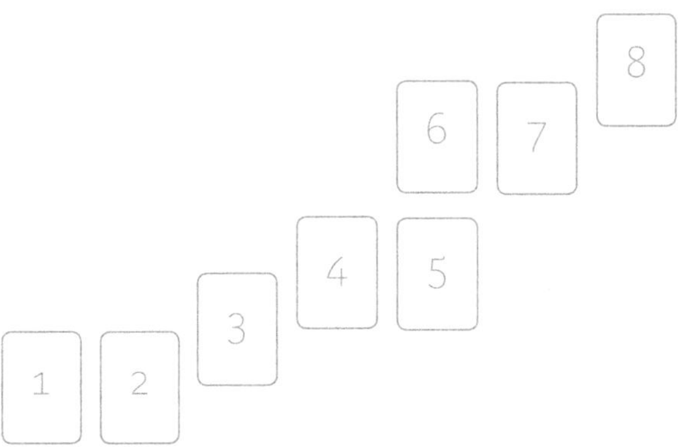

Acts of kindness are medically proven to make us healthier. Emotional warmth produces the hormone oxytocin in the brain, which moves through the body and reduces blood pressure. Elevated levels of dopamine, often referred to as "helper's high," leave us feeling tingly and good.

The Queen of Cups is the most empathetic personality in the deck. The deep oceans surrounding her refer to her deep reserves of altruism, empathy, and emotional support for others.

Gertrude Moakley's Problem-Solving Spread

Moakley suggests the female Pope (High Priestess) card is based on a distant relative of the Visconti family. Elected Popess by a small group of Guillemites, the Inquisition burned her at the stake in autumn of 1300.

On This Day

Gertrude Moakley was born this day in 1905. Moakley researched and wrote about Renaissance tarot while working as a librarian at the New York Public Library. She was the first scholar to suggest that tarot trumps are based on Renaissance parades, where each float "trumps" the next. The trumps represented easily understood allegories. These allegories were translated into a deck of cards as a playable game for both nobles and the general public.

Summation of Spread

Gertrude Moakley set out to solve tarot's biggest questions: where, how, and what is tarot? This spread uses the library detective for inspiration to help us resolve any issue or any problem.

The Justice card relates to problem-solving skills. Her upward-pointing sword seeks clarity, while the balancing scales represent the weighing of information. Notice she does not wear a blindfold, as she is keenly aware of the situation surrounding any issue.

Cast Your Cards

The cards are cast in a straight line to ease your flow of information.

1. What is my intended outcome?
2. What helps me gather information?
3. What is the insight I require?
4. Who inspires me?
5. What do I already know?
6. Should I rest, letting this incubate?
7. Once I achieve my goal, how do I develop it?

Qualities of Pisces Spread

On This Day

Today marks the first day of the astrological sign of Pisces, the fish.

Summation of Spread

The spread is based on the essential qualities of Pisces: fluctuation, depth, imagination, reactive, receptive, mystical, and compassion.

Cast Your Cards

Cast the cards in the shape of the Pisces symbol, or glyph:

1. Why is it important to remain malleable?
2. What do I discover moving into my deepest depths?
3. How do I make the most of my imagination?
4. How can I become less reactive?
5. How do I become more receptive to good?
6. How does mysticism serve me?
7. How do I walk with compassion?

Pisces is ruled by the planet Jupiter, lilac is the primary color, the lucky day is Friday, and the best locations for success are seashores and coastal cities. Pisces rules the twelfth house of the zodiac, governing the deepest, darkest secrets and desires.

The Moon card, like Pisces, is all about evolution and the changing nature of any situation. Representing the deep subconscious and urges springing from below, the moon's reflective light causes hidden desires to surface. Pisces is the watery child of the moon.

February • 20

Forgive Someone Spread

Forgiveness does not guarantee the end of the pain an offense has caused. It does, however, help you deal with the emotions you possess toward the offender. Every one of us has control over the emotions we choose to hold or release.

On This Day

The last recorded witchcraft trial took place in England on this day in 1712. Jane Wenham, the "Witch of Walkern," was found guilty and sentenced to death. Thankfully, she was given a royal pardon from Queen Anne.

Summation of Spread

Forgiveness is powerful medicine when we realize it has little to do with the other person and everything to do with ourselves. This spread helps pave the path to forgiveness so that you may be set free.

Cast Your Cards

Step back, take a breath, and cast the cards as follows:

1. Is holding on to anger causing me pain?
2. How will the act of forgiveness change me?
3. Will forgiveness allow me to move on?
4. Will forgiveness help me create a new future?
5. What action should I take?
6. What is my lesson?

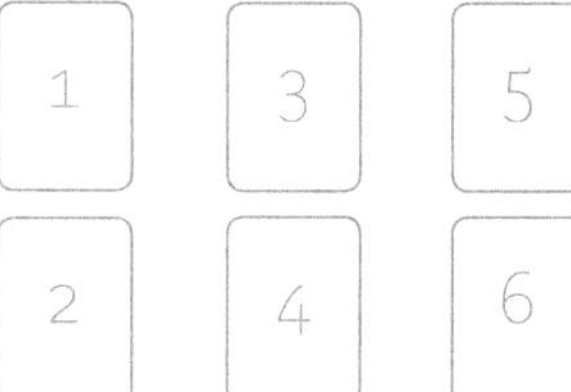

The Judgement card represents a new awakening. True forgiveness regarding a deep and plaguing issue can spur great transformation, especially for a long-term or long-held issue. Surprising consequences include a rash of new growth—precisely what the Judgement card depicts.

Erotic Thoughts Spread

On This Day

Anaïs Nin, writer and diarist, was born on this day in 1903. Beginning her literary career in Paris, she moved to New York in the 1940s. Hailed as one of the finest writers of female erotica, she was one of the first women to fully explore the realm of erotic writing.

Nin was a friend—in some cases, lover—of many literary figures, including Henry Miller, John Steinbeck, and Gore Vidal.

Summation of Spread

Eroticism is not simply the physical act of sex; rather, it is the arousal and anticipation of sex and sensuality. A pleasurable and subtle activity that is often overlooked, eroticism can last for hours, days, and months, while the sex act itself occurs in a relatively short period of time. Nin's spirit inspires this spread.

The Star card is about being completely at ease in one's body and with one's sensuality. The Star depicts vulnerability, allowing the body to be in an open and receptive state. Here we can discover new and uncharted pleasures.

Cast Your Cards

1. What is romance?
2. What is my greatest aphrodisiac?
3. What turns me on?
4. How can I send myself empowering messages?
5. How can I be brazen?
6. Who am I obsessed with?
7. Who wants to sleep with me?
8. What should I spend the afternoon doing?
9. How do I want them?
10. How can I have them?

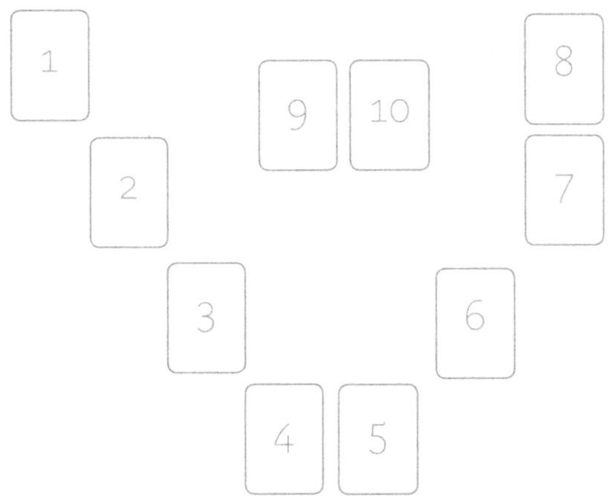

Sybil Leek's Mount of Venus Spread

Sybil Leek was born to a well-to-do, influential British family and was taught astrology by her grandmother.

On This Day

Sybil Leek, English witch, astrologer, psychic, and leader in the formation of modern Wicca and Neopagan witchcraft, was born this day in 1917.

Summation of Spread

Sybil Leek explained palmistry's connection with astrology. Beneath each finger and the thumb are fleshy mounds called mounts, each derived from an astrological connection, given names of the planets, and associated with planetary qualities. This spread's questions are inspired by the mounts.

Leek remarks, "The Tarot reader gives a performance that has elements of suspense as the client waits to know what the future holds. Personally, I know of no other form of divination which offers this Hitchcock-like suspense…With a good reader the ornate figures seem to begin to take on a life of their own, staring with benevolent faces as they lie on the table."

Cast Your Cards

Cast your cards in the shape of the human palm:

1. Mount of Venus (base of the thumb): How do I express sensuality?
2. Mount of Jupiter (base of the index finger): How does ambition lead me?
3. Mount of Saturn (base of the middle finger): What is the seat of my destiny?
4. Mount of the Sun (base of the third finger): How does my charisma radiate?
5. Mount of Mercury (base of the little finger): How does intellectuality serve me?
6. Mount of Mars (below the Mount of Mercury): How am I most courageous?
7. Mount of Moon (below Mount of Mars): How do I encourage the flowering of my imagination?

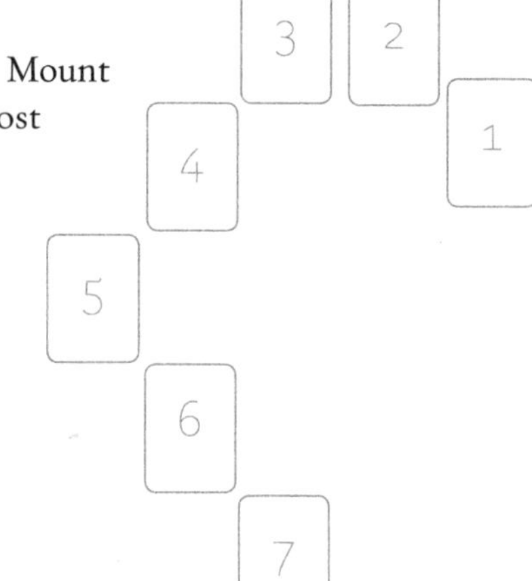

Seeking the Light Masonic Mystery Spread

On This Day

Sir Arthur Conan Doyle, author of the famed Sherlock Holmes series, received his second degree from his Masonic Lodge on this date in 1887. Masonic membership, popular among English and American gentlemen in the last century, uses devices called tracing boards for their studies.

A candidate entering the Masonhood must state that they believe in a supreme being; however, the Masons do not insist on naming who the supreme being should be. Belief in a higher power, any power, is required upon entry.

Summation of Spread

Tracing boards, like tarot cards, are symbolic learning devices. Used by Masons to advance through their grades, different boards offer different lessons. The Seeking the Light Masonic Mystery Spread uses the first degree tracing board as inspiration.

Cast Your Cards

1. Physical world (checkered floor tiles): What binds me?
2. Essence of soul and psyche (columns): Who am I?
3. The Heavens: How do I make contact with the divine?
4. Center Star (divinity): What is the nature of divinity?
5. Ladder (Jacob's ladder): How do I discover my true path?

Three Rungs of the Ladder:

6. Faith (Apprentice):
   How can I trust?
7. Hope (Fellowcraft):
   What do I yearn for?
8. Charity (Master):
   How do I give back?

3 4 8 5 7 6 2 1

The Three of Pentacles in the RWS deck contains Masonic symbolism: an apron, bench, and Masonic tool. Many Golden Dawn members were Masons, and they used Masonic structure in the Golden Dawn's own grading and initiations.

Innovation Spread

Observation and experience lead to truly ingenius solutions because life is like a jigsaw puzzle. The more you live, the more pieces you see, increasing the likelihood you'll assemble these pieces in a way no one else has thought of.

The Two of Wands represents placing a visionary plan into action. The figure with the world in his hands is looking at the big picture. Stay true and persevere to see your vision through to the end.

On This Day

Steve Jobs, the visionary and creative genius behind Apple computers, was born on this day in 1955.

Summation of Spread

Jobs exemplified the American dream: a self-made man whose parents, two graduate students, gave him up for adoption, he realized his dream through intelligence and determination. Connecting creativity with technology, Jobs inspires a spread you can use to jump-start a revolution.

Cast Your Cards

Create the shape of a light bulb going off as you cast your cards:

1. What is my vision?
2. Where is my passion leading me?
3. How can I nurture my creativity?
4. What helps me become brave in my actions?
5. Can I allow myself to fail so I may succeed?
6. What helps me embrace the idea of possibility?
7. What tremendous possibility have I overlooked?
8. What changes as a result of innovative thinking?
9. What do I need to start doing right now?

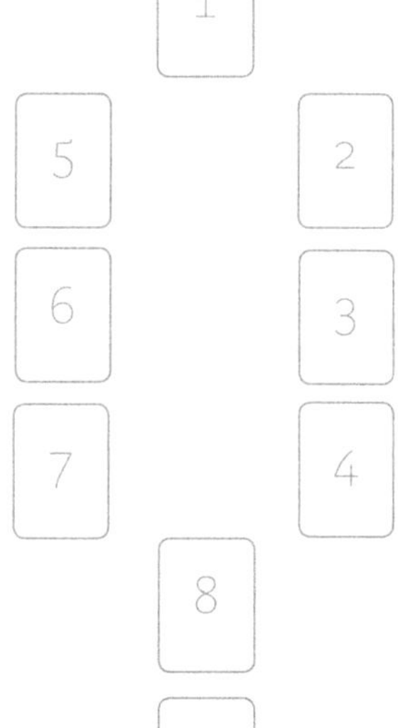

Defensiveness Spread

On This Day

The Battle of Los Angeles occurred on this date in 1942. Three months after the United States entered World War II, tensions were high after the attack on Pearl Harbor. Objects were spotted in the sky and, thinking the city was under enemy fire, a blackout was ordered and air raid sirens rang. Over 1,400 shells were fired into the sky, killing seven people and damaging buildings. Eventually deemed a false alarm, the press and media sensed a cover-up.

Modern-day UFO experts have suggested the government fired at extraterrestrial spacecraft, but we may never know the truth.

Summation of Spread

While we may never know what flew over Los Angeles that night, it is true that in normal life defensiveness becomes problematic, blocks growth, and shuts out new possibility. This spread examines the degree to which you may or may not be defensive.

Cast Your Cards

The Defensiveness Spread is useful when your feathers feel ruffled and you have a desire to soothe them. Cast your cards as follows:

1. What pushes my buttons?
2. What do I really like about myself?
3. What helps me accept my imperfections?
4. What helps me be honest with myself?
5. How can I respond rather than react?
6. What helps me see other people's perspectives?
7. What am I afraid of?

The Two of Swords sometimes represents a person so deeply ingrained inside their own psyche, trapped in their mind, that they act cold and defensive to others. An abundance of twos in a spread reflect myriad choices to be made.

February • 26

Hugo was planning a novel on social misery and injustice as early as 1830, but Les Misérables *would take seventeen years to become realized and published. Clearly, it was worth the wait.*

The Justice card connects to a sense of social justice and knowing the difference between right and wrong. Sadly, it is those without a voice who often go undetected by the sword of Justice.

Les Misérables Spread

On This Day

Victor Hugo was born on this day in 1802. Author of *The Hunchback of Notre Dame* and *Les Misérables*, Hugo is widely regarded as the most famous French Romantic writer and poet.

Summation of Spread

Set in nineteenth-century France, *Les Misérables* is the story of Jean Valjean. Hunted by the ruthless policeman Javert, he agrees to care for factory worker Fatine's daughter, Cosette. This decision will alter their lives forever. The Les Misérables Spread is based on themes found in the novel and musical adaptation.

Cast Your Cards

1. Forgiveness: Who need I forgive?
2. Self Sacrifice: What is worth everything to me?
3. Prejudice: What hidden prejudice do I hold?
4. Plight of Women: How can I help women in need?
5. Social Issues: What social issue do I care about most?
6. Poverty: How can I help break cycles of poverty?
7. Fight: What is worth fighting for?
8. Dream: What do I dream of?
9. Hope: What is the greatest good possible?
10. Compassion: What breeds compassion?
11. Philanthropy: What small step can I take to heal the world?

1		6
2		7
3	11	8
4		9
5		10

Haunted House Spread

On This Day

The Borley Rectory, a creepy Victorian mansion known as the most haunted house in England, was destroyed by fire on this day in 1939. This misfortune occurred due to an overturned oil lamp.

Summation of Spread

The Haunted House Spread is useful to perform in a home or space with ghosts bumping about. Discover the story of a place as you learn how to clear the energy of a house, apartment, or dwelling. Perform this spread at your own risk. Once the information comes to light, there is no way to unlearn it.

Cast Your Cards

Grab your flashlights and candles. The Haunted House Spread's cards are cast as follows:

1. What is the energy of this place?
2. Is there a rational explanation for the phenomena?
3. Is this space haunted?
4. Do I really want to know what occurred here?
5. Who lived here?
6. What was their life like?
7. Who died here?
8. What holds the energy captive?
9. How may I release this energy?

The Borley Rectory was built on the site of a thirteenth-century monastery where, according to legend, a monk and a beautiful young woman were killed attempting to elope. The monk was hanged and the bride-to-be was bricked alive within the walls.

The reversed Death card represents residual energy resulting in hauntings. Past energy that hasn't dissipated affects the present. It is by letting go that evolution is possible.

Moina Mathers's Clairvoyance Spread

Moina Mathers's brother was philosopher Henri Bergson, the first Jewish man to receive the Nobel Prize for Literature.

On This Day

Moina Mathers was born on this day in 1865. Moina—artist, occultist, and the first member initiated into the Golden Dawn—was married to Golden Dawn founder Samuel Liddell MacGregor Mathers. Working closely with her husband, he as magician and she as oracle, they brought forth information for the order using Moina's clairvoyant skills.

Summation of Spread

Clairvoyance is the ability to gain information through visualization or mental imagery. It means "one who sees clearly." The Clairvoyance Spread examines aspects of clairvoyance and suggests questions to activate your own clairvoyant qualities.

The Queen of Cups is a deeply clairvoyant woman. Her cups contains watery visions of truth and imagination. Truly metaphysical and artistic, she dreams for those who cannot.

Cast Your Cards

You can use these questions as a jumping-off point for the further development of psychic skills.

1. What is the best way to cultivate focus?
2. How can I foster a moment-to-moment awareness?
3. Do I dream in color, with vivid images?
4. What helps me create powerful visualizations?
5. Can I make use of my visual/artistic talent?
6. Do I see auras or lights around people?
7. Do I often sense things moving in my peripheral vision?
8. How do I trust in my visions?
9. Why is it important to pay attention to my gifts?
10. What is the result of nurturing my clairvoyance?

Lunar Eclipse Spread

On This Day

On this night in 1504, Christopher Columbus tricked Jamaican natives into giving his sailors food, even after his sailors had stolen from the natives. He did so by correctly predicting a full lunar eclipse visible on this night. Using his almanac knowledge, Columbus pretended the eclipse was a sign from his god and used the trick to manipulate the natives.

Summation of Spread

Lunar eclipse magic is very potent. A lunar eclipse only happens during a full moon as the earth's shadow passes over the moon's face. Evoking the Triple Goddess, this spread's questions regard aspects of deep magic for clarity and wisdom in daily life.

Cast Your Cards

The Lunar Eclipse Spread can be performed anytime but has extra strength on the night of an eclipse. Cast in the shape of a waxing moon, indicative of growing abundance.

1. What lies at the heart of my magic?
2. What is the lesson of early life?
3. What is the challenge of middle life?
4. What is the wisdom learned in later life?
5. What must be removed?
6. What must emerge?
7. How do I harness the power of the moon?

Ancient Egyptian stories regaled lunar eclipses as a sow swallowing the moon. Mayans interpreted it as a jaguar swallowing the moon. Many cultures viewed lunar ellipses as demons swallowing the moon. They would chase the eclipse away by yelling and throwing stones at it.

The High Priestess and her triple crown—a reference to the waxing, full, and waning moon—is connected to the Maiden, Mother, and Crone Triple Goddess concept. A sliver of moon weaves through her luminescent robes.

Procrastinating Spread

Psychologists distinguish between three types of procrastinators. This includes avoiders (people with strong fear of failure and success), thrill seekers (who enjoy a last-minute euphoric rush sensation), and decisional procrastinators (who can't make decisions).

The Two of Swords figure has blindfolded herself in an effort to move within. Will she accept the challenge at hand? Can she free herself to move outward?

On This Day

Today was the due date for Truman Capote's manuscript *Answered Prayers*. The author of *In Cold Blood* and *Breakfast at Tiffany's* would have been paid one million dollars had it been delivered today in 1968. The manuscript was never submitted, and he was quoted as saying, "I'm either going to kill it or it's going to kill me." Capote died in 1984.

Summation of Spread

Why put off till tomorrow what you can do today? Does procrastination ever paralyze you? Can you work through the fear, block, or issue holding you back? This spread will get you moving if you feel stuck on a project or activity.

Cast Your Cards

Visualize your project successfully completed and imagine how you will feel. Cast the cards as follows:

1. The project at hand.
2. How can I break this down into small, achievable steps?
3. What is my first step?
4. What is my second step?
5. How can I reward myself for taking the first step?
6. What will happen when I get down to work?
7. Why is it essential I finish this?
8. How can I remove my ego from the process?

Dr. Seuss's Feeling Grinchy Spread

On This Day

Dr. Seuss, beloved children's author, was born on this day in 1904. Writing his way into the hearts of millions, Theodor Seuss Geisel's books have become fixtures of the childhood experience.

Summation of Spread

Geisel based his famous Grinch from *The Grinch Who Stole Christmas* on himself. He found himself cranky and unexcited for the holidays and decided to write the Grinch to discover if he could find something about Christmas he'd obviously lost.

Cast Your Cards

Cast your cards in the shape of an umbrella so you can turn that frown upside down and let a smile be your umbrella.

1. What is the root of what's bothering me?
2. Is there someone I can talk to?
3. Can I treat myself to something fun right now?
4. What am I grateful for?
5. Is there a new exercise I can take up?
6. Should I change my diet?
7. Should I go somewhere different?
8. How can I express myself creatively?
9. What will it take to drive this bad mood away?

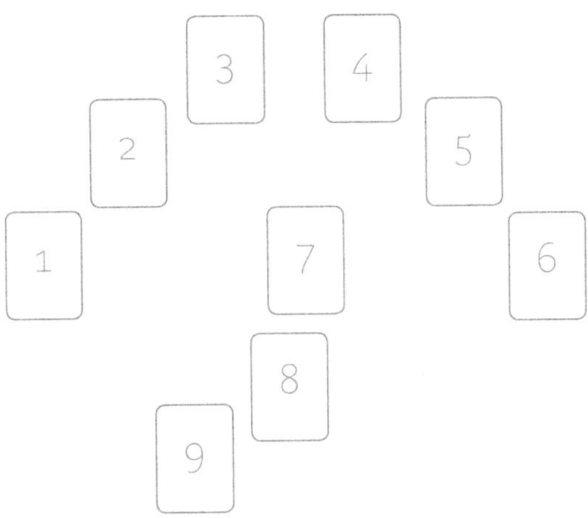

Dr. Seuss was bet $50 by a publisher that he couldn't write a book with fifty assorted words or less. The classic Green Eggs and Ham *was the result.*

The Four of Pentacles is often considered the grinchiest card in the entire deck. Seen as a miser, he holds his pentacle tightly and defensively. But don't be so quick to judge—it can also be understood as the card of stability due to the solid nature of the number four.

Secrets of the Forest Spread

What you put out comes back threefold; the rule of three applies to more than just witchcraft. While hiking or camping, remember this: a person can go three minutes without air, three hours without heat, three days without water, and three weeks without food.

The Ace of Pentacles is a seed, the Seven of Pentacles the harvest, and the Ten of Pentacles the culmination of the cycles and natural rhythms of life.

On This Day

The Shoshone Forest became the first nationally protected forest in the Unites States today in 1891. Covering over 2,500,000 acres in Wyoming, from craggy mountain peaks to dense spruce and fir forests, the abundant land is rich in biodiversity and home to over 335 animal species.

Summation of Spread

The modern world makes it easy to forget we are a part of nature, not separate from it. Forests speak to those with ears to listen, whispering truths and magic, beauty and wonder. This spread uses woods, streams, and rocks to inspire questions about personal revelation.

Cast Your Cards

With your favorite tree in sight or in your mind's eye, cast your cards:

1. What can the forest teach me?
2. What secrets lie in the heart of the forest?
3. How do I connect to my wild side?
4. How can I encourage metamorphosis?
5. What is blossoming in my life?
6. What is passing away?
7. What lies in the pools of my subconscious?

Cinderella's Jealousy Spread

On This Day

The film *Cinderella* came out on this day in 1950. Cinderella suffers at the cold, cruel hands of her wicked stepmother and evil stepsisters until she reigns triumphant in the end. Envy and greed make Cinderella's life miserable until she marries her prince and moves to the castle.

Summation of Spread

Jealousy is a familiar feeling that everyone deals with. This spread has been written for when you feel the pangs of envy. It looks closely at what elicits this response in you, what you can learn about yourself, and how you can let it go.

Cast Your Cards

Prepare for a ball, expect magic to happen, and cast your cards.

1. What is the situation triggering jealousy?
2. Why am I jealous over this?
3. What am I trying to keep?
4. Why do I feel threatened?
5. What false belief have I created?
6. How can I build my self-confidence?
7. How can I avoid comparing myself to others?
8. How can I learn to trust?

Most Disney movies contain hidden Mickey Mouse images. Cinderella is no exception. Look closely when Cinderella sings "Sing, Sweet Nightingale"—three bubbles converge to form Mickey's face.

The reversed Queen of Wands represents a person burning up, sweating, and fuming with jealousy. If you discover a reversed card you don't like, simply turn it right-side up to release its negative hold on the situation.

Justice Card Spread

Justice is one of the four cardinal virtues, along with Temperance, Fortitude (Strength), and Prudence. Females depicted these virtues in fifteenth and sixteenth century icons. Mysteriously, Prudence is absent from the tarot pack, though her sisters all make an appearance.

The Justice card expresses the need for balance and harmonizing conflicting needs through actions, thoughts, and words. Justice is highly aspected with work and serves as a reminder that we reap what we sow.

On This Day

On this day in 1956, the Supreme Court upheld the ban on segregation in public schools, colleges, and universities. This action corrected an injustice that never should have existed in the first place.

Summation of Spread

Using the highest US court as inspiration, this spread examines symbols found within the Justice card.

Cast Your Cards

Pull the Justice card from your deck. Place it in the center of the Justice Card Spread and cast your shuffled cards around it as follows:

1. Double-edged sword: How can I see clearly?
2. The scales: Are my actions balanced?
3. Hanging veil: What is hidden?
4. The crown: What authority do I possess?
5. The throne: Do I feel secure?
6. Foot pointing out: How can I move in the right direction?
7. Lack of blindfold: What do I see?
8. Yellow and gold colors: What action do I take?

Embrace Your Creative Process Spread

On This Day

Painter, poet, architect, and sculptor Michelangelo was born on this day in 1475. Considered one of the greatest artists to have ever lived, his volume of work and influence on the development of Western art remain voluminous. His best-known works include sculptures of David, the Pietà, and sublime frescoes in the Sistine Chapel.

Summation of Spread

Working creatively, you can invoke the spirit of Michelangelo the same way you might invoke a god for a magical ritual. Utilizing his genius for inspiration, this spread sheds light on your creative process.

Cast Your Cards

Call upon Michelangelo's consciousness and cast your cards in the shape of a painter's circular palette.

1. What helps me accept my creative gifts?
2. How do I dedicate a specific amount of time to it?
3. Do I have the space to work in?
4. Should I work in the same place each day?
5. Can I recognize and utilize creative spurts?
6. Is there a muse lingering near me?
7. What am I capable of?
8. What helps me let go of the end result?

Michelangelo claimed he only had to look inside the stone to discover the image he sought to create. While making David, he said he needed only to chip away at what was not the image to release the truth of his masterpiece.

Have you noticed that all the Aces contain a mysterious hand emerging from a cloud? Renaissance art often depicts the hand of God stretching from mysterious clouds.

Roommate Spread

The Odd Couple series was based on the play by Neil Simon of the same title.

On This Day

Today marked the last airing of popular sitcom ***The Odd Couple***. The show followed two divorced male roommates sharing a Manhattan apartment, one neat and tidy, the other messy and sloppy. Comedic conflict and television history ensued.

Summation of Spread

Roommate selection is one of the most important decisions you will ever make, due to the intimate nature of living with another person. The Roommate Spread helps ease the process by giving you an overview of your potential roommate. Use this spread when you have a particular roommate in mind.

The Seven of Cups reminds us to cast our net widely before making our choice. Each cup offers glittering possibility, just as people contain unknown possibilities. We will only truly know the contents of the cup once it has been selected. Mutual respect and responsibility between house mates is paramount. Choose wisely.

Cast Your Cards

Cast the Roommate Spread's cards in two columns.

1. Roommate in question.
2. How will we get along?
3. Will we have fun together?
4. What rules need to be placed in advance?
5. Are they clean?
6. Will they be considerate?
7. Can I trust them enough to live with them?
8. Will they be financially responsible?
9. What hidden qualities do I need to be aware of?
10. What does our living relationship look like?

1	6
2	7
3	8
4	9
5	10

Female Nature Spread

On This Day

Today is International Women's Day, first celebrated in the United States in 1909. The United Nations advocates awareness and action on this day regarding the social, political, and human rights of women around the world.

Summation of Spread

Pondering human rights, a survey of humanity begs the question as to why any sane species would inflict so much brutality and degradation upon half its population—especially the half that gives birth to the entire species! Having no say over their future or their bodies, the world unacceptably looks the other way and chalks it up to "foreign culture." This spread takes a look at control, repression, and expression operating in your life, regardless of your gender.

Cast Your Cards

Control

1. Why is feminine nature terrifying to those in control?
2. Why is there a need to control feminine nature?

Repression

3. In what way have I been repressed?
4. What part of my personality is considered dangerous by others?

Expression

5. What do I need to express?
6. What happens if I operate at the height of my potential?
7. What would the world be like if women held the power that men do?
8. What can I do to empower women?

Female domination and oppression continue in many parts of the world where women legally live as prisoners, unable to leave their homes unless under male guardianship and not possessing essential equal human rights.

The High Priestess and the Empress combined create the complete female archetype. A woman's dual nature is represented in the two cards, as the High Priestess echoes inner truth and reflective nature while the Empress represents birth and creative potential.

Limiting Belief Spread

Barbie's real name is Barbara Millicent Roberts. Boyfriend Ken was named after the son of Mattel founders Ruth and Elliot Handler.

On This Day

Today is Barbie's birthday. Mattel launched the miniature blond bombshell on this day in 1959. Barbie bore the brunt of controversy when criticized that she was an unrealistic role model for young girls. The power of Barbie prevails as she remains a popular doll and the figurehead of an empire.

Summation of Spread

Using unrealistic physical expectations of beauty as an example, this spread examines a lie that is told or believed as truth. Big growth moments occur when we realize that a truth we hold is false. This spread asks you to choose a limiting belief you believe is true. You will then pull cards to discover otherwise.

The Eight of Swords figure is bound and blindfolded in the same way limiting beliefs or long-held negative assumptions paralyze growth and opportunities.

Cast Your Cards

Write a limiting belief on a small piece of paper. Limiting beliefs are easy to spot. Choose something you want. Verbalize or write down the reason you aren't doing it. Then fill in the blank: "I can't do this because _____." Write this on a piece of paper.

Place the written belief on the table, then cast your cards beneath it:

1. Why do I believe this to be true?
2. What would happen if it weren't true?
3. Why did this belief become ingrained in my mind?
4. What can I do to erase this as truth?
5. What will happen as a result?

Lord Shiva's Find a Mate Spread

On This Day

Today is the Hindu festival for Lord Shiva. This deity is considered the supreme god and matchmaker god. As dawn breaks and humid temperatures rise, devotees flock to temples, worship, bathe, and fast.

Summation of Spread

Looking for a long-term relationship? This spread is for you. Describing steps for bringing the relationship closer, it will also suggest what to do while waiting for love to come your way.

Cast Your Cards

Prepare for the love of your life by casting your cards.

1.–3. What three characteristics should I look for in a mate?
4. What must heal from a previous relationship?
5. What unrealistic expectation must I release?
6. Where will I meet my soulmate?
7. What is his or her best quality?
8. Why will we be happy together?
9. What should I focus on in the meantime?

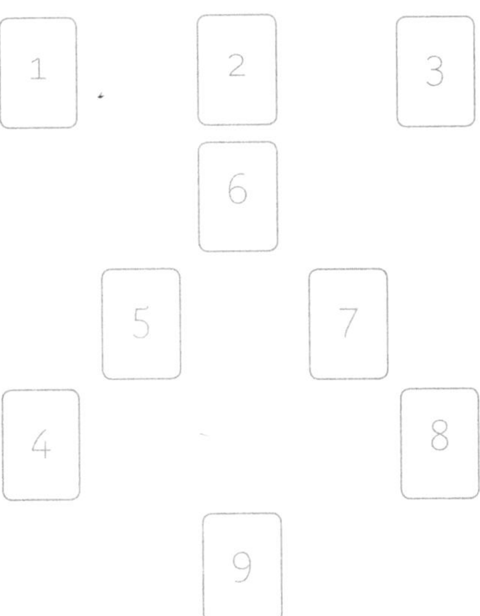

Hindu fasts—the denial of physical need for the sake of spiritual gain—exist for almost every deity. Fasts are held on certain days depending on the deity. For instance, Monday is Shiva's day in northern India. One looking for a good mate and harmonious family would fast on this day.

The Two of Cups is a matchmaker's dream. The card depicts two souls who are perfect for each other. The uniting source is not similarities to one another but complementary differences. Just as the Lovers card ponders the union of opposites, this is the moment of excitement and wonder when a new union is formed.

Unexpected Storm Spread

The East River between Manhattan and Queens froze over in 1888. The brave souls who crossed the river on foot were in for a rude awakening when the tides changed. The surface broke, leaving them stranded on ice floes.

The Tower card aligns with issues of unexpected or sudden change. The RWS Tower card reveals a circular crown knocked off a square tower. This small but subtle reference reminds us that what is unexpectedly destroyed never fit to begin with.

On This Day

One of the greatest recorded blizzards of all time occurred on this day in 1888 when 55 inches of snow fell in New York City and surrounding states. During the blizzard, transit shut down and people were confined to their homes for more than a week.

Summation of Spread

Unforeseen surprises can pop up like unexpected storms. Temperatures the day before the blizzard of '88 hovered in the mid fifties until two fronts collided. The resulting snow tempest is an example of the surprises life can throw our way. Tarot helps to cope with unforeseen circumstances by guiding us toward the highest possible path.

Cast Your Cards

The cards are cast in the form of a massive snow drift.

1. The situation at hand.
2. What is the best way to keep this situation in perspective?
3. What is good about being knocked out of my comfort zone?
4. How can I accept what I have no control over?
5. Who is available to help me with this?
6. What unexpected strength do I draw from?
7. What is the good that arises?

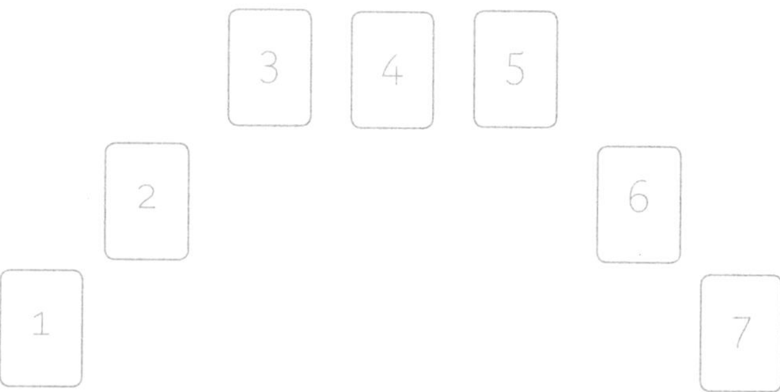

Summer Flowers Spread

Victorian women used the secret and unspoken language of flowers to express sentiments that rigid social norms of the time would not allow them to articulate.

On This Day

Today is National Plant a Flower Day. It reminds the public to get a head start on the growing season. Many summer blossoms can be started early indoors in early spring, saving time and money. Utilize items bound for your recycling bin—including eggshells, newspaper, and toilet tubes—for early planters. They can be popped right into your garden with the young plants.

Summation of Spread

The romantic, mystical Victorians assigned meanings to each and every flower under the sun. This generalized spread is inspired by floral fantasies and the meaning given to each blossom.

Cast Your Cards

Cast your cards like pollen in the wind.

1. Chrysanthemum: What makes me a good friend?
2. Cockscomb: What helps me laugh?
3. Impatiens: Why is my mother proud of me?
4. Baby's Breath: What brings me joy?
5. Calla Lily: What does my heart want to express?
6. Cosmos: What brings balance to my life?
7. Aster: Who am I thinking of?
8. Gardenia: Who is my secret love?
9. Jasmine: What increases general pleasure?

The Nine of Pentacles is a gardener's dream landscape. The card bursts with bounty, animal and vegetable coexist, and the female on the card is content and secure, at home in the garden of herself.

March • 13

Qualities of Uranus Spread

Uranus is the coldest planet in our solar system with an average temperature of -350 degrees F. Its orbit lasts the equivalent of 84 Earth years, and it has 27 moons. Seasons on Uranus last more than twenty years because the planet is tilted on its side.

On This Day

The planet Uranus was discovered today in 1781 by astronomer William Herschel. Observing the heavens though his telescope in his garden, it was the first discovery of a planet by telescope. Herschel distinguished it as a planet, not a star as had been previously believed. He also discovered two of its twenty-seven moons, Titania and Oberon.

Summation of Spread

This spread contains questions based on the astrological associations of the planet Uranus. This general spread uses a heavenly body to offer you greater clarity in life.

Like Uranus, the Fool card has rebellious, radical ideas. Both the Fool and Uranus rule originality and progress, operating outside of societal norms. The Fool is a free thinker whose purpose is to foster new beginnings in life. He is so fresh, so new, and so blank that he is numbered zero. He is pure potential in action.

Cast Your Cards

Cast your cards in the shape of a cross, which forms part of Uranus's astrological symbol.

1. Radical ideas: What outlandish idea must I follow up on?
2. Progression: What area of life am I making the greatest progress in?
3. Adventure: What adventure awaits?
4. Surprise: What hidden surprise will delight?
5. Disruption: What must be destroyed?
6. Awakening: What must be awakened?

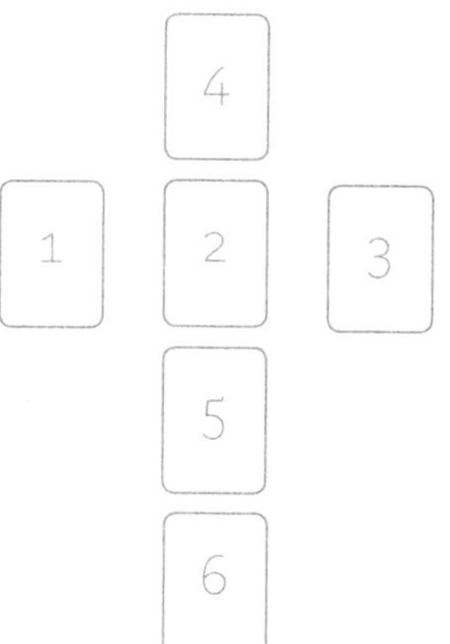

Reciprocation of Love Spread

On This Day

White Day is a Japanese romantic holiday celebrated today. Japanese Valentine's Day differs from the States as women bestow chocolate gifts upon men. On White Day, men who received chocolate now return the favor. They offer gifts of white chocolate, white lingerie, white cookies, or marshmallows to the women in their life.

Sinfully sweet chocolate has long been considered an aphrodisiac. Aztec chief Montezuma would consume a "choclati" drink flavored with vanilla and spices before visiting his harem.

Summation of Spread

Reciprocity, the simple give and take of love and affection, is core to any relationship, romantic or otherwise. Japan's White Day is an opportunity for you to explore the state of give and take in your romantic realm.

Cast Your Cards

Shuffle the cards. Think of the one you love. Imagine their sparkling eyes, warm hands, and soft kisses as you cast the cards in the shape of your affectionate and generous heart.

1. Whom do I love?
2. Are they a good partner for me?
3. How do they make me feel special?
4. How do I make them feel special?
5. What is the greatest gift I can give my love?
6. What is the gift they give to me?
7. How do we lift each other up?
8. How do we tear each other down?
9. Why is this relationship worth the effort?
10. What special, fun, unique gift can I surprise them with?

The angel in the Temperance card hovers above the water, actively mixing fluids. These fluids move back and forth like the give and take of a relationship, keeping everything in symbiotic balance.

Is My Crush Crushing Back Spread

Romeo and Juliet is the most widely retold and restaged love story, with seventy-seven movie versions made to date. Through the play, the lovers speak of their fate as if they are being guided by a supernatural force.

The Lovers speak of important choices one makes upon finding the reflection of your heart in another. The Lovers raises issues of sexuality and sensuality, the possibility of creation and discovery, and of the undulating line where your skin ends and your lover's begins.

On This Day

Based on information Shakespeare gave to us within the *Romeo and Juliet* text, today is the day the world's most famous lovers were married.

Summation of Spread

Is the apple of your eye eyeballing you back? These star-crossed sweethearts inspire a juicy love spread. Will your feelings be returned? Survey the situation with your cards to know exactly how to proceed.

Cast Your Cards

Thrice whisper your crush's name at midnight beneath the light of the full moon and cast your cards.

1. Myself.
2. My crush.
3. What does their body language indicate?
4. Do they make good eye contact with me?
5. Do they make physical contact with me?
6. Do they treat me differently than other people?
7. Are they showing interest in things I like?
8. Do they seem nervous around me?
9. Are they interested?
10. Should I make a move?
11. Will my heart get crushed?
12. Will it be worth it?

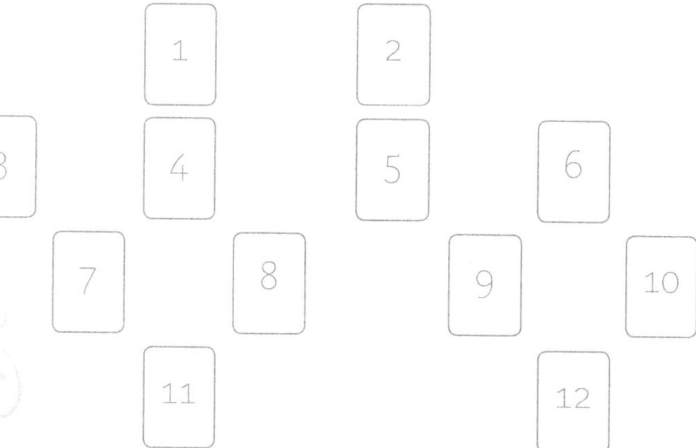

Alice Hoffman's Practical Magic Spread

On This Day

Author Alice Hoffman was born on this day in 1952. Her extraordinary *Practical Magic* describes two bewitching sisters struggling to use their gift of hereditary magic in life and in love.

Summation of Spread

This spread, inspired by Alice Hoffman's magical realism, reflects on the magical currents coursing through your life. Pay close attention to energetic reserves that are yours for the taking when you reach out to become who you truly are.

Cast Your Cards

Invoke magic and cast your cards like a field of fireflies illuminating the night.

1. What is the nature of magic?
2. How does magic weave itself through my life?
3. Do I know how powerful I am?
4. What helps me harness my power?
5. Where should I focus my attention?
6. What must I cultivate?
7. What must I let go?
8. What spell/intention should I cast?

Hoffman admits her childhood was not always a happy one. Speaking of the magic she discovered amidst the escapism of books, the young Hoffman was often found in the library.

The Page, or Knave, of Pentacles is most likely to be found lost in the beauty of prose, expanding her mind through the words of others, and buried in a book. The most studious and serious of all pages, this page's love of learning is unparalleled by any other card in the deck.

St. Patrick's Shamrock Spread

Cause and effect applies to the Wiccan Rule of Three, stating that any energy or magic released into the world will return to the caster three times.

On This Day

St. Patrick's Day celebrates the anniversary of the death of St. Patrick. Kidnapped, sold into slavery, escaping, then receiving religious training, St. Patrick returned to Ireland in 432 CE as a missionary. Upon his return, he explained the concept of the Holy Trinity to the uneducated public using the shamrock as an allegory. This is why the shamrock is the symbol associated with St. Patrick's Day. The Irish have observed this holiday for over one thousand years.

Summation of Spread

The Shamrock Spread uses the concept of three to inform its questions. Using the Holy Trinity of Christianity, the Three Jewels of Buddhism, and the Threefold Goddess of Wicca, you'll look into various aspects of your identity.

The Empress card is assigned the number 3. Representing possibility, creativity, growth, wealth, and marriage, she is a generous and protective woman.

Cast Your Cards

Four-leaf clovers bring luck, too. Find one, keep it close, and cast your cards.

1. Father: How do I relate to my father?
2. Son: How am I different from my father?
3. Holy Ghost: What is my mystery?

1. Buddha: What is my highest spiritual potential?
2. Dharma: How can I follow a path to enlightenment?
3. Sangha: What does community mean to me?

1. Maiden: How do I differ from my mother?
2. Mother: How do I relate to my mother?
3. Crone: What is my destiny?

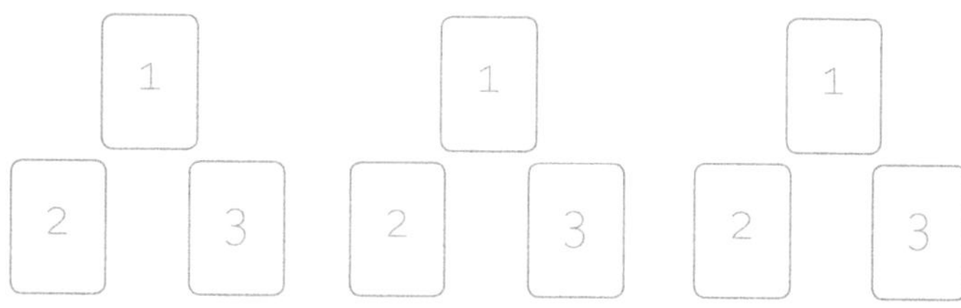

Edgar Cayce's Aura Spread

On This Day

American psychic, prophet, mystic, and seer Edgar Cayce was born this day in 1877. Cayce's method of prophesy involved lying down and entering a sleep state to answer a subject's questions. Cayce's purported abilities included astral projection, mediumship, and seeing auras.

Summation of Spread

Auras are an energy field, a reflection of the subtle life energies within a body. Holistic healers attribute emotional states to auras. This spread is inspired by Cayce and the qualities attributed to aura colors.

Cast Your Cards

Select a significator card representing how you are feeling at the moment. Cast your cards around the significator.

1. Significator card representing you.
2. Red: Health status.
3. Orange: Am I in a creative place?
4. Yellow: What is the state of my intellectuality?
5. Green: Am I feeling balanced?
6. Blue: What is my spiritual state?
7. Indigo: What is a spiritual state I cannot deny?
8. Violet: My love life.
9. Brown: What am I feeling negative about?
10. White: Can I wipe the slate clean?

Cayce felt his life's work was healing the sick and conducting spiritual inquiry and study. Gaining celebrity status near the end of his life, he feared the public paid more attention to his prophesies than to the work he deemed important.

The Hanged Man has a yellow halo around his head like an aura. Allegorically, it represents a state of spiritual illumination. From the Roman gods to Jesus Christ and from Buddhist deities to Persian miniatures, these halos are found cross-culturally in religious iconography.

Wisdom of Minerva Spread

Minerva's Greek counterpart was Athena, for whom the city of Athens was named.

On This Day

Ancient Romans held the festival of Minerva, goddess of war, wisdom, arts, crafts, and sciences, on this day. Minerva is often depicted with a sheath of armor and helmet; her sacred creature is an owl, symbolizing ancient wisdom.

Summation of Spread

Gods, like archetypes, stand as shining examples for us mortals roaming the earthly realms. Gods offer us a gold standard, a specialty, a bar to strive for. This spread uses Minerva's archetype to deeply explore, cultivate, and disseminate the roots of your wisdom.

The High Priestess represents the wisdom of Minerva, while all four knights represent fierce warrior qualities. True wisdom lies in how you utilize the tarot deck, a metaphysical machine awaiting your gentle touch and unique interpretations.

Cast Your Cards

Cast your cards in the shape of owl eyes:

1. What do I see that others do not?
2. What do I see when I look into darkness?
3. What do I understand about life?
4. What do I understand about myself?
5. What am I here to do?
6. What knowledge do I carry with me?
7. How do I open to receive wisdom?
8. How do I free my mind?

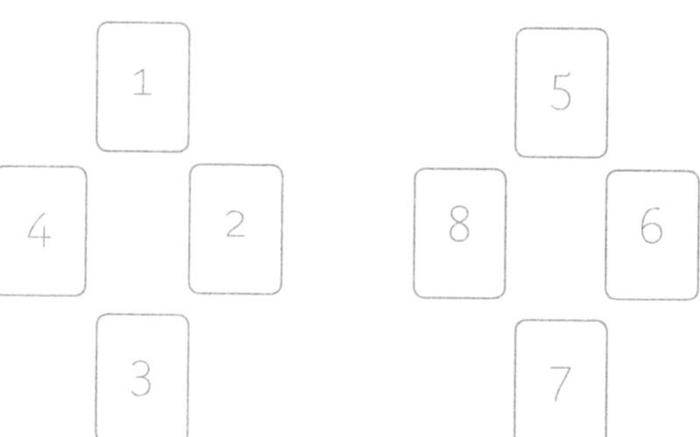

Ostara Serpent Magic Spread

On This Day

Ostara is the Anglo-Saxon spelling of the name for the Germanic deity of spring. Her attributes include eggs, babies, and bunnies, coinciding with Easter but holding Pagan rather than Christian resonance.

Summation of Spread

Spring, in addition to its fertility rites, marks the awakening of all slumbering creatures, ideas, and plans. In Scotland, Highlanders traditionally pounded the ground with a stick until a serpent emerged. The reptile's behavior gave an indication of how early spring would come. The Ostara Serpent Magic Spread seeks to discover what slumbers within you.

Cast Your Cards

An excellent spread to perform on a warm spring day, be sure not to rush through it. Arrive at specific answers to each question before moving ahead. Cast the cards as a snake uncoiling itself:

1. What is reborn this year?
2. How do I activate my passion?
3. How can I stimulate my intellect?
4. What must become conscious?
5. How do I become an active participant in my life?
6. What does metamorphosis mean to me?
7. What can I uncoil and free?
8. What message does the serpent whisper in my ear?

Germanic tribes that honored Ostara, a lunar goddess, explain how she mates with her fertility god at this time of year. She gives birth nine months later during the Yule celebration.

The Judgement card is the card of resurrection and metamorphosis. While an awakening of consciousness may occur anytime, spring provokes a general sense of renewal in almost everyone. Be sure to keep your ears open to whatever calls you.

Qualities of Aries Spread

Aries is ruled by the planet Mars, red is the primary color, the lucky day is Tuesday, and the best location for success is in any big city. Aries rules the house of the self, physical appearance, and first impressions.

Aries' ram's horns glyph is often next to the Emperor. The Emperor is the pure embodiment of this sign as he displays an action-oriented, forward-thinking mind. Never afraid of taking charge, the Emperor is a fearless defender, like the Greek god of war for whom this sign was named.

On This Day

Today marks the first day of the astrological sign of Aries, the Ram.

Summation of Spread

This spread is based on the essential qualities of Aries, including being demanding, ambitious, and effective, as well as exhibiting courageousness, leadership, and determination.

Cast Your Cards

The Aries Spread's cards are cast in the shape of the Aries symbol, or glyph, in the shape of the ram's horns.

1. What needs to be expressed at this moment?
2. In what ways do I lead others?
3. In what ways am I headstrong?
4. What do I demand of myself?
5. Where does ambition lead me?
6. When am I most effective?
7. How am I courageous?

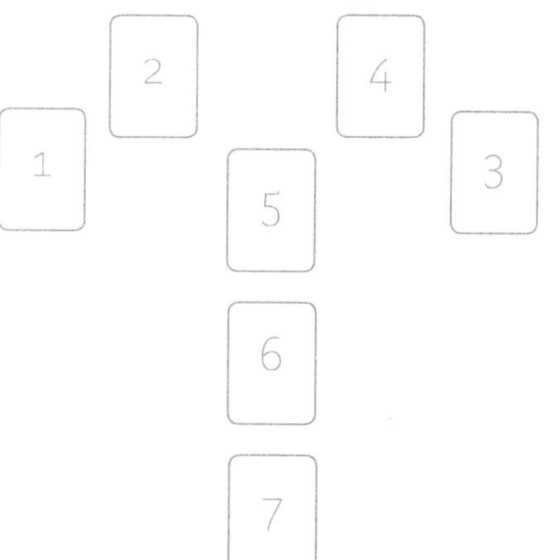

Wheel of Fortune Spread

On This Day

You wouldn't want to be caught with a deck of tarot cards in the Massachusetts Bay Colony on this day in 1630. Town officials enacted a law banning possession of cards, dice, and gaming tables.

Summation of Spread

Gambling often references the icon of the Wheel of Fortune. This spread is based on symbols found upon the Wheel of Fortune card and looks at where this lucky symbol could lead you.

Cast Your Cards

Use this spread to answer any question. Format your question before casting the spread or simply let the cards answer the questions posed. Pull the Wheel of Fortune card from your deck. Placing it in the center of the spread, cast your cards around it.

1. Wheel: Where is my energy moving?
2. Sphinx: What is the riddle?
3. Serpent: What is potent right now?
4. Jackal: What is rising?
5. Lion (Leo): What do I need to be strong about?
6. Ox (Taurus): What am I being stubborn about?
7. Person (Aquarius): What makes me human?
8. Eagle (Scorpio): What ideas take flight?

Older than any tarot deck, the Wheel of Fortune icon is displayed in medieval manuscripts and on church walls throughout Europe. The symbol endures because it serves as a reminder of the temporary nature of life.

The Wheel of Fortune portends the beginning of a new cycle, but unlike the Fool, who starts afresh, the Wheel makes use of past lessons learned. The Wheel also denotes changing fortunes, a rash of luck, and sometimes a windfall of cash. Fortune spins her wheel, and the fates of those attached rise and fall at her whim.

Philosopher's Spread

Nietzsche suffered a psychotic breakdown at age 44. Sending letters to friends, he signed them "Dionysus the Crucified." Placed into asylums and then into his mother's care, he lived in a semiconscious state until his death at age 56.

Philosophy is the study of knowledge, reality, and the nature of existence. The High Priestess's reality is entirely based in her inner realm of knowing and understanding.

On This Day

Friedrich Nietzsche, one of the world's most profound and influential modern philosophers, was awarded his doctorate from the University of Leipzig on this day in 1869.

Summation of Spread

Nietzsche questioned reality, the world, and everything we live in and by, believing life's basic doctrines should be examined no matter the consequence. The Philosopher's Spread utilizes basic philosophical questions to discover your opinions regarding the nature of existence.

Cast Your Cards

This is an excellent spread to perform with a friend or a small group of people. Each question may be posed as fodder for a group discussion. The card will retain your group's focus. Taking turns, answer the questions based on the card received.

Cast in the shape of a circle, the symbol of infinity, with the final question posed in the center.

1. Why is there something rather than nothing?
2. Is our universe real?
3. Do we have free will?
4. Does God exist?
5. Is there life after death?
6. Can I really experience something objectively?
7. How do we know what's right or wrong?
8. What are numbers if you can't really see them?
9. What is being?

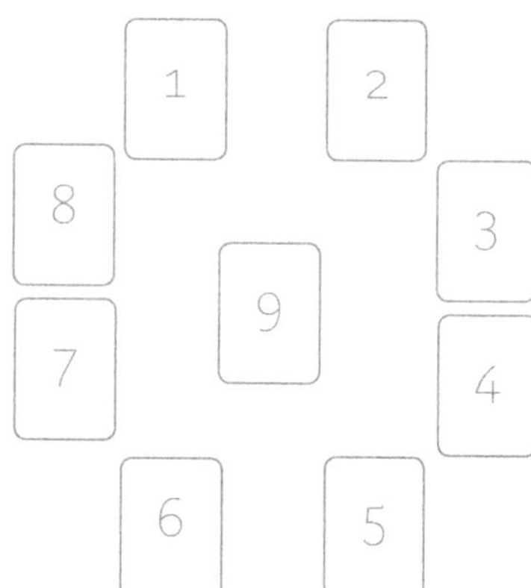

Conflict Resolution Spread

On This Day

Today is archangel Gabriel's feast day in the Roman calendar. Gabriel is the messenger angel because he told Elizabeth and Mary about the impending births of their sons, John the Baptist and Jesus. He also dictated the spiritual text of Islam, the Koran, to Mohammed. Hmmm, sounds a touch like fortunetelling and mediumship, doesn't it?

Summation of Spread

Feeling a Mercury retrograde? Suffering through a misunderstanding? The patron saint of communications and messengers, Gabriel inspires questions posed to ease communications between people, coworkers, colleagues, friends, loved ones, or family members when conflicts arise.

Cast Your Cards

Cast the Conflict Resolution Spread's cards in a gentle arch, representing the bridge to communication.

1. Can I make the first move?
2. What helps me understand that I can't change them?
3. What is one realistic expectation?
4. What helps communication?
5. How can I be a better listener?
6. How can I repair the damage quickly?
7. What would I see standing in their shoes?
8. What helps me forgive?
9. Can we agree to disagree?
10. Final outcome.

Unresolved conflict leads to resentment, which causes negative impacts on health and longevity. Resolve conflicts now to avoid future negativity.

The archangel Gabriel is seen blowing a trumpet, indicating God's return to earth to the souls beneath him. This image is translated in modern times as a wake-up call that inner transformation is at hand.

Olympian Advice Spread

The Titans were a primeval race of powerful deities who ruled during the Golden Age. They were overthrown by the Olympians, a race of younger gods, during the War of the Titans.

On This Day

Today is Greece's national independence day. Greece's successful revolt against the Ottoman Empire is celebrated with street parades and parties.

Summation of Spread

In addition to Greece's contributions of art, philosophy, mathematics, and science to the modern world, they have passed on their unique pantheon of gods. This spread makes use of twelve gods who offer advice from their vantage point atop Mount Olympus.

Cast Your Cards

The answer for each card is to be given in the form of advice. Imagine each god speaking to you through the card.

1. Zeus: fatherly advice about your life.
2. Hera: motherly advice about your family.
3. Poseidon: watery advice about your emotional life.
4. Aphrodite: beautiful advice about romantic love.
5. Demeter: active advice about your creative ability.
6. Dionysus: sensual advice about cultivating more pleasure in your life.
7. Apollo: divine advice about owning your knowledge.
8. Artemis: loving advice about communication with animal friends.
9. Hermes: firm advice about being in the driver's seat.
10. Athena: serious advice on anger management.
11. Ares: profound advice on death and birth.
12. Hephaestus: sage advice on passion.

Greek gods contain the same archetypal patterns as major arcana cards. In a separate exercise, discover if you can connect the gods mentioned in the Olympian Advice Spread with the corresponding major arcana cards. There is no right or wrong answer; it's simply a thought exercise to discover the underlying power of archetypes.

Joseph Campbell's Hero's Journey Spread

On This Day

Joseph Campbell, mythologist, writer, and lecturer, was born this day in 1904. Coining the term "follow your bliss," he is best known for the popularization of the Hero's Journey.

George Lucas credits Joseph Campbell's influence on Star Wars, *which he wrote after reading Campbell's* Hero with a Thousand Faces.

Summation of Spread

This hearty spread offers an opportunity to examine where you are and where you are heading in the near future.

Cast Your Cards

1. Ordinary World: The present moment.
2. Call to Adventure: What adventure is calling me?
3. Refusal of the Call: What stops me from accepting the challenge?
4. Supernatural Aid: Who is my guide/helper along the way?
5. The Road of Trials: What is my challenge?
6. Meeting with the Goddess: What or whom do I love most?
7. Woman as Temptress: What do I desire more than anything?
8. Atonement with Father: What person or thing holds ultimate power in my life?
9. Ultimate Boon: What happens when I confront this power?
10. Master of Two Worlds: How do I accept the duality of my journey and integrate it into my life?
11. What strength do I draw upon confronting this challenge?
12. What is my reward?
13. How am I changed?

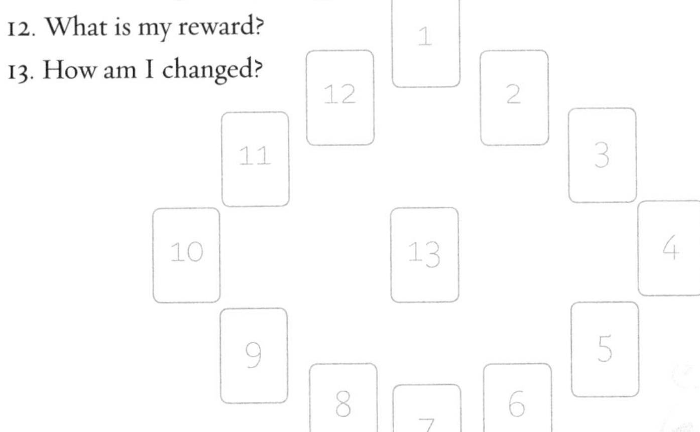

The Fool can be seen as the soul embarking on the Hero's Journey. Moving through the cards with a nose for adventure and a knack for all things supernatural, he learns lessons, transforming into a hero.

March • 27

Titanic's Unrequited Love Spread

Kate Winslet campaigned for the role of Rose, sending James Cameron daily notes that included a rose and the sign-off "From your Rose." Cameron originally envisioned the character as "an Audrey Hepburn type," but Kate eventually won him over, and the rest is film history.

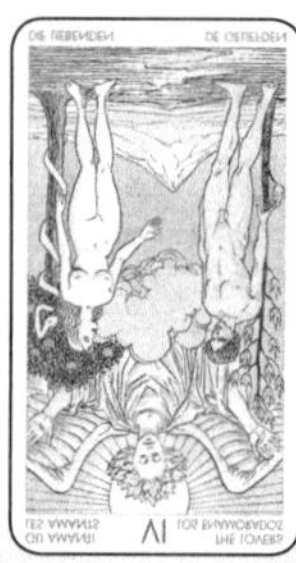

Unrequited, impossible, or doomed love is represented by a reversed Lovers card. Reversals can often relate to the card's opposite meaning. The Lovers card typically represents love and romance, so its reversal could metaphorically signify a lover on the bottom of the ocean.

On This Day

The 3D version of James Cameron's *Titanic* premiered on this day in London in 2012. This epic romantic-disaster movie broke box office records, picked up scores of Academy Awards, and left audiences sobbing.

Summation of Spread

Nothing sears the heart like unrequited love. The tragedy of Jack and Rose was like that of Romeo and Juliet: their love never had time to mature or blossom. The dazzling, luminous question of "what if" lingers. This spread examines a love that, for whatever reason, cannot be.

Cast Your Cards

Remember, it is better to have loved and lost than not to have loved at all. Cast your cards as follows:

1. Myself.
2. Our attraction.
3. The object of my love.
4. Why I love them.
5. Why they love me.
6. Why can't we be together?
7. What would have happened if we were together?
8. Why is it best we are apart?
9. How can I express love anyway?
10. What is learned?

Kuan Yin's Compassion Spread

On This Day

Today is the birthday of beloved Eastern Buddhist deity Kuan Yin, the bodhisattva (buddha-to-be) of infinite compassion and mercy. In Malaysia, devotees bearing fresh fruit, flowers, and sweet cakes gather at her temple to honor her. Immensely popular among Chinese Buddhists, she is seen as a source of unconditional love, a savior, and a protector of women and children.

Summation of Spread

Reflecting upon the nature of compassion, Kuan Yin is perfect inspiration for this spread. The deity inspires questions posed to open your heart and soul.

Cast Your Cards

Release resistance and cast the Kuan Yin Compassion Spread's cards as follows:

1. What does compassion mean to me?
2. How am I compassionate?
3. In what area do I not show compassion?
4. What can I let go of to have a more compassionate heart?
5. What feelings do I experience when I offer compassion?
6. How can I find empathy for someone I dislike?
7. Who has shown compassion to me?
8. How can I recognize commonalities rather than differences?

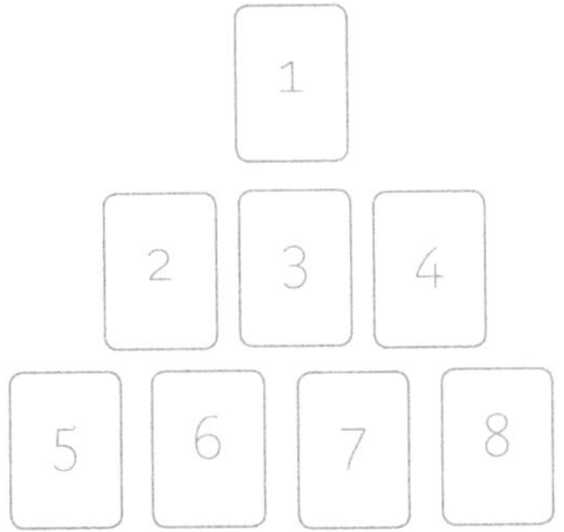

Kuan Yin is associated with vegetarianism due to her empathetic state. Chinese vegetarian restaurants are often decorated with her image, and she appears in many Buddhist vegetarian pamphlets and magazines.

The Ace of Cups represents the waters of true tenderheartedness as the universal source for the soul of humanity. It is the ability to experience emotions, love, joy, and suffering—the entire range of human experience.

March • 29

To have a mercurial nature means displaying qualities of eloquence, shrewdness, and swiftness. It also means having a quick, changeable, sometimes volatile personality.

The quality of communication belongs to the entire suit of Swords. The King and Queen of Swords are the great communicators of the tarot deck, using their eloquence, razor-sharp intellect, and oratory skills to communicate precisely what is on their mind.

Mercury's Business Communication Spread

On This Day

The Messenger spacecraft sent the first orbital image of the planet Mercury to Earth on this day in 2011. The spacecraft arrived after a six-year journey, sending back images of the spidery craters and barren landscapes of valleys, mountains, highlands, and plains of this innermost planet.

Summation of Spread

Astrologically, Mercury rules all messages, day-to-day expression, and thought. Unemotional and curious, Mercury can be called upon to increase the quality of all communications, business or otherwise. This spread examines conversation and growth in terms of business.

Cast Your Cards

Place your business vision in the center and surround it with important questions. Envision the growth and blooming of your business and cast as follows:

1. What is my vision?
2. What opens my perception to hear others?
3. How do I present myself in the best way possible?
4. How do I maintain clarity?
5. Do I adequately express enthusiasm?
6. What helps me negotiate?
7. Am I following up in the best way possible?
8. What stands in my way?
9. How can I use communication to grow my business in the best way possible?

Goddess of Health Spread

It is a proven fact that laughter and connecting with friends boosts your immune system and decreases stress hormones.

On This Day

Today is the Roman festival date for Salus, goddess of health and preservation, success and good fortune. Her name literally means "salvation."

Summation of Spread

Looking to become healthier? Spring is the perfect time of year to contemplate health as greens and veggies sprout from the ground and days grow longer. The heavily bundled clothes of winter are shed, making way for lighter fabrics. Using this ancient goddess of health, the questions of this spread are inspired by all the aspects of a wholesome lifestyle.

Cast Your Cards

Cast your cards in the shape of an apple because an apple a day keeps the doctor at bay:

1. Am I getting enough sleep?
2. Am I tending to my relationships?
3. How can I increase the health of my diet?
4. What helps me eat healthy whole foods?
5. What exercise do I love?
6. What increases my happiness?
7. What increases my creativity?
8. What action can I take to improve my health?
9. Why am I worth it?

The Nine of Pentacles is a woman who is comfortable in her skin and who takes excellent care of herself, representing the harmony of what one wants and what one has. She understands real wealth is the value of what you already have, body included, and thereby exemplifies the present enjoyment of it.

Secrets of the Moon Spread

Scientists believe the moon was once part of Earth, and it was formed when a Mars-sized object crashed into the earth 4.5 billion years ago.

On This Day

Today is the Roman festival of Luna according to Ovid, who describes this ritual worship on Aventine Hill in Rome. Luna, the Roman divine embodiment of the moon, is represented as the female complement to the sun.

Summation of Spread

The moon is associated with magic, the psychic, and the feminine. Transformations evolve during her cycles and lunar events. All these lunar aspects inspire the spread's questions.

Cast Your Cards

Feel her glow and cast cards during the waxing moon. It is a time of magnetism and of attracting good things into your life:

1. New: What is possible?
2. Waxing: What am I drawing to me?
3. Full: Where does my power lie?
4. Waning: What do I need to shed?
5. Lunar Eclipse: What darkens my mood?
6. Dark Side of the Moon: What lurks within my hidden side?
7. Tidal Pull: In what area of life do I have the greatest effect?
8. What is now possible?

The Moon card is evocative of the perceived dangers of the unconscious. The sun broadly shines while the moon remains elusive, ever changing, and mysterious. The crawfish crawling out of the pool appears to be under the moon's spell. Something surprising is brought to the surface. You learn and confront something new about yourself.

Fool's Spread

In the ruling days of monarchy, fools or court jesters were often the only members of the court with the freedom to do or say anything they pleased. While fools and simpletons act outside the bounds of normalcy, this ultimate outsider status actually brought them freedom.

On This Day

Today is April Fool's Day, twenty-four hours of light-hearted pranks and jokes. No resource explains how or why the practical jokes began, but it is likely connected to the oldest fertility rites of spring, when the sun's return echoed the continuance of human life.

Summation of Spread

Today was made for the Fool card, on whom this spread is based. The questions are based on symbolism found within the Fool card.

Cast Your Cards

Use this spread to answer any question. Format your question before casting the spread or simply let the cards answer the questions posed.

Pull the Fool card out of your deck. Place it in the center of the spread and cast your cards around it:

1. Dog: What do I have faith in?
2. Bag: What do I carry with me from the past?
3. Cliff: What unseen danger lies ahead?
4. White Rose: What do I strive for?
5. Mountain: Where do I feel most enlightened?
6. Fool's Upturned Face: What happens when I follow my bliss?
7. Fool's Question: Am I following my dreams?
8. Number Zero: What potential exists?

The Fool represents a fresh start and a new beginning. Because he harbors no fear, the Fool represents freedom. If you follow the Fool's path, new possibilities evolve and your landscape will inevitably change.

My Fairy Tale Spread

Hans Christian Andersen had a habit of falling in love with unattainable women. Upon his death, a small pouch was found on his chest. The pouch contained a letter from his first unrequited love of many decades earlier.

The magic found in fairy tales also thrives in the suit of Wands. In addition to representing fire and passion, they are actual magical wands reverberating with power and the ability to achieve anything the bearer sets their mind to.

On This Day

Hans Christian Andersen, beloved Danish author of fairy tales such as *The Little Mermaid*, *The Princess and the Pea*, and *The Emperor's New Clothes*, was born on this day in 1805.

Summation of Spread

Did you know your life is a fairy tale? All fairy tales contain common themes and motifs. These essential components can be found in your life and are activated by this spread.

Cast Your Cards

Make a wish upon a star, roll up your sleeves, and cast the cards as follows:

1. Hero: Who am I?
2. Villain: What is my challenge?
3. Magic: How do I weave enchantment?
4. Nature: What natural elemental do I have a close affinity to?
5. Word, Potion, or Object: What is my power object?
6. Supernatural Helper: Who is watching and helping me?
7. Helpful Animal: Who is my animal spirit guide?
8. Magic of Three: What is the role of creativity in my life?
9. Ending: What is the culmination of my current journey?

Rolling the Dice Fortunetelling Spread

On This Day

The El Rancho Vegas opened today in 1941, becoming the very first resort on the infamous Las Vegas Strip.

Summation of Spread

Cards, throwing dice, gambling, luck, and fortunetelling have always been intertwined. Dice can be thrown for divination too. Sybil Leek explains in her book *On Fortune Telling* how dice are tossed into a 360-degree circle. The circle is divided into twelve 30-degree sections. The information in each sector is based on the number reflected in the dice. This spread is based on Sybil's method, using tarot cards instead of dice.

Cast Your Cards

Sector 1: Events of your next year.
Sector 2: State of your finances.
Sector 3: Chances for travel.
Sector 4: Home life atmosphere.
Sector 5: Business enterprises.
Sector 6: Health outlook.
Sector 7: Marriage and partnerships.
Sector 8: Inheritances and deaths.
Sector 9: General state of mind.
Sector 10: Your profession and occupation.
Sector 11: Your friendships.
Sector 12: Your enemies.

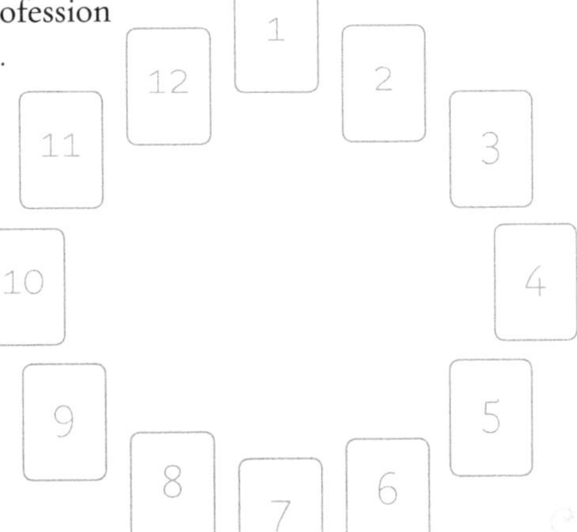

Love flows as freely in Vegas as cards and dice. Anyone over the age of sixteen can obtain a marriage license in Las Vegas for $55. The average cost of filing for divorce is $450.

The Wheel of Fortune card reflects life's ups and downs and is likely the only tarot motif on plenty of slot machines.

April • 4

Where Should I Live Spread

About 62 percent of people still live in the state where they were born. Florida has the lowest percentage of people born there who still live there.

On This Day

Actress Grace Kelly, along with family, bridesmaids, poodle, and over eighty pieces of luggage, boarded an ocean liner in New York Harbor bound for the French Riviera on this day in 1956. Thousands of New York fans waved goodbye. In Monaco, over 20,000 onlookers lined the streets to greet their future princess.

Summation of Spread

While the fanfare of Grace Kelly's move was extraordinary, making the personal decision to move can be challenging. One of the most important decisions you will ever make, this spread is designed to help you find the living situation of your dreams.

The Eight of Cups and Six of Swords are both "moving" cards. Each card suggests better times lie ahead. The Eight of Cups signifies a move alone; the Six of Swords, a move with others.

Cast Your Cards

1. Should I move somewhere completely new?
2. Will I be disappointed if I don't leave?
3. What environment do I enjoy?
4. What type of dwelling feels cozy to me?
5. Do I want to move far away?
6. Should I move to a new country?
7. Where am I passionate about living?
8. What size town is good for me?
9. Is culture important to me?
10. Is it important to live near my friends?
11. How much are other people influencing my decision?
12. What is my final outcome?

Writing a Will Spread

On This Day

Howard Hughes, one of the wealthiest men in the world, died on this day in 1976 without a will. His estate was in dispute over thirty-four years after his death and was ultimately split between twenty-two cousins in 1983.

The oldest will was found in a tomb in Egypt. Dating from 2548 BCE, a man named Uah left all his property to his wife, Teta.

Summation of Spread

Have you written a will? Writing a will is more for the people you love than for yourself. It protects loved ones and your estate, and it makes sure your intentions are carried out. This spread is best performed before writing or revising a will.

Cast Your Cards

Remember, these may be the last words and wishes you will convey. Cast the cards as follows:

1. How do I find the right lawyer?
2. What do I want them to do with my body?
3. Who will make sure my intentions are carried out?
4. How should I express my intentions?
5. Have I inventoried and categorized my assets?
6. Do I understand how taxes affect what I give away?
7. Is there a charity I'd like to support?
8. What choice do I need to make regarding my living will?

Justice embodies the need for people to harmonize possibilities, thoughts, and words so the independence of the mind is attained and expressed. This is especially important in writing wills and in all contractual matters.

The Temple of Apollo's Know Thyself Spread

Apollo Delphinus was the god Apollo's dolphin form. It was believed he commandeered a Cretan ship in dolphin form and forced it to land on Delphi's coastline, where the sailors became the island's first priests.

The Knight of Cups, like dolphin-formed Apollo Delphinus, combines warrior qualities with a shapeshifting ability to make for a sensual and powerful knight.

On This Day

The ancient Greek festival Delphinia, held in honor of Apollo, was celebrated today with a procession of virgins, athletic games, and sacrifices. Apollo was the handsome, eternally young god of prophecy, archery, music, and medicine.

Summation of Spread

How well do you know yourself? *Know thyself* was inscribed at the Temple of Apollo in Delphi, according to writer Pausanias. This spread inquires about you and just how well you know the person living in your skin.

Cast Your Cards

Gaze in the mirror. Did you know you are much more than the shapeshifter looking back at you? Cast in the shape of the laurel wreath that often graced Apollo's head.

1. What is my understanding of the universe?
2. What is my understanding of the earth?
3. What role do my parents play in my life?
4. What is the relationship between my body and my mind?
5. How free am I to create possibility for myself?
6. What invokes my curiosity?
7. What fascinates me?
8. What helps me follow my true path?

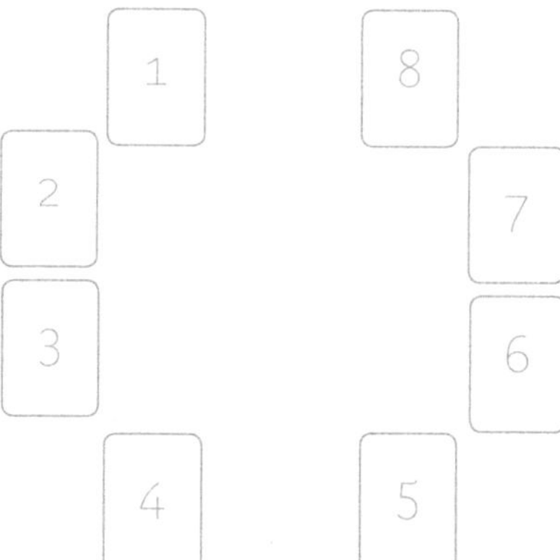

Reason to Celebrate Spread

On This Day

Wine and spirit lovers, rejoice: today marks the "soft opening" of the repeal of Prohibition. On this day in 1933, FDR signed an act so that manufacturers could legally produce and sell beer of 3.2 percent alcohol.

Summation of Spread

Feel like celebrating? The Reason to Celebrate Spread examines the amazing qualities of your life so you can raise a glass (of whatever you like) and toast yourself.

Cast Your Cards

1. What is my best quality?
2. What makes my body unique?
3. Who loves me?
4. Why is my family amazing?
5. What is my most unique talent?
6. Why do I make the world a better place?

1 2 3 4 5 6

Speakeasies, places illegally selling alcohol, were called this due to the fact one would often have to whisper a password to get inside. Once inside, guests were asked to "speak easy" so as not to make too much noise and alert the authorities to its existence.

The social movement of temperance was the force leading to Prohibition. The temperance movement promoted complete abstinence from drinking. It holds little in common with the concept of balance and what the Temperance card actually refers to.

Wisdom of Swords Spread

The Salem witch hysteria began with a group of young girls playing fortunetelling games, which were forbidden by rigid Puritan dogma.

On This Day

On this day in 1692, arrest warrants were issued for Elizabeth Proctor and Sarah Cloyce for the practice of witchcraft. Both women ultimately escaped the gallows where nineteen others had swung in an unnecessary and deathly case of mass witch hysteria.

Summation of Spread

Tarot reflects the spectrum of the human condition. The decision to end someone's life falls under the darkest aspect of the suit of Swords. Nothing is more destructive than a mind set on bloodlust and violence, and the extreme qualities of any suit can be deadly. Swords, typically the most frightening tarot suit, represent the quality of Air—our minds, thoughts, reasoning, and comprehension. Swords represent our intellectual understanding and what we tell ourselves about the world around us. This spread is based on the typical qualities of the suit of Swords.

Swords reflect the metaphor of the double-edged sword. For every decision, idea, or judgment you make, there is always another side that may be just as correct as the assumption you have arrived at.

Cast Your Cards

Cast in the shape of a knight's sword:

1. Change: What do I need to change?
2. Power: How can I best exercise my power?
3. Oppression: How do I oppress myself?
4. Courage: How am I strong?
5. Conflict: What is bothering me?
6. Intellectuality: How can I reexamine my current situation?
7. Mind: How do I best expand my mind?
8. Action: What action should I take today?

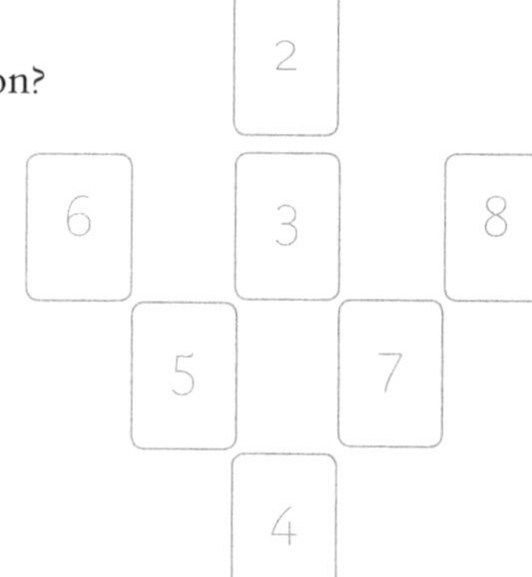

Vacation Spread

On This Day

Times Square was officially named on this day in 1904. Always the cultural hub of New York City, its history reflects the glittering lights of Broadway theater, dance halls, restaurants, and hotels. From the seedy peep shows, go-go bars, and prostitution of the '70s to the current Disneyfication and gentrification, it remains a number-one tourist attraction, with over 39,200,000 visitors annually.

Summation of Spread

Have you planned a vacation? Cast this spread after you have decided upon a destination to see what the travel gods have in store for you.

Cast Your Cards

Grab your passport, sunglasses, and guidebook, then cast your cards in the shape of an airplane.

1. Will there be delays in traveling?
2. If so, what can I do to circumnavigate the issue?
3. What is the most important thing about this vacation?
4. What new thing should I try while away?
5. Will a romantic spark be ignited?
6. How do I make the most of my vacation?
7. What unexpected awesomeness may happen?

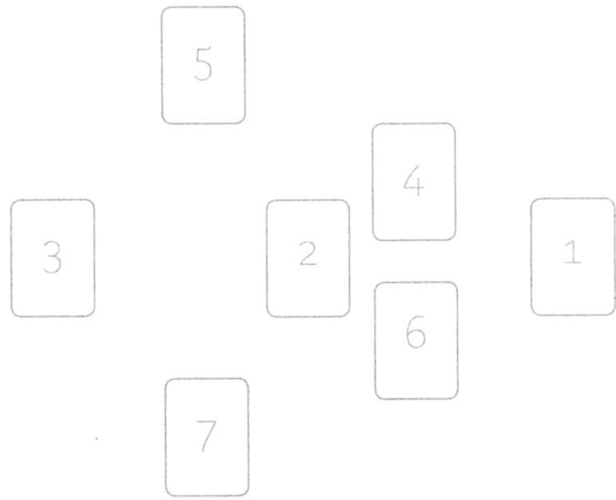

Vacations have been proven to shrink stress and anxiety. Relationships are enriched, tension is eased, and childlike wonder is renewed. Consider a three-day weekend if a longer vacation is out of the question.

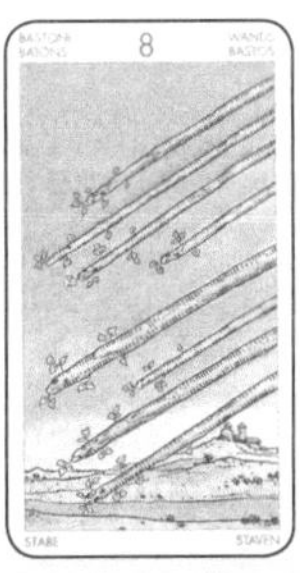

The Eight of Wands represents safe, quick travel over long distances. The card reflects high levels of energy springing you forward in any direction you choose. The key is conducting the energy as you wish rather than letting it run wild.

Magical Trees Spread

Trees are the longest-living organisms on our planet, receiving 90 percent of their nutrition from the atmosphere and only 10 percent from the soil. Acting as lungs for our planet, they breathe in carbon dioxide and exhale oxygen.

The Four of Cups depicts a Tree of Knowledge behind the seated figure. Trees are sacred symbols that represent strength, knowledge, and wisdom on any tarot card. They stand as a reminder of reach, root, and sturdiness.

On This Day

On this day in 1872, Nebraskans celebrated the first Arbor Day. Created as an observance to plant and maintain trees, it is now celebrated by many other countries, usually in springtime.

Summation of Spread

Herbs, gems, and flowers all have magical associations, and so do trees. This spread is infused with the magical attributes of wise trees that remind us to slow down, take life at our own pace, and bask in the value of patience.

Cast Your Cards

Feel your roots in the rich earth, reach for the sky, and cast your cards in the shape of a tree branch.

1. Willow: What increases my intuition?
2. Apple: Who loves me?
3. Birch: What increases my health?
4. Fir/Pine: What gives me power?
5. Hazel: What increases my creativity?
6. Oak: What makes me strong?
7. Maple: What brings me success?
8. Rowan: What kindles my magic?

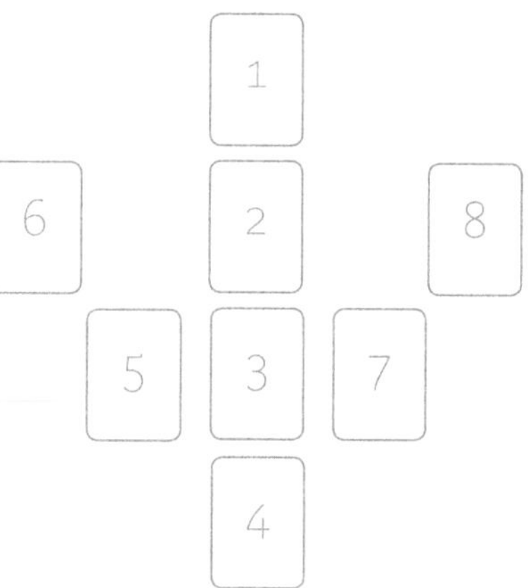

Imagination to Reality Spread

On This Day

The Apple 1 computer was released on this day in 1976. Brainiac Steve Wozniak hand-built the machine and designed it after his friend Steve Jobs suggested they sell them. About 200 units were produced.

Summation of Spread

What are you dreaming of? All inventions and innovations begin with thought. An invisible, intangible idea exists in the mind before existing on the physical level. The Imagination to Reality Spread examines recurring thoughts in your mind, helping you to bring them into reality.

Cast Your Cards

1. What am I dreaming of?
2. Why should I make this thought a reality?
3. What would happen in my life if I created this?
4. What would happen in the lives of others if I created this?
5. What step can I take to make it happen?
6. What challenge confronts me?
7. How do I face it?
8. What lessons do I learn?
9. Final outcome.

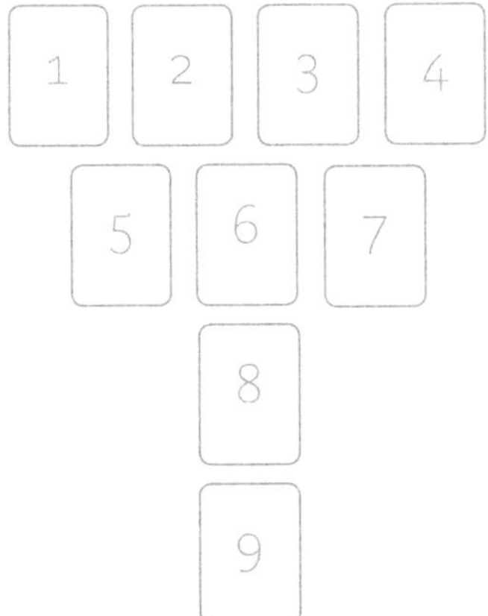

To finance their creation, Jobs sold his VW van and Wozniak hocked his high-end calculator for $500. Their personal computers went on sale for $666.66 because Wozniak enjoyed repeating digits.

Innovation belongs to the suit of Wands, whose energy is Fire. The King of Wands carries unstoppable energy; this visionary won't rest until his job is complete. King of Wands personality types are responsible for inventions like computers, light bulbs, airplanes, etc., and change culture and history as we know it.

Interview with the Vampire Spread

Anne Rice wrote Interview with the Vampire *in only five weeks, shortly after the devastating death of her five-year-old daughter.*

On This Day

On this day in 1976, Anne Rice published *Interview with the Vampire*, innovative as the first gothic novel displaying sympathetic supernatural creatures. Her monsters were philosophical, lonely, and experienced moral conflict. It was a far cry from previous gothic novels that contained frightening supernatural creatures.

Summation of Spread

The themes and characters from *Interview with the Vampire* are at play in your life, and the questions in this spread are inspired by them.

The Knight of Cups, like sensitive vampire Louis, is a gentle, thoughtful soul. This knight is least prone to violence. The fish on his cloak represents spirit and creativity, while his winged feet and helmet represent an active and creative imagination.

Cast Your Cards

Cinch your corset, stay out of sunlight, and prowl the evening streets after casting your cards.

1. Louis: What is my sensitivity level?
2. Lestat: How do I show off?
3. Claudia: How am I childlike?
4. Immortality: What lives forever?
5. Change: What helps me accept change?
6. Loss: What have I lost?
7. Sexuality: How can I satisfy my sensual needs?
8. Power: Where should I exercise more power in my life?

The Noble Eightfold Path Spread

On This Day

Today is the beginning of the Songkran Festival celebrating the Buddhist New Year in Thailand, Burma, Cambodia, and Laos. Families and friends celebrate by visiting temples and sprinkling water on each other's hands for good luck.

The Songkran Festival's tradition of sprinkling water has turned into an excuse for marvelous water fights. Participants armed with buckets, water guns, and hoses splash everyone in their path, even police.

Summation of Spread

Seeking wisdom? The Noble Eightfold Path is the principal teaching of Buddha. Buddha describes the path as a way to end suffering and achieve self-awakening. The word "right" denotes completion, coherence, wisdom, and skillfulness.

Cast Your Cards

With stillness in your heart, cast your cards.

1. Right View: How does the nature of reality work?
2. Right Intention: What issue do I need to resolve?
3. Right Speech: How do I best use my words?
4. Right Action: What is the best action to take in the world?
5. Right Livelihood: Am I ethical in the work I do?
6. Right Effort: How can I evoke kindness for myself and others?
7. Right Mindfulness: How do I best experience the moment at hand?
8. Right Concentration: How do I cultivate complete awareness of the task at hand?

WISDOM		ETHICAL CONDUCT			MENTAL DEVELOPMENT		
1	2	3	4	5	6	7	8

Buddhism's Noble Eightfold Path is often represented by the dharma wheel symbol, which, like the Wheel of Fortune card, is a reference to the changing nature of life's circumstances.

Right Relationship for Me Spread

Tragedy struck when a 23-year-old Oxford graduate perished at the Abbey. His death was blamed on participation in a Crowley ritual. Mussolini promptly ejected Crowley from Sicily in 1923, though the crumbling structure still stands to this day.

The Devil card represents power and control issues existing in any relationship. Emotional dependency, enslavement to another, and codependent destructive behavior are darker aspects of the card.

On This Day

Aleister Crowley signed his lease for the Abbey of Thelema in Sicily on this day in 1920. Sex magic, yoga, ritual practices, and the pursuit of free will and pleasure ran wild at Crowley's utopic commune.

Summation of Spread

Have doubts about your relationship? Objectivity can be tough when viewing a relationship from the inside. The salacious activity taking place inside Crowley's commune had members reevaluating their situation from time to time. This spread poses questions to check on the status of your relationship. Mainly written as a romantic relationship spread, you could also use this to examine a close friendship.

Cast Your Cards

1. Am I hiding in my relationship from other people?
2. Am I hiding anything from my partner?
3. Do I ask my partner to resolve issues I should resolve on my own?
4. Have I completely lost myself in the other person?
5. What is the level of drama in this relationship?
6. Do we inspire each other to be better?
7. Do we make enough time for each other?
8. Do I feel respected by my partner?
9. Are my needs being met?

Leonardo da Vinci's Creative Solution Spread

On This Day

On this day in 1452, a peasant woman gave birth to an out-of-wedlock son who grew up to embody the Renaissance humanist ideal. A sculptor, inventor, mathematician, architect, botanist, musician, anatomist, writer, and one of the most famous painters of all time, her little bundle of joy was Leonardo da Vinci.

Summation of Spread

Seeking solutions? All geniuses have something in common that sets them on a path to greatness: they ask questions. This spread reminds us that when searching for answers to a problem—be it healing, painting, or inventing—your final answer lies in a leap of awareness that only creative thinking will bring. Use this spread to jump-start the creative process for any project, idea, or problem.

Cast Your Cards

1. What is my intended outcome?
2. How do I gather as much information as possible?
3. What pattern do I discover?
4. Can I surrender to the process?
5. What helps me see this situation in a new light?
6. What actions encourage inspiration?
7. Have I given myself enough incubation time?
8. What missing element do I need?
9. Final outcome.

Leonardo stole corpses from graveyards to study human anatomy. A compulsive draftsman, he filled scraps of paper with sketches, doodles, and drawings, about 4,000 of which survive to this day.

Those with a strong affinity to da Vinci's work will find the Leonardo da Vinci Tarot by Iassen Ghiuselev and Atanas Atanassov of great interest.

Castle of Crossed Destinies' Inversion Spread

The Castle of Crossed Destinies *is divided into two sections. The first takes place in a castle and uses the the Visconti-Sforza Tarot. The second, taking place in a tavern, uses the Marseilles Tarot.*

The entire major arcana can be read as the storytelling arc of initiation and is symbolic of the Hero's Journey.

On This Day

The Castle of Crossed Destinies by Italo Calvino is published on this day in 1979. The characters in Calvino's story have lost their power of speech due to traumatic events. Each character relates their tale using tarot cards instead of words. A narrator interprets the cards for them, but because the cards are open to interpretation, the story the narrator relates is not necessarily the story intended by the characters.

Summation of Spread

Ever notice how the same life event can be interpreted in different ways? Accessing the power of storytelling, this spread asks you to pull specific cards rather than randomly drawn cards to tell a story from your life.

Cast Your Cards

Use tarot to tell a tale. Think of a dramatic or poignant part of your life open for exploration. Select cards to represent the story and people. Add as many cards as needed for important details. After completing, ask a friend to interpret the story based on your cards, with no information from you. How close or far do they come to the truth? Do you discover something new in their rendition?

Consider the following when creating your spread:

- Who were you at the beginning of the story?
- Which people had the greatest influence on you? (Use the court cards for this.)
- What did you want?
- What actually happened?
- What did you learn?
- What was the result?

J. P. Morgan's Financial Responsibility Spread

On This Day

American financier J. P. Morgan was born this day in 1837. One of the most influential bankers in history, Morgan was also a notable collector of books, paintings, and other art objects.

Summation of Spread

Could your financial philosophy use a boost? Using this giant of banking, we can take a look at our own financial habits through the lens of tarot.

Cast Your Cards

Summon the financial wisdom of J. P. Morgan and cast your cards.

1. Financially, what would happen to my family if I died tomorrow?
2. Do I have an emergency fund set aside?
3. How can I maximize my savings?
4. What can I do to make the most of my income?
5. What is the state of my credit rating?
6. How will I live in retirement?
7. Will I thank myself later for the financial decisions I make today?
8. What should I be doing that I'm ignoring?
9. What step can I take today to improve my financial situation?

Morgan was a passionate collector of antiquities. Tarot was one of his prized possessions. He owned one-third of the original Visconti-Sforza deck; it sat near his desk in his private study until he died.

The Ten of Pentacles may be the wealthiest card in the deck, but the jam-packed card begs the question of where one's attention goes once the material world has been conquered.

April • 18

Beauty and the Beast's Inner Beauty Spread

More than 3,300 people auditioned for the original Beauty and the Beast *Broadway show, but only 30 were cast.*

On This Day

Beauty and the Beast opened on Broadway on this day in 1994. Based on the fairy tale published in 1740, the beloved story reveals the inner nature of grace and the lessons one learns while discovering it.

Summation of Spread

Can tarot make you more beautiful? Inner beauty reflects the nature of the soul. It has nothing to do with external appearance. This spread is created to cultivate and explore elements of your own inner beauty.

The Nine of Pentacles portrays a woman completely secure, surrounded by animal friends, and lacking nothing. Satisfied with her own company, she is quite content to turn her attention only to what fascinates her. She also represents achieving a comfortable lifestyle and is tactful and diplomatic.

Cast Your Cards

Cast your cards like a mirror reflecting your soul rather than your lovely looks.

1. What builds my confidence?
2. What helps me stay healthy?
3. What gives me real satisfaction?
4. What gives me pride about who I am?
5. What makes me laugh?
6. How can I be generous to others?
7. How can I recognize the beauty of others?

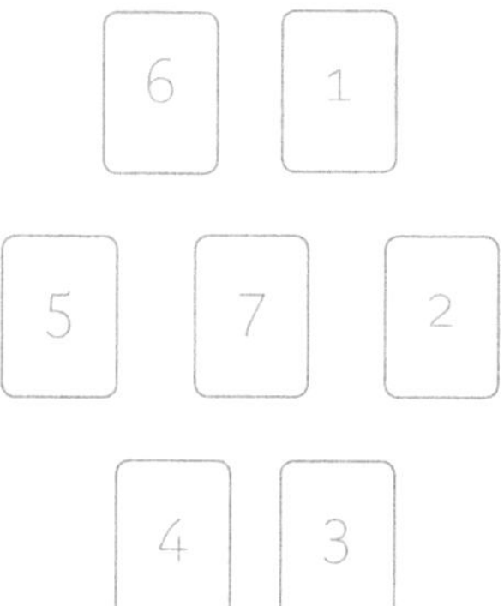

Primrose Magic Spread

On This Day

Primrose Day is celebrated today in England. The entire plant is edible and can be placed into salads or jam. Medicinally, it cures headaches and coughs and acts as a mild sedative. Primrose, an early flower of spring, is also a fairy flower. Plant it to attract fairies to your property.

Summation of Spread

Looking for help from the fairy realm? Extremely magical, the questions of this spread are based on the lore and meanings behind this lovely flower.

Cast Your Cards

Cast the Primrose Magic Spread's cards like pollen in a light spring breeze.

1. How can I create more beauty in my home?
2. What attracts love?
3. What encourages lust?
4. If I appease them, how will fairies aid me?
5. What keeps my children loyal?
6. What protects me from adversity?

Primroses have long been considered a literary flower. Katniss's little sister in the Hunger Games series is named for the flower, Shakespeare refers to its cosmetic properties in A Midsummer Night's Dream, *and poet John Donne connects the primrose with womanhood.*

The Seven of Cups reflects shamanistic visions of otherworldly realms and creatures, including the fairy world. The Seven of Cups reminds us of the worlds existing beyond our normal doors of perception. Will you explore such places? Do you dare?

Qualities of Taurus Spread

Taurus's ruling planet is Venus, blue and violet are the primary colors, the lucky day is Friday, and the best location for success is a quiet place. Taurus rules the second house of the zodiac, governing money, possessions, and their spiritual values.

Representing time-honored beliefs and traditions, the Hierophant shares his knowledge and teaches material and spiritual lessons. His strength and patience endure through the ages. Like the High Priestess and Justice cards, he sits like a middle pillar. His fingers are lifted in a sign of blessing to his loyal followers and students.

On This Day

Today marks the first day of the astrological sign of Taurus, the Bull.

Summation of Spread

The spread is based on the essential qualities of Taurus: instruction, security, appreciation, patience, practicality, a loving nature, creativity, and strength.

Cast Your Cards

Cast in the shape of the Taurus symbol, or glyph, which looks like a ring in a bull's nose.

1. What do I teach others?
2. What area of my life lacks security?
3. How can I show more appreciation to those I love?
4. How can I be more patient?
5. What must I be extremely practical about?
6. What do I love more than anything?
7. What is my artistic gift?
8. What is my greatest strength?

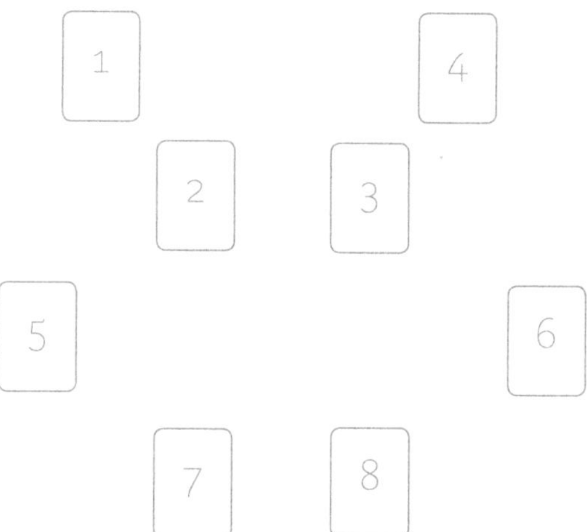

Secrets of Rome Spread

On This Day

Myth and oral legends claim Rome was formed on this day in 753 BCE. Romulus and Remus, abandoned twins of the god Mars and a vestal virgin, decided to build a city. Disagreeing on a specific location, Romulus killed his brother. He founded the city, named it Rome after himself, and created the legions and senate.

Some ancient Romans placed the symbol of a phallus on their front door as a symbol of fertility and luck. Miniature phalluses were often worn as lucky charms.

Summation of Spread

Need a quick vacation? Visit Rome through tarot. Rome was known as the Eternal City even among ancient Romans. Filled with sacred, mythological sites and a history spanning over two thousand years, the sites of Rome provide inspiration for this spread.

The Emperor card connects with Rome through its history of imperialism and ruling Caesars as well as being the Vatican's ultimate seat of power. The Emperor represents dominion over others and is a completely masculine principle and the ultimate patriarch.

Cast Your Cards

The Secrets of Rome Spread's cards are cast in the shape of a Roman arch.

1. The Forum: What lies at the center of my life?
2. The Vatican: What does spirituality teach me?
3. The Sistine Chapel: How do I connect with the Divine?
4. The Colosseum: What spectacle offers me pleasure?
5. The Catacombs: What secret do I conceal?
6. The Trevi Fountain: Who wants to kiss me?
7. Italian Cuisine: How can I indulge myself every day?

Voice of the Earth Spread

Earth Day is now celebrated on the global level. Over 1 billion people take part, and, according to the Earth Day Network, this makes it the largest secular civic event in the world.

On This Day

Today is Earth Day, an annual event created to promote awareness of and appreciation for our environment. Founded in 1970, it is a day of education about environmental issues. Its formation was inspired by the antiwar movements of the 1960s.

Summation of Spread

Do you gain wisdom from natural places? There is no denying we are part of the natural world, not separate from it. This spread's questions are written to foster a connection with the whispering of the earth and her elements.

Cast Your Cards

Feel the grass between your toes and the wind in your hair while casting the cards in the shape of our blue planet:

1. How do I reconnect to the earth?
2. What helps me embrace natural forces?
3. Where is my favorite natural place?
4. What does the wisdom of a tree offer me?
5. What does the wisdom of water offer me?
6. What does the wisdom of air offer me?
7. What does the wisdom of birds offer me?
8. How can I heal the earth?
9. How does this help to heal myself?

The Page of Pentacles represents a young person who is not only concerned about the state of the earth but likely to facilitate change. The pentacle resting in the page's hand represents a deep willingness to look inside environmental issues, and the plowed field represents the potential for growth.

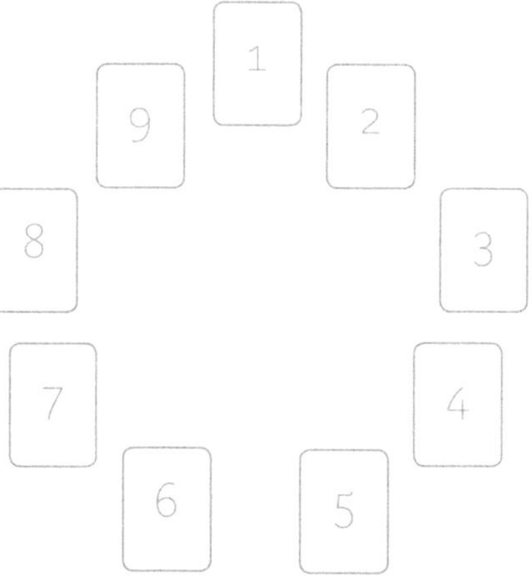

St. George's Slay the Dragon Spread

St. George is considered a martyr in the Islamic faith as well as in Christianity.

On This Day

Today is St. George's Day in England. The legend of St. George states that while traveling through the countryside, he discovered a village under the spell of a horrible dragon. They kept the dragon at bay by feeding it one maiden every day. By the time St. George arrived, the only maiden remaining was the daughter of the king. Slaying the dragon, he rescued the princess and the town. Subsequent English knights used his name as a battle cry, shouting it as they plunged into the fray.

Summation of Spread

Ready to stop something in its tracks? Using St. George for inspiration, this spread prepares you for radical change by helping slay a negative issue you have grown accustomed to.

Cast Your Cards

St. George, like the Knights Templar, wore a red cross on a white background. Cast this spread in the shape of a cross.

1. What is the issue that must be addressed?
2. What do I sacrifice?
3. How do I stop this behavior?
4. How do I approach the source?
5. What physical action can I take?
6. How does life change as a result?
7. What has been learned?

Like St. George, the Knight of Wands is eager and quick to battle. Wands represent spiritual passion, the same quality burning in the heart of this patron saint of England. The violence of religious persecution and intolerance of others can be understood as a Wands reversal, where spiritual energy has turned destructive.

Flirting with Danger Spread

The remains of Pompeii are so well preserved that you can see Greek-inspired buildings, water fountains, brothels, bathhouses, residences, and an amphitheater standing along cobblestoned streets.

Wands echo the energy, force, and potential destruction of a volcano. It is important to channel passions and energy. Will you bottle your passion up, let it snuff out, or use it wisely to guide and light your way?

On This Day

Mount Vesuvius, the volcano responsible for the 79 CE eruption burying the Roman cities of Pompeii and Herculaneum, erupted again on this day in 1872. It blocked the escape route of twenty spectators, who then perished in the lava.

Summation of Spread

Is your middle name Danger? Mount Vesuvius is the most deadly volcano in the world due to its heightened activity and the high density of population living nearby in Naples. This spread is based on the fact that we all take risks, real and imagined. The questions look at what you are risking at the moment.

Cast Your Cards

Cast your cards in the shape of a volcano as a reminder that the ground we walk on is not always as stable as we might believe.

1. What stability exists?
2. Is there a risk I need to take?
3. What risk am I already taking?
4. Is it a needed risk?
5. What happens if I walk away?
6. What happens if I up the ante?
7. How does this risk define me?
8. What is the lesson learned?

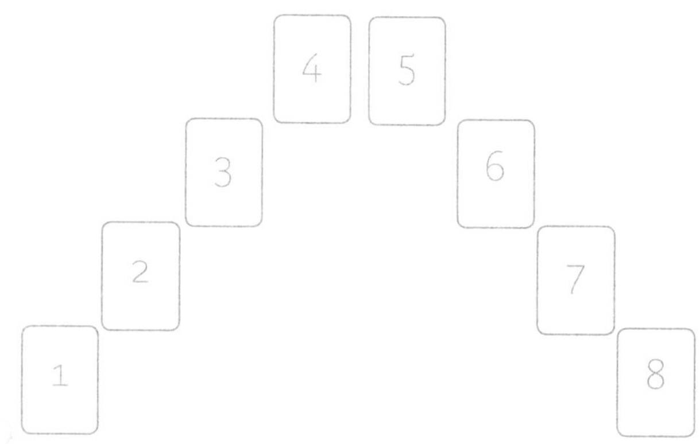

Should I Tell Them I Love Them Spread

On This Day

A feast honoring St. Mark, patron saint of Venice, is held on this day. Traditionally, men give the women they love a single budded long-stem red rose. It is called Le Festa del Boccolo: the celebration of the rose bud. A gondola race takes place in the Bacina di San Marco to mark the occasion.

Roses are symbolic of love. For alchemists, the entire process of psychic transformation takes place under a rose or "sub rosa."

Summation of Spread

Is now the time to bare your soul to your beloved? The romance and intrigue winding through Venice's watery alleys is inspiration for a spread regarding matters of your heart.

Cast Your Cards

Listen to the cards and your intuition while casting your cards in the shape of a gondola:

1. What is the status of this relationship?
2. How do I feel about them?
3. How do they feel about me?
4. Are we destined to be together?
5. What is the root of attraction?
6. Why are they good for me?
7. Should I tell them I love them?
8. What is their reaction?
9. What is the ultimate outcome?

Nakedness on any card in the tarot deck represents vulnerability. The decision to reveal strong personal feelings can leave you feeling especially vulnerable, but it shouldn't stop you from expressing yourself.

April • 26

Goal Setting Spread

Achieving a goal produces dopamine, a neurotransmitter responsible for the feeling of pleasure. It also activates neural circuitry, making you eager to pursue new challenges.

On This Day

A massive cache of mummies surrounding the Lahun Pyramid in Egypt was discovered on this day in 2009. Their sarcophagi were decorated with bright green, red, and white images of the deceased. Over thirty of them were well preserved, with afterlife prayers inscribed upon them.

Summation of Spread

Are you ready to take action and get what you want? Pyramids, like church spires, point toward the heavens. You'll do the same with a spread that examines what you want to create in your life. Writing goals is pleasurable and productive. It defines where you are going in measurable steps and successes. Rather than asking questions for this spread, you will write down your goals aligned with the time frame.

Small, achievable goals fall into the Emperor's realm of rule and stability. Because goals keep you on track and because meeting them makes you feel good, they keep you moving. The Chariot uses an action plan to plot his course to success.

Cast Your Cards

Be realistic when writing your six-month, twelve-month, and five-year goals. Deal the cards face-down. Cast the Goal Setting Spread's cards in the shape of a pyramid. Each card gives specific help and guidance in achieving each goal.

1. A six-month achievable goal.
2. A six-month achievable goal.
3. A six-month achievable goal.
4. A twelve-month achievable goal.
5. A twelve-month achievable goal.
6. A five-year achievable goal.

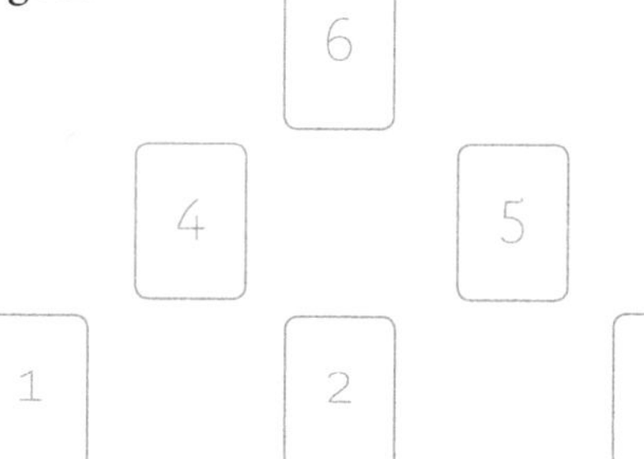

Tornado Spread

On This Day

This day in 2011 marked the largest tornado outbreak ever recorded: 358 tornadoes in over 21 states were confirmed by the National Weather Service in a three-day period. The most, 205, occurred on this day.

Summation of Spread

Feeling a little out of control? Twisters and cyclones form when warm air meets cold. Unpredictability, damage, and the massive scale of tornadoes make them fascinating and terrifying. This spread uses tornado energy to examine what happens emotionally when the unexpected occurs.

Cast Your Cards

Look to the clouds, feel the direction of the wind, and cast the cards calmly upon the table.

1. What should I focus on when things are calm?
2. What gets me hot under the collar?
3. What cools or calms me down?
4. What damage am I capable of?
5. What happens when I'm out of control?
6. Who or what is usually in my path?
7. How do I pick up the pieces?
8. Is there a way to express myself in a calm way?

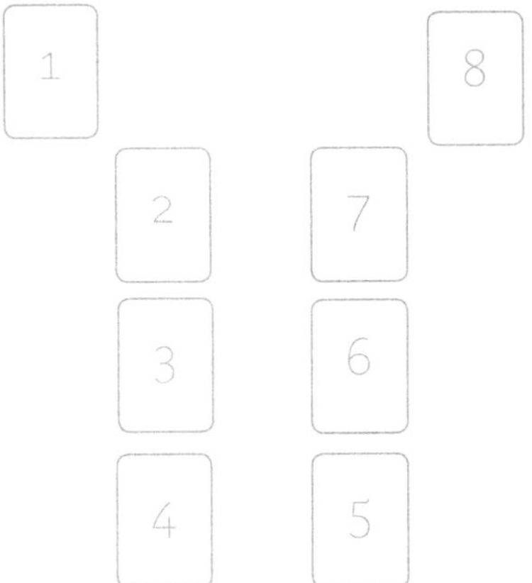

Tornados can occur anytime but usually happen between 3 and 9 PM. Tornadoes contain the fastest winds on earth. They sometimes hop along their path, destroying one house and leaving the next one untouched.

Like tornadoes, the Tower card is violent and unpredictable, signaling destruction, upheaval, and an event or situation occurring out of the blue.

Floralia's Flowers of Spring Spread

Flora was depicted wearing a crown of flowers, and her image was engraved on Roman coins. Her nemesis was an antagonistic deity called Robigus, whose wrath caused the destruction of crops.

The Nine of Pentacles and her lush landscape is a reminder of the restorative quality of time spent in the garden and alone in nature. Enveloped in the natural world, one discovers the earth gently whispering wisdom and symphonies of sweetness to those with ears to listen.

On This Day

The Floralia festival began in Rome on this date in 238 BCE to please the goddess Flora. Flora is the goddess of flowers, spring, and fertility. Celebrated with public games and theatrical presentations, the final day of her festival was devoted to circus games.

Summation of Spread

Looking for inspiration from the garden bed? This spread uses goddess Flora's spring flowers and their Victorian meanings to inform its questions.

Cast Your Cards

Imagine yourself in a field under the warm spring sun, the earth springing to life around you, and cast the cards in the shape of a flower:

1. Apple Blossom: Whom do I love?
2. Daffodil: Who is true to me?
3. Dahlia: What should I be careful of?
4. Hyacinth: What is worth waiting for?
5. Delphinium: What brings me peace?
6. Poppy: What helps me to rest?
7. Snowdrop: What can I hope for?
8. Iris: What can I trust?

Happy Marriage Spread

On This Day

Kate Middleton and Prince William were married on this day at Westminster Abbey in 2011. All of Britain and the world rejoiced at this fairy tale come true. Engaged on private holiday in Kenya, Prince William offered Kate the same engagement ring his father, Prince Charles, had given his mother, Princess Diana.

Summation of Spread

The Happy Marriage Spread's questions are inspired by issues to consider before agreeing to tie the knot.

Cast Your Cards

Juno is the Roman goddess ruling marriage. She inspires her namesake month, June, the most popular month for weddings. Cast your cards in the shape of the rainbow found on the Ten of Cups.

1. Do we care for each other like friends?
2. Can I be honest and vulnerable with my mate?
3. Do we reach good solutions for our problems?
4. Do we care for each other's needs?
5. Do we respect each other?
6. Do I trust my mate completely?
7. Do we want the same things out of life?
8. What do I need to know?

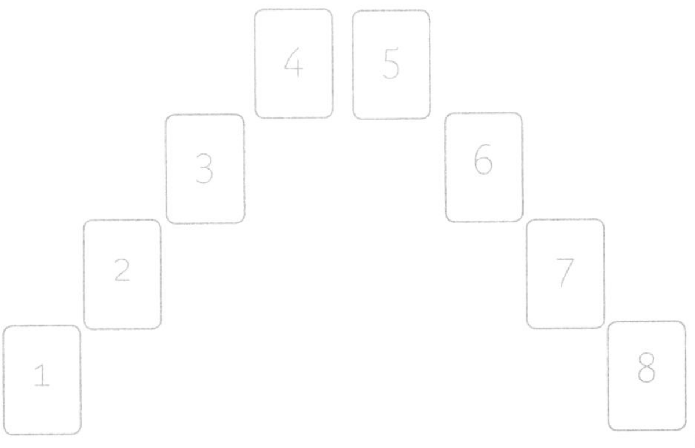

Ancient Greeks claimed the fourth finger contained the "vein of love" running straight to the heart. This is why engagement rings are worn on the fourth finger of the left hand. The first recorded wedding rings, with the circles representing eternity, were from ancient Egypt.

The Ten of Cups represents wedded bliss, a happy home, and familial contentment. The "happily ever after" card, it marks the satisfactory end of a chapter with the optimism of what is to come.

Lover's Baggage Spread

Walpurgis Night is celebrated exactly six months from Halloween.

On This Day

Tonight is Walpurgis Night, the traditional spring festival in central and northern Europe, often celebrated with dancing and bonfires. Tonight is an auspicious night for sorcery.

Summation of Spread

Distracted by pains of the past? Feeling held down by a previous relationship? Uncover what previous relationship baggage you and your loved one carry. By the light of the spring moon, this spread sheds light on you and your love's connections to the past.

Cast Your Cards

Burn angelica incense for release from the past as you cast the cards:

1. Card representing me.
2. What do I carry from the past?
3. Can I set myself free?
4. Card representing my lover.
5. What do they carry from the past?
6. Can they set themselves free?
7. Is their past problematic?
8. Are they devoted to me?
9. Is there a step I should take?
10. Are we meant to be?
11. What is the lesson of this relationship?

The Eight of Swords represents a person bound to past issues. Reliving past events over and over in her mind does not allow her to move forward in her life. Let this bound image remind you to heal what pains you've faced and move forward.

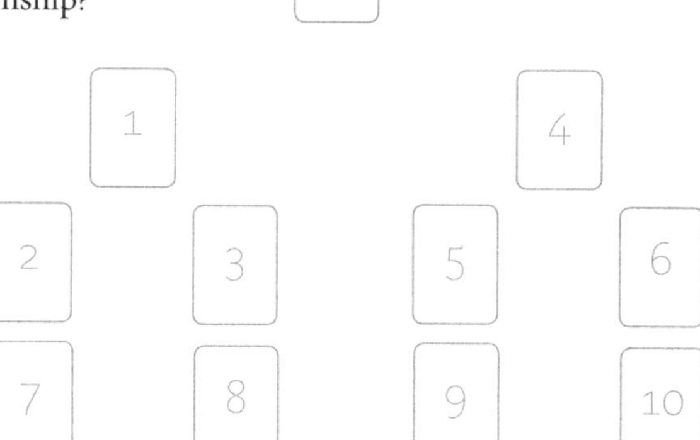

Beltane Crossing Over Spread

On This Day

Celtic Beltane begins at moonrise the night before the first day of May. Beltane marks the second half of the Celtic year, opposite Samhain. Like Samhain, the veil between worlds is at its thinnest right now. Instead of our ancestors and ghosts passing into our world as they do in October, this is the opportunity for us to pass through into theirs.

Summation of Spread

Ever wonder what it's like on the other side? The Beltane Crossing Over Spread lets you enter the netherworld. Indulge your curiosity and include as many original questions as you like.

Cast Your

1. Wha ... l like?
2. H
3. V
4

regular world?

5

4 6

9

11

Beltane is symbolic of birth and regeneration. Earth's reproductive and sexual energies are at their peak this time of the year. Kiss the one you love under the Beltane moon.

The Death card is a doorway to the great beyond of spirits and departed souls. Let the wisdom of those who walked before come to you. Remember the lessons you offer in return with the light and warmth of your life in a symbiotic dance.

The Loch Ness Magical Scotland Spread

Scotland's official animal is, unsurprisingly, the unicorn.

On This Day

The first sighting of the Loch Ness monster was reported on this day in 1933. The event made news when a well-known businessman and his wife informed the local paper of a great beast spotted in Loch Ness.

Summation of Spread

Do you long for the romance of the Scottish Highlands? Nessie is but one of many attributes of Scotland, land of kilts, bagpipes, William Wallace, and the inspiration for Hogwarts castle. It's easy to understand why Scotland is the land of magic. This spread weaves Scottish enchantment in your life.

Cast Your Cards

1. Castles: What security do I have?
2. Islands: Where can I escape to?
3. Highlands: What elevates me to a higher place?
4. Mist: What mystery is rolling into my life?
5. Tartan: Where do I belong?
6. Heather: What magic is growing in my life?
7. Whiskey: What end-of-day activity should I indulge in?
8. Fairy: What supernatural aid is available to me?

The Celtic Cross Spread, first published by A. E. Waite in his *Pictorial Guide to the Tarot,* is likely the most popular tarot spread ever created. Today it is found in most books accompanying new tarot decks. A Celtic Cross is a cross with a circle around it. Scotland, Ireland, and Britain are filled with Celtic cross monuments, found especially in graveyards.

Tower Card Spread

On This Day

The beloved Old Man of the Mountain, also known as the Great Stone Face, in the White Mountains of New Hampshire collapsed on this day in 2003. The cliff, shaped like a man's face, was revered by many who took comfort in anthropomorphizing the side of a mountain.

Summation of Spread

Collapse and destruction are hallmarks of the Tower card. This card's appearance and catastrophic events signal enlightenment and humility before nature. This spread is based on symbols found on the Tower card.

Cast Your Cards

Use this spread to answer any question. Format your question before casting the spread or simply let the cards answer the questions posed. Pull the Tower card from your deck. Placing it in the center of the Tower Card Spread, cast your cards around it.

1. Lightning bolt: What is my wakeup call?
2. Crown: What is pushed aside?
3. Tower: What situation did I create?
4. Mountain: How high can I reach?
5. Falling: Can I release control?
6. Male/Female: How do I maintain duality?
7. Fire: What must burn away?
8. Clouds: What is the higher truth I must learn?

Nathaniel Hawthorne used New Hampshire's Old Man as inspiration for a short story, The Great Stone Face, *published in 1850. The Old Man's profile has been New Hampshire's state emblem since 1945.*

In addition to destruction, the Tower card represents a flash of understanding, a moment of illumination, and a transcendental state where one moves beyond a normal state of awareness to a higher consciousness and enlightenment.

Anger Management Spread

In Marvel comic books, the Hulk is able to leap great distances, traveling far before meeting the ground and bouncing up again.

On This Day

The iconic Incredible Hulk comic book character came to life on the big screen in the film *The Avengers*, released on this day in 2012. Physicist Dr. Bruce Banner, after accidental exposure to the detonation of a gamma bomb, involuntarily transforms into the Hulk whenever angry or threatened.

Summation of Spread

Feeling volatile? The Anger Management Spread is helpful to perform when you're feeling edgy or "Hulk-like" and need to bring your emotions down a notch. This spread, provoked by the green superhero, examines how you experience personal anger.

The Devil card carries darker aspects of extreme anger and destruction, both physical and psychological. Unchecked tyranny and obsession spiral out of control when not tempered with love and forgiveness.

Cast Your Cards

Breathe deeply and cast the cards as follows:

1. Why am I so angry?
2. What led to this situation?
3. What will happen if I express my anger?
4. What will happen if I suppress my anger?
5. What will happen if I calm my feelings?
6. What action should I take?
7. What is my outcome?

Cinco de Mayo Against All Odds Spread

On This Day

Today is Cinco de Mayo, a Mexican holiday celebrating an "against all odds" victory over the French army in 1862. The French army was seven times larger, well trained, and better equipped. However, the French were defeated at the Battle of Puebla, where the smaller Mexican army made a shocking victory.

The French army eventually regrouped and moved on to take Mexico City. Regardless, the euphoria of the unlikely Mexican victory against overwhelming odds is remembered every May fifth.

Summation of Spread

What do you want more than anything? This spread, in honor of insurmountable odds, asks what impossible goal you want to accomplish. Go out on a limb—be brave and ask for what you really, truly want. How else will your wildest dream come true?

Cast Your Cards

Using tactical maneuvers, you will attack oncoming challenges in a wall of cards. Once you reach the other side, you will reap the rewards of victory. Dream large and cast your cards.

1. What do I want to do?
2. What is my first challenge?
3. What is my second challenge?
4. What is my third challenge?
5. How should I meet the first challenge?
6. How should I meet the second challenge?
7. How should I meet the third challenge?
8. What is unexpected?
9. How will I change?
10. What is my prize?

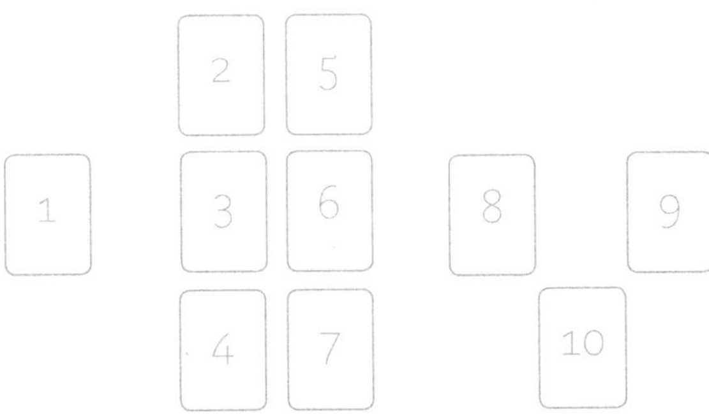

The power and passion to meet any challenge is found in the energetic reserves of the four knights and kings of the tarot. Each king wears armor under his regal robes, a reminder of his strength and prowess.

May • 6

Freudian Analysis Spread

At age 83, while losing a battle with cancer, Freud requested a doctor end his life. He died of a physician-assisted morphine overdose.

The crawfish emerging from the Moon card's pool of water represents an unconscious urge or need coming to light. This is marked for you in a moment of discovery, when you realize you desire something new or have desired something all along without realizing it.

On This Day

Sigmund Freud, the founding father of psychoanalysis, was born on this day in 1856. Freud harbored a morbid fear of ferns and the number 62, so much so that he would not book himself into any hotel with more than 61 rooms for fear he would be given room 62.

Summation of Spread

Ready to lie on an analyst's couch? Using Freud's key terms and essential concepts as a springboard, this spread examines the mysteries that make up the complex and wonderful creature reading these words.

Cast Your Cards

Nature loves pairs. This spread makes uses of pairs to compare and contrast aspects of personality.

1. Conscious Mind: What weighs heavily on my mind?
2. Unconscious Mind: What wants to emerge?
3. Superego: What is my main focus and most urgent need?
4. Ego: Who do I think I am?
5. Id: What is the unnamed center of my wants, needs, and desires?
6. Sublimation: How do I redirect unfulfilled desires into something useful?
7. Pleasure Principle: What feels good?
8. Reality Principle: What must be done?

Bourbon Street Spread

On This Day

The city of New Orleans was founded on this day in 1718 by Jean-Baptiste le Moyne de Bienville. The city's distinct European flair is due to its previous French and Spanish ownership.

Summation of Spread

Feeling hedonistic and wicked? Bourbon Street marks the oldest part of New Orleans and focuses its tourist center. Known for its bars and strip clubs, it has transformed from a red-light district to a corporate tourist center. This spread uses the shadier elements of old Bourbon Street to inform its questions.

Cast Your Cards

Jazz notes linger in humid air and the past whispers in your ear as you duck into a shop for a tea-leaf reading. The Bourbon Street Spread wants to examine your delicate soul.

1. Prostitution: How do I sell myself short?
2. Gambling: What is the biggest risk I take?
3. Jazz: How am I innovative?
4. Dancing: How can I let myself be free?
5. Drinking: How well do I moderate myself?
6. Voodoo: What wicked magic do I possess?

Not much separates the living from the dead in New Orleans. With a violent Civil War history, slavery, and catastrophes like Hurricane Katrina, it's no wonder New Orleans is a paranormal gumbo and one of the most haunted cities in the United States.

Bourbon Street's long history as a red-light district and hedonistic spot of overindulgence falls under the Devil card's auspices. The Devil represents temptation, instant gratification, and, above all, the ability to have a great time.

Seven Themes of Van Gogh Spread

The day Van Gogh threatened artist Paul Gauguin with a razor, Van Gogh ran off in angst to a brothel, where he sliced off the lower part of his left ear and handed it to a prostitute for safekeeping. Gauguin later discovered him lying unconscious, his head covered with blood.

The Empress card evokes the creativity of artists. She is the uniting force and link between the physical and the spiritual. The Empress is present the moment paint touches canvas, words manifest upon paper, and bodies move to music.

On This Day

Vincent Van Gogh, painter of supremely supernatural visions, committed himself to a hospital on this day in 1889. The clinic's buildings and gardens became subjects of his paintings, including the famous *Starry Night*.

Summation of Spread

You may share more with Van Gogh than you realize. The Vincent Van Gogh museum reflects upon the seven main themes appearing in Van Gogh's work. These themes have been crafted into a tarot spread examining your inner qualities and motivations.

Cast Your Cards

Cast the cards in a signature Van Gogh swirl.

1. Practice Makes Perfect: What am I practicing?
2. Style of Your Own: What is my unique style?
3. Effect of Color: What color do I need to bring into my life?
4. Peasant Painter: How do I make life simpler?
5. Japanese Influence: What foreign culture influences me the most?
6. Modern Portrait: What does it mean to be modern?
7. Wealth of Nature: What is my relationship to nature?

T. S. Eliot's Poets & Writers Spread

On This Day

Poet T. S. Eliot makes reference to his poem *The Wasteland* in a letter to patron John Quinn on this day in 1922. Eliot makes reference to tarot cards in his landmark poem: a section of *The Wasteland* highlights Madame Sosostris, a fortuneteller known to be the wisest woman in Europe, who reads from a "wicked pack of cards."

Summation of Spread

Are you working on a book, memoir, or piece of poetry? This spread has been created for the writer, poet, or artist about to embark on a new piece of work.

Cast Your Cards

Cast your cards as T. S. Eliot would place words on a page.

1. The project at hand.
2. What must I create?
3. What must be expressed?
4. Why is it so important for me to do this now?
5. What will this work help me to uncover?
6. How can I accomplish my task in the most eloquent way possible?
7. Focus card: what helps me retain my focus for the entire project?

Writing affects the mind the same way as meditation. Breathing slows down as the writer enters a zone where words flow freely. Stream of consciousness writing has proven to be an effective method of destressing oneself.

The King and Queen of Swords are the novelists of the deck. Their gifts of articulation and mental acuity provide them with the ability to communicate precise thoughts, use appropriate words, and express exactly what's on their mind.

Court de Gébelin's Under Your Nose Spread

Court de Gébelin and Benjamin Franklin were Masonic brothers in the Les Neuf Seurs lodge and served as Voltaire's conductors in his Masonic initiation.

On This Day

Antoine Court de Gébelin passed away on this day in 1784. He is important to tarot's history because all of tarot's occult associations began with him. He was the first person in recorded history to claim that tarot is a repository of ancient secrets.

Summation of Spread

Is something hiding from you in plain sight? Truth and wisdom can be directly in front of us, yet we don't see them till we are ready. De Gébelin explained to all of Paris society that tarot was the Egyptian Book of Thoth—an ancient book of secrets hidden in plain sight. His Egyptian theory was eventually disproved, yet his influence is undeniable.

The King of Swords, like Court de Gébelin, is a well-educated scholar who has the capacity of reaching a large audience due to his seat of power.

Cast Your Cards

Let's assume a piece of wisdom or an answer you need is hiding in front of you. Use this spread to uncover it. Cast far apart in the vein of your expanding consciousness.

1. What answer is right in front of me?
2. How do I cultivate hidden truths?
3. What limiting belief must I release?
4. Am I willing to change?
5. What would I embrace if I allowed myself to?
6. Can I look at myself and see what the universe sees?
7. What possibility exists that I can't possibly imagine or comprehend at the moment?

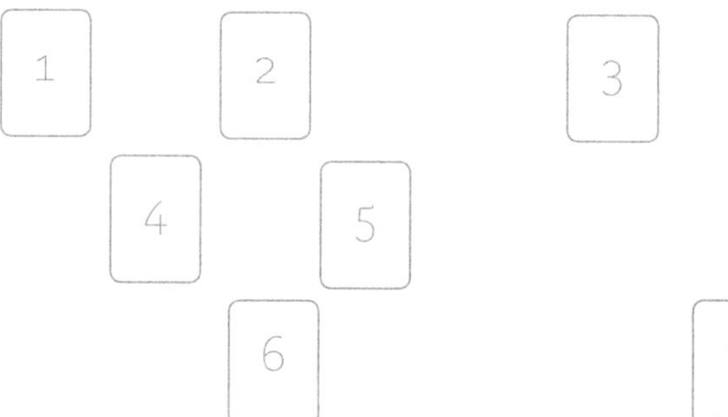

Frieda Harris's Painter's Palette Spread

On This Day

Artist Frieda Harris passed away on this day in 1962. Harris collaborated with Aleister Crowley, and she painted the Thoth tarot deck.

Summation of Spread

Did you know an artist's paintbox can offer clues to your personality? Frieda Harris used watercolors to paint the Thoth deck. Using her palette as inspiration, this spread is based on the magical significance of color.

Cast Your Cards

Cast your cards as paints on a palette.

1. Red: What energizes me?
2. Orange: What gives me confidence?
3. Yellow: What ignites my imagination?
4. Green: What balances me?
5. Blue: What calms me?
6. Purple: What engages my intuition?
7. White: What helps me find peace?
8. Brown: What grounds me?

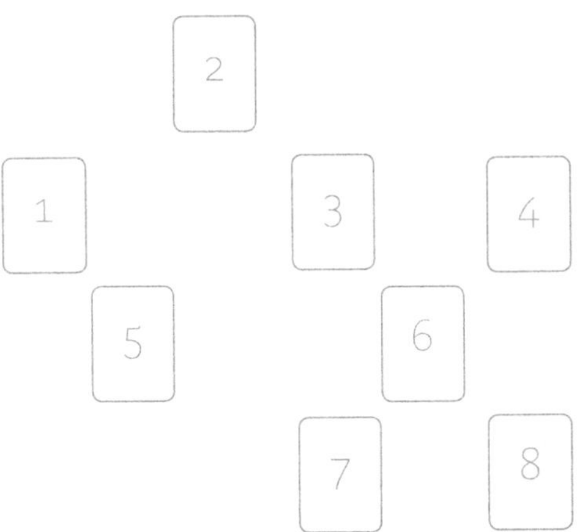

Although Harris took notes from Crowley for the Thoth deck, he offered her full credit. He said it was Harris who kept the deck's momentum afloat. She insisted he consider each and every card as a masterpiece, able to stand on its own, independent from the rest of the deck.

The Empress card, ruled by Venus, is the embodiment of creativity. Symbolized by wheat, pomegranates, and pregnancy, her fertility is not only literal but also figurative. She represents ideas and talent springing forth.

Mother's Day Spread

Mothers in the 1700s gave birth to an average of 7 to 10 children; in the 1950s, they averaged 3.5 children; and today's moms average 2 children. A mother changes 7,300 diapers by the time her baby turns two, and no mother could ever be described as average.

The Empress represents the archetypal Mother figure, while the queens represent mothers you'd meet on a day-to-day basis. The Queen of Pentacles represents a chef, decorator, gardener, and crafter type of homemaker.

On This Day

The first Mother's Day was celebrated today in 1907. Anna Jarvis campaigned for a Mother's Day holiday in memory of her deceased mother. The elder Jarvis had created Mothers' Day Work Clubs to improve sanitary and health conditions in burgeoning cities around the United States.

Summation of Spread

The mother-child relationship is evident for everyone regardless of form. The Mother's Day spread examines this delicate relationship in order to better understand it. Doing so, you come a step closer to understanding yourself.

Cast Your Cards

1. What is the state of my relationship with my mother?
2. What great gift has my mother given me?
3. What great challenge does my mother offer me?
4. How am I similar to my mother?
5. How am I unlike my mother?
6. How do I define myself in comparison to her?
7. How can I best honor our relationship?

Exorcism Spread

On This Day

The ancient Roman Lemuralia—a feast to exorcise unwanted spirits from the home—was held today. It was standard for the head of the family to rise at midnight, walk barefoot around the home, and throw black beans while reciting incantations. Other family members banged pots and pans to rid the home from the wandering, restless spirits.

Summation of Spread

Let's hope you won't ever have to exorcise an actual demon from your life. Every now and then, though, there are habits, people, or situations we'd be better off without. The Exorcism Spread takes a look at issues hindering us so they may be removed.

Cast Your Cards

Cast your cards in the shape of an X.

1. What do I fear most?
2. How am I my own worst enemy?
3. What behavior must be sent away?
4. How do I abandon what doesn't work?
5. What should I create?
6. What must be reborn?
7. What empowering belief must I incorporate?
8. How do I make the best of who I am?

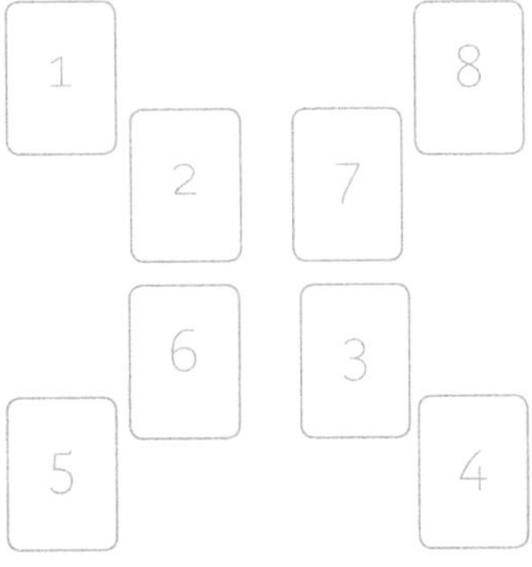

The US yearly average of requests for exorcism comes in at about 400, but only two or three are usually approved by the church. Pope John Paul the Second carried out an unsuccessful exorcism in 2000. It took many more sessions from another priest to "cleanse" the victim.

The Devil card represents the demon long blamed for the horrific actions of humanity. People find it easier to blame an external influence for wrongdoing rather than look within themselves.

Rockefeller's Balanced Budget Spread

John D. Rockefeller abstained from alcohol and tobacco all his life. Saving most of his income, he spent it on philanthropy, revolutionizing its modern concept. He thanked his mother for his philosophy, as it was she who taught him "willful waste makes woeful want."

Despite the Four of Pentacles' reputation for being a financial miser, this card represents the essential element of financial balance. The number four represents stability and structure. It is with stability and structure that money and investments grow and flourish.

On This Day

The philanthropic Rockefeller Foundation was created on this day in 1913. From establishing institutions like the Johns Hopkins School of Health and the American Shakespeare Festival to funding initiatives, fellowships, and scholarships, the foundation is responsible for a dizzying array of philanthropy. Rockefeller himself has been called the greatest philanthropist in American history.

Summation of Spread

Looking to balance your checkbook? Rockefeller became the richest man in the world before becoming its greatest philanthropist. His financial books were balanced. Using his inspiration, this spread examines money and balancing your budget.

Cast Your Cards

Feel the abundance and cast your cards.

1. What does money mean to me?
2. What is my relationship to the energy of money?
3. What does money offer me?
4. How can I make the most of my money?
5. Do I have a budget surplus or shortfall?
6. Is there an expense I should eliminate?
7. What is my next realistic financial goal?
8. What will help me reach this goal quickly?
9. What is the best thing I can spend my money on?

Qualities of Mercury Spread

On This Day

The Romans believed May 15 to be the birthday of Mercury, messenger of Zeus, who travels at the speed of thought. The planet Mercury revolves around the sun in a speedy 88 Earth days; this early observation was made by an Assyrian astronomer in the fourteenth century BCE.

Mercury is the ruler of Gemini and Virgo. Its surface is barren, and, like our moon, it is peppered with craters and contains no weather systems or atmosphere to protect it.

Summation of Spread

The Qualities of Mercury Spread contains questions based on the astrological associations of the planet Mercury. Using these associations, questions are posed to offer greater clarity in life.

Cast Your Cards

Cast in the shape of the Magician card's upheld wand.

1. Intelligence: How do I best use my intelligence?
2. Language: What needs to be said?
3. Communication: What helps me communicate clearly?
4. Memory: What trick does my memory play?
5. Expression: What is my best mode of expression?
6. The Mind: How do I cultivate mental acuity?

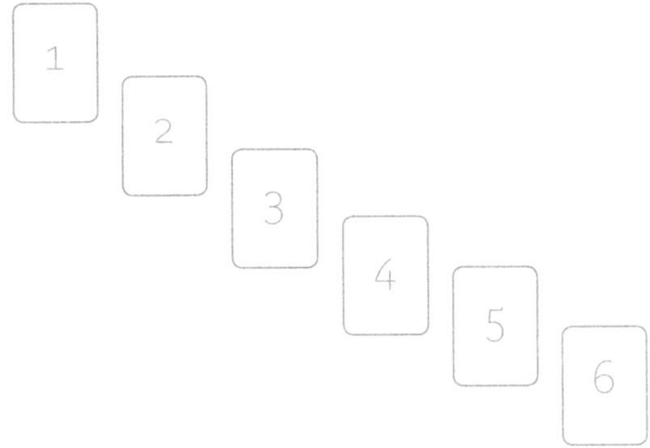

Mercury connects to the Magician card due to his magic, eloquence, and ability to change reality. The Magician's stance demonstrates the Hermetic concept of "as above, so below." The microcosm (you) and macrocosm (universe) each lie within the other. By comprehending one, you can understand the other.

May • 16

Tickets to the first Oscar event cost $5; 270 people attended, and the ceremony lasted only 15 minutes.

Academy Awards Spread

On This Day

The first Academy Awards, commonly known as the Oscars, was held on this day in 1929. A gala private dinner was given at the Hollywood Roosevelt Hotel in Los Angeles. It was a far cry from the pomp and circumstance accompanying its modern ceremony.

Summation of Spread

You are the star of your life. The Academy Awards Spread channels the glitz and glamour of the Oscars to inform its questions. (For a fortunetelling experiment, pull cards to make predictions on who will take home the gold on Hollywood's biggest night.)

Cast Your Cards

Avoid those pesky paparazzi, don a pair of shades, and cast the cards in the shape of a martini glass.

1. Best Actress/Actor: Who would play me in the movie of my life?
2. Best Supporting Actress/Actor: Who is my most supportive friend?
3. Best Foreign Film: Where must I travel?
4. Costume Design: How should I revamp my wardrobe?
5. Production Design: How should I redecorate my living space?
6. Visual Effects: What new perspective should I embrace?
7. Makeup and Hairstyling: How should I revamp my look?
8. Best Director: What direction should I point my life in?
9. Best Picture: What is theme of my life narrative/story?

Like an Academy Award winner, the Ace of Pentacles depicts a gold object in hand. Will you walk through the garden gate of opportunity? The Ace of Pentacles signifies financial gain, prosperity, and a chance to begin afresh.

Pendulum Spread

On This Day

Edgar Allen Poe published *The Pit and the Pendulum* on this day in 1845. Poe's gothic story of torture at the hands of the Spanish Inquisition appeared in *The Broadway Journal.*

Summation of Spread

You can use a pendulum for a unique one-card tarot reading. A pendulum is a weight suspended by a freely moving pivot. Purchase one or easily make one by slipping a ring over a necklace chain to create a makeshift pendulum.

Cast Your Cards

Prepare your pendulum as you see fit. Some practitioners cleanse it as they would a card deck. Shuffle the cards; prepare and state your question. Select seven cards, placing them face-down in front of you. The pendulum will begin swinging toward the card with the answer. Once you have determined which card, flip it over to discover your answer.

Ask any question you like and answer with one card.

1	2	3	4	5	6	7

Golden Dawn member William Butler Yeats was a critic of Poe, finding his work vulgar. Yeats said The Pit and the Pendulum *"does not seem to me to have any permanent literary value of any kind...analyze [it] and you find an appeal to the nerves by tawdry physical affrightments."*

The razor-sharp Ace of Swords represents the genesis of a genius idea. Reversed or swung outward, the Ace of Swords becomes a deadly weapon, ready to slice its foes to shreds. It reflects the potential of any person to be brilliant or destructive, and if it appears for you, you should follow through on your most recent good idea.

Empress Card Spread

The Empress marks the female counterpart to the High Priestess. While the High Priestess contains knowledge, it is the Empress who uses and expresses knowledge. Their duality creates the ultimate female archetype.

The Empress is complete intelligence expressing itself in every creative aspect. The epitome and essence of femininity, she is the Mother archetype who not only creates life but sustains it.

On This Day

Eleanor of Aquitaine, one of the most powerful and wealthy women of the Middle Ages, married Henry II of England on this day in 1152. Queen Consort of France, then England, she bore ten children, three of whom would become kings. She outlived all her children except for two.

Summation of Spread

Eleanor of Aquitaine provides inspiration with which to view the symbols found on the Empress card. These symbols and associations inspire the Empress spread.

Cast Your Cards

Use this spread to answer any question. Format your question before casting the spread or simply let the cards answer the questions posed. Pull the Empress card from your deck. Placing her in the center, cast your cards around her.

1. Symbol of Venus: What do I love?
2. Wheat: How do I nurture others?
3. Waterfall: What emotion is flowing?
4. Zodiac Crown: Who am I?
5. Scepter: What power do I exert?
6. Throne: What stability do I maintain?
7. Hidden Pregnancy: What is being born?
8. Pomegranates: What fertile grounds await?

Marilyn Monroe's Flames of Desire Spread

On This Day

Marilyn Monroe sang "Happy Birthday, Mr. President," to John F. Kennedy at Madison Square Garden on this day in 1962. One of Marilyn's last public performances, it was iconic not only because Marilyn was the epitome of a sex symbol, but also because of the presumed affair between her and the president. Her tragic death occurred three short months later.

Joe DiMaggio sent roses to Marilyn Monroe's crypt three times a week for over twenty years.

Summation of Spread

Consumed with the thought of someone? Is desire driving you wild? Marilyn Monroe provoked desire; women wanted to be like her and men wanted to have her sexually. Using this icon of sensuality, this spread examines the nature of desire in our personal lives.

The Lovers card contains many symbols of desire, including twelve burning flames, juicy apples, a snake, full nudity, the solar power of the sun, and a phallic mountain rising in the background.

Cast Your Cards

1. Why does this person provoke my desire?
2. Will my cravings for them be met?
3. Will this turn into a long-term relationship?
4. Is this person a soulmate?
5. Should I trust my feelings?
6. What am I projecting?
7. Can I trust this person?
8. What is the worst thing that could happen?
9. What is the best thing that could happen?
10. What does this relationship teach me?

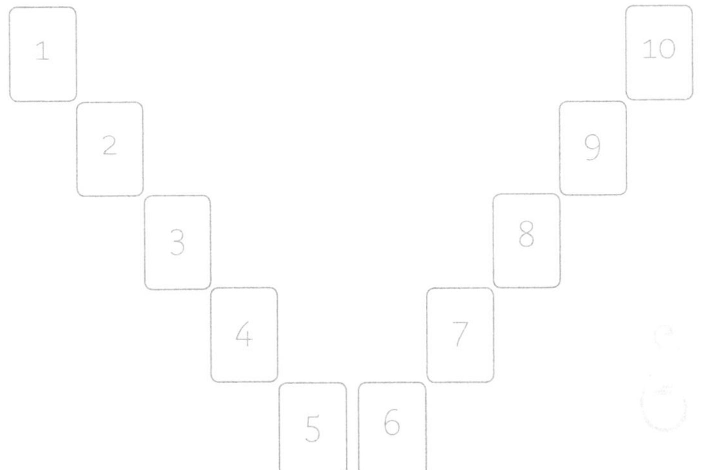

Slow It Down Spread

Light moves at 186,000 miles per second, sound moves at 1,142 feet per second, a storm moves 52 feet per second, and a person walks 4 feet per second.

The Star card evokes action without physical movement. She is pouring yet moves nowhere, content to focus on the task at hand. This is a reminder that movement occurs within the subtle body. Energetic changes within will affect and color outward actions.

On This Day

The first speeding arrest was made on this day to—who else?—a New York City cabbie. The year was 1899, and Jacob German was arrested and jailed for driving his horseless carriage 12 mph down Lexington Avenue.

Summation of Spread

Careening a little too fast? Feeling out of control? A 12 mph speeding ticket is comical in comparison to the rate at which modern drivers fly down roadways—a reminder of relativity and the accelerated speed of modern life. This spread is inspired by questions designed to help you slow it down a bit.

Cast Your Cards

Cast your cards...slowly.

1. What do I need to slow down and pay attention to?
2. What am I trying to avoid?
3. How can I enjoy my ride more?
4. What is my reward for stopping to smell the roses?
5. What will happen if I don't slow down?
6. What toll does this take on my physical body?
7. What small adjustment shall I calculate on my internal GPS?

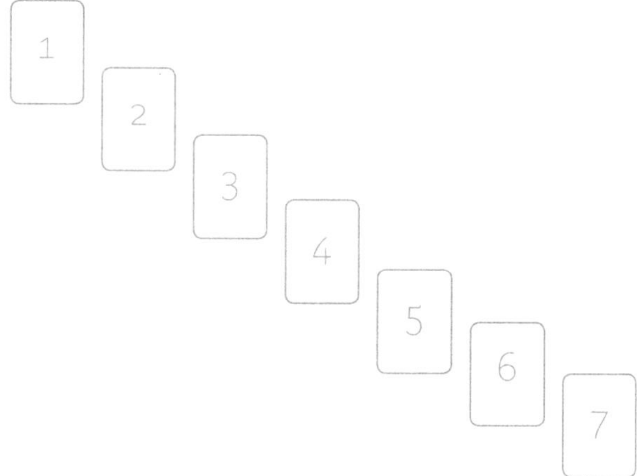

Qualities of Gemini Spread

On This Day

Today marks the first day of the astrological sign of Gemini, the Twins.

Summation of Spread

This spread is based on the essential qualities of Gemini: communicative, intelligent, inquisitive, expressive, changeable, flirtatious, playful, and energetic.

Cast Your Cards

The Gemini Spread's cards are cast in the shape of the Gemini glyph, which looks like the roman numeral for two.

1. What improves my communication with others?
2. In what area am I remarkably intelligent?
3. Where is my inquisitive nature leading me?
4. What needs to be expressed through me?
5. Why is it important to be flexible?
6. What is my most flirtatiously appealing quality?
7. How can I let loose and have some fun?
8. Where is duality operating in my life?
9. What personal relationship should I focus on?
10. What sector of my life requires energy?

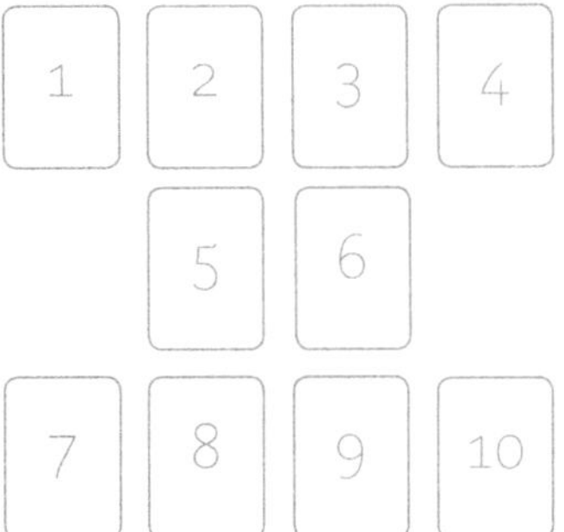

Gemini's ruling planet is Mercury, its primary color is yellow, its lucky day is Wednesday, and the best place for success is high above sea level. Gemini rules the third house of the zodiac, governing elementary education, communication, and sibling relationships.

Duality is found within the couple on the Lovers card. Soulmates often feel they complement each other—that true love is the heart's counterpoint in the soul of another. While two come together to create one in the Lovers card, duality and individuality are both essential.

May • 22

Gothic Torture Spread

Gothic subculture formed in the eighties as a subgenre in the London music scene and quickly spread. The name is derived from the gothic literary genre of the nineteenth century.

On This Day

Bring your dark side to the surface, whip out some Depeche Mode, and don some crushed velvet and lace. Today is World Goth Day.

Summation of Spread

Ready to explore the sublime? The Gothic Torture Spread does not examine literal torture but rather the transcendental experience of darkness through themes prominent in goth culture.

Cast Your Cards

The Gothic Torture Spread's cards are cast in the shape of the ankh, an ancient symbol of life.

The Death card represents the beginning of something rather than its end. Gothic style and substance are based on those things we find moving in the shadows, among flickering candles, and teetering on the boundary of pleasure and pain.

1. Grotesque: What truth have I distorted?
2. Horror: What scares me?
3. Romance: What excites me?
4. Curse: What plagues me?
5. Ghostly: What haunts me?
6. Mysterious: What mystery must be unraveled?
7. Desolate: What makes me feel bleak and empty?
8. Death: What has been lost?
9. Angst: What hope fills me with the sense of overcoming this useless situation?
10. Creativity: What makes my darkness so beautiful?

Mesmerizing Spread

On This Day

Franz Anton Mesmer was born this day in 1734. Using a theory called animal magnetism, he cured a wide variety of diseases. Animal magnetism was based on the idea that everything in the universe is interconnected. He postulated that when our energy, or "universal fluid," is blocked, we become sick. His name is the root of the English verb "mesmerize."

Mesmer was discredited when a royal commission investigated his findings and concluded he was a charlatan. Regardless, his legacy persists, and his efforts aided the development of modern hypnosis.

Summation of Spread

How are your energy levels? Are you feeling vibrant or drained? This spread uses Mesmer's theory as a commentary on personal states of energy. It examines what your energy is attracting and how to adjust it for your greatest good.

Describing optimal health and an open energy flow, the Sun card is auspicious in all matters pertaining to health. Representing vitality and splendor with the enlightenment of the spirit and knowledge, you will succeed.

Cast Your Cards

Cast the Mesmerizing Spread's cards in groups of three:

1. What is the state of my energy?
2. How can I keep it flowing?
3. What is my greatest energy block?
4. How do I eliminate this block?
5. What keeps me healthy?
6. Does this energy draw others to me?
7. Am I attracting good people into my life?
8. Am I attracting romance into my life?
9. Am I attracting money into my life?
10. What final adjustment should I make?

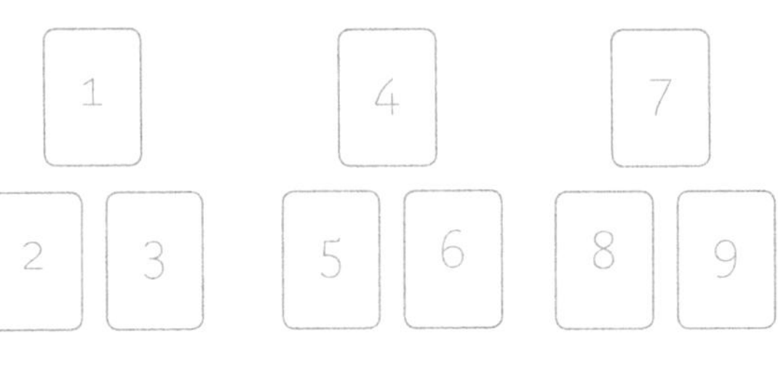

Celebrate like a Queen Birthday Spread

Divination was a popular Victorian pastime. Young women used tea leaves, palm reading, dripping wax, fruit cakes, scrying, and cards, among other objects, in attempts to discover the names of their future husbands and answer all their questions.

Tarot queens express fully mature feminine qualities, intrinsic to all women as well as men. Each queen represents nurturing, personal security, and a sense of self. A queen appearing in the past position of a tarot spread can indicate the influence of a mother figure or strong female.

On This Day

Today is the birthday of England's Queen Victoria, born in 1819. The Victorian era was named for the queen and spanned her reign between 1837 and 1901. Victorians enjoyed the heyday of Spiritualism, when séances, spirit writing, and Ouija boards were all the rage.

Summation of Spread

Celebrate your own special day by performing this spread on your birthday. Nine questions have been crafted, as nine is the number of wish fulfillment.

Cast Your Cards

Shuffle the cards. Count down the number of cards to the age you are turning. Place these aside and lay out your spread with the remaining cards like glowing candles on the perimeter of your favorite cake.

1. What was I born to do?
2. What will mark the upcoming year as different?
3. What will I do better this year?
4. What new thing should I bring into my life?
5. Why am I so special?
6. How can I appreciate myself?
7. What gift should I give myself?
8. What is my birthday blessing?
9. What is my birthday message?

Star Wars Spread

On This Day

Star Wars was released on this day in 1977.

Summation of Spread

This epic film uses the Force, described by Obi-Wan Kenobi as the energy field surrounding and enveloping all living things. Like magic, the Force binds all organic beings and the galaxy together. The Star Wars Spread uses the concept of the Force to inquire about the electric, magical energy coursing through your life.

Cast Your Cards

Cast your cards in the shape of an X-wing fighter, the chosen space vehicle of the Rebel Alliance:

1. What is the Force?
2. What energy courses through me?
3. How can I train myself to be more sensitive to my power?
4. What creates a disturbance in my force?
5. Am I tempted by the Dark Side?
6. How do I filter emotions like fear?
7. Can I use my Force for compassion?
8. What is the destiny I must fulfill?

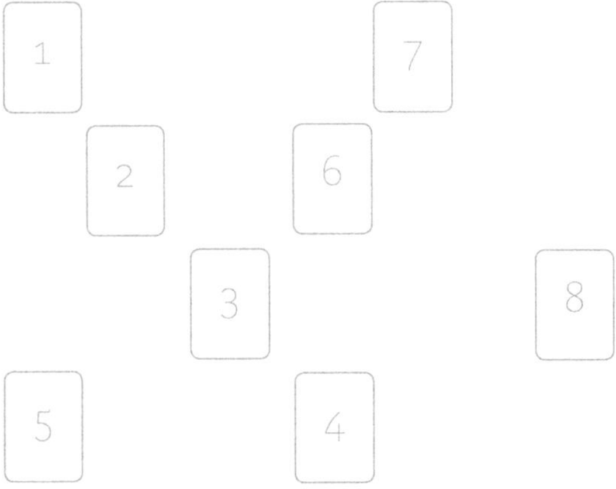

George Lucas used archetypal mythological constructs to create Star Wars. *The film has been compared to the practices and beliefs of many major religions, including Taoism, Buddhism, Hinduism, and Christianity.*

Obi-Wan Kenobi and Yoda live alone, sequestered in isolation, until Luke discovers them. Their powerful knowledge is unleashed when Luke shows he is ready to learn. The Hermit's lamp is indicative of all the knowledge he would share with those who are ready—a reminder of the age-old concept that when the student is ready, the teacher appears.

Dracula Spread

Bram Stoker and Pamela Colman Smith, illustrator of the RWS deck, were dear friends and worked together at the Lyceum Theater in London.

Artist and author Robert Place created the Vampire Tarot, based upon the novel *Dracula*. He posits that the vampire's thirst for blood is a metaphor for the Holy Grail quest—the life-giving substance and fountain of youth for which all philosophers and alchemists strive.

On This Day

Bram Stoker published *Dracula* on this day in 1897. In doing so, he defined the modern form of vampires as we know them today.

Summation of Spread

Feeling a touch of bloodlust? *Dracula*'s bloody tale regales the count's attempt to relocate from Transylvania to England and the ensuing battle between perceived forces of good and evil. Stoker invoked themes of Victorian female sexuality, immigration, and post-colonialism. The Dracula Spread uses themes from the iconic novel to inform its questions.

Cast Your Cards

Cast the Dracula Spread's cards in the form of two wooden stakes. Hold tight—they may save your life.

1. Traveler: Where am I going?
2. Intruder: How do I feel like an outsider?
3. Prisoner: What holds me captive?
4. Disguise: What do I pretend to be?
5. Fear: What do I fear and desire?
6. Isolation: Do I feel alone?
7. Sexuality: Can I express my sensual needs?
8. Blood Lust: What do I crave more than anything?

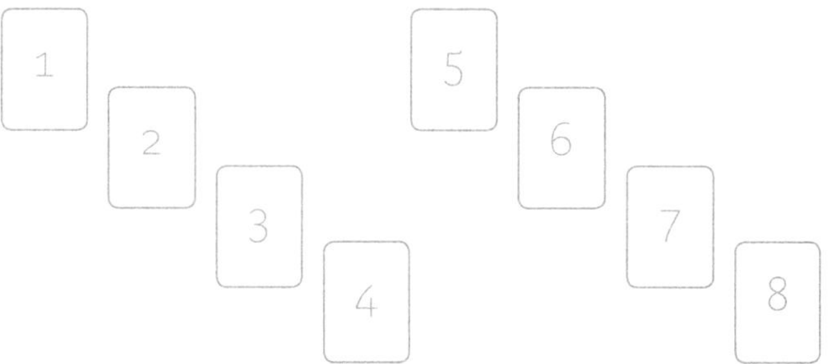

Marie Anne Lenormand's Palm Reading Spread

On This Day

French fortuneteller Marie Anne Lenormand was born on this day in 1772. Lenormand was a cartomancer and palm reader for more than forty years. Famous in her day, she is enjoying a renaissance among modern card readers.

Summation of Spread

The general questions of this spread are inspired by the lines palm readers look at when analyzing a client's palm.

Cast Your Cards

1. The Simian Line: How do I manage thoughts and emotions?
2. Marriage Line: Will I have a long marriage?
3. Children Line: How many children will I have?
4. Health Line: Will my health be good?
5. Line of Intuition: How sensitive am I?
6. Medical or Teaching Lines: How do I help others?

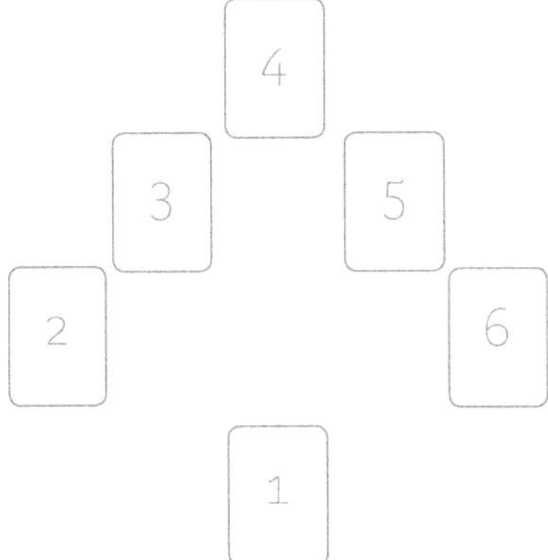

In 1807 Lenormand read Napoleon's palm and predicted his intention to divorce Josephine. He imprisoned Lenormand for twelve days in December while he finalized his divorce. This incident propelled her into notoriety, making her the most sought-after reader of her time.

All tarot aces connect to the palm. Note the hand on each ace where the symbol of each suit rests. All aces are connected to the number 1 and represent the beginning of a cycle, issue, or chapter in your life.

May • 28

Freedom Spread

Amnesty International was awarded the Nobel Peace Prize in 1977 for securing peace, justice, and security in the world.

On This Day

Amnesty International was born on this day in 1961. It is the largest human rights movement, with more than 3 million members in over 150 countries. Their mission is to end all grave abuse of human rights worldwide.

Summation of Spread

How truly free are you? Countless people have lost their lives so freedom could be passed on to future generations. We sip tea and read a book while a woman on the other side of the world lies naked in the corner of a jail cell for voicing her political opinion. Our children run off to school in the morning while in other countries a young girl is shot and killed on her school bus simply for wanting an education in a country repressing female rights. This spread explores everyone's right to basic and essential human freedoms.

The Devil card's darkest aspect is human rights violations, while the Star card represents ultimate freedom. The seven small stars represent the chakras of the human body, while the large star represents the free flow of cosmic energy.

Cast Your Cards

Cast the Freedom Spread's cards in the shape of a candle. The candle is Amnesty's symbol, based on the Chinese proverb "it is better to light a candle than curse the darkness."

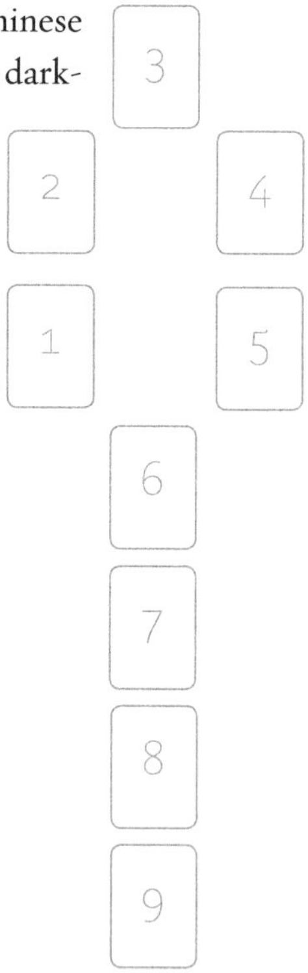

1. Am I free?
2. Do I have my dignity?
3. Do I have basic essentials?
4. Do I suffer at the hands of another?
5. Am I free to speak my opinion?
6. Am I free to leave my situation?
7. Do I have a support system?
8. Can I freely express my political opinion?
9. What can I do to help those who do not have basic human rights?

Einstein's Examining a Solution Spread

On This Day

On this day in 1919, a solar eclipse provides proof of Einstein's general theory of relativity.

Summation of Spread

Are you rethinking an important decision? Having arrived at any big solution, examination is the best way to be sure you've made the best possible choice. Einstein's Examining a Solution Spread is inspired by considerations you may have overlooked when first making your decision.

Cast Your Cards

1. Have I chosen this solution to please someone else?
2. Did I choose this because it is what other people expect of me?
3. Did I choose this because it is the way everyone else does it?
4. Did I choose this because it is easy?
5. Have I made the best choice for myself?
6. Is there any last thing I should consider?

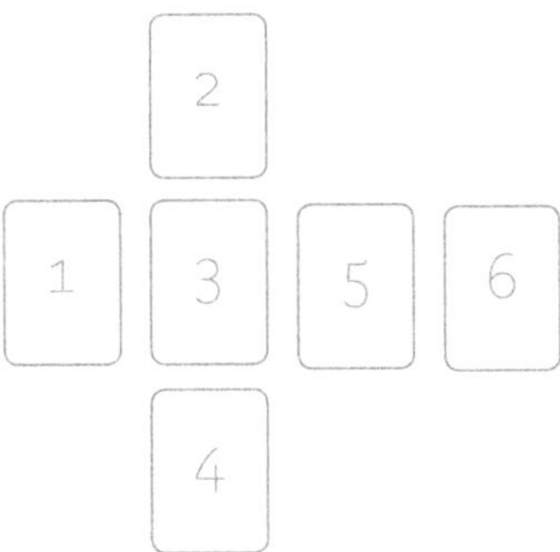

After his death, slices of Einstein's brain were sent to scientists all over the world, who concluded that Einstein's brain had more glial cells than normal. Glial cells are responsible for synthesizing information.

The Page, or Knave, of Swords represents a keen and quick calculating mind that is decisive in action. Diplomacy, grace, energy, and spying are qualities associated with this card. Look to this page for aid in making any decision.

May • 30

Wisdom of Pentacles Spread

Pope Benedict recently asked Spanish priests to distance themselves from El Colacho to downplay this Pagan tradition's connection with Catholicism.

On This Day

Today is the mysterious baby-jumping festival of El Colacho in Castrillo de Murcia, Spain. Dating back to 1620, all babies born in the previous twelve months are placed on mattresses in the street. Men dressed as devils jump over the babies while crowds watch and cheer. The ritual is performed to absolve the babies from original sin.

Summation of Spread

This spread is informed by the suit of Pentacles, which represents anything in the material world—and that includes people as well as money, objects, and things. The little babies tucked onto mattresses represent Pentacles.

Pentacles represent the physical and external level of consciousness, acting as a mirror of your health, finance, work, and creativity. Pentacles represent our outer surroundings and how we create, shape, and grow our lives from an external point of view.

Cast Your Cards

Cast the cards in the shape of a five-pointed pentagram.

1. Manifestation: What am I manifesting?
2. Realization: What do I realize is true?
3. Prosperity: What brings me prosperity?
4. Health: How do I best maintain optimal health?
5. Finance: How can I attract wealth?
6. You: Who am I?

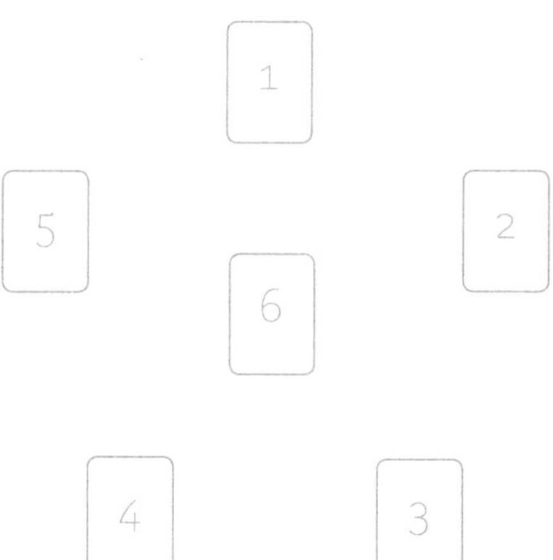

31 • May

Yoga Asana Archetype Spread

On This Day

On this day in 1893, Swami Vivananda began his journey to America from India. Speaking at the Chicago World's Fair, this was the first time yoga was introduced to America on a large scale.

The om mantra is found in Hindu and Tibetan philosophy. It is said to be the primordial sound of the universe and is connected to the third eye (consciousness) chakra.

Summation of Spread

This spread's questions are based on basic yoga poses to explore the meaning and metaphor behind them. This spread is helpful whether you are familiar with the practice or not. If you do keep a personal yoga practice, you might want to ponder these questions when performing these asanas, or positions.

Cast Your Cards

The cards of this spread are cast in the shape of Downward-Facing Dog, an all-around rejuvenating stretch.

1. Downward-Facing Dog Pose: What helps me turn inward?
2. Tree Pose: Why is it important to be strong yet flexible?
3. Headstand: What helps me to see the world from a different perspective?
4. Eagle: Can I see what is truly important in life?
5. Cobra: Can I rise above the material world and peer into the unknown?
6. Child's Pose: How do I cultivate a youthful attitude?
7. Corpse Pose: How can I let go of everything?

Like a yogi, the Hanged Man's inversion places him upside down, looking at the world from a new perspective. The Hanged Man is associated with artists, seers, and mystics. He represents arriving at a crossroads and sometimes signals a pause leading to wisdom and prophetic power.

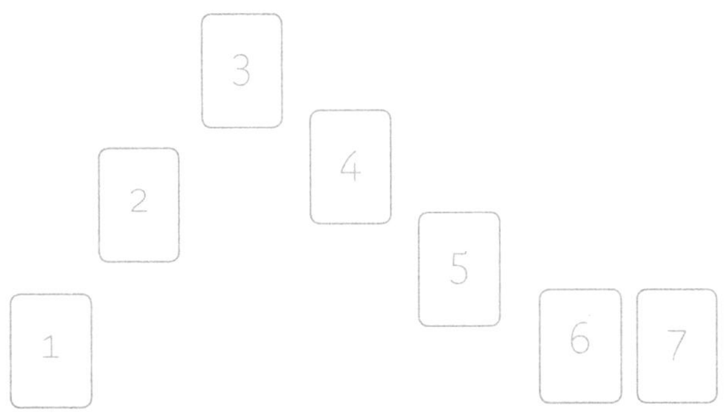

Find True North Spread

Standing at the North Pole, all directions point south. The North Pole is actually located in the Arctic Ocean, covered by sea ice that constantly moves amidst the icy waters.

On This Day

Magnetic north was discovered on this day in 1831. Two norths lie in the Arctic: magnetic north varies from place to place due to magnetic abnormalities, while true north is the northernmost point on Earth's surface. True north sits at the top of Earth's axis, the point upon which it spins. Magnetic north moves, while true north is fixed.

Summation of Spread

Where are you going? Finding true north is essential for proper navigation. Navigating our life's journey, we sometimes find ourselves off track, rendering us unsure of our standing. This spread can help you follow the right path for yourself.

Cast Your Cards

The Moon card displays a crawfish about to embark on a journey. Cast your cards in the shape of his path.

1. What path am I on?
2. What path should I be on?
3. How do I adjust where I am moving?
4. What signs point me in the right direction?
5. Whom do I meet along the way?
6. What distracts me?
7. What challenges me?
8. What should I pay attention to?

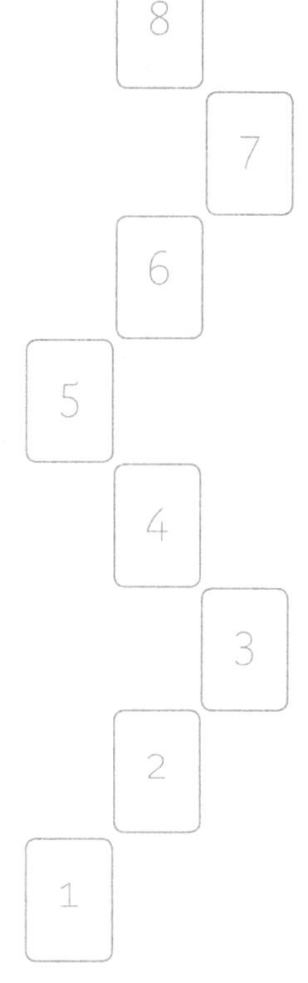

Tarot's directional attributes differ among practitioners, but it is generally agreed that the Pentacles represent North.

Pentacles (Earth) = North

Wands (Fire) = South

Cups (Water) = East

Swords (Air) = West

Circus Spread

On This Day

Legendary huckster P. T. Barnum began touring with his circus on this day in 1871, calling it P. T. Barnum's Grand Traveling Museum, Menagerie, Caravan, and Hippodrome.

P. T. Barnum was over sixty years old when he entered the circus business. He was also an author, publisher, philanthropist, and even a politician. He served in the Connecticut legislature and was mayor of Bridgeport, CT, for one year.

Summation of Spread

Does the big tent and roar of the crowd fill you with childlike wonder and delight? This spread uses classic circus elements to inform a general spread about your life.

Cast Your Cards

Cast your cards like a three-ring circus.

1. Ringmaster: What am I taking charge of?
2. Clown: What issue am I not taking seriously?
3. Acrobat: What area of my life requires more flexibility?
4. Tightrope Walker: How can I achieve more balance?
5. Daredevil: What is worth risking everything?
6. Juggler: What happens when I stop trying to juggle everything?
7. Knife Thrower: What should I be aiming at?
8. Freak Show: What scares yet fascinates me?
9. Human Cannonball: What direction am I headed in?

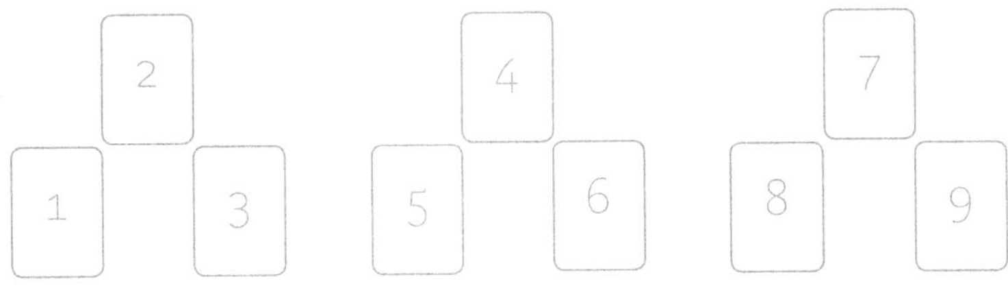

The Two of Pentacles looks like a juggler or circus performer as he balances two Pentacles. The card speaks of balance and the need to eventually make a decision. It is important to remain flexible regardless of the outcome.

June • 3

Bellona's Fury Spread

The Latin word for war is bellum, *relating to the modern word* belligerent, *whose literal interpretation is "war-waging."*

On This Day

Today is the Roman festival date for Bellona, goddess of war. The feminine aspect of warfare, she is depicted wearing a helmet and armed with spear and torch. All Roman senate meetings relating to foreign wars were conducted at her temple. Though the role of the female was suppressed in ancient Rome and women were not allowed to battle, mythology still allowed the female component in warfare.

Summation of Spread

What gets you steaming angry? Ever hear the expression "hell hath no fury like a woman scorned?" Bellona informs this spread, crafted to explore the elements of the psyche that get you rip-roaring mad.

The Queen of Wands acts as goddess of war when scorned. Wands, the suit of Fire, renders her dangerous, volatile, and explosive. One need only ponder this decisive and destructive element to understand just how hot under the collar this queen is likely to become when crossed.

Cast Your Cards

Take a breath and cast your cards as follows:

1. What makes me angry?
2. How do I express my fury?
3. How does emotion make me strong?
4. How does emotion weaken me?
5. Do I forgive myself?
6. Can I find forgiveness for others?
7. How can I let the anger go?

Improve My Sex Life Spread

On This Day

Dr. Ruth Westheimer, sex therapist and media personality, was born on this day in 1928. Dr. Ruth rose to fame in the 1980s as a cultural icon with her free, frank talk about sex and relationships on radio and television.

Citing a headache as a reason not to have sex won't work anymore. Scientists have discovered the endorphins released during sex naturally reduce the pain of a headache.

Summation of Spread

Need to spice it up? Dr. Ruth has helped the masses improve their sex lives. Channeling Dr. Ruth's openness and sage advice, this spread looks at how to improve the quality of your sex life.

Cast Your Cards

1. Am I living healthfully?
2. Do my partner and I take enough time out for each other?
3. How do we break out of our bedroom rut?
4. How do I best communicate what I need?
5. What does my partner need?
6. What can I indulge in that I haven't before?
7. What am I dying to try?
8. What unexpected quality comes from revitalizing my sex life?

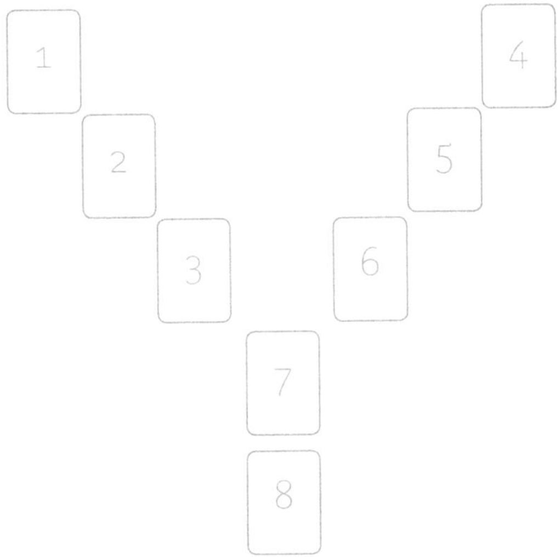

Note the phallic and explosive nature of the Tower card. It represents the ultimate male orgasm. The watery Star card follows the Tower and represents the ultimate female orgasm and receptiveness.

Qualities of Venus Spread

Venus rules Taurus and Libra. One day on slowly rotating Venus lasts 243 Earth days, while the average surface temperature is 867 degrees F. No wonder Venus represents the slow burn of passion, beauty, and love.

Venus's aspects emerge through the Empress card as a reminder to focus attention on passions, loves, and what brings pleasure. The symbol of Venus is placed on the heart-shaped shield at her feet.

On This Day

Venus went into transit on this day in 2012. Transit occurs during a rare astronomical alignment. Passing directly between Earth and the sun, Venus is seen as a tiny dot gliding across the face of the sun. Because Venus is visible to the naked eye, it is present in many mythologies, including written accounts of the ancient Babylonians. Venus is named after the Roman goddess of love and beauty.

Summation of Spread

The Qualities of Venus Spread contains questions based on astrological associations of the planet Venus. Using these associations, questions are posed to offer greater clarity in life.

Cast Your Cards

Cast your cards in the shape of a heart:

1. Love: How can I cultivate love?
2. Beauty: What makes me feel beautiful?
3. Passion: How can I kindle passion?
4. Pleasure: How can I feel pleasure each day?
5. Charm: What is my most charming quality?
6. Relationships: Which relationship in my life needs attention?
7. Money: What small thing can I do to increase my money?
8. Harmony: What adjustment brings a greater sense of harmony to my life?

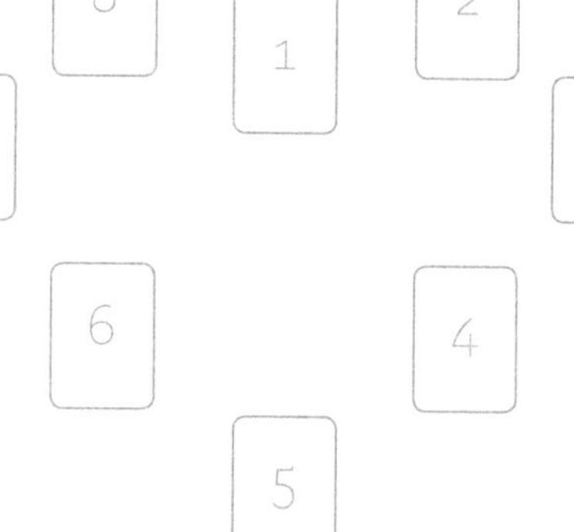

Summer Fun Spread

On This Day

The first drive-in movie theater opened on this day in New Jersey in 1933.

Summation of Spread

Drive-in movies are synonymous with summer fun. Summer's warmth stirs the inner child no matter your age. The Summer Fun Spread explores a variety of elements to be sure that this year you have the best summer of your life.

Cast Your Cards

Cast your cards in the shape of a drive-in movie screen:

1. What trip should I plan?
2. What new thing can I try?
3. How can I attract summer romance?
4. Is there a relationship I should begin?
5. Is there a relationship I should let go of?
6. What is the theme of my summer style?
7. Should I pick up a new sport or exercise?
8. Is there something I've always wanted to do but haven't done yet?
9. What can I focus on to have the best summer ever?

One of the biggest drive-in theaters was in Copiague, Long Island, New York. It covered 29 acres, parked 2,500 vehicles, had a full-service restaurant with seating on the roof, and a trolley system that shuttled children and adults to a playground.

The Three of Cups represents the carefree joy of living and abundance of friendship typical of the summer season. Joy, growth, and the pleasure of community are all connected with the Three of Cups.

Vesta's Happy Home Spread

A priesthood of women, the vestal virgins were Rome's only full-time group of female priests. The vestals were considered essential to the continuance and security of Rome, caring for a sacred fire that was never allowed to go out.

The Queen of Pentacles is goddess of the house and home. Taking full advantage of all she has acquired, she recognizes the value of everything from people to objects. Her unique talents always benefit those around her. Practical and wise, she promotes good health, proper manners, and kindness to others.

On This Day

Vestalia, the celebration of Vesta—goddess of house and home, hearth and fire—began on this day in ancient Rome. Her temple doors opened only today for mothers to make offerings of sacrificial foods in hopes of her blessings.

Summation of Spread

Ready for a bit of housekeeping? Vesta's Happy Home Spread calls to Vesta for inspiration on the cultivation and maintenance of a happy home.

Cast Your Cards

Cast as follows:

1. What is the state of energy in my home?
2. How can I connect to my home as I would a person?
3. How can I make my home more comfortable?
4. How do I protect against unwanted guests?
5. What is the state of my family?
6. What do I love about my family?
7. What gives my family its roots?
8. What action can I take to make my home a sanctuary?

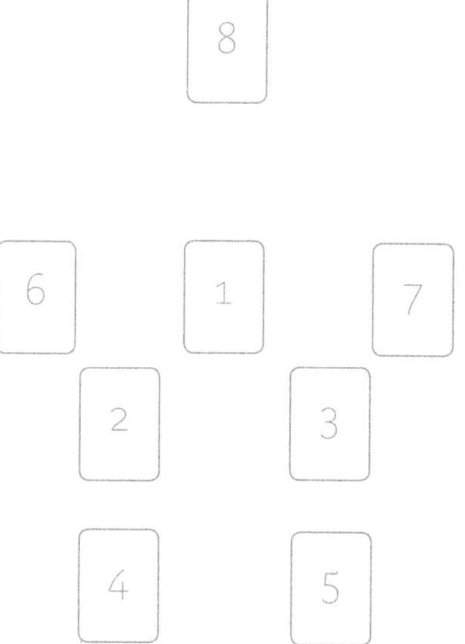

Ghost-Hunting Spread

On This Day

The comedy film *Ghostbusters* was released on this day in 1984, becoming an instant classic. The film follows three parapsychologists in New York City who open a ghost-catching company.

Dan Aykroyd was the initial driving force behind Ghostbusters *as interest in the afterlife ran in his family. His grandfather had constructed a special radio in an attempt to reach the spirit world.*

Summation of Spread

Cast this spread when you are planning a ghost-hunting expedition for yourself.

Cast Your Cards

Consider three locations you will visit and investigate for specters. Cast the cards as follows:

1. First location.
2. Second location.
3. Third location.
4. Who makes the perfect ghost-hunting partner?
5. What special equipment do I need?
6. Will I be placing myself in danger?
7. What will I find?
8. Will it be scary?
9. Can I stay objective?
10. Will I make a good ghostbuster?

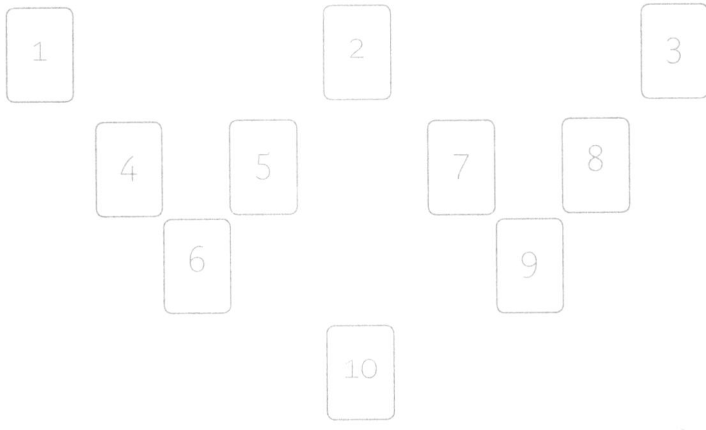

The Seven of Cups represents ghostly activity, as the cups hover in the air like specters. Will they and their treasure disappear into thin air or shall they manifest as realities? Only time will tell.

Partnership Spread

Crowley had been looking for an artist for a tarot project and had his friend Clifford Bax help him find one. When the artist he'd planned to introduce to Crowley didn't materialize, he invited Harris instead. The rest is tarot history.

Two of Cups is the partnership card, representing romantic, platonic, or business partnerships. Balance and harmony manifest as a result. The caduceus of Hermes represents the healing element present in the relationship.

On This Day

Aleister Crowley was introduced to Frieda Harris on this day in 1937. Together, they created the Thoth tarot. The project, which was supposed to last six months, spanned over five years. Sadly, neither one of them would live to see their deck published.

Summation of Spread

This spread considers the theme of partnership and how you can work best with the other person or entity. It can be read for romantic, business, or platonic partnerships.

Cast Your Cards

Think of a current partnership and cast the cards to examine it.

1. Card representing me.
2. Card representing my partner.
3. What I am hoping for?
4. What are they hoping for?
5. What I bring to the relationship.
6. What they bring to the relationship.
7. What brings us together?
8. Why I aid them.
9. Why they aid me.

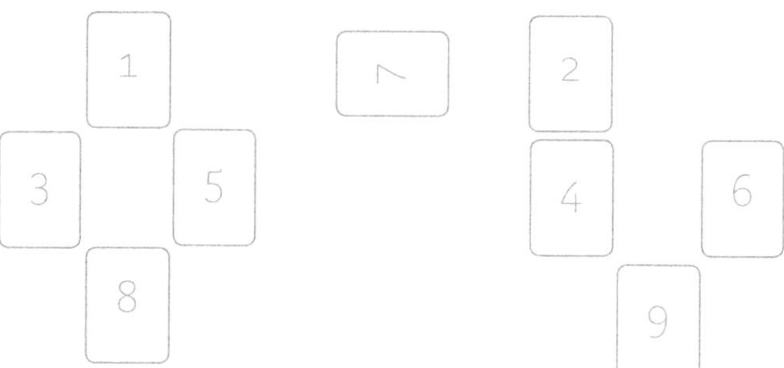

Unhappiness at Work Spread

The average employee spends over 90,000 hours on the job in their lifetime.

On This Day

The Equal Pay Act was passed on this day in 1963. It stated that men and women must receive equal pay for equal work.

Summation of Spread

Feeling unsatisfied at work? The questions examine the reasons why. Once the problem is defined, a solution will present itself.

Cast Your Cards

As a child dreaming of the future, what did you imagine yourself doing? Do your former dreams align with your current state? If not, cast the cards to get closer to your vision.

1. The state of my current job.
2. What do I like about it?
3. What do I dislike about it?
4. Am I settling for less than I'm worth?
5. Do I like the people I work with?
6. Am I appreciated and valued?
7. Do I find this job fulfilling?
8. Am I paid what I am worth?
9. Is this field or industry interesting to me?
10. Does this job align with my future goals?
11. What action should I take?

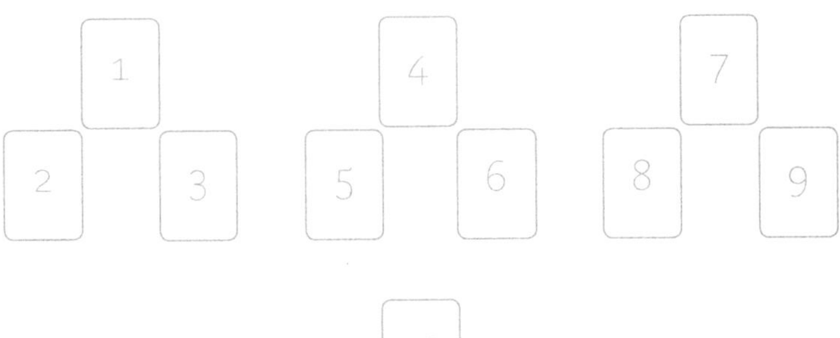

The Eight of Pentacles represents a person thoroughly engaged in the work they do and laboring with pride and craftsmanship.

Trojan Horse Spread

Both The Iliad *and* The Odyssey *began as oral tradition and were transcribed centuries after their composition.*

Attraction and energy are associated with the suit of Wands. Wands are the element bringing life to our body, intention to our actions, and passion to our projects. Wands can change our world if we let them light our way.

On This Day

Troy was sacked and burned on this day in 1184 BCE. Virgil's *Aeneid* describes how, after ten warring years, the Greeks devised a new strategy. Constructing a massive wooden horse and hiding men inside, they pretended to sail away, leaving the horse behind. The Trojans, thinking it a victory prize, brought the horse inside the gates. Under the darkness of night, the Greeks crept out of the horse, opened the gates, sacked Troy, and ended the war.

Summation of Spread

Do you have a Trojan horse in your life? The metaphor is useful whenever someone has used trickery to bring an enemy inside. This spread was created to examine elements you invite into your life that may not be in your best interest. This is especially helpful for the person who finds themselves re-creating similar situations and wants to break the habit. Often the enemy behind the gate is ourselves.

Cast Your Cards

Cast your cards with a warrior's determination.

1. What false truth have I allowed in?
2. What negativity do I attract with this belief?
3. Why must I stop doing this?
4. What step can I take to get rid of it?
5. How does my life change as a result?
6. What new belief can I fill the space with?
7. What helps me do it effortlessly?

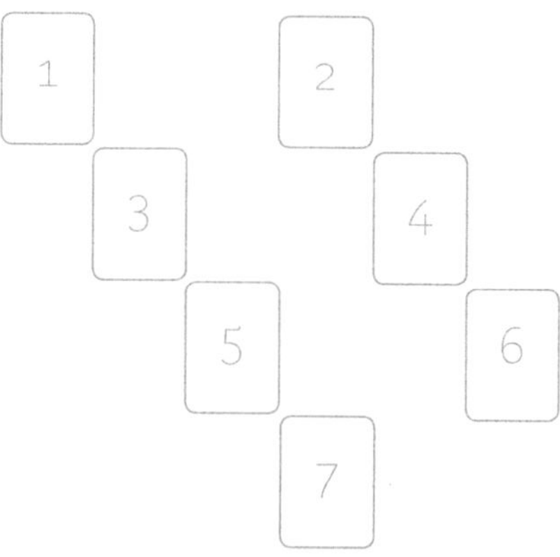

Magician Card Spread

On This Day

Today is National Magic Day. Whether you prefer the magical meandering of Harry Potter, feats of modern magicians like David Blaine, or the hallowed grounds of the ceremonial magicians, you can celebrate the day by performing the Magician Card Spread.

Summation of Spread

The Magician Card Spread is based on symbols found on the Magician tarot card. It probes your connection to matters of personal power.

Cast Your Cards

Use this spread to answer any question. Format your question before casting the spread or simply let the cards answer the questions posed. Pull the Magician card from your deck. Placing it in the center of the Magician Card Spread, cast your cards around it as follows:

1. Magic Wand: Where do I receive power?
2. Pointing Finger: Where do I direct my power?
3. Lemniscate: How do I keep positive energy moving?
4. Items On Table: What tools sit at my disposal?
5. Roses: What is manifesting?
6. White Lily: What is transforming?
7. Uroboros (snake belt): What is reborn?
8. Yellow Background: How does my imagination serve me?

The Magician's iconography in historical tarot depicts him as swindler or slight-of-hand artist. Not until the formation of esoteric decks did occultists get hold of the Magician and elevate him to the level of magus.

The Magician represents pure will; he is able to cast magic as he pleases. He represents the ability to make something happen—a reminder of inner strength, resolve, mastery, and charisma.

Papus's Tarot Discovery Spread

Papus was only 24 years old when he wrote his complicated treatise Tarot of the Gypsies: The Most Ancient Book in the World, *otherwise known as* Tarot of the Bohemians.

On This Day

Gérard Encausse, or Papus, was born on this day in 1865. He didn't alter the course of tarot's history, but he did keep the momentum going by forging a deep connection between tarot and Kabbalah, the two largest Western magical traditions.

Summation of Spread

Papus's Tarot Discovery Spread was created to examine a personal journey with the cards. A tarot practice takes many forms; this spread inquires about your path.

Cast Your Cards

1. What does tarot mean to me?
2. What magic will the cards unlock in my life?
3. How do I best gather information from the cards?
4. What should I do if I ever become scared?
5. Am I ready to read for others?
6. Is this deck the one for me?
7. How can I find my truth?
8. How can I work with tarot in a unique way?
9. What is today's message?

The Eight of Cups connects to all journeys, tarot or otherwise. The figure moving up the mountain is the Hermit, who sets off on his journey to enlightenment. Leaving all worldly possessions behind him as he goes, this is a metaphor for abandoning what you have gained in search for something more.

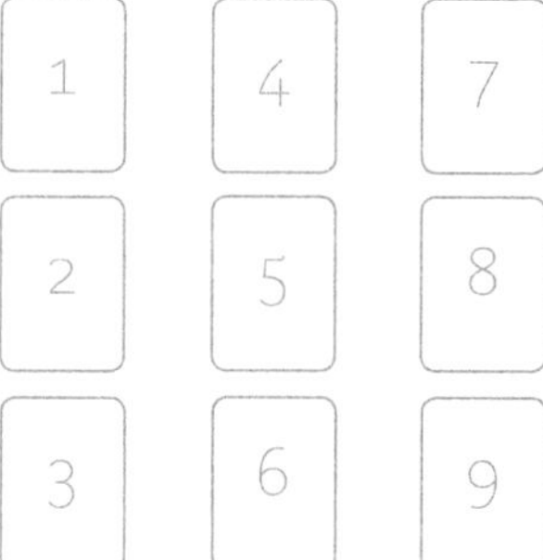

Six Realms of Existence Spread

On This Day

Tibet celebrates a three-day festival today at the Tashilhunpo Monastery, a massive monastery founded by the first Dalai Lama. It is marked with the hanging of a giant *thangka*, a painting on silk or cloth with embroidery.

Summation of Spread

The Tibetan Book of the Dead is a funerary text describing the levels of consciousness between a soul's death and next rebirth. This spread is inspired by each realm of consciousness.

Cast Your Cards

Cast your cards and proceed into the Tibetan land of the dead.

1. Realm of Hell (tortures): What tortures me?
2. Realm of Hungry Ghosts (greed): What do I crave?
3. The Animal Realm (dullness): What bores me?
4. The Human Realm (balance): How do I inhabit my body?
5. The Realm of Jealous Gods (jealousy and envy): What do I want that others have?
6. The Realm of the Gods (delight and endless pleasure): What brings me utmost pleasure?

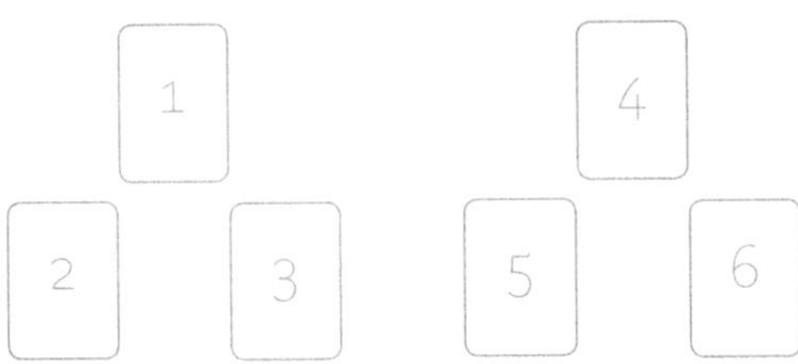

The key to entering and exiting spiritual realms is to understand that they are actually empty. They exist as products of the human mind; this is why death is instant spiritual liberation. This also teaches us how to live within the constant flow of life and death.

The six realms are depicted as segments on the Wheel of Life, corresponding to the Wheel of Fortune card.

Spiritualism Spread

Early séances were theatrical, dramatically conjuring and materializing spirits. Today's séances are concerned with mental mediumship, though messages received remain profound and insightful. Modern Spiritualism is similar to any other religion in its rituals and services.

The Page of Cups is the medium, psychic, and intuitive card. Her great sensitivity is a reminder of the open nature of children and why children are often the first members of a household to sense ghosts and spirits. The fish popping out of her cup represents a vision or psychic flash.

On This Day

The Spiritualist Church selected a grove in upstate New York on this day in 1873 that would eventually become the Lily Dale Assembly, a town of spiritualists and mediums. The year-round population hovers near 275 residents, but an average of 22,000 people come each year to attend workshops, lectures, and have private readings. An early believer of Spiritualism included Arthur Conan Doyle, author of the Sherlock Holmes mysteries.

Summation of Spread

Would you like to speak with the dead? Spiritualism, a religious movement that began in the nineteenth century, acknowledges life after death via contact with the spirit world. Male and female reverends are certified mediums, and séances are often conducted after church services. This spread is based on the general information that comes through a medium.

Cast Your Cards

Cast your cards in a razor-sharp line.

1. Who is here?
2. What do you look like?
3. Why have you come through today?
4. What do I need to know?
5. Why is this important?
6. What is your message?
7. What will happen if I follow your advice?

Summer Lovin' Spread

On This Day

The rollicking stage musical *Grease* was turned into a film and premiered in New York City on this day in 1978.

Summation of Spread

Are you ready for a summer love? Characters Sandy and Danny fall for each other over summer vacation. One of the film's memorable scenes and songs is "Summer Nights," upon which this spread is based.

Cast Your Cards

Cast the cards of the Summer Lovin' Spread when the air turns warm and evenings are optimal for long walks on the beach. Feel the wind touch your skin, tuck your toes into the sand, and cast as follows:

1. Card symbolizing my summer fling.
2. How do we meet?
3. What do they look like?
4. What is their personality like?
5. How do they make me feel?
6. What sort of fun do we have?
7. Will we stay in touch after the summer?
8. Does the fling turn into a long-term relationship?

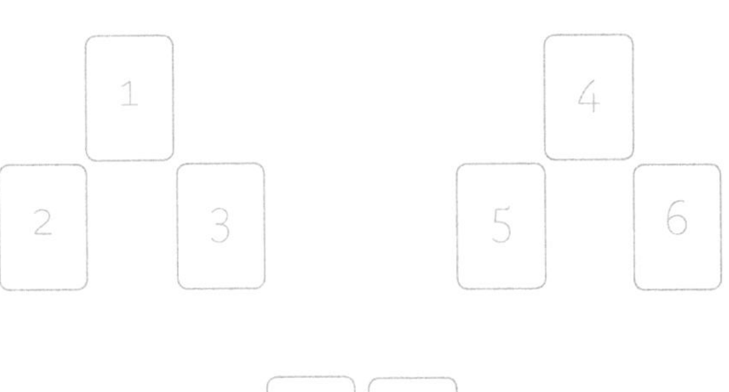

Some psychologists say people fall in love with a person similar to a parent when there are unresolved childhood issues. Unaware, people seek to resolve this childhood conflict as an adult.

The Six of Wands is the triumphant celebration of victory, describing the emotional high of falling in love. Wands represent the fire, passion, and excitement of new love, and parades are often held during the warm days of summer.

Pushing Boundaries Spread

Stravinsky was romantically linked with Coco Chanel. He ruthlessly promoted his work in order to support a lavish lifestyle that included living in Switzerland, Paris, the South of France, Hollywood, and New York City.

On This Day

Igor Stravinsky, widely considered the twentieth century's most important and influential composer, was born on this day in 1882. A musical revolutionary, he continually pushed boundaries, collaborating with Picasso, Jean Cocteau, and George Balanchine.

Summation of Spread

Are you ready to move out of your comfort zone? Great artists remind us of what is possible in both life and art. This spread uses Stravinsky as inspiration for questions regarding the pushing of your boundaries in work, relationships, and life, so your end result is evolution and growth.

The Five of Wands pushes boundaries. The energy and excitement created by the five sparring youths is indicative of the energetic blast needed to take on new challenges. They joust and spar in good fun, serving as a reminder of the joy occurring when one expands one's comfort zone.

Cast Your Cards

1. What do my personal boundaries stop me from doing?
2. Where am I heading?
3. What must be destroyed?
4. What is my strongest fear?
5. What helps me take emotional risks?
6. How can I shake up my routine?
7. When is it okay to cross the line?
8. What's the worst that can happen?
9. What outrageous action should I take right now?

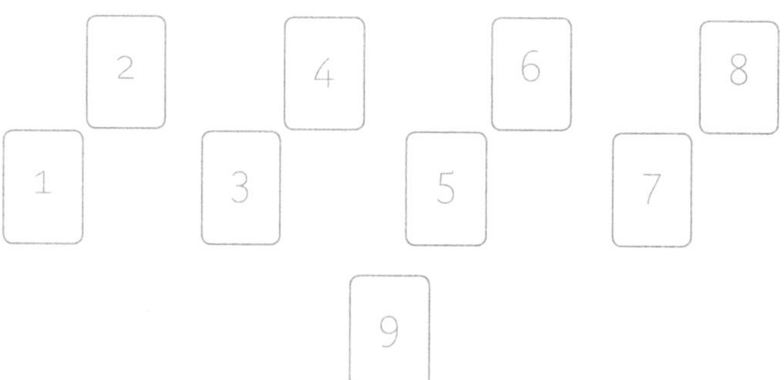

Picnic Spread

On This Day

Today is International Picnic Day, celebrating one of the most pleasurable aspects of summer: outdoor feasts with family and friends. The Victorians held the art of picnicking in high regard. Elaborate meals were served in pastoral landscapes at the height of nature's beauty.

Summation of Spread

This spread takes inspiration from aspects of the time-honored pastime of picnicking.

Cast Your Cards

Cast the cards as you might lay out a sumptuous feast while pondering the warm summer days ahead.

1. Blanket: What protects me?
2. Ants: What is bothering me?
3. Sunshine: What fills me with joy?
4. Sandwich: What sustains me?
5. Cupcake: What sweet thing can I look forward to?
6. Lemonade: What refreshes me?
7. Wine: What intoxicates me?

While we enjoy picnic pleasures in modern life, eating outside was a necessity for our ancestors. The idea of a slow and elegant meal outdoors, rather than a harvest worker's dinner in the fields, came into fashion during the Middle Ages.

The Ten of Cups, representing familial bliss, is connected to nature's beauty, represented by the rainbow. The social pleasure of human company is represented by the family and frolicking. This card is the culmination of happy times and good feelings among family and friends.

Father's Day Spread

Ties are the most traditional gift bought around the world on Father's Day.

On This Day

The first celebration of Father's Day took place on this day in 1910. Upon hearing of the newly created Mother's Day, Sonora Dodd—of Spokane, Washington—felt fathers were due their own day of recognition. Wanting to honor her widowed father, who took care of his six children during the Civil War, she lobbied for a Father's Day.

Summation of Spread

This spread examines the relationship you have with your father in order to better understand it and, therefore, yourself.

Cast Your Cards

1. What is my relationship to my father?
2. What is the great gift my father has given me?
3. What is the great challenge my father has given me?
4. How am I similar to my father?
5. How am I unlike my father?
6. How do I define myself in comparison to him?
7. How can I best honor our relationship?

The Emperor card represents the archetypal father figure, while the tarot kings represent father types you'd meet on a daily basis.

Litha Midsummer Solstice Spread

On This Day

Litha was originally intended to coincide with the summer solstice, and on modern calendars it is often celebrated between June 20–24. A fire and water festival, it marks the convergence of the sun and moon, and it is considered optimal for harvesting magical and medicinal plants.

Summation of Spread

This spread is based on the seven sacred directions. It is a powerful meditative opportunity for reflection during the excitement of midsummer's magic, manifestation, and abundance.

Cast Your Cards

Cast the Litha Midsummer Solstice Spread's cards as follows. Upon completion of this spread, go outside to pick flowers or a bouquet of herbs and bring the splendor of summer inside.

1. East (Air): What do I know?
2. South (Fire): What is my potential?
3. West (Water): What do I understand?
4. North (Earth): What should I nurture?
5. Above: What divine wisdom is mine?
6. Below: What do I inherit?
7. Within: How do I connect with what is inside me?

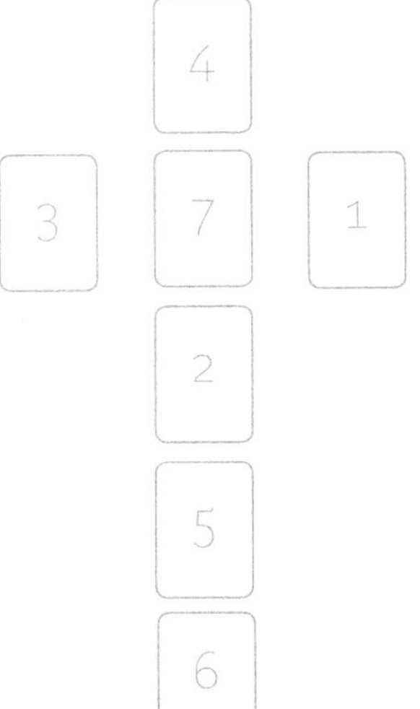

Russian witchcraft states the most powerful botanicals are ritually harvested on Midsummer's Eve. Unique plants like the fern seed offer invisibility on this night only. Now is a magical time for divining, finding true love, and flirting.

The Sun card corresponds to this high day of summer. On an intellectual level, the sun represents being able to communicate, while on the physical plane it represents victory, success, recognition, and glory.

Qualities of Cancer Spread

Cancer's ruling planet is the Moon, silver is the primary color, the lucky day is Friday, and the best place for success is near or on the water. Cancer rules the fourth house of the zodiac, governing home, family, and nurturing influences.

The Chariot card represents plotting a course and being in the driver's seat. The star-filled canopy represents the grace of the heavens and the zodiac, which aid you in victory. A union of opposites is suggested by the black and white sphinxes, so subtle control is required.

On This Day

Today marks the first day of the sign of Cancer, the Crab.

Summation of Spread

This spread is based on the essential qualities of the astrological sign of Cancer, including emotions, intensity, diplomacy, impulsiveness, selectiveness, and intuitiveness.

Cast Your Cards

1. How does my emotional depth serve me?
2. Why should I embrace intensity?
3. In what area of life do I need to be diplomatic?
4. When is it okay for me to be impulsive?
5. Why is it important to be selective?
6. Where does my intuitive strength lie?

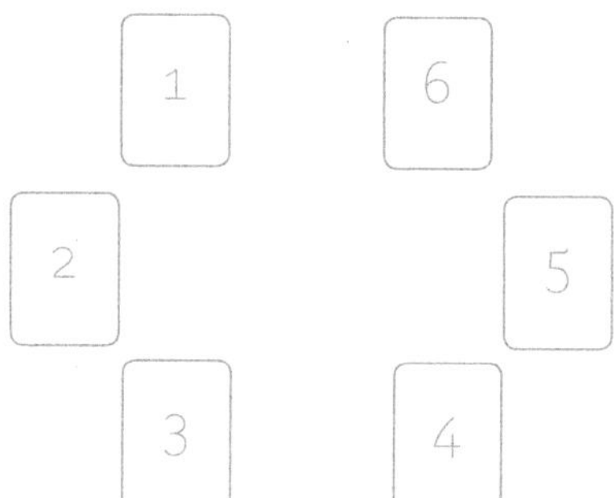

Sensitive Breakup Spread

On This Day

Henry VIII told his first wife, Catherine of Aragon, they would separate on this day in 1527. The king, upset with Catherine's inability to produce a male heir, engaged in a salacious affair with Anne Boleyn. Catherine was banished from court and forced to take residence elsewhere. Till the end of her life she ascertained her right as Henry's only lawful wife and England's only rightful queen.

Henry VIII married six times, beheading two of his wives. Catherine Howard was only eighteen years old when Henry sent her to the guillotine.

Summation of Spread

Are you ready to call it quits? Breakups are never easy for either party. The Sensitive Breakup Spread helps to evaluate the situation, explore all options, and conduct the breakup in the most graceful manner possible.

Cast Your Cards

The cards are placed in three groups. The first examines the how, when, and where of the breakup. The center represents emotional reactions and how to best deal with them. The third represents future ramifications.

1. When is the right time to break up?
2. Where is the correct place?
3. How can I be honest yet sensitive?
4. What will their reaction be?
5. How can I not react to their reaction?
6. Will we remain friends?
7. How will I feel a few weeks from now?
8. Will I be happier if we aren't together?

Three tarot cards embody the emotions and situations of any breakup. The Tower is indicative of shocking change and loss of control when a relationship deteriorates. The Three and Five of Swords reflect damaged feelings, especially with a third party in the mix.

Indiana Jones Life's Adventure Spread

Most of the snakes used in the Well of Souls scene were not snakes but legless lizards. Causing trouble on the set, the lizards were not afraid of fire but instead tried to get closer to the flames to keep warm.

The tarot knights embody Indiana Jones's sense of adventure. The Knight of Wands connects to Indy's passion, the Knight of Swords to thinking quick on his feet, the Knight of Pentacles for his love of objects and antiques, and the Knight of Cups for his romantic feelings toward Marion.

On This Day

Filming of the epic *Raiders of the Lost Ark* began on this day in 1980. An instant classic, *Raiders* flew into the hearts of millions who wished they, like Indy, could run off to adventure and intrigue.

Summation of Spread

Seeking excitement? You might not be a globe-trotting archaeologist, but it is possible to use inspiration from *Raiders of the Lost Ark*'s scenes and themes to find adventure in your own backyard.

Cast Your Cards

Cast the Indiana Jones Life's Adventure Spread's cards in the shape of Indy's iconic hat:

1. Boulder: What is chasing me?
2. Bullwhip: What is my secret weapon?
3. Fedora: What is my signature symbol?
4. Air Travel: Where do I need to go?
5. Romance: Whom should I kiss?
6. Snakes: What scares me?
7. Submarine: How deep am I willing to go?
8. The Ark: What power or magic lies inside me?

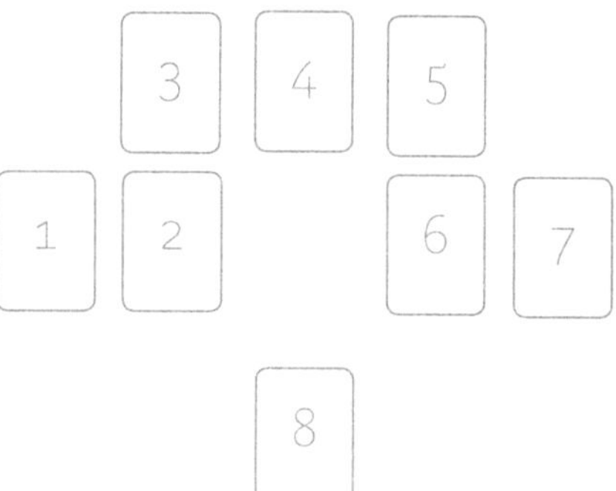

Midsummer Magical Love Spread

On This Day

Today is Midsummer's Day, the exact middle of summer. Magic, witches, fairies, dancing, rites, and rituals are associated with this long summer's day and Midsummer's Eve. Bonfires and fortune-telling mark celebrations in countries and communities acknowledging Midsummer's Day.

Summation of Spread

Ready to inquire about your true love? In Italy, young girls gather the buds of a houseleek, one bud for each suitor. The opening bud was her future husband. Such an auspicious day for love divination inspires this Midsummer Magical Love Spread.

Cast Your Cards

By the dance of candlelight, let the cards reveal your true love:

1. Who is the object of my love?
2. Do they love me back?
3. Are we soulmates?
4. What brings us together?
5. What tears us apart?
6. Why am I drawn to this person?
7. What draws them to me?
8. What is my love history?
9. What is their love history?
10. What is the likely outcome?
11. What should I focus on?

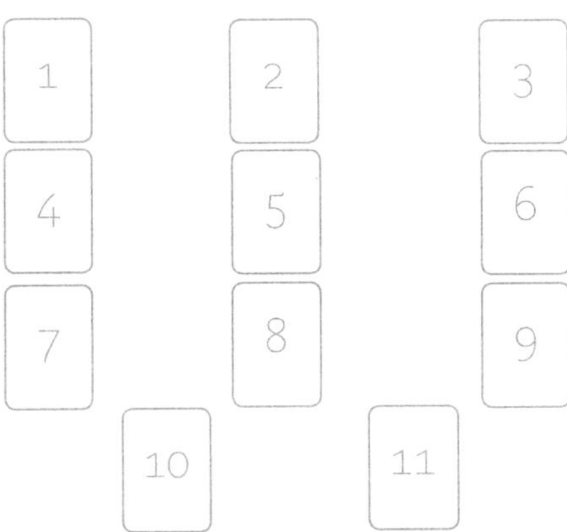

To discover the initial of a future husband, peel an apple in one continuous long strip. Toss the peel over your left shoulder; the peel will land in the shape of their initial.

The World card is indicative of living and fully experiencing love, be it spiritual, emotional, sacred, or profane. The victory ribbon around the World dancer is emblematic of success.

Jacques Cousteau's Adventure Spread

Cousteau discovered that dolphins use sonar to navigate after observing their behavior in the Mediterranean. It was also he and his team who discovered the wreck of Britannic, Titanic's *sister ship, off the coast of Greece.*

The King of Cups sits on a throne amidst rolling oceans, as certain as Cousteau. He has reached a maturity at which he can claim true authenticity and self-confidence. The King of Cups is a creative guide and mentor, just as Cousteau educated others on the wonders of the sea that so captivated his imagination. This is an excellent card for someone in the creative arts.

On This Day

Jacques Cousteau, diver, author, conservationist, and filmmaker, left the earth on this day in 1997. To many generations, his name is synonymous with the thrill of undersea adventure.

Summation of Spread

What mysteries await you? Everyday life offers myriad opportunities to glimpse unexplored realities, be they people, places, or things. All you need to do is give yourself over to the adventure.

Cast Your Cards

The Jacques Cousteau's Adventure Spread's cards are cast as a path leading into the depths of the unknown:

1. Am I ready for adventure?
2. What adventure awaits me?
3. What action do I take this moment to begin my adventure?
4. What must be explored?
5. Where shall I travel?
6. What will terrify me?
7. What will excite me?
8. What challenges me?
9. What changes me?

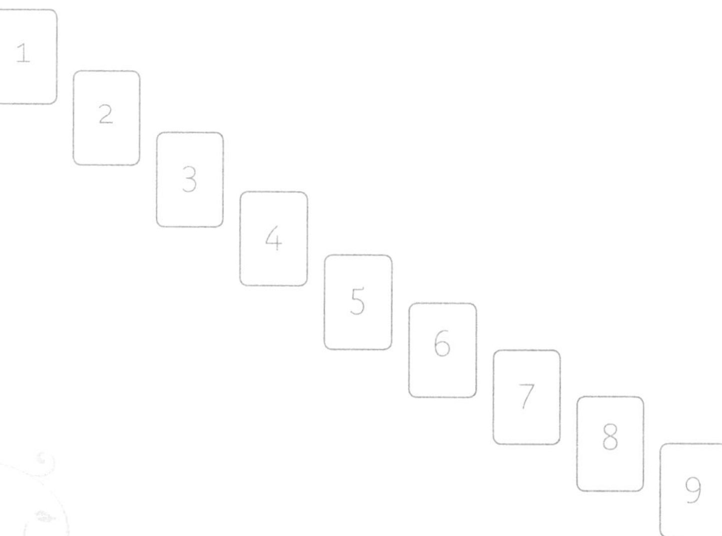

Your Personal Symbol Spread

On This Day

Mercedes, the luxury car company, registered their symbol on this date in 1903. Their familiar sign, the three-pointed star, represents their perceived dominance over land, sea, and air.

Summation of Spread

It is empowering to create or discover your own personal symbol. A personal symbol raises energy to higher concepts, identifies you with a higher idea, and can be a reminder of your personal power. Once the power symbol is identified, create or select it so you can carry it with you—placed on a piece of jewelry, tattooed, or tucked away where no one else can see it. Use it as you see fit.

Cast Your Cards

This spread poses questions to get you thinking about what your appropriate symbol is. Answer the questions using drawn cards as prompts.

1. My personal motto is...
2. My most influential element is...
3. My best color is...
4. My spirit animal is...
5. My power number is...
6. My most ardent belief is...
7. I feel powerful when...

1

7 2

6 3

5 4

Symbols communicate directly to our unconscious. Deep thoughts and beliefs about human life are conveyed in a single, immediate, and powerful image.

The entire tarot deck operates under the power of symbol. Symbols—like poetry or facial expressions—convey what cannot be said in words. A symbol is the doorway to something new, sublime, and unspoken.

Vampire's Kiss Spread

Some scholars suggest the term vampire *derives from the Greek word* nosophoros, *meaning "plague carrier." The many cross-cultural terms for vampire suggest that the vampire myth or archetype is deeply embedded in human consciousness.*

Kissing of all forms, vampire or otherwise, stems from the suit of Wands, representing passion and primal instincts. Wands are the fire of life throbbing within you, the blood in your veins making your skin warm and cheeks blush.

On This Day

Dark Shadows premiered on this day in 1966. This American gothic soap opera gave teenagers a reason to run home after school to watch vampire Barnabas Collins along with werewolves, ghosts, zombies, witches, and warlocks.

Summation of Spread

Are you ready to embrace the darkness and snuggle with the supernatural? The world's most famous vampire soap opera offers inspiration for this spread, based on the intense allure of a vampire's kiss.

Cast Your Cards

Cast your cards on a moonless night as you dwell amidst the shadows. Are you feeling brave enough to greet dark desires and discover who or what is waiting for you?

1. What should I give myself over to?
2. What happens when I abandon rational thought?
3. Who wants to kiss me?
4. How do I embrace my darkness?
5. What thrives in darkness?
6. What thrills me?
7. What increases immortality?
8. What lives forever?
9. What action do I need to take?

1	2	3
4	5	6
7	8	9

Should I Take This Job Spread

On This Day

Labor Day became a federal holiday on this day in 1894. Now recognized as the formal end of summer, an excuse for shopping, and the supposed last day to wear white, Labor Day was originally formed to celebrate the economic and social contributions of workers in the United States.

The first nineteenth-century Labor Day rally was to gain support for an 8-hour workday. Up till then, a 12-hour workday was the norm.

Summation of Spread

Are you considering a job offer? This spread uses Labor Day as inspiration for questions concerning employment opportunities coming your way.

Cast Your Cards

1. Is this a long-term career move?
2. Am I moving toward something I want?
3. Does this position challenge my mental abilities?
4. Am I capable of doing this job?
5. Do I fully understand the expectations of this role?
6. Does this offer a fair salary?
7. Am I proud to be associated with the company's brand, product, or services?
8. Will my coworkers be friendly?
9. Will the work feel professionally satisfying?
10. Will this offer me the lifestyle I desire?
11. Is there opportunity for future growth?
12. What potential pitfalls do I need to be aware of?
13. Final word.

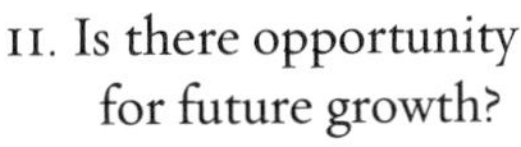

1 2 3 4 5 6

7 8 9 10

11

12

13

Wands are the suit representing career, while Pentacles represent the money earned while working.

Gender-Bending Spread

The Beatie family filed for divorce, and a legal mess ensued. It challenged the validity of the marriage and raised issues of reproductive rights and abilities for a transgendered person to legally maintain his or her legal identity.

The World card is seen by many cartomancers and occultists as a hermaphrodite, a figure equally male and female, representing the reconciliation of opposites and the experience of union.

On This Day

Thomas Beatie, known as the world's first pregnant man, gave birth to a daughter on this day in 2008. Beatie, a female-to-male transsexual, was legally recognized as a man when he married his wife, Nancy, who could not conceive. Thomas used artificial insemination to become pregnant and ultimately gave birth to three children.

Summation of Spread

Gender issues may be deeper in our consciousness than we realize. This spread provokes deep, thoughtful questions about what it means to be male and female. These questions also will aid in understanding masculine (swords and wands) and feminine (cups and pentacles) suits of tarot.

Cast Your Cards

1. What does "female" mean to me?
2. What does "male" mean to me?
3. How am I feminine?
4. How am I masculine?
5. What are the boundaries between gender?
6. How do I embrace both?
7. How would my life have been different if I had been born of the opposite sex?
8. What personal quality remains the same regardless of gender?

Full Moon Spread

On This Day

Today is National Full Moon Day, set aside to appreciate the moon's beauty and eloquence. No other astral body creates such magic, mystery, and speculation.

Summation of Spread

The moon's effect is a subtle yet vital pull on the forces of life. The Full Moon Spread takes into account the intrinsic qualities of the moon to craft its questions.

Cast Your Cards

Cast the Full Moon Spread in a circle like the moon itself.

1. What mystery does the moon reflect?
2. Who looks at the moon and thinks of me?
3. What hidden truth does moonlight illuminate?
4. Am I comfortable reflecting the light of others?
5. How do I affect the world with my presence?
6. What lies at the heart of my truth?
7. What cycle am I experiencing?
8. To what place am I transitioning?
9. What wondrousness lurks in the shadows?

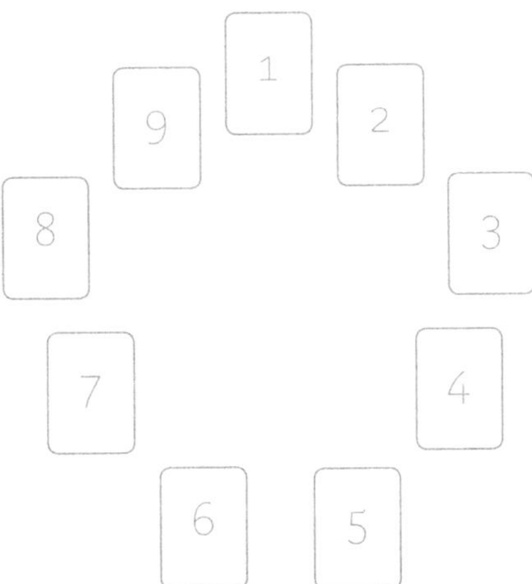

Seen from the moon, Earth goes through its own phases. The phases are always in reversal. There is a full Earth when it's a new moon for us, and there's a new Earth when we look up and see a full moon shining down upon us.

The Moon card signifies a journey or passage through the unknown. Truly reflecting our changing interior state through its cycles, this skyward object, locked in Earth's gravitational pull, connects all of humanity who have gazed upon it and thought, wondered, marveled, and wished.

Qualities of Saturn Spread

Epic storms can rage on Saturn for months, even years. Saturn rules the astrological sign of Capricorn, and Saturday is named after Saturn.

The World card offers success, euphoria, travel, and completion. Those who recognize their limits, maintain discipline, and embrace structure are able to grasp this card's glory for themselves.

On This Day

The Cassini space probe entered into orbit around Saturn on this day in 2004. The probe's mission was extended until 2017 to study a full period of Saturn's seasons. Saturn was named after the Roman god based on the Greek Cronus.

Summation of Spread

The Qualities of Saturn Spread contains questions based on the astrological associations of the planet Saturn. Using these associations, questions are posed to offer greater clarity in your life.

Cast Your Cards

The Qualities of Saturn Spread's cards are cast in the shape of the planet and its rings.

1. Structure: Why is structure good for me?
2. Limitations: What is my greatest limitation?
3. Authority: How do I grapple with authority issues?
4. Discipline: What area of my life needs more discipline?
5. Concentration: What do I need to focus on?
6. Striving: What am I aiming for?
7. Responsibility: What should I stand up and take responsibility for?
8. Teaching: What can I teach others?

Halfway There Spread

Famous prophet Nostradamus died on this date in 1566. Nostradamus twice married, was father to several children, and was known to spend entire nights in his study, withdrawn in intense meditation, where he claimed to channel supernatural knowledge from God.

On This Day

When the clock strikes noon today, it is the exact midpoint of the year: the 183rd day of the year in the Gregorian calendar. It is considered the midpoint because there are 182 days before and 182 days after today.

Summation of Spread

This spread is designed to take stock of the last six months and plan ahead for the six ahead. Examine and revisit what was relevant when the New Year's ball dropped. What were you looking forward to? Did you set resolutions or intentions?

Cast Your Cards

Lay the cards in a half circle:

1. How have I grown since the New Year?
2. What has helped me accomplish my goals this year?
3. What can I be proud of?
4. What challenge have I overcome?
5. What theme should I focus on for the next six months?
6. What unexpected surprise waits for me?

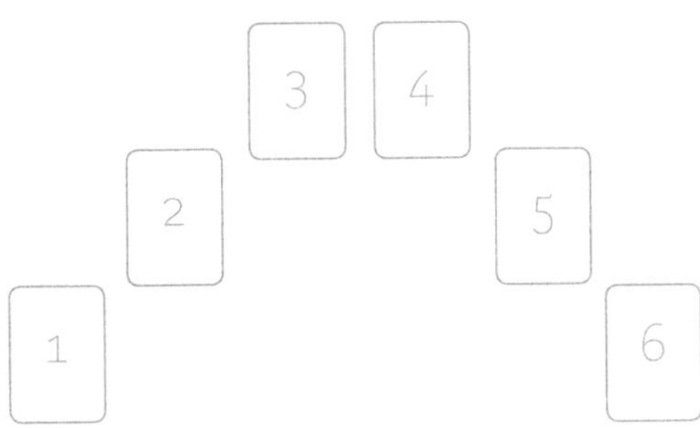

The halfway point of the minor arcana rests at the fifth card. All fives in tarot imply challenge, sorrow, loss, and drama. Five is Geburah (Judgment) on the Tree of Life, a place shaking the stability felt in the preceding four. When feeling sad or confronted, let the fives of tarot remind you challenges push us forward, spur growth, and define who we are.

Savings Spread

In 1819, the price of bacon was 16 cents a pound; tea was $1 a pound, and shoes were $2 a pair. A skilled workman earned $1 a day, a laborer 75 cents, and a servant earned $2 a week plus room and board.

The Seven of Pentacles represents an accumulation of wealth and the thought process regarding what to do next. Effort and responsibility are still required to see a project through to fulfillment, and there is much more to come.

On This Day

The Bank of Savings, the first savings bank in the United States, opened in lower NYC on this day in 1819. The Bank of Savings was built to help those struggling financially to maintain a savings account.

Summation of Spread

What is your financial philosophy? The Savings Spread examines your conceptions of finance—how and why you save.

Cast Your Cards

Make magic over your money. Place a reversed triangle over the pyramid found on the dollar bill to create a six-pointed star. Cast your cards in this shape.

1. My current and prevailing attitude about money.
2. My negative perceptions about money.
3. My positive perceptions about money.
4. What can I do to put more money in the bank?
5. What happens as a result of new financial investments and savings?
6. What is the great financial lesson of my life?

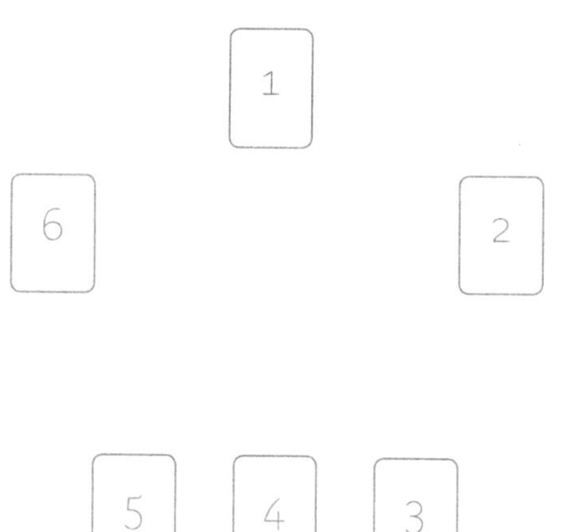

Declare Your Independence Spread

On This Day

Today commemorates the United States's independence from Great Britain. The day is usually celebrated with sparkly firework shows, patriotic parades, summer picnics, and lively parties.

Summation of Spread

We all have something in our lives we would like to declare independence from—it may be a habit, a relationship, addictive behavior, or a way of thinking. To perform this spread, you must pick something you want or need to get rid of. Once you have selected what you are letting go of, this spread marks the beginning of your independence.

Cast Your Cards

This spread takes on the shape of a firework, with the ninth card exploding in the center.

1. Why is it important to declare my independence right now?
2. What are the negative effects of my old pattern or habit?
3. What lessons has it taught me that I can now leave behind?
4. What positive effects will come of my independence?
5. How can I come up with a new habit or routine?
6. Who supports me?
7. How can I reward myself for this change?
8. What should I focus on as I forge a new direction?
9. What will be the most exciting result of my independence?

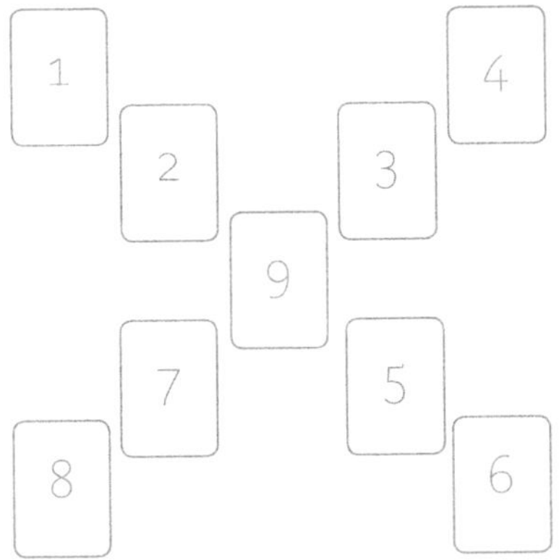

Thomas Jefferson and John Adams, two signers of the Declaration of Independence who also served as US presidents, died on this day in 1826. This date happened to be the fiftieth anniversary of the Declaration of Independence.

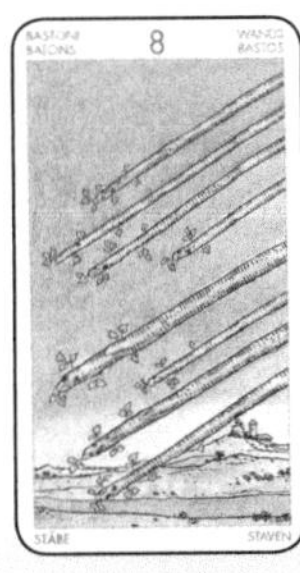

The Eight of Wands represents energetic movement. Changes like gaining independence will alter the course of this energy, sending it to new and exciting places.

Seven Planetary Metals Spread

Isaac Newton's principle and recipe for the philosopher's stone—the substance that could turn base metals like iron, tin, and lead into gold—was accidentally discovered amidst a collection of old chemistry books at the Chemical Heritage Foundation in 2010.

The number 7 has esoteric and occult significance relating to all sevens in tarot, including the Chariot. Secret and mysterious, there are 7 days of the week, 7 visible planets, and 7 notes on the musical scale; lucky sevens mark a fortunate gambler.

On This Day

Sir Isaac Newton, one of the world's most influential scientists, published the work *Principia* on this day in 1687. Stating the three universal laws of motion, it enabled advances in the Industrial Revolution. Newton, an alchemist, sought calculations and created blueprints of the philosopher's stone.

Summation of Spread

Use alchemy to inform your life. The oldest branches of alchemy concerned themselves with creating an earthly paradise. Merging the cosmic and terrestrial, alchemy created a correspondence between planetary influences and the spirits of Earth's metals. This spread is based on the seven planetary metals found on Earth.

Cast Your Cards

Cast the cards in the circular shape of our solar system.

1. Gold (Sun): How am I authoritative?
2. Silver (Moon): How am I intuitive?
3. Copper (Venus): How do I love?
4. Iron (Mars): What gives me willpower?
5. Tin (Jupiter): What brings me success?
6. Mercury (Mercury): What helps me learn?
7. Lead (Saturn): What grounds me?

Hold Me, Thrill Me, Kiss Me, Kill Me Spread

Why is kissing so much fun? Our lips are packed with sensitive nerve endings. The slightest brush triggers a cascade of neural messages to our brains and bodies. Lips are our most exposed erogenous zone.

On This Day

Today is International Kissing Day, recognized in Great Britain, the United States, and Canada.

Summation of Spread

Pucker up! Kisses convey messages and intimacy. Whether lip-locking a lover, pecking a child good night, or smooching a friend on the cheek, kisses convey love and affection. The Hold Me, Thrill Me, Kiss Me, Kill Me Spread uses kissing clichés to discern salacious information about life and love.

Cast Your Cards

Lick those sexy lips and cast your cards.

1. Judas Kiss: What can I not trust?
2. Kiss the Cook: What am I creating?
3. Blowing a Kiss: Does someone need extra love from me right now?
4. Kiss and Tell: Who is talking about me?
5. Kiss of Death: What is transforming?
6. Kiss My Derrière: How do I rebel?
7. Kiss Your *%$ Goodbye: What should I avoid?
8. French Kiss: Who has a crush on me?
9. Chocolate Kiss: Is there someone I should be kissing right now?

The Lovers card represents kissing and implicit sensuality. The Golden Dawn assigned an attribute to each major arcana card. The Lovers card was assigned smell, and rightly so. Kissing engages most of our senses, tastes, textures, secrets, and emotions. Through scent we instinctually examine the pheromones of our lover.

Houdini's Transformation Spread

Houdini was an avid aviator and the first person to achieve controlled, powered flight over Australia in his biplane. He made a few movies and debunked fraudulent mediums after vain attempts to contact his mother after her death.

The Eight of Swords in the Rider-Waite deck looks like a Houdini escape act, as the figure is blindfolded and bound. Have you ever voluntarily placed yourself in this position? If so, how can you free yourself? The answer may lie in this spread.

On This Day

Harry Houdini first performed a handcuffed escape from a nailed, roped packing crate lowered into the East River in New York City on this day in 1912. When police forbade him to use a pier, he hired a tugboat and invited the press on-board. He escaped in fifty-seven seconds.

Summation of Spread

Ready for a change? For many fans, Houdini's stunts weren't about breaking out of shackles; rather, his feats represented a magical transformation. This spread is based on the next transformation you will experience.

Cast Your Cards

1. Where am I right now?
2. Where do I want to be?
3. What is the first step I should take?
4. What is the second step I should take?
5. What is the third step I should take?
6. What is a new belief I must incorporate now?
7. What happens as a result?

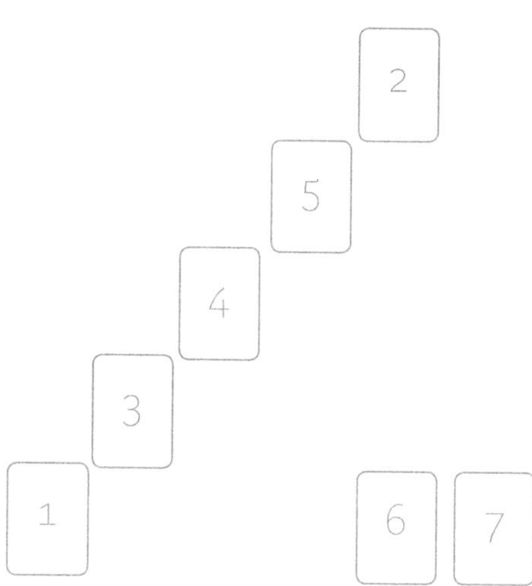

UFO Spread

On This Day

On this date in 1947, a press statement was issued saying the army had recovered a crashed "flying disk" from a ranch near Roswell, New Mexico. The UFO story emerged thirty years later when a major involved in the original recovery expressed his belief the military had recovered an alien spacecraft.

Summation of Spread

The UFO Spread asks the tarot questions we all want to know regarding the existence of flying saucers.

Cast Your Cards

The UFO Spread's cards are cast in the shape of the mysterious flying disks you may have seen in the sky:

1. Do UFOs exist?
2. What do they want?
3. Where do UFOs come from?
4. What do UFOs look like?
5. Why do people believe in UFOs?
6. Have I ever seen a UFO?

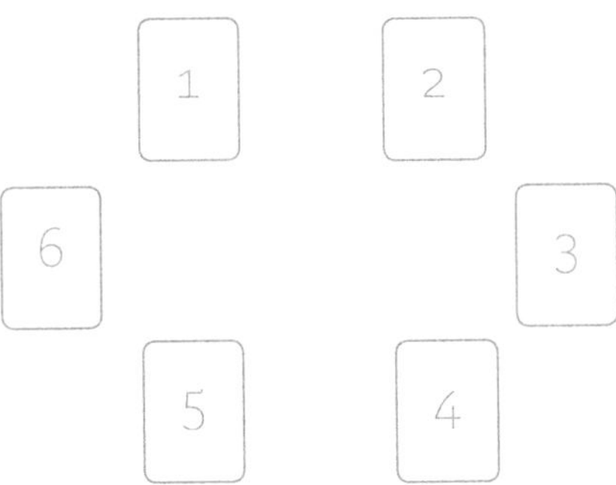

Project Blue Book was the name of the Air Force's official investigation of UFO phenomena. The term was coined by Captain Edward J. Ruppelt.

It has been suggested that a UFO hangs quietly in the background of the Temperance card. A glowing golden crown hovers over the mountain range to the left of the Temperance angel. Could Temperance, who hovers over the water, possibly be a visitor from another world? You be the judge.

July • 9

Four Chambers of the Heart Spread

The heart can always be opened to receive and give more love. Never forget: the Law of Attraction states we receive what we give.

The Three of Swords is usually considered a heartbreak card due to the Rider-Waite and Sola Busca image. Add a new and slightly different understanding of the Three of Swords: recall that the threes in tarot imply creativity, and Swords represent the mind. The Three of Swords may be understood as extreme creativity of the mind.

On This Day

Physician Daniel Hale Williams performed the first successful human open-heart surgery on James Cornish today in 1893—without anesthesia. Ouch.

Summation of Spread

Give yourself over to your most valuable organ. The Four Chambers of the Heart Spread is based on the four chambers of your precious heart. Two of the heart's chambers are the superior atria, which are receiving chambers, connecting to the suits of Cups (Water) and Pentacles (Earth)—the feminine, soft, and receptive suits. The heart's other two chambers are the inferior ventricles, which are discharging chambers, connecting to the suits of Swords (Air) and Wands (Fire)—the masculine, hard, and domineering suits.

Cast Your Cards

Receiving and Accepting

1. What blocks me from receiving love?
2. What can I proactively do to open myself to receive more love?

Discharging and Offering

3. What blocks me from giving love?
4. How can I offer more love to those around me?

Wild Card

5. What surprise does my heart have in store?

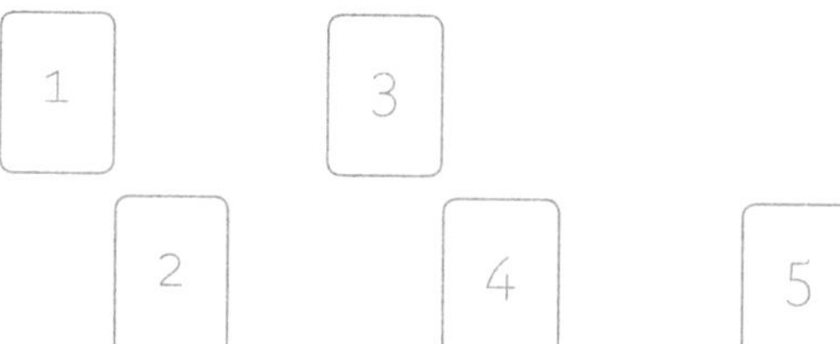

Lady Godiva Spread

On This Day

Lady Godiva rode her horse naked though the streets of Coventry, England, today in 1040. She did so to lower the tax burden her husband had unfairly placed upon its residents.

Summation of Spread

Are you ready to be brazen? Lady Godiva's legend, extremely sensual in nature, is symbolic of having the nerve and daring to do the right thing even if it means moving out of your comfort zone. The Lady Godiva Spread asks if there isn't someone or something in your life who could use a little help.

Cast Your Cards

Be bold and cast your cards:

1. Who is being treated unfairly?
2. Why does this issue resonate with me?
3. What action can I take to help them?
4. Can I count on others for help?
5. What happens as a result of my action?
6. What do I learn in the process?
7. Why is this important?

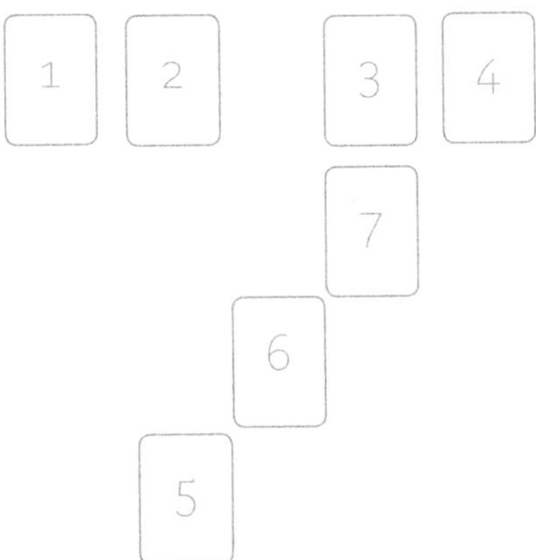

Out of respect for Lady Godiva, all residents remained inside, barring their windows and doors during the duration of her ride. One man named Tom peeked out a window. Before he saw anything, he was struck blind. The phrase "peeping Tom" stems from this story.

The Knight of Cups represents Lady Godiva's famous slow ride. The suit of Cups is female in nature, representing the imagination springing around her myth. The river flowing before the Knight of Cups represents the nature of compassion moving freely, and the slow gait of the knight's horse represents Lady Godiva's meandering ride through town.

Setting Boundaries Spread

The Europeans were slow to discover the Great Barrier Reef, while Australian Aboriginals have been aware of the reef for over 40,000 years.

The Ace of Swords is always at your beck and call to draw a line in the sand, in the air, or even in the soft flesh of your adversary. Slay all barriers with it. Standing for a great idea, this sword is your most powerful ally when you wield it fearlessly.

On This Day

On this day in 1770, Captain James Cook's ship ran aground. Unknowingly, he had just discovered the Great Barrier Reef. A system of over 3,800 coral reefs and islands along the coast of Australia and the largest living thing on earth, it supports a wide variety of life including fish, whales, dolphins, and sea turtles.

Summation of Spread

Do you protect yourself well? The Great Barrier Reef, which can be seen from outer space, is inspiration for a spread concerning the boundaries you set to secure your mental and physical state.

Cast Your Cards

Remember how precious you are as you cast your cards.

1. What helps me become more self aware?
2. What boundaries do I find hard to set?
3. What helps me stop this?
4. What should people not ask of me?
5. What do I have the right to ask for?
6. Why is it okay to protect my time and energy?
7. Who is supportive of me?
8. What is the first boundary I must set?

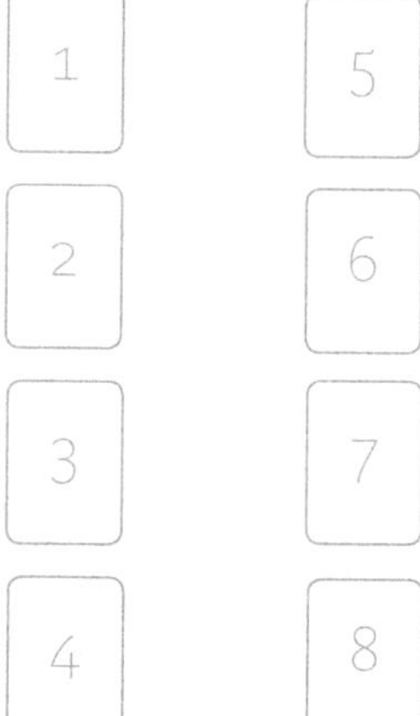

Transcendental Spread

On This Day

Henry David Thoreau was born on this day in 1817. Poet, philosopher, and author of *Walden; or, Life in the Woods*, Thoreau was a leading Transcendentalist.

Summation of Spread

Are you ready to embrace the sublime? Transcendentalism is a philosophical movement. It places importance on the purity of the individual and nature, outside of organized religion. It claims people are at their best when they are truly self-reliant and independent rather than following pre-set, predetermined dogma. This spread is inspired by the ideas of leading Transcendentalists.

Cast Your Cards

The Transcendental Spread's cards are cast moving upward, as its title suggests.

1. How do I move from an identity crisis to personal authenticity?
2. How do I move from a crisis of discontent to a quest for happiness?
3. How do I move from meaningless anxiety to movement and purpose?
4. How do I move from isolation to a sense of community?
5. How do I move toward personal responsibility?
6. How do I move from death anxiety to death acceptance and self-transcendence?

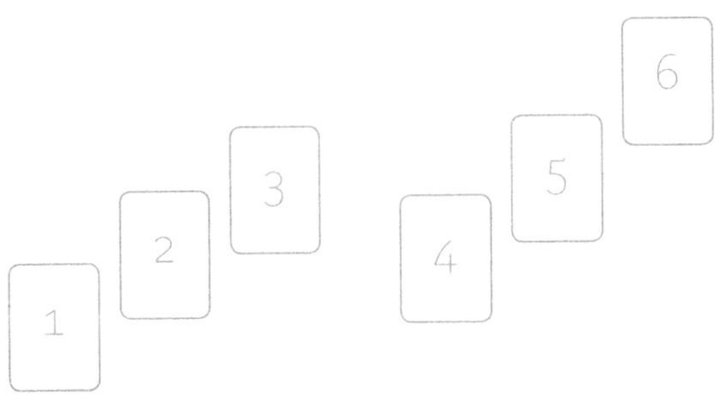

Transcendental meditation is a form of mantra meditation introduced to the United States by Maharishi Mahesh Yogi in the 1960s. This form of meditation is not connected to the Transcendentalist movement, but both are meant to move a person beyond the limits of themselves.

The Hanged Man connects to all forms of transcendence. He is willing to sacrifice creature comforts, look at the world through a new perspective, and perform the ultimate surrender of moving beyond one's physical limits.

John Dee's Horoscope Spread

John Dee practiced divination openly, holding séances, raising spirits, and using a famous magic mirror for scrying. This polished black stone can be seen at the British Museum in London.

Each tarot card is assigned an astrological correspondence. *Tarot and Astrology*, a book by Corrine Kenner, contains excellent detailed information linking the cards and the stars.

On This Day

John Dee was born on this day in 1527. Court astrologer and friend to Queen Elizabeth I, he was a mathematician, astronomer, and occultist.

Summation of Spread

This spread is inspired by the queen's legendary astrologer. Use John Dee's Horoscope Spread for a large question affecting every area of life. Each card corresponds with an astrological house found in an astral chart.

Cast Your Cards

Cast in the shape Babylonians first used for the twelve astrological houses.

1. Aries: Physical appearance, traits, ego, beginnings.
2. Taurus: The material world, money, possessions.
3. Gemini: Childhood environment, communication, achievements.
4. Cancer: Ancestry, heritage, roots.
5. Leo: Recreation, love, sex.
6. Virgo: Skills, health, well-being.
7. Libra: Marriage, partners, diplomacy.
8. Scorpio: Death, rebirth, sexual relationships, transformation.
9. Sagittarius: Journeys, culture, knowledge, religion.
10. Capricorn: Ambition, career, status.
11. Aquarius: Friends, fortunes, hopes.
12. Pisces: Mysticism, secrets, the unconscious.
13. Final word.

10 11 9 12 8 1 13 7 2 6 3 5 4

Bastille Day Start a Revolution Spread

On This Day

The Bastille, a French prison and symbol of a king's tyranny, was stormed on this day in 1789. This was the flashpoint that ignited the French Revolution. During the following ten years, French society underwent an epic transformation. Absolute monarchy and feudal society were challenged as democracy spread through Europe and ultimately the world.

Storming the Bastille was a symbolic act, as it only held seven prisoners the day it was taken. Four of the prisoners being held were there for check forging.

Summation of Spread

Why not start a revolution in your life? What have you been putting off? What have you waited to do? Using the French Revolution as inspiration, there's no time like the present to storm your own gates.

Cast Your Cards

1. What must I do?
2. Where does my power lie?
3. Who is my ally?
4. Who is my enemy?
5. What stands in my way?
6. What is symbolic of my struggle?
7. What happens as a result of my bravery?

The Five of Wands represents sparks of revolution. The sparring youths mimic warfare with their wands. Conflict is difficult yet necessary, moving the aggressors to new territory. Reflecting both inner and outer challenges, action is required.

Wisdom of Thoth Spread

Thoth, credited with the invention of hermetic arts and magic, is the patron of scribes. Thoth lives in many realms at once, teaching magical skills in the land of the living.

On This Day

The Rosetta Stone was discovered during a Napoleonic campaign in Egypt today in 1759. Egyptian hieroglyphics were untranslated until this discovery; their meanings were open to speculation. Once the stone was discovered, though, Egyptologists were able to unlock the entire hieroglyphic language and writing system.

Summation of Spread

Are you ready to invoke godlike powers? Thoth was the "large and in charge" Egyptian god who maintained the universe. The god of writing, communications, and magic, this spread invokes his attributes with its questions.

The Magician summons the power of alchemy and magic, using his fingertips to create and effect change in his life and circumstance. A true magician sees through artificial reality and embarks on psychological change to venture into the truth of life and reality itself.

Cast Your Cards

Cast the cards as you might a cast a spell to uncover the truth of your situation.

1. Wisdom: What do I know?
2. Writing: What must I read or write?
3. Record Keeping: What must be remembered?
4. Magic: What power do I possess?
5. Imagination: Where will my imagination lead me?
6. Trickery: Who is deceiving me?
7. What is my past?
8. What is my present?
9. What is my future?

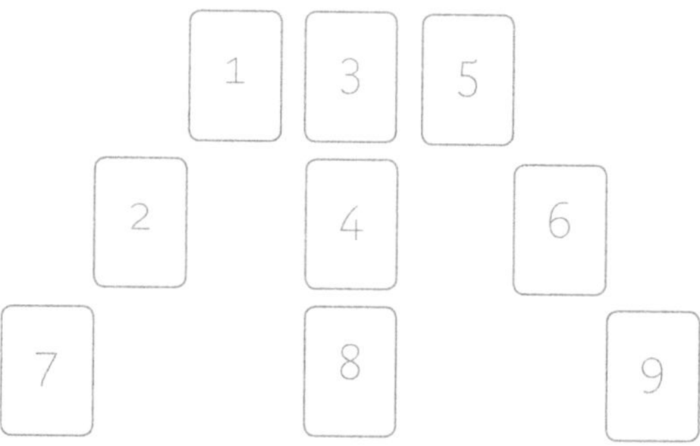

Moving Spread

On This Day

New York City was once the capital of the United States. On this day in 1790, Congress declared the city of Washington, in the District of Columbia, as the permanent capital of the United States. It was promptly moved.

Most moves—42 percent—are made for personal reasons. Job-related moves make up about 40 percent, and 18 percent are represented by military or government relocations.

Summation of Spread

Are you considering a move? The Moving Spread's questions are crafted to help decide whether or not to take a leap and move to a new location, be it across town or in a completely new place.

Cast Your Cards

1. Is changing my location a good idea?
2. Why is moving a good idea?
3. Should I make this move?
4. Can I afford to move?
5. Will I be happy there?
6. Will this be the fresh start I'm looking for?
7. How can I make the move without stress?
8. What problems will I leave behind?
9. What new adventure will I embark upon?
10. What do I need to know that I don't see yet?

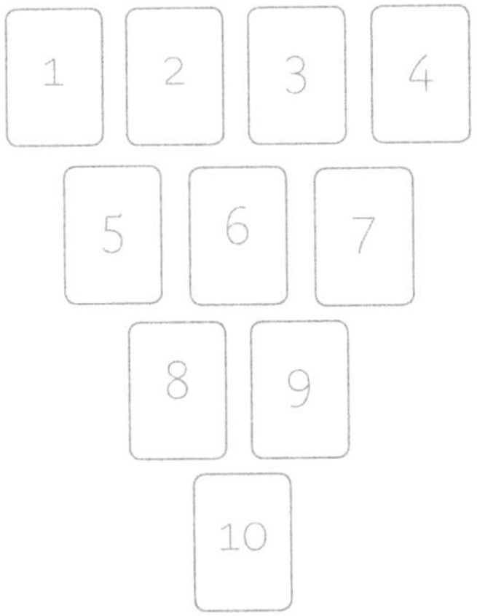

The Queen of Pentacles represents a delicious, happy home. She is the master of the material world, living with passion and decorating her home with beauty and style. Every person who crosses her threshold is impressed by her manner of living. Call upon her energies when creating a comfortable and cozy home.

John Jacob Astor's Financial Investment Spread

John Jacob Astor's great-grandson, John Jacob Astor IV, was an inventor, built the Waldorf Astoria Hotel, was the author of a sci-fi novel set in the year 2000, and tragically died when the Titanic *sank. His pregnant wife took refuge on a lifeboat, and their son was born four months later.*

The King of Pentacles rules over investments and the rising and falling of fortunes. Representing King Midas, everything he touches turns to gold. He is master and commander of the material domain.

On This Day

John Jacob Astor was born on this day in 1763. He became America's first multimillionaire after building a massive fur-trading empire.

Summation of Spread

Are you considering a large investment? This spread uses Astor's energy and ideas to pose questions when you are considering a big financial commitment.

Cast Your Cards

Cast in the shape of a dollar sign. Place the final card on the outside of the $ symbol to discover the probable outcome.

1. My current financial position.
2. Why am I choosing to do this now?
3. Do I have a large time frame for this money?
4. Can I afford to invest this money?
5. What is my goal?
6. Is this investment consistent with my life goals?
7. Do I understand the pros and cons of this investment?
8. Will I be okay if the investment goes belly-up?
9. Have I calculated an excellent exit strategy?
10. Outcome.

Root of the Problem Spread

On This Day

Ted Kennedy accidentally drove his car off a bridge in Chappaquiddick, Massachusetts, today in 1969. Mary Jo Kopechne was fatally trapped inside. Kennedy wondered aloud if some terrible curse hung over his family, due to a string of tragic incidents including the deaths of his brothers, president John F. Kennedy and senator Robert Kennedy.

The shocking plane crash deaths of John Kennedy Jr., his wife, and his sister-in-law in 1999 left us all questioning if a curse didn't, in fact, linger over this family of American royalty.

Summation of Spread

Is there an issue that needs to be eliminated? While it is tempting to blame horrific circumstances on external influences such as curses or evil eyes, more often than not, a close examination of a situation will reveal the root of the problem. This spread aims to reveal the root of the problem so it may be removed.

Cast Your Cards

Cast these cards with delicacy. A careful eye will reveal the truth of the situation and propose a singular course of action:

1. Why is this happening?
2. What control do I have over the situation?
3. What is the root of the problem?
4. What should I stop doing?
5. What should I start doing?

The Two of Swords takes a meditative stance, often used when journeying inside oneself to discover the root of all feelings. Silence and seclusion make deep, eloquent answers reachable. They can be used to transform and reveal everything in life.

Ballerina Spread

Degas consciously chose to paint his ballerinas off-guard, showing them backstage in awkward moments or exhausted after practicing for hours.

On This Day

Impressionist painter Edward Degas was born on this day in 1834. Also a renowned sculptor, he is most remembered for painting ballet dancers.

Summation of Spread

Ballet is the martial arts of dance. The Ballerina Spread brings elements of this art form together, building a spread examining how these qualities are at play in your life.

Cast Your Cards

The Ballerina Spread's cards are cast in the shape of a ballerina's first position.

1. Grace: How am I graceful?
2. Physicality: How can I care for my body?
3. Dedication: What should I dedicate myself to?
4. Focus: What do I need to focus on right now?
5. Practice: What daily practice should I perform?
6. Beauty: How do I cultivate beauty in my life?
7. Storytelling: What stories do I need to pay attention to?
8. Art: What am I creating?

Like ballet, the Temperance card is associated with balance. The toes of Temperance remind us of ballet, one foot dipped in water, representing the unconscious, and one foot on land, representing grounding. Balance exists between the meeting of conscious and subconscious.

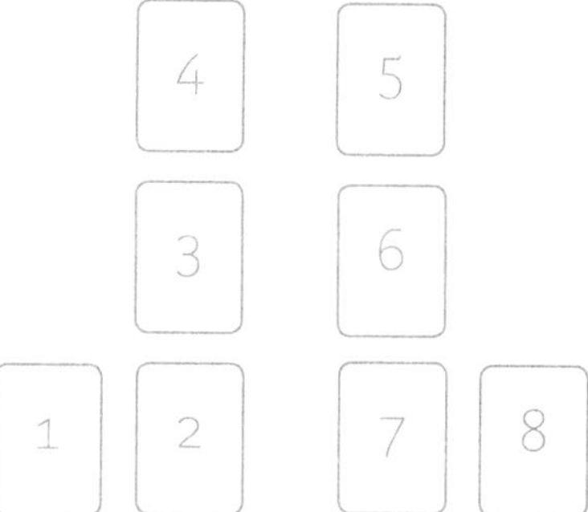

Moon Mystery Small Step Spread

On This Day

Neil Armstrong became the first person to set foot on the moon on this day in 1969. Doing so, he uttered the famous phrase, "That's one small step for a man, one giant leap for mankind."

Summation of Spread

This date brings two important concepts to the fore: small steps that lead to big evolution and the mystery of the moon. Combining these two elements creates the Moon Mystery Small Step Spread.

Cast Your Cards

Cast in the shape of a waxing moon helping to usher new habits into your life.

1. What I want to do.
2. Why I want to do it.
3. What holds me back?
4. What changes when I accomplish it?
5. What is one small step?
6. Will I really do it?
7. What will I do differently today?

Small steps meet almost no resistance from the subconscious mind; this is why they create big change. A few days of small successes create enjoyment, and the mind wants more. It is almost as if you are tricking the mind into change.

The Moon card's crawfish reveals a small-step story. His perilous journey has only just begun. Up the path, past the beast, and through the towers, he will slowly, surely make progress until one night, a night like any other, he finds that just as he once lay at the bottom of the pool, he is now at the summit of the mountain. Every step counts.

July • 21

Hemingway Spread

Hemingway lived in Paris at the height of Gertrude Stein's "lost generation," drank with F. Scott Fitzgerald and James Joyce, and was married four times.

On This Day

American literary giant Ernest Hemingway was born on this day in 1899. Hemingway redefined the writing style of the time with his taut, economical prose. Offering utmost respect to his reader, he wrote using the "principle of the iceberg" theory, which states that seven-eighths of a story lies underneath the surface. Allowing his readers to fill in the blanks, using repetition, rhythm, and repeated images, his stories resonate with large themes and complex emotions.

The Death card resonates strongly with Hemingway as it is a central theme in his work. Hemingway claimed it was only by looking death directly in the face—via war or big-game hunting—that he was able to come to terms with life.

Summation of Spread

Tarot, like Hemingway's prose, allows readers to fill in the blanks with their intuition. The Hemingway Spread's questions are informed by the themes prevailing through Hemingway's work.

Cast Your Cards

Cast the Hemingway Spread's cards in the shape of a bullfighting sword.

1. What is my relationship to men?
2. What is my relationship to women?
3. How do I find dignity under pressure?
4. What does life teach me?
5. What does death teach me?
6. How do I focus on the essential?
7. How may I communicate better?
8. What lies beneath the tip of my iceberg?

Sun Card Spread

On This Day

The longest solar eclipse in recorded history happened on this day in 2009, casting its shadow over parts of Asia and the Pacific Ocean.

The word eclipse *is from the Greek* ekleipsis, *meaning "abandonment, cessation, omission, or flaw." Solar eclipses mythically portended inauspicious events or hidden dangers.*

Summation of Spread

Solar events offer us an opportunity to ponder and examine the symbols found inside the Sun card, upon which the questions of this spread are based.

Cast Your Cards

Use this spread to answer any question. Format your question before casting the spread or simply let the cards answer the questions posed. Pull the Sun card out of your deck. Placing it in the center of the Sun Card Spread, cast your cards around it as follows.

1. Sun: How do I let my highest, best energy flow through me?
2. Child: How do I retain innocence?
3. Nudity: Where can I let down my guard?
4. Banner: What do I express to others?
5. White Horse: What is magical about my life?
6. Wall: How can I remain open?
7. Sunflowers: How do I find truth?
8. Sun's Rays: How can I radiate warmth to others?

The Sun card represents a breakthrough, energetic growth, and—above all things—hope. Sun worship exists in all cultures because the sun represents life. The horse on the card represents the new direction life is taking. When the Sun card appears, it is a reminder that each and every day is a gift and an opportunity for expansion.

Qualities of Leo Spread

Leo's ruling planet is the sun, golden-yellow is the primary color, the lucky day is Sunday, and the best location for success is anyplace outside. Leo rules the fifth house of the zodiac, governing creativity, procreation, and recreation.

The Strength card features an image of a lion and always represents the use of gentle persuasion over brute force. It is a card of extreme power and control.

On This Day

Today marks the first day of the sign of Leo.

Summation of Spread

This spread is based on the essential qualities of Leo: generosity, warmth, expansiveness, artistry, self-confidence, authority, self-discipline, magnetism, and a brave and calm demeanor.

Cast Your Cards

Cast in the shape of the Leo symbol, or glyph, looking like a lion's tail:

1. In what way can I be more generous?
2. Where should I extend my warmth and love?
3. In what direction is my life expanding?
4. How can I best use my artistic gifts?
5. In what area of life do I need to exhibit more confidence?
6. How can I exude authority without being bossy?
7. How have I become more self-disciplined?
8. Who am I drawing toward me?
9. How am I brave?
10. In what area of life do I need to calm down?

Triple Goddess Spread

On This Day

Robert Graves, English poet, scholar, translator, and writer of antiquity, was born on this day in 1895.

Summation of Spread

Graves popularized the conception of the Triple Goddess in his famous book *The White Goddess*. Graves theorized there was an archetypal triad of goddesses found in the mythology of Europe and the ancient Middle East. This Triple Goddess represents the three stages of female life, the cycles of the moon, and the realms of earth, underworld, and heavens. This spread uses the gentle beauty of Robert Grave's legacy and the Triple Goddess to inform its questions.

Cast Your Cards

The structure of Maiden, Mother, and Crone offers insight at any stage of life. Cast in three groups: Maiden (Waxing), Mother (Full), and Crone (Waning).

1. What enchants me?
2. What am I enthusiastic about?
3. What is beginning?

4. What do I know?
5. What has grown?
6. What stirs in me?

7. How am I wise?
8. What do I understand?
9. What is ending?

1 2 3 4 5 6 7 8 9

Graves sometimes wrote under a process called "analeptic thought," a term he created for throwing one's mind back in time and receiving impressions.

The Triple Goddess symbol, also a symbol of Wicca, rests on the crown of the High Priestess. The symbol emulates the simultaneous waxing, full, and waning moon, and, therefore, the Triple Goddess.

Salacia's Secrets Spread

To honor Salacia on this day, Romans fashioned olive boughs into arbors to encourage an abundance of water.

On This Day

Salacia, female divinity of the sea and Neptune's wife, was honored today with a Roman festival. She is represented as a gorgeous nymph sitting with or driving Neptune in a pearl shell chariot drawn by dolphins or seahorses. She was personified as the calm, sunlit aspect of the sea.

Summation of Spread

Why does the sound of water relax us and crashing waves captivate us like watching the flickering embers of a fire? Salacia inspires this spread by provoking questions pondering personal connections to the element of water and the mysteries of the deep.

The Queen of Cups is often depicted as a mermaid queen. Gentle and tranquil, this queen also connects to the calm and restorative element of the ocean, unlike her husband, the King of Cups, who floats amidst stormy seas.

Cast Your Cards

Cast in the form of a seashell.

1. How does the element of water play a role in my life?
2. What is the best way for me to foster connection with the element of water?
3. What sea creature is a spirit guide for me?
4. How and where do I cultivate a special place near a body of water for myself?
5. What strength do I draw from water?
6. How do I inspire others with my gifts?
7. How do I feel like the ocean?
8. How can I feel more deeply?
9. Why is depth important?

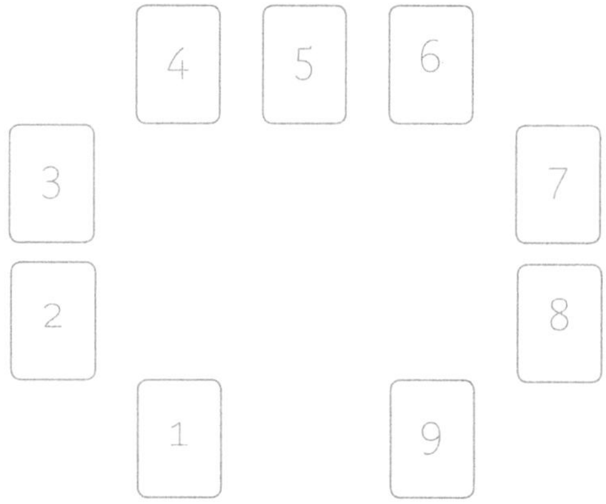

Jungian Archetype Personality Spread

On This Day

Carl Gustav Jung was born today in 1875. The most complex, important, and controversial of psychological theorists, he was a prolific writer and thinker. Influencing psychology, the study of religion, and literature, he is also the founder of analytical psychology.

Jung's doctoral dissertation explored the occult. In it, he analyzed the séances of a fifteen-year-old medium who also happened to be his cousin.

Summation of Spread

Who are you? Using Jung's twelve archetypes, or primary human motivations, this spread seeks wisdom and reflection about who we are and what motivates us.

Cast Your Cards

Cast the cards in three groupings representing Ego, Soul, and Self.

Ego

1. The Innocent: What makes me happy?
2. The Orphan: How do I connect with others?
3. The Hero: How do I prove myself?
4. The Caregiver: How do I care for others?

Soul

5. The Explorer: How do I expand?
6. The Rebel: How do I change what doesn't work?
7. The Lover: How do I experience intimacy?
8. The Creator: What is my vision?

Self

9. The Jester: How do I have fun?
10. The Sage: What is my truth?
11. The Magician: How do I make dreams come true?
12. The Ruler: Where should I exercise control?

Jung's theories of archetypes prove why tarot works so well, operating as a door to opportunity and insight. It is through symbol and archetype that the reader is able to cultivate personal truth.

Dream Inspiration Spread

Mary Shelley dreamed Frankenstein, Robert Lewis Stevenson dreamed Dr. Jekyll and Mr. Hyde, Paul McCartney found the tune for "Yesterday" while sleeping, and Jasper Johns dreamed his famous flag painting, as did Henri Rousseau for his painting aptly titled The Dream.

The Seven of Cups is the dreaming card, while the Four of Swords reflects sound sleeping.

On This Day

Today Finland celebrates National Sleepyhead Day. Traditionally, the last person found asleep in the house is woken up by either being tossed into a lake or the sea or having water splashed upon them. Waking up during a dream is often the best way to remember it. Dozens of works of literature, art, and science sprang from dreams; the periodic table of elements is said to be based on the dream of scientist Dmitri Mendeleev.

Summation of Spread

Have you had a good dream lately? This spread helps you decipher why your subconscious responded in the form of a particular dream and suggests an action to take in your waking life.

Cast Your Cards

Analyze as follows:

1. Dream's essential theme.
2. Why did the dream evoke these feelings?
3. Why is this lingering in my subconscious?
4. Is there a practical action I should take in responding to the message of the dream?
5. Is there something in the material world that I can birth as a result of this dream?
6. Is any part of this dream prophetic?
7. What truth have I discovered about myself?

Should or Shouldn't I Spread

On This Day

Austria-Hungary made the decision to declare war on Serbia today in 1914. This action officially began the First World War, and the decisions of a few would affect millions of lives. The estimated casualties of World War I, ranging from eight million to over fifteen million, rank this war as one of the deadliest conflicts in human history.

Some psychologists suggest making important decisions in the morning, before your energy reserves are depleted, in order to make the most well-informed decision.

Summation of Spread

Are you struggling with a decision? Sometimes odds and outcomes are weighed and the solution still remains unclear. This spread is crafted to help make tough decisions with clarity and insight and for the highest good possible.

Cast Your Cards

Cast the cards face-down. Take your time as you flip and reveal the cards through the spread.

1. The issue at hand.
2. Why am I grappling with this?
3. Why is this occurring at this point in time?
4. Why is this so important to me?
5. What does my intuition say?
6. What does my logical mind say?
7. What should I do?
8. What shouldn't I do?

The Two of Pentacles represents the weighing of decisions. It reminds the viewer to remain alert and agile while juggling life, family responsibilities, and decisions.

Heartbreak Spread

The Greeks believed the heart was the seat of the spirit, the Egyptians thought all emotions and intellect arose from it, and the Chinese believe the heart to be the place of happiness.

The Three of Swords represents the pain and sorrow of a broken heart with the piercing of this delicate, fleshy organ. Ominous storm clouds hover, bringing rain and tears, yet—like all storms—this too shall pass.

On This Day

On-again, off-again couple Elizabeth Taylor and Richard Burton divorced for the second and final time on this day in 1976.

Summation of Spread

Are you feeling the pain of heartbreak? Everyone fears it, and everyone's faced the devastation of heartbreak and rejection. Despite all efforts, some cherished relationships cannot continue. This spread poses important and comforting questions when licking love wounds.

Cast Your Cards

The cards are cast in the symbol of a peace sign to help you find it.

1. Can I allow myself to feel the pain?
2. Am I strong enough not to see them again?
3. What will help me heal?
4. What activities make me happy?
5. Can I try something new?
6. Can I revel in my independence?
7. Do I have a strong support system of friends?
8. What is the lesson of this relationship?
9. How can I care for myself?
10. When will I be ready to love again?

1

2 9 3

7 8

4 10 5

6

Starting a Business Spread

On This Day

On this day in 1953, the US Small Business Administration was formed. It began providing millions of counseling sessions, loans, contracts, and other forms of assistance to small businesses.

Summation of Spread

Thinking of starting a business? The Starting a Business Spread is based on the questions that should be asked at the beginning of a new business venture.

Cast Your Cards

Cast the cards in the shape of a pyramid, the icon found upon the one-dollar bill.

1. Why am I starting a business?
2. Who is my ideal customer?
3. What do I provide?
4. Am I prepared to spend time and money on this business?
5. What makes my business different from others?
6. Do I need to take out a loan?
7. How long before I start making a profit?
8. Who is my competition?
9. How will I advertise this business?
10. Will my business be successful?

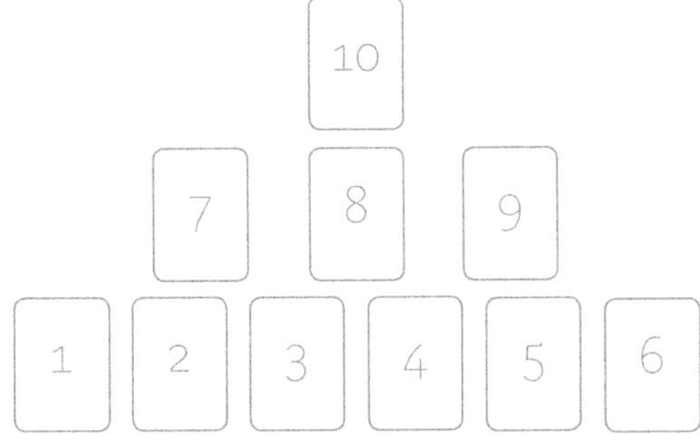

The average age of people who begin companies is forty.

The Two of Wands, like an entrepreneur at the onset of a business venture, holds the world in his hands. The Wands invigorate the card with fire, energy, and excitement. This card also suggests forging a business partner relationship and securing the financing needed. It is the card of the visionary about to execute his plan.

July • 31

Failure and Imagination Spread

Rowling conceived of the idea for the Harry Potter series while riding on a train from Manchester to London. Rowling lived in poverty until the first Harry Potter book was released.

On This Day

British novelist J. K. Rowling, author of the Harry Potter series, was born today in 1965.

Summation of Spread

Are you afraid of failure? It may be just the very thing provoking you forward. This spread is inspired by the commencement speech J. K. Rowling gave to Harvard's 2008 graduating class. In her speech, she mentioned the essential importance of failure as a learning tool. Rowling claims failure facilitates change, forces creativity, and fuels determination.

Cast Your Cards

The Failure and Imagination Spread's cards are cast in two groups, with a final independent card.

1. How does failure strip away the inessential?
2. How is rock bottom a solid foundation to build upon?
3. How does my imagination transform me?
4. What am I capable of?
5. How does my imagination allow me to understand the lives of others?
6. How do I touch other people's lives by simply existing?
7. How can I empower those who are powerless?
8. How can I imagine better?
9. Final word.

The Five of Cups is the failure and imagination card. The spilled cups represent unfulfilled hopes and dreams. A bridge looms in the background, his exit point to salvation and reinvention. The Five of Cups stands as a reminder not to wallow too long in sadness. The two remaining cups suggest that not all is lost.

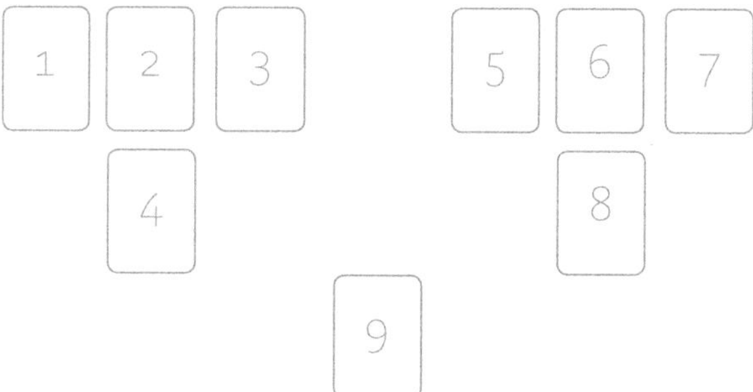

Lammas/Lughnasa Herb Garden Spread

On This Day

Lammas and Lughnasa, ancient Celtic festivals, celebrate the agricultural harvest. Today was the culmination of a month of celebration, while the three days preceding Lughnasa were especially sacred and devoted to purification.

Summation of Spread

Lammas, filled with romantic components, is an occasion for the blessing and harvesting of botanicals. The height of summer brings them to the peak of their power, just before decomposition begins. Collect and harvest herbs on this night for good luck and powerful magic. This spread is based on the magic associated with herb gardens.

Cast Your Cards

Cast the cards as you would sprinkle seeds in a garden:

1. Basil: How do I exorcise negativity from my life?
2. Chamomile: What calms me?
3. Yarrow: How can I improve my psychic ability?
4. Parsley: What protects me?
5. Sage: What do I know?
6. Mint: What attracts money?
7. Dill: What provokes lust?
8. Thyme: What healing action should I take?

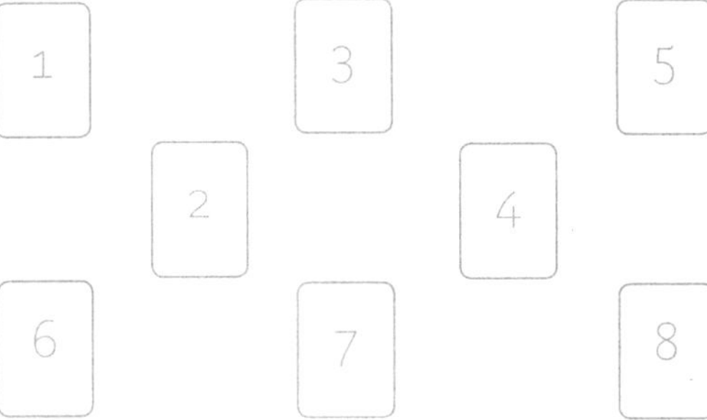

Lughnasa means "the marriage of Lugh," an important Celtic deity. At least fourteen European cities are named after him, and it has been suggested that many European churches dedicated to St. Michael the archangel were built over sites once dedicated to Lugh.

The Seven of Pentacles is the harvest card. The figure pauses and reflects. His crop is bountiful, yet something has led him to reevaluate the situation. This card reflects the concept of being very productive at what you are naturally talented at. What is easy for you may be challenging for others.

Contractual Matters and Legal Documents Spread

Celebrities have been ridiculed for the outrageous riders placed in their contracts. While the Foo Fighters request coloring books and comedy DVDs in their rider, when they are finished, their contracts state all food leftovers be delivered to a local homeless shelter or soup kitchen.

The gentle Knight of Cups often represents legal papers and the signing of contracts. His steady, slow progress is a reminder never to rush into any legal matter—be sure you are covered and completely understand your rights.

On This Day

While the Fourth of July celebrates our nation's independence, the actual signing of the document occurred on this day in 1776.

Summation of Spread

Signing a contract soon? Important moments in life—purchasing a home, marriage, entering school, etc.—often involve the signing of legal documents. This spread has been created for contemplation when in the midst of signing a contract. This spread ensures you have your bases covered.

Cast Your Cards

1. What is the matter at hand?
2. Are my best interests covered?
3. Does the contract clearly state what I am receiving?
4. Does the contract clearly state what I am providing?
5. Am I giving too much away?
6. Is there anything I don't understand?
7. Is this something I really want to do?
8. What is the ultimate outcome?

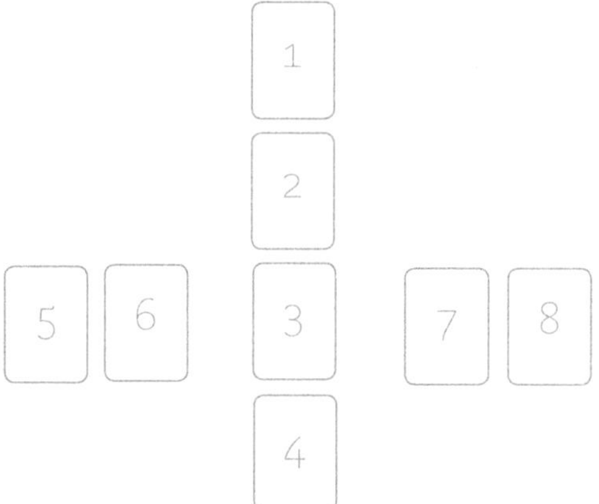

Chalchiuhtlicue's Regeneration Spread

On This Day

Chalchiuhtlicue is the Aztec goddess of water, rivers, seas, storms, and tempests. This goddess of youthful beauty and ardor was associated with any day of the Aztec calendar containing the number 3.

Summation of Spread

Are you ready for the waters of renewal? Chalchiuhtlicue's aquatic connection ties her to fertility and childbirth. Aztec midwives cut an infant's umbilical cord and washed the new baby while saying the customary greeting of Chalchiuhtlicue. Flowing waters, evocative of regeneration and renewal, inspire this spread.

Cast Your Cards

Cast in the shape of a drop of regenerative water from your favorite spa or swimming spot.

1. What needs to be washed away?
2. How do I let it go?
3. Why do I grasp and cling tightly to it?
4. What fills its place?
5. How can I rejuvenate myself?
6. What action must I take?
7. What is the result?

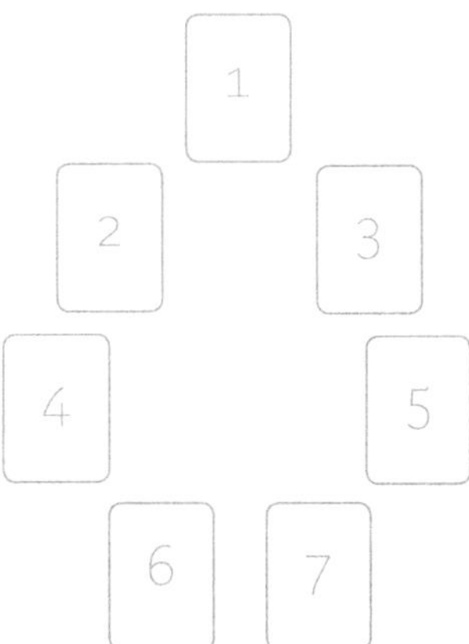

Chalchiuhtlicue's celebration days were celebrated by priests diving into lakes and imitating the movements and croaking of frogs, hoping to bring rain.

The High Priestess is the first card in the deck depicting water. A river flows behind her veil; it is said that all waters—the rivers, streams, and waterfalls—flowing through the tarot spring from her. She springs forth water as a fountain of wisdom and connection.

Toast Yourself Spread

Champagne is a specific region in France, and only grapes from this geographical location may be legally called champagne.

The Nine of Pentacles is evocative of vineyards, wine, and champagne. A woman stands amidst a lush harvest of grapes. The background castle is indicative of generational winemakers who have stepped before her. The castle stands for the familial and cultural heritage handed to you; it is your birthright.

On This Day

Champagne is said to have been invented on this day in 1693 by Dom Perignon, a French Benedictine monk. The story claims Perignon was making wine, and he couldn't get rid of the bubbles. Tasting it, he exclaimed, "Come quickly! I am drinking the stars!"

Summation of Spread

Need a pick-me-up? Raise a glass to yourself. Champagne's invention, though likely more legend than truth, inspires a spread that would raise a thousand glasses.

Cast Your Cards

Cast your cards in the shape of champagne flute. As each bubble pops, may a wish come true.

1. Why should I be proud of myself?
2. What can I accept about myself?
3. What do I love about myself?
4. What do others celebrate me for?
5. Why should I be celebrating?
6. Can I allow myself to celebrate every day?
7. Who should I celebrate with?
8. What intention is coming true?

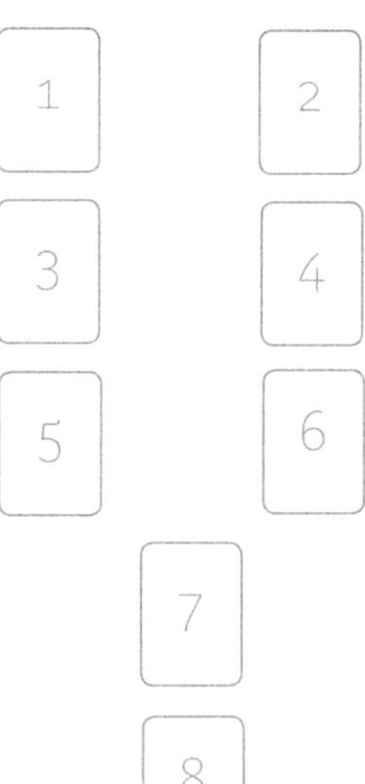

Salus's Healing Spread

On This Day

The Roman festival of Salus, goddess of health, was celebrated on this day. Representing public safety, health, and welfare, her father was Aesculapius, the god of healing. His symbol was a staff with a single snake coiled around it, used in the modern symbol of medicine and healing. Salus had the job of looking after this sacred snake. The staff is similar to Mercury's caduceus, a staff with two snakes and wings at the top.

Summation of Spread

Do you have a health issue? This spread of health and wellness is inspired by the ancients to help discover healing for whatever ails you.

Cast Your Cards

Imagine perfect health and cast your cards.

1. What is causing discomfort?
2. How can I ease my pain?
3. First step to healing.
4. Second step to healing.
5. Third step to healing.
6. What steps can I take toward future well-being?

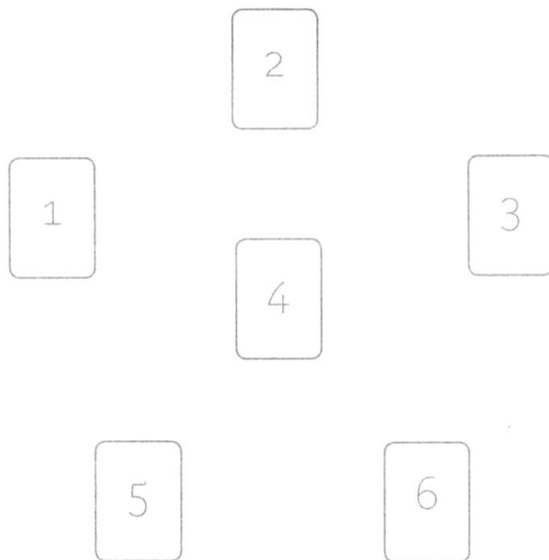

Studies have shown that having safe sex is one of the healthiest things you can do. An average tryst burns about 200 calories, boosts the immune system, and helps people live longer and happier lives.

The Star card represents healing on the highest spiritual and physical levels, the quiet after the storm, the openness of the psyche, and a free emotional flow—the integration of mind, body, and spirit. The Star is a complete holistic picture of health and happiness coming together as the soul channels higher powers, doing work promoting the greater good for all.

Engage Intimacy Spread

Four Vedic Sanskrit texts written in 1500 BCE contain the first recorded mention of a human kiss.

On This Day

Don Juan, the movie holding the record for most onscreen kisses, was released on this day in 1926. John Barrymore kisses over 191 different women in this romantic film.

Summation of Spread

Do you wish to get closer to your partner? Kissing is not always a promise of true intimacy, but it is the physical steppingstone helping humans exchange scents, tastes, textures, secrets, and emotions. Invigorating your relationship or getting back into the game after a breakup or dry spell, this spread is based on essential points of true intimacy. Use this spread as a reminder or springboard to reengage in the most pleasurable of art forms.

The Lovers card represents the emotional and sexual components of falling in love, physical attraction, and love at first sight. The union of the two people pictured on the card carries the eroticism, choices, and ramifications that follow all matters of the heart.

Cast Your Cards

1. What helps me release unrealistic expectations?
2. How can I nurture myself?
3. How can I focus attention on my partner?
4. What helps me to share and communicate?
5. Am I comfortable showing affection?
6. What simple, sweet thing can I do for my partner?
7. What helps me own who I am?
8. How can I focus on giving love?

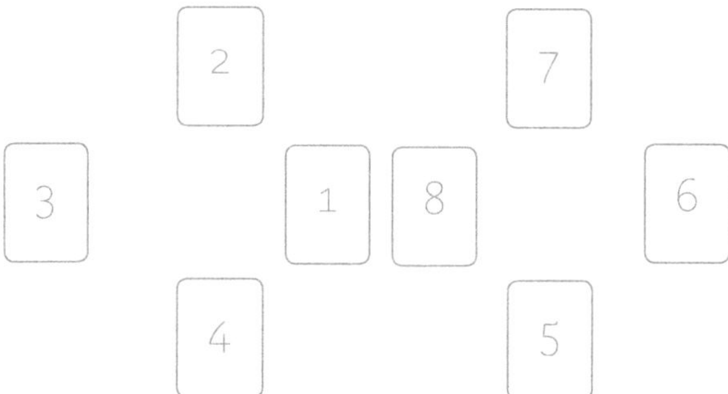

Florentine Magic Spread

On This Day

Construction began on this day in 1420 on the dome of the Duomo, Florence's great cathedral. Standing in the city center, it is proclaimed by many to be the most beautiful in all of Europe.

Summation of Spread

Access Italian magic. Birthplace of the Renaissance, home to Dante Alighieri, Galileo, Roberto Cavali, and the Medici family, this miraculous city is the inspiration for a spread using the jewels of Florence to inform its questions.

Cast Your Cards

Cast the Florentine Magic Spread's cards the way one might shave black truffle upon a plate of fresh pasta.

1. Renaissance: What revival am I experiencing?
2. Boboli Gardens: What is blooming?
3. Uffizi Gallery: How am I creative?
4. Pitti Palace: How can I treat myself like royalty?
5. Vecchio Bridge: What helps me get where I'm going?
6. Statue of David: What helps me tone my muscles?
7. Cuisine: How can I make healthy food feel indulgent?

Streets in Florence often have different names from one end of the street to the other, and this is reminiscent of life's journey. Sometimes you begin in one place and it brings you down a path, leading you where you least expect it to.

Italy is the birthplace of tarot insofar as historians can trace it. The cards were first a game among noble courts and families; it soon became a tavern game enjoyed by the masses. Used for gaming long before divination, few could have foreseen the evolution of modern tarot.

August • 8

Should I Quit This Job Spread

Quitting a job usually involves a high degree of emotion. Leave on a high note by building bridges, providing adequate notice, expressing gratitude, and making peace with adversaries.

On This Day

President Richard Nixon announced that he would resign from office today in 1974. Shocking the country, he did so the following day in a live resignation speech from the oval office.

Summation of Spread

Is it time for you to quit your job? While few people leave jobs with the high drama, intrigue, and media speculation surrounding the Watergate scandal, it can be tough to know when it is time to throw in the towel. This spread examines when to take the leap and cut the bonds to your current job.

Cast Your Cards

Career is an essential element of your lifestyle, personality, and social situation. Nothing is more valuable than time. Cast your cards with a true heart and clear conscience to make the best possible choice.

The Seven of Swords cuts his losses. This card is indicative of leaving a situation and carrying only what is needed into the future. He leaves the safety of camp, which represents the known comfort zone, and he walks alone into the unknown—a scary yet brave decision.

1. Do I enjoy what I do?
2. Am I challenged by my work?
3. Do I feel stressed?
4. What is my relationship with management?
5. What is my relationship to my coworkers?
6. Do I have good employment options around me?
7. Outcome if I stay.
8. Outcome if I leave.
9. Should I quit this job?

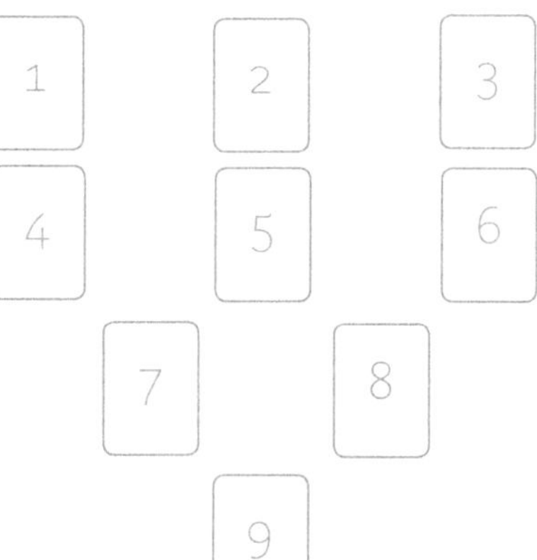

9 • August

Am I Being Lied To Spread

On This Day

Megastars Rihanna and Eminem collaborated on a smash single and released "Love the Way You Lie" today in 2010.

Summation of Spread

Do you think you are being lied to? This is an excellent spread to perform when your intuition is screaming for you to pay attention that something is not right. This spread examines the situation and gets to the heart of the matter.

Cast Your Cards

1. Am I following my instincts correctly?
2. Is there a chance I am worrying for nothing?
3. Are my doubts justified?
4. How do I find out the truth of the situation?
5. Am I being lied to?
6. Am I willing to forgive and move forward?
7. What sort of change must be made?

The lyrics of "Love the Way You Lie" deal with the issue of domestic violence, something both artists have had a history of grappling with.

Swords represent the ideal of truth because they illuminate the mind, intellect, and reasoning. Swords often carry conflict with them, an inevitable outcome of lies and half truths. The Ace of Swords is used to discern truth and is found on the Justice card for this reason. Moral choice and ethical quandaries are settled using this sword.

August • 10

Meteor Shower Spread

The meteor shower is named after Perseus, the Greek hero best known for decapitating the fearsome, snake-haired Medusa. Some Catholics refer to the Perseids as the "tears of St. Lawrence" due to the fact that August 10 is the date of this saint's martyrdom.

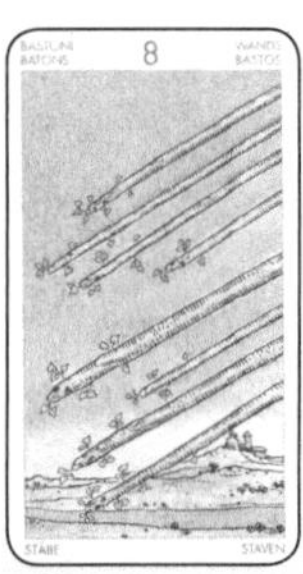

The Eight of Wands race across the sky like shooting stars of energetic, volcanic nature. Rather than burning up in the atmosphere, the Eight of Wands brings its energy toward the ground. Where shall the wands land, and will you be the one to direct them?

On This Day

Today marks the approximate peak of the Perseid meteor shower. Observable for over 2,000 years, it is visible through the Northern Hemisphere. It produces up to sixty meteors an hour when viewed at its optimal point in the wee hours of the morning.

Summation of Spread

Who was the first person to wish upon a star? During the Perseids shower it looks as if the stars are answering back. This spread is inspired by the meteor showers of summer.

Cast Your Cards

Assuming a meteor shower offers celestial messages, the Meteor Shower Spread cards are cast in the shape of a shooting star.

1. What surprising opportunity is racing toward me?
2. How do I best prepare for it?
3. What happens if I embrace it?
4. What happens if I ignore it?
5. What old issue must burn away?
6. What does the element of fire have to teach me?
7. Will my wish come true?

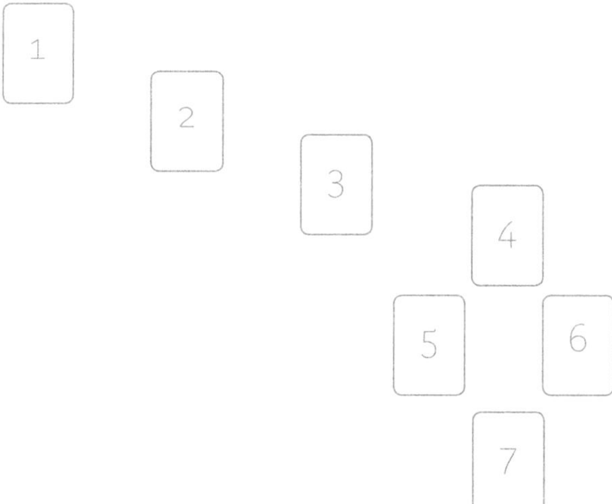

11 • August

Imprisonment Spread

On This Day

At 9:40 AM on this day in 1934, the first prisoners were taken to Alcatraz Island Penitentiary. Designed to hold prisoners who caused problems at other penitentiaries, this infamous jail became home to America's most notorious bank robbers and murderers.

During Alcatraz's 29 years of operation, no prisoner successfully escaped. Shut down due to the high price of operation, it now serves as a tourist site and inspiration for pop culture films, TV shows, and literature.

Summation of Spread

Are you held captive by something? Prison bars are not the only facility to hold people in. Destructive ideas, social expectations, limiting beliefs, and even other people can hold someone captive. This spread looks at what holds a person captive so they are empowered to break free of the ties that bind.

Cast Your Cards

Cast the cards like window bars in a dank prison cell begging to be broken.

1. What holds me captive?
2. What drains my happiness?
3. What do I wish I didn't know?
4. How am I my own worst enemy?
5. What do I fear most?
6. What is worse than death?
7. How do I make my escape?
8. What lesson do I bring with me?
9. What lies on the outside?

A fortification like Alcatraz looms on the cliffs behind the bound figure in the Eight of Swords. It appears to fade into the background, symbolic of the past disappearing and the figure's ability to break free. Her floating nature represents the supernatural quality of this card. Interior walls and shackles can be destroyed with a single thought.

High Priestess Card Spread

Some scholars link the High Priestess with the image of Pope Joan, while others believe she is based on an Umiliata nun, Sister Manfreda. A relative of the Visconti family, she was elected pope by a heretical Guglielmite sect and was later burned at the stake.

The High Priestess is custodian of all knowledge. She is where all feminine aspects of the divine thrive and live. She embodies the complete understanding of spiritual mysteries and is indicative of your own wells of personal knowledge.

On This Day

Helena Blavatsky was born on this day in 1831. This Russian spiritualist and author was cofounder of the Theosophical Society. Theosophy is an esoteric philosophy combining Eastern and Western teachings that exerted a tremendous influence among nineteenth-century occultists.

Summation of Spread

Ready to examine your hidden knowledge? Blavatsky's historical footprints, books, and legacy qualify her as High Priestess of the esoteric. This spread is based on symbols found within the High Priestess tarot card. The High Priestess appeared in historical decks as the Popess.

Cast Your Cards

Use this spread to answer any question. Format the question before casting the spread or simply let the cards answer the questions posed. Pull the High Priestess card from your deck. Placing it in the center of the spread, cast your cards around it.

1. Triple crown: What is changing?
2. Book/Scroll: What do I know?
3. Dress: What is my magic?
4. Cross: What is the nature of reality?
5. Veil: What is hidden?
6. Pomegranate: What is growing?
7. Water: What continues?
8. Moon: What is illusion?

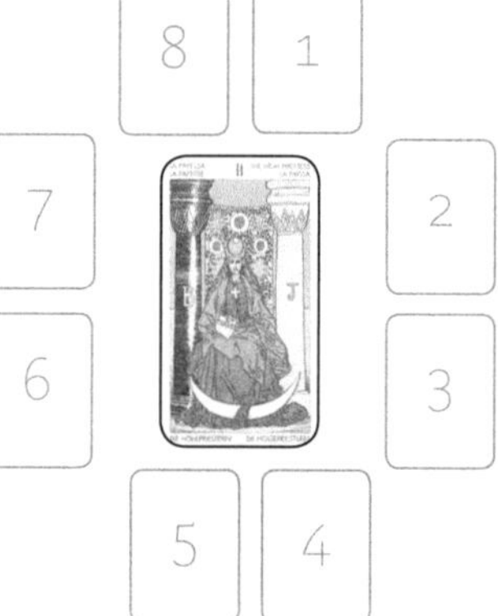

Moon Card Spread

On This Day

Ancient Romans celebrated Nemoralia, Festival of Torches, on this day. It honored Diana, goddess of the hunt, the moon, and birthing. Adopted by Catholics as the Feast of the Assumption, worshipers carried torches to the dark waters of Lake Nemi, where the reflected torchlight intermingled with the moon's light.

Summation of Spread

Diana's connection with the moon makes this the perfect day to explore aspects of the Moon tarot card, whose symbols inform the questions of this spread.

Cast Your Cards

You may use this spread to answer any question. Form your question before casting the spread or simply let the cards answer the questions posed. Pull the Moon card from your deck. Placing it in the center of the spread, cast your cards around it as follows.

1. Dual Towers: What false towers have I built?
2. Dog: What is the loyal, responsible thing to do?
3. Wolf: What is my primal urge screaming for?
4. Moon: What does intuitive clarity tell me?
5. Sun: What harsh reality exists?
6. Pool: What does my subconscious mind contain?
7. Crawfish: What is emerging from the depths of my soul?
8. Path: Where will this new illumination lead me?

Offerings to the goddess Diana on this day included small messages written on ribbons and tied to the altar or trees; small baked clay or bread statues of body parts in need of healing; clay images of mother and child; small sculptures of stags; dancing and songs; and fruit.

The Moon reflects changes and transformation. Be it the metamorphosis of a werewolf or the tidal pull of the ocean, nothing remains the same.

Lizard Wisdom Spread

The tail some lizards leave behind wriggles in order to confuse the enemy. This defense gives the lizard time to escape.

The Eight of Cups leaves every single cup behind as he proceeds on his journey up the mountain. Evocative of deep internal and emotional transformation, this card sets the subject off on a new path.

On This Day

Today is World Lizard Day, celebrating reptilian fascination. It is celebrated by a niche of reptile lovers, conservationists, and educators.

Summation of Spread

Are you ready to shed what is not needed? Some lizards can escape a deadly situation by leaving part of themselves behind. They can break off their tail to escape a predator, but it will only grow back once. This unique action inspires the Lizard Wisdom Spread. Utmost bravery is required when letting go of what one holds dear. A willingness to loosen tight grips, a belief that what came once will come again, contains the power to transform a life.

Cast Your Cards

Think about what needs to be discarded as you cast the cards.

1. What is disturbing my peace?
2. What am I fighting against?
3. Why is this happening?
4. What action must I take?
5. What will be left behind?
6. What will grow in its place?

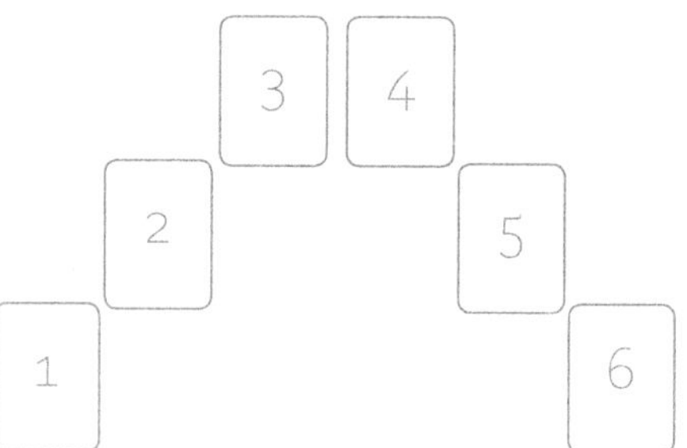

Julia Child's Never Too Late Spread

On This Day

Julia Child was born on this day in 1942. Famous for her revolutionary cookbooks and a television icon long before the era of cooking shows, Julia Child did not enter cooking school until the age of thirty-seven.

Summation of Spread

Are you seeking a fresh direction? No one is too old, too set in their ways, or too comfortable to change their life. Julia Child is proof positive that it is never too late to embark on a passion, follow a dream, or begin something new.

Cast Your Cards

Nothing but possibility and probability lie ahead as you cast your cards.

1. What unique ability do I possess?
2. What is my passion?
3. Why do I stifle what I am capable of?
4. What small, specific change can I make?
5. How do I make better choices as I move forward?
6. What do I gain as a result of my effort?
7. What is the worst thing that will happen if I begin afresh?
8. What is the best thing that will happen if I begin afresh?
9. What support systems do I have in place to aid this change?
10. How does my life transform?
11. What wonderful quality should I recall and honor on a daily basis?

During World War II, Julia worked as a research assistant for the Office of Strategic Services. Playing a key role in the communication of top-secret documents, this is where she met her future husband, diplomat Paul Child.

The Three of Wands suggests the beginning of a new enterprise. Business and investment partners are found easily, and ideas are blooming.

Horse Lovers Spread

Romans linked horses with Mars, god of fury and war. Celtic mythology held them as harbingers of good fortune, and the white horse was especially sacred. Folk wisdom states that if many horses are seen standing together, a storm is coming.

All four knights and the Death card depict horses. To detect the energy and direction of a situation, look carefully at any horse appearing in a spread. They can indicate the direction, speed, and energy of the situation at hand.

On This Day

Today marks the famous, frantic horse race in Sienna, Italy, called Il Palio. This morning, competing horses are taken to the local churches to be blessed. It is a sign of good luck if the horse leaves droppings.

Summation of Spread

Humankind owes a massive debt of gratitude to the horse. From the moment they became domesticated, horses have been one of the largest contributors to human civilization. The Horse Lovers Spread uses the symbolism of the horse to inspire its questions.

Cast Your Cards

Cast in the shape of a horseshoe and catch your luck inside of it:

1. What is the driving force of my life?
2. How do I harness personal energy to drive me further?
3. What will I work hard for?
4. What gives me freedom?
5. How can I become stronger?
6. How am I noble?
7. How am I graceful?
8. How am I free?

Rachel Pollack's Mysterious Dr. Apollo Spread

On This Day

Rachel Pollack was born today in 1945. Her book ***Seventy-Eight Degrees of Wisdom*** is considered a modern tarot classic, and she has published twelve tarot books, six novels, over thirty short stories, and dozens of comic books.

Summation of Spread

Rachel was given this tarot spread on her fifth birthday by the Mysterious Dr. Apollo. She has been kind enough to allow me to reprint it here for your enjoyment.

Cast Your Cards

Cast carefully—this spread can change a life if the suggested action is taken.

1. Known!
2. Unknown!
3. Danger!
4. Opportunity!
5. Action!

	2	
3	5	4
	1	

Rachel's first experience with tarot came during a cold winter in Plattsburgh, New York, in 1970. A teacher offered Rachel a tarot reading in exchange for a ride home.

Like Rachel Pollack, the Hierophant is a revered teacher who is happy to impart wisdom and advice. Compassionate and knowledgeable, the Hierophant conveys mysteries and spirituality and shares ideas with the public.

August • 18

Ancestral connection reminds us we are not alone on our journey. Interesting synchronicities occur once you begin honoring ancestors. Stay aware of dreams and look for messages from unexpected places.

The Ten of Pentacles represents the cycles of family life, connection between generations, and the wisdom and knowledge of the old mixed with the enthusiasm and brightness of youth.

Honor Your Ancestors Spread

On This Day

Today is the culmination of the Bon Festival, a Japanese Buddhist festival honoring the spirits of ancestors. Familial sites are visited, family reunions occur, and ancestors are believed to visit family altars. Lanterns, candles, and luminaries are lit and sent down-river, helping spirits find their way back to the netherworld.

Summation of Spread

Honoring ancestors can be an immensely rewarding spiritual experience. Acknowledging the web of life, we connect to what is greater than the sum of our parts. This spread is inspired by the people who have walked before you.

Cast Your Cards

Pull one card for each ancestor you would like to honor—the number is up to you. For this spread, three ancestors are called. These ancestor cards should be dealt face-up and the rest face-down, to be flipped one at a time when you read them.

1. Ancestor card.
2. What is your message?
3. How can I honor you?

4. Ancestor card.
5. What is your message?
6. How can I honor you?

7. Ancestor card.
8. What is your message?
9. How can I honor you?

10. What is my family legacy?
11. How do I best honor it?

Coco Chanel's Revamping My Wardrobe Spread

Advice from Miss Chanel: "A woman has to apply perfume wherever she wants to be kissed."

On This Day

Coco Chanel was born on this day in 1883. She would revolutionize the fashion world by freeing women from binding corsets and introducing the famous little black dress, ballet flats, the Chanel suit, the quilted purse, and Chanel No. 5, a staple fragrance popular to this day.

Summation of Spread

Ready for a style change? Use this spread to mix up your personal style sense. It helps you establish a new direction and think about what might be interesting to explore.

Cast Your Cards

The cards of this spread are cast in the shape of the lemniscate, the same shape as a woman's body.

1. What is my style?
2. What new element do I want to embrace?
3. Do I dress to express my inner self?
4. How can I change up my shopping habits?
5. What am I most comfortable wearing?
6. What clothing makes me feel powerful?
7. What makes me feel sexy?
8. Do I accentuate my body's natural assets?
9. What do I want to accomplish in the near future?
10. Do I trust my style instincts?
11. How will a revamped wardrobe make me feel?

1

2 3

4 5

6

7 8

9 10

11

The Nine of Pentacles is associated with style and panache. Clearly a woman of means, she dresses for no one other than herself. Entirely sure of who she is, this woman is comfortable in her skin and knows who she is down to her perfectly pedicured toes.

August • 20

Lovecraftian Horror Spread

Lovecraft's biggest influence was Edgar Allen Poe; he claimed that Poe was his "god of fiction." Both lost their fathers at a young age, loved poetry, and used antiquated language in writing, and they both worked against contemporary literary styles to create their own worlds of fantasy.

Swords represent the articulation of thoughts, the mental process by which we take our emotions, sensorial reactions, and perceived facts to make sense of our reality—a reality which, upon examination, is never as solid as we think.

On This Day

H. P. Lovecraft, prolific author of essay, horror, fantasy, and science fiction, was born on this day in 1890.

Summation of Spread

Lovecraft spurred an entire literary genre called Lovecraftian horror. He emphasized the cosmic horror of the unknown rather than typical symbols of gore and fear. He wrote about prehuman, supernatural, and terrestrial elements operating under a thin shell of reality that, when revealed, would damage the sanity of any ordinary person. It is upon these themes that the Lovecraftian Horror Spread has been crafted.

Cast Your Cards

Answer the following questions at your own risk.

1. How thin is the skin of reality?
2. What does the past teach me?
3. When do I feel most isolated?
4. How do I overcome a sense of helplessness?
5. How can I accept unanswered questions?
6. How close do I hover to the brink of insanity?
7. What is strange about my relationship with my parents?
8. What truly underlies my reality?

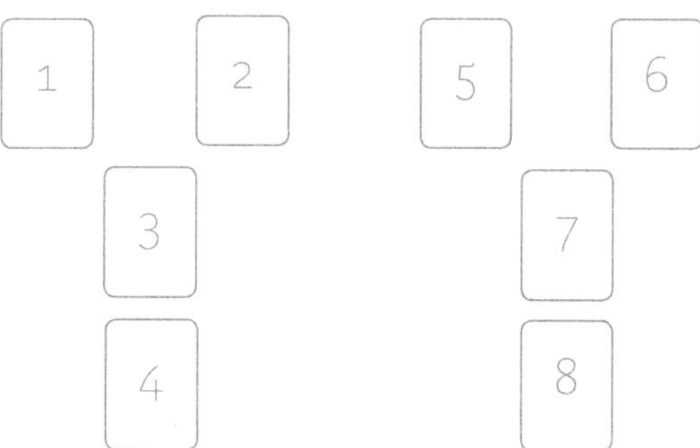

Grow Your Business Spread

On This Day

Today is the ancient Roman festival Consualia, held in honor of Consus, deity of the harvest and stored grain. Harvest grains were held in underground vaults, as was Consus's temple. Consus's shrine, covered all year, was uncovered and worshiped on this day.

During this Roman celebration, all horses and mules were exempted from labor. The animals were led through the streets and adorned with garlands of flowers.

Summation of Spread

Ready to chart new business growth? Late August is harvest time, a time to appreciate what has grown. It is also the time to look ahead to the future, at what we hope to accomplish as the weather turns cool. This spread is inspired by ancient grains, building upon what you have already accomplished.

Cast Your Cards

1. My business as it stands.
2. How should I expand this business?
3. What is working for me?
4. What is my biggest challenge?
5. How do I rise to meet the challenge?
6. Should I join forces with another?
7. How can I diversify?
8. How can I tap into new markets?
9. What is my greatest strength?
10. What is the growth potential for next year?

The Three of Cups evokes celebration, friendship, and the harvest. Fruits are seen in the field, the season has been a success, and now is the time to celebrate with the people who have touched you most. This is, above all, the card of friendship and the value of human companionship, sister- and brotherhood, and togetherness.

Stealing Beauty Spread

Vincenzo Peruggia, a Louvre employee, hid the Mona Lisa *in a broom closet and walked out with it under his coat. The painting was stored in a trunk for two years before Peruggia was caught trying to sell the* Mona Lisa *to the directors of the Uffizi Gallery in Florence.*

The Empress manifests beauty. Every concept of beauty bursts forth in the manner of sheer creativity. The universe expresses itself through the Empress, who is as present in the act of a blooming flower as she is at the canvas of an artist. Self-expression is the epitome of beauty in the Empress's eyes.

On This Day

On this date in 1911 the *Mona Lisa* was reported missing from the Louvre. The Louvre closed for a week while the investigation was underway. Even Pablo Picasso was brought in for questioning.

Summation of Spread

How does the idea of beauty inform your life? This spread uses the idea of stealing beauty to ponder long-held concepts and attitudes toward the perceptual experience of pleasure and satisfaction.

Cast Your Cards

Cast the Stealing Beauty Spread's cards in the shape of a brightly shining diamond.

1. What does the concept of beauty mean to me?
2. What do I consider beautiful?
3. Who is the most beautiful person I know?
4. Where is the most beautiful place I visit?
5. Do I consider myself beautiful?
6. When has beauty deceived me?
7. When has beauty inspired me?
8. Is beauty in the eye of the beholder?

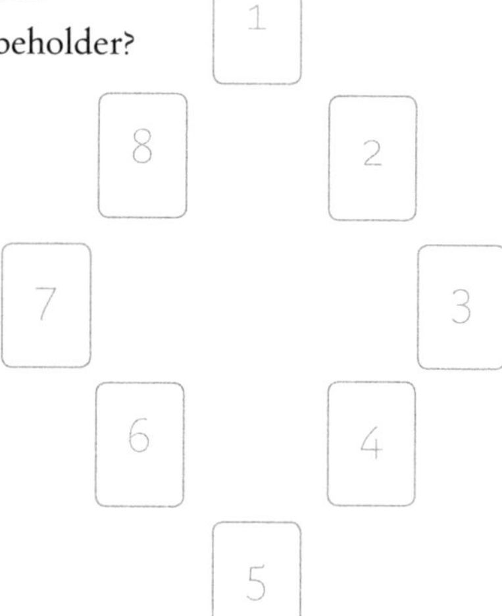

Qualities of Virgo Spread

On This Day

Today marks the first day of the astrological sign of Virgo, the virgin.

Summation of Spread

This spread is based on the essential qualities of Virgo: thoughtful, observant, reflective, shy, meticulous, precise, and intelligent.

Cast Your Cards

Cast in the shape of a V.

1. How can I be more thoughtful of others?
2. What should I pay close attention to at this moment?
3. What issue needs to be carefully reflected upon?
4. What can I let out into the world?
5. Where should I be most meticulous?
6. Who needs to know precisely how I am feeling?
7. In what area is my intelligence most effective?

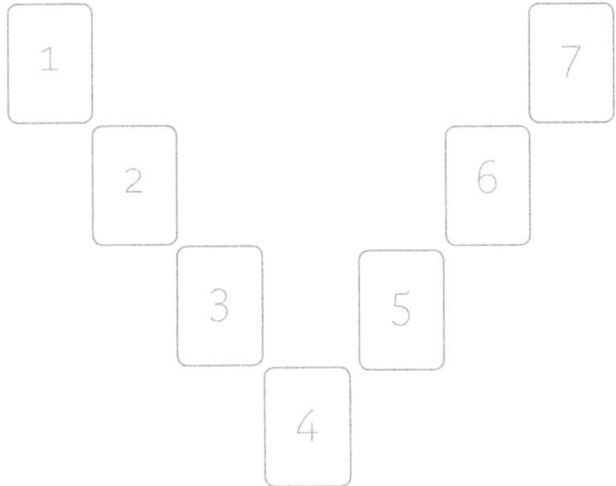

Virgo's ruling planet is Mercury, blue is the primary color, Wednesday is the lucky day, and the best location for success is found in small cities. Virgo rules the sixth house, governing work and service to others.

Virgo's introspective qualities match well with the Hermit, the retainer of human knowledge and wisdom. The quality of virginity, or purity, also connects to the Hermit, who removes himself from society. The Hermit's lesson is not to completely withdraw from the world lest growth becomes hindered. The Hermit must return to share his knowledge with others.

Goddess of the Dead Spread

During this festival, Rome's "ghost stone"—the cover to Hades and the underworld—was lifted so ghosts had easy access back and forth between worlds.

The Six of Swords is connected to the ferrying of souls across the river of the dead. In Greek mythology, Charon is the ferryman of Hades. The swords in the boat suggest past pains are carried with you. The card reassures us that better times are ahead and indicate a quietly transformative journey.

On This Day

The Roman festival of Mania was held on this day. Roman and Etruscan mythology claimed Mania was the goddess of spirits. Greek mythology named Mania the goddess of insanity and madness.

Summation of Spread

Are you ready to unleash hell? Brace yourself for the cavernous shadows of the underworld, wormholes to lower consciousness, and rivers of dread. The Goddess of the Dead Spread's questions are informed by the attributes of the goddess Mania and aspects of darkness from the underworld.

Cast Your Cards

Cast in the shape of a triangle:

1. Ghost: What am I holding on to that must be released?
2. Undead: What walks among us?
3. Spirit: Who watches over me?
4. Ancestors: What does my house of spirits want for me?
5. Insanity: What makes me feel crazy?
6. Madness: What do I discover amidst madness?
7. Darkness: What creativity lies in darkness?

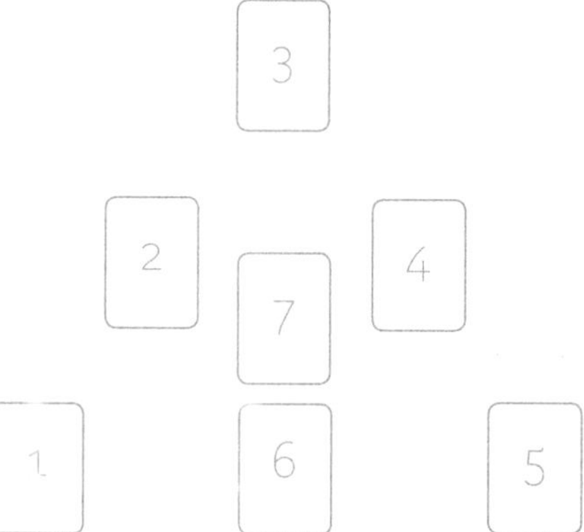

Qualities of Neptune Spread

On This Day

Voyager 2 made its closest approach to Neptune on this day in 1989. Neptune is named after the Roman god of the seas and is identified with the Greek god Poseidon.

Neptune rules Pisces and visual communication such as painting, writing, dance, photography, and film. It is the farthest planet in our solar system.

Summation of Spread

The Qualities of Neptune Spread contains questions based on astrological associations of the planet Neptune. Using these associations, questions are posed to offer greater clarity in life.

Cast Your Cards

Cast in the shape of Poseidon's trident:

1. Spirituality: What is calling my spirit?
2. Dreams: What dream will manifest itself into reality?
3. Imagination: To what should I pay attention to capture my imagination?
4. Inspiration: What inspires me?
5. Illusions: What false illusion should I shatter?
6. Idealism: What is my highest goal and noblest principle?
7. Mystical: What activity best cultivates my mystical qualities?
8. Visions: What dancing visions may I turn to reality?

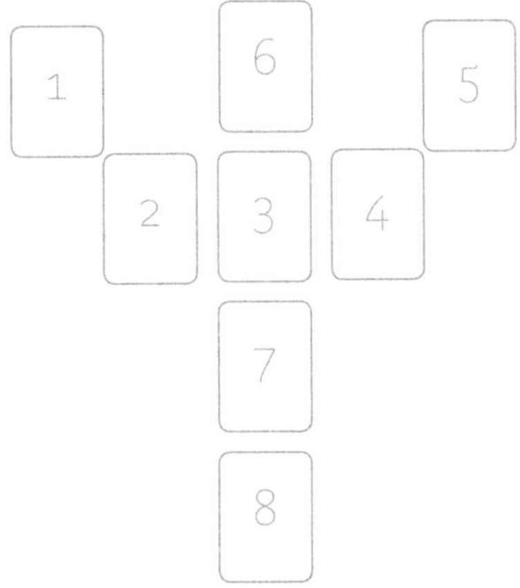

Lost in his dreams and visions, the Hanged Man looks at the world through transcended consciousness. Representing suspension, not death, his face does not reflect suffering. His gallows is in the form of the Tao cross; his head bears the halo of enlightenment. A. E. Waite claimed this card reflected an aspect of the Divine relating to the universe.

August • 26

Loyalty of a Pooch Spread

Dog owners have lower blood pressure and live longer. Perhaps dog owners get more exercise, leading to an increase in overall health and well-being.

On This Day

Today is National Dog Day, a day to give extra love and smooches to your puppy and all canine friends.

Summation of Spread

Examine the relationship between you and your pet today. The Loyalty of a Pooch Spread is based on the notion that dogs have a more highly developed emotional life than any other creature. It is a spread that can be performed regarding your dog or pet of choice.

Cast Your Cards

This spread can be done with a particular pooch in mind or you can ask these same questions of a person in your life who demonstrates great loyalty and companionship to you. Cast the Loyalty of a Pooch Spread's cards in the shape of a bone.

1. Card representing my loyal friend.
2. Card representing me.
3. How we are together.
4. How can I show them love?
5. What do we enjoy most together?
6. How does their unconditional love feel to me?
7. How does this help me open to others?
6. How can I become as joyful and carefree as a canine?
7. What treats do the dog(s) in my life deserve?

The Chariot card denotes loyalty, faith, and motivation. If this steadfast card appears in a spread, it can represent a person or pooch who will always travel at your side. It also signals the wells of loyalty and devotion residing inside yourself.

Stephen King's Terror Spread

On This Day

Stephen King published a collection of four novellas collectively called *Different Seasons* on this day in 1982. A prominent and prolific horror author, King is our modern-day Dickens.

Summation of Spread

Isn't it fun to be scared? King's voice has dragged us kicking and screaming in fear and delight to some of the darkest literary landscapes ever imagined. Although King is a master storyteller, most associate his name with fear. The creepy-crawlies inspire this spread. Warning: this spread is not for the faint of heart.

Cast Your Cards

Fear not, constant reader, he knows the way—he's been there before. Cast your cards as follows:

1. What do I fear more than anything?
2. What is the worst that could happen?
3. Who is watching me?
4. What hides in my closet?
5. What lurks under my bed?
6. Who wants to devour me?
7. What protects me?

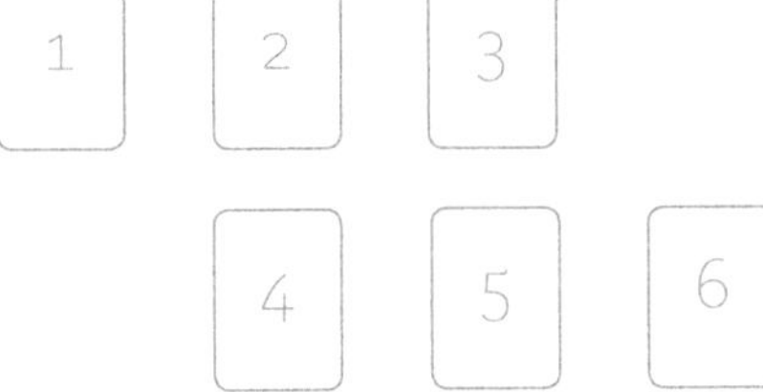

Three of the four stories in Different Seasons *were turned into films:* Stand By Me, Apt Pupil, *and* The Shawshank Redemption, *which went on to be nominated for an Academy Award for Best Picture.*

The Two of Swords represents the refusal to look at a frightening situation, believing something doesn't exist if we can't see it—fooling ourselves into thinking the truth is other than what it seems. Conversely, it can be a needed retreat and meditation. The key lies in the reasoning behind the blindfold's placement.

Northern Lights Goddess Aurora Spread

The Northern Lights occur over 35 miles above Earth and are visible from space.

On This Day

On this day, a geomagnetic storm causes the Aurora Borealis to shine so brightly that it is seen over the United States, Europe, and even as far as Japan. Said to be Viking spirit dancers, Eskimo spirit animals, Greek portents of war, and Algonquin reflections of the Creator's fire, the Northern Lights have inspired cross-cultural mythology from the moment they first danced above human eyes.

Summation of Spread

Do you enjoy morning hours? The Aurora Borealis are named for the Roman Aurora, goddess of the dawn, and Boreas, the Greek name for the north wind. This spread takes inspiration from Aurora, who renews herself every morning and flies across the sky announcing the sun's arrival.

The Fool card shows us that each and every day is an opportunity for a fresh start. The Fool represents freedom of all things—free love, free travel, and freedom to think. He is pure potential.

Cast Your Cards

1. What is renewed every day?
2. Why does morning hold special magic?
3. What can I do better tomorrow?
4. What is the most important thing I can accomplish tomorrow?
5. What new thing can I try tomorrow?
6. What special morning ritual can be cultivated?
7. What should be left behind with my night's sleep?

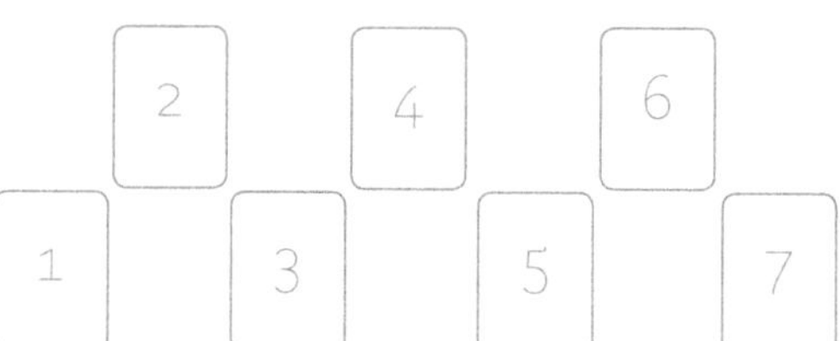

Mary Poppins Spread

On This Day

The film version of *Mary Poppins* was released on this day in 1964. The story of a magical nanny who works for an emotionally detached banker's unhappy family sang and danced its way into the hearts and memories of millions.

Summation of Spread

The Poppins story is rife with wonderful lessons and life advice. This spread is inspired by spoonfuls of sugar, loving rules, and examples set by the most famous nanny of all time.

Cast Your Cards

Cast in the shape of a magical flying umbrella.

1. Where do I need to set boundaries?
2. How can I make disagreeable work fun?
3. How can I live in the moment?
4. How can I be authentic?
5. What helps me develop my personal voice?
6. Do I keep my promises?
7. How can I stay flexible?
8. How can I make a difference in other's lives?
9. How can I become closer with my family?

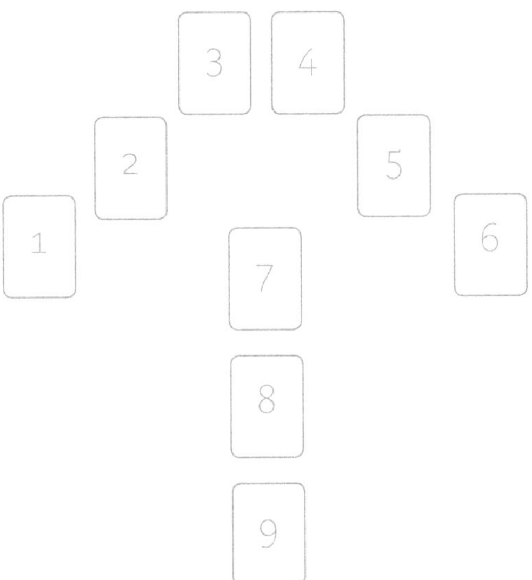

The film originally included a scene where all of the toys in the nursery jumped to life. Proving too scary for children, it was edited out. However, the Broadway musical would go on make use of this magical device.

The Three of Cups is indicative of the joy, dancing, and singing that accompanies any musical theater production. Joy of self-expression lies at the heart of musical theater, and this is precisely what the three women celebrate.

August • 30

Frankenstein Spread

Frankenstein was conceived amidst a wet, rainy summer at Lake Geneva with Lord Byron and her future husband Percy Shelley. Confined by terrible weather, they amused themselves by reading German ghost stories, and, at Lord Byron's suggestion, each wrote a supernatural tale.

With his display of authority and rigid, controlling, and unbudgeable qualities, the Emperor card carries shades of the Frankenstein monster.

On This Day

Author Mary Shelley was born on this day in 1797 in London, England. Shelly wrote the dark and gloomy archetypal gothic novel *Frankenstein*, which she began writing when she was eighteen.

Summation of Spread

Frankenstein is the classic tale of a manmade monster seeking acceptance—a cautionary tale of what goes tragically wrong when man makes Promethian-like attempts to control the nature of life and death. The Frankenstein Spread uses the themes and symbols from the tale to shed light on your life.

Cast Your Cards

Cast in the shape of two lightning bolts:

1. Rebellion: How do I move against the grain?
2. Life Creation: What do I create in my life?
3. Shaping Destiny: What destiny should I embrace?
4. Alienation: What makes me feel like an outsider?
5. Monstrosity: What terrifies me?
6. Madness: What makes me crazy?
7. Secrecy: What do I repress from others?
8. Guilt: Does guilt influence my actions?
9. Desire: What do I crave more than anything?
10. Occult Knowledge: How does occult knowledge help me understand my reality?
11. Dangerous Knowledge: What do I know that I wish I didn't know?

Wisdom of Wands Spread

On This Day

Today is the Flaming Fireball festival in Nejapa, El Salvador. Men dress as skeletons, divide into two teams, and hurl burning gasoline-soaked rag balls at each other. Commemorating a volcanic eruption in 1922, the local churches say it was Saint Jeronimo fighting off the Devil with balls of fire.

Summation of Spread

Are you ready to get moving? This night of hurling fire is associated with the suit of Wands, the raging magical flames of tarot. Wands represent the power of desire, spirituality, action, and inspiration. This spread is inspired by the suit of Wands.

Cast Your Cards

A wand is the first instrument associated with magical will. Cast your cards in the shape of a wizard's wand:

1. Movement: Where am I going?
2. Action: What should I be doing?
3. Initiative: What stand should I take?
4. Personality: What is the highlight of my personality?
5. Ambition: What do I want?
6. Spirit: What is my highest good?
7. Determination: Why will nothing stop me?
8. Expression: What needs to be expressed?

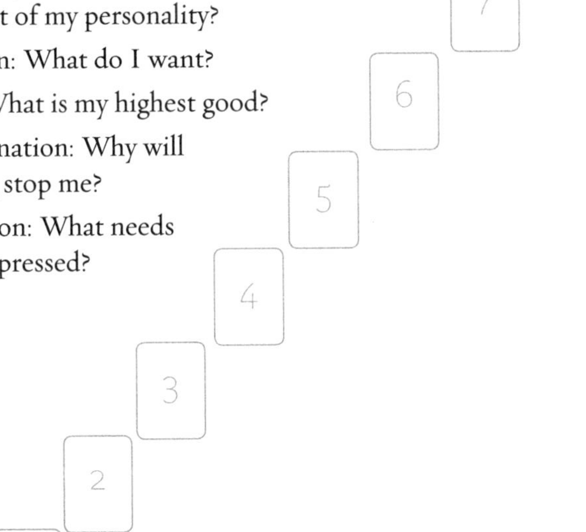

Fire is an event, not a thing. Heating wood or fuel releases volatile vapors that can readily combust with oxygen, and the incandescent bloom of gas further heats the fuel, perpetuating the cycle.

Wands address what makes us tick, why we get out of bed in the morning, and why we do what we do. Spiritually, they represent what is important to you at the core of your being—your passions and desires.

September • 1

Natalie Portman met her future husband, choreographer Benjamin Millepied, while working together filming Black Swan.

The Devil card connects to the dark, repressed parts of the personality. Representing passion, instincts, and hedonism, he can also represent the distortion of repressed desire expressing itself in harmful ways.

Embrace Your Dark Side Spread

On This Day

Black Swan, the dark psychological thriller starring Natalie Portman, opened the Venice Film Festival on this day in 2010. The movie's plot swirls around ballet dancer Nina, who is cast as the lead in *Swan Lake*.

Summation of Spread

What do you keep hidden? What thrives in your dark side? In *Swan Lake*, Nina must embody both the purity of the White Swan and the darkness of the Black Swan. While the innocence of the White Swan sits sweetly in her comfort zone, Nina slowly loses her mind while finding her dark and sensual Black Swan qualities. This spread pulls back the curtains on your personal Black Swan by utilizing themes from the film.

Cast Your Cards

Cast your cards in the shape of a swan:

1. What part of myself am I afraid the world will see?
2. What part of myself am I afraid to see?
3. How do I respond to this fear?
4. What walls do I create?
5. What part of myself feels dangerous?
6. Do I command my sexual power?
7. Can I express love toward those dark parts of my psyche?
8. Can I accept and protect my darkness without allowing it to hurt others?
9. Who is my doppelganger?

2 1 3 4 5 6 9 8 7

Nike's Success Spread

On This Day

The Greeks celebrated winged goddess Nike, goddess of speed, strength, and victory, on this day. Assuming the role of charioteer, which is how she is often portrayed in Greek art, she flies around battlefields rewarding the victors with fame and glory.

Summation of Spread

Are you prepared for victory in any area of life? Nike inspires the questions of this spread and sheds light on the situation.

Cast Your Cards

Cast Nike's Success Spread's cards in the shape of one of Nike's wings:

1. What is in my favor?
2. What opposes me?
3. What will guarantee my success?
4. What will destroy it?
5. How does success change me?
6. How do I stay the same?
7. What must I give up?
8. What is gained?

Nike's Roman equivalent was named Victoria, from whom we inherit the word for victory.

The Chariot card, like Nike, shares common qualities of speed, success, conquest, and ambition. The Chariot represents a person who has found and reached success due to their own labors and ingenuity. A sense of motion prevails—of being in control and having reins in hand regarding the forces of life.

Burning Man Spread

A temporary airstrip is set up every year at Burning Man and completely erased afterwards.

On This Day

The Burning Man Festival has occurred on and around this date since 1986. The festival, a temporary experimental community built in a Nevada desert, is dedicated to radical self-expression and self-reliance. A ritual wooden effigy is always burned.

Summation of Spread

Burning Man founder Larry Harvey wrote ***Ten Principles of Burning Man*** in 2004, reflecting the culture and ethos of the event. They inform the questions of the Burning Man Spread.

Cast Your Cards

Cast your cards in the effigy of the burning man:

1. Radical Inclusion: How do I welcome and respect people I don't know?
2. Gifting: How can I give unconditionally?
3. Decommodification: How can I place less value on "things"?
4. Radical Self-Reliance: How do I best discover and rely on my inner resources?
5. Radical Self-Expression: How do I express my unique gifts?
6. Communal Effort: How do I cooperate with others?
7. Civic Responsibility: How can I become a better community member?
8. Leaving No Trace: How can I reduce my carbon footprint?
9. Participation: How do I achieve being through doing?
10. Immediacy: How do I overcome the barrier between myself and the recognition of my inner self by participating in the experience of life?

The Hanged Man and the Burning Man both reject the ego. Placing self-interest aside is a key component of the Hanged Man. Placing the needs of others first and dedicating yourself to a higher cause link to the sacrificial aspects of this card.

City of Angels Spread

On This Day

Spanish settlers founded Los Angeles, California, on this day in 1781. Little did they know their enclave would rise to become the entertainment capital of the world. Hundreds of films and records are produced in LA each year—the second largest city in the United States next to New York City.

In Los Angeles County, approximately 100,000 women a year get their breasts enhanced, an average of 65 people change their legal name to Jesus Christ, and the average citizen consumes 250 tacos a year.

Summation of Spread

Do you find yourself California dreamin'? The City of Angels Spread is crafted with questions inspired by the city's themes and explores how these topics relate to your life.

Cast Your Cards

Cast in the shape of a star on the Hollywood Walk of Fame:

1. Starlet: What drama do I create?
2. Glamour: What can I do today to make myself feel glamorous?
3. Red Carpet: What image do I project to the world?
4. Glitz: How can I indulge myself?
5. Beaches: How can I connect with the element of water?
6. Sunshine: What makes me feel healthy?
7. Rock 'n' Roll: What makes me want to dance?
8. Movie Sets: What fantasy is close to becoming reality?

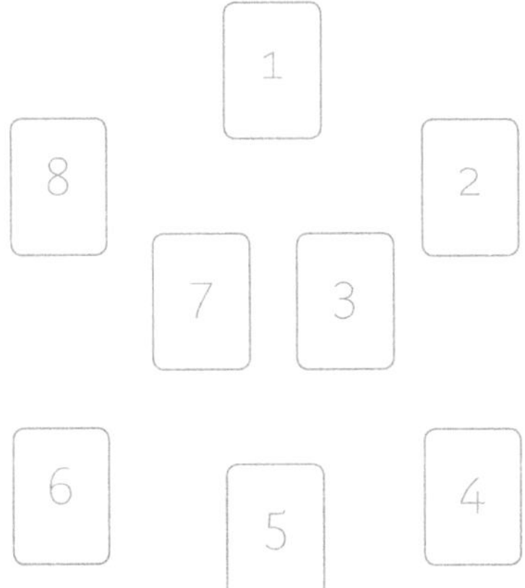

The Seven of Cups, like Los Angeles, has a strong association with movies and the imagination. It looks as if the silhouetted figure stands in front of a projector. The cups, like cinematic visions, swirl before him, representing possibilities that have not yet unfolded.

Should I Start This Project Spread

Winchester's fascination with the number 13 reflects everywhere in the house. Bathroom number 13 has 13 windows, the kitchen sink has 13 drain holes, and she even modified a 12-light gas chandelier to hold 13 lights.

The Four of Pentacles shows a man clinging to his money while a city is built up behind him. He clings to objects as if this will save him from the inevitable fate of death. Yet no one—not even Sarah Winchester, with her massive amounts of money and never-ending house construction and decoration—can escape the fate awaiting us all.

On This Day

Sarah Winchester, owner of the famed Winchester House and heiress to the Winchester gun fortune, died on this day in 1922. The Winchester house, a project she undertook after a medium told her to do so, was under construction 24 hours a day for 38 years. The Victorian house, located in California, is renowned for its rambling size, rooms, and lack of a master building plan.

Summation of Spread

Are you debating the beginning of a major project? Projects can look appealing at the onset, then diminish in fun and usefulness. This spread examines whether or not to embark upon a new project.

Cast Your Cards

Cast your cards in an upward line.

1. Is this project worth doing?
2. Will the results yield a lasting benefit?
3. Does the process or result justify the time spent?
4. Does the process or result justify the money spent?
5. What is at the core of what I want to accomplish?
6. Will I enjoy the process?
7. What is the result of my effort?

Accepting Loss Spread

On This Day

Diana Spencer, Princess of Wales, was laid to rest in a public funeral at Westminster Abbey today in 1997. Her body was interred on a small island in an ornamental lake on the Spencer family estate. Of the over two billion people watching the funeral, few will forget the image of her sons, William and Henry, walking behind her coffin as it wound through the streets of London.

A path of 36 oak trees, one for each year of her life, leads to the lake where Diana is buried. Four black swans swim beside water lilies that line the lake. An arboretum planted by Diana, William, Harry, and other family members stands nearby.

Summation of Spread

Have you lost someone dear? Nothing prepares us for the loss of a loved one. While a tarot spread will not hold all the answers, this spread sheds light and offers options when experiencing the heartbreak of loss.

The Ace of Cups is a fountain of love with the power to heal a broken heart.

Cast Your Cards

1. How can I face this loss?
2. How do I let the pain come out?
3. Who can I share this with?
4. Can I relish the beauty of the natural world?
5. How can I be gentle with myself?
6. Can I allow myself the time I need to heal?
7. What mind/body activity can I perform that offers peace?
8. Looking directly into this loss, what do I see?
9. Can I find the gift and good of this situation?
10. What moves with me into the future?

Strength Card Spread

The virtue of Fortitude usually depicts a lion or broken column. The Visconti-Sforza deck, however, shows Heracles attacking a lion, which is a likely allegory of Sforza, the man who commissioned the deck, and his military victories.

The Strength card often represents an obstacle allowing you to overcome your fears. Energy and calmness reign over brutality and force. Strength of character, high moral standing, physical stamina, and health are all represented.

On This Day

A solar eclipse on this day in 1251 BCE may mark the birth of legendary Heracles, divine hero of Greek mythology. Heracles displayed strength, courage, and ingenuity; Hercules is his Roman equivalent.

Summation of Spread

Heracles is depicted in the Visconti-Sforza deck as the Strength card, with his signature club and the Nemean lion. This spread is based on symbols found within the traditional Strength card.

Cast Your Cards

Use this spread to answer any question. Format your question before casting the spread or simply let the cards answer the questions posed. Pull the Strength card from your deck, place it in the center of the spread, and cast your cards around it.

1. Female: How am I reasonable?
2. Lion: What are my instincts telling me?
3. Lemniscate: How can I expand my thinking?
4. Hand Gesture: How can I be gentle to others?
5. Garland Belt: Where should I place a boundary?
6. White Gown: How can I bring about peace?
7. Mountain: What is the long-term goal?
8. Yellow Background: How does my intelligence serve me?

Sibling Issues Spread

On This Day

The psychological drama *Dead Ringers* was released on this day in 1988. Jeremy Irons plays identical twin gynecologists who pretend to be each other. Taking full advantage of the fact no one can tell them apart, they lie to everyone until their own relationship deteriorates over a woman, leading to a gruesome ending.

Summation of Spread

Are you feuding with a brother or sister? Sibling fights and misunderstandings can be extremely painful. This spread gives you an opportunity to step back and survey the situation, finding a new way to express your needs and bring a solution to sibling squabbles.

Cast Your Cards

1. The situation.
2. What I'm feeling.
3. What they are feeling.
4. What I see that they don't see.
5. What they see that I don't see.
6. What is truly possible for the two of us.
7. What action can I take to heal the relationship?

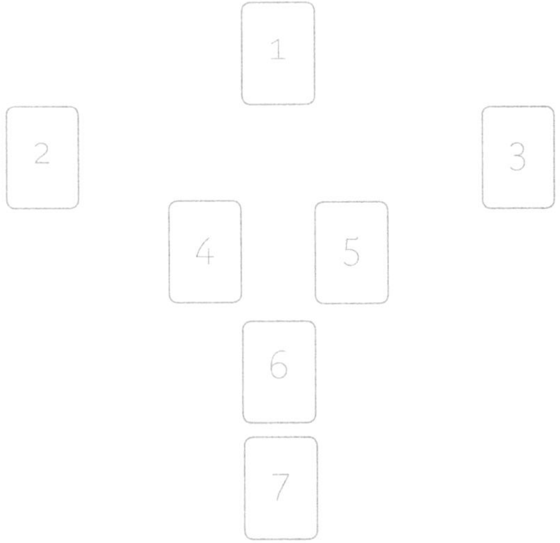

Researchers have found that hour for hour, children spend more time with their siblings than with friends, parents, teachers, or even alone. While they may not always get along, by the time a child is 11 years old, they have spent about 33 percent of their time with their siblings.

The Three of Cups is the representation of bliss, cooperation, and the joy of togetherness. While the card appears intensely female, it represents both genders in the accomplishment and achievement of a common emotional goal.

September • 9

Reincarnation research is a branch of parapsychology that specifically studies young children who make spontaneous remarks about past lives. These children supposedly carry knowledge from a previous life into this one.

The Wheel of Fortune is the idea of karma, evolution, and eternal rotation. The endless cycles, ups and downs, and the representation of eternity are found within this most iconic and enduring of images.

Past Lives of Lovers Spread

On This Day

Cloud Atlas, the film adaptation of the novel by David Mitchell, premiered at the Toronto International Film Festival on this day in 2012.

Summation of Spread

How did you and your soulmate know each other in past lives? *Cloud Atlas* contains six storylines, all of which, excluding one, are reincarnations of the same soul in different bodies. Seizing upon the idea of reincarnation and soulmates, this spread is inspired by the unfolding mystery of eternal love and connection.

Cast Your Cards

Feel the connection and cast your cards.

1. Who was I in a past life?
2. Who was my soulmate in a past life?
3. What was our relationship?
4. Was it a stable relationship?
5. Did we have children?
6. Were we together a long time?
7. What lesson did we learn together in our past life?
8. What lesson are we learning in this life?
9. Are we evolving and moving forward?

Marie Laveau's Voodoo Spread

On This Day

Marie Laveau, the Queen of Conjure, was born on this day in 1794. Marie was the most infamous Voodoo figure in American history. Transforming the religious practices of African slaves into social and cultural institutions, her rituals served as public spectacle, entertainment, and even political influence. Working as a hairdresser in New Orleans, she offered private consultations and led public rituals, including exorcisms and sacrifices to the spirits.

Every year, thousands of people visit Marie Laveau's grave, offering her tribute in the form of random offerings, hoping she will grant favors and wishes from beyond the grave.

Summation of Spread

Are you ready to work some mojo? Marie Laveau's Voodoo Spread is based on core elements, items, and lore from New Orleans Voodoo, ritual, and spellwork.

Cast Your Cards

Be wary of the crossroads after midnight, and cast the cards as follows:

1. Amulet: What do I need protection from?
2. Crossroads Mojo: What choice must I make?
3. Bayou Swamp: What lurks in my subconscious?
4. Gris-Gris Bag: What magic or energy should I focus on and carry with me?
5. Spirit House: What energy must be repelled?
6. Black Cat Juju: What area of my life contains good luck?
7. Conjure Oil: What must I create?
8. Zombie: What must die?
9. Wanga Paquet: In what area of my life should I concentrate all my power?

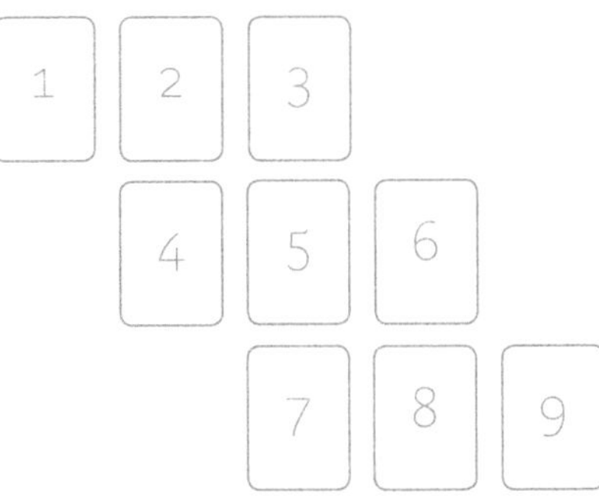

The Queen of Wands casts powerful magic. The black cat sitting at her feet is an often-overlooked aspect of this queen's magical work. Fierce, determined, and containing vast reserves of energy, of all the tarot queens, she provokes change and alters her reality the quickest.

Forgiveness Spread

The Mayo Clinic says letting go of grudges and bitterness makes way for peace, kindness, and compassion. It also leads to healthier relationships, lower blood pressure, and many other desirable qualities.

The Ace of Cups represents the emotional flow, growth, and openness that occurs when true forgiveness is offered.

On This Day

A series of suicide attacks occurred in New York City, Arlington, Virginia, and Shanksville, Pennsylvania, on this day in 2001. Nearly 3,000 people were murdered when terrorists altered American landscape, history, and foreign policy forever.

Summation of Spread

Forgiveness does not make offending acts acceptable, but it frees the person harboring anger. The ramifications of retaliation versus forgiveness were considered when creating this spread. Forgiveness is a mental and sometimes spiritual act of ceasing feelings of resentment, anger, and indignation.

Cast Your Cards

1. Can I express my emotions without apologizing for them?
2. Do I have a support system around me?
3. What can I turn this pain into?
4. What is causing me to hold on to anger and resentment?
5. Can I find empathy for the person who hurt me?
6. How do I rid myself of anger?
7. Can I set the boundaries I need?
8. Can I give thanks for the good in my life?
9. How do I deal with the fact that my anger may return?
10. Imagining myself in the future, is my life better without vengeance?
11. Final word.

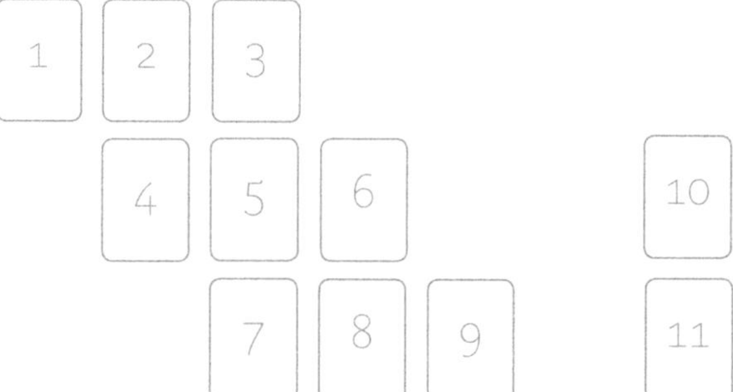

Peek-a-Boo Burlesque Spread

On This Day

The first burlesque show opened in New York City on this day in 1866. Called *The Black Crook*, it ran for 475 performances and made over a million dollars for its producers.

Summation of Spread

Are you a tease? Modern burlesque, often called neo-burlesque, invokes glamour girls' pinup style while reveling in the art of the striptease. Partial clothing is removed while pasties and g-strings remain, leaving audiences a little something to the imagination. This alluring idea of the hidden informs this spread.

Cast Your Cards

Every second card, the "what I keep hidden" cards, is cast face-down. Cast the "what I show" cards face-up. Moving through the spread, examine how you play peek-a-boo with the world around you.

1. What I show to the world.
2. What I keep hidden.
3. What I show to my ex.
4. What I keep hidden.
5. What I show to my lover.
6. What I keep hidden.
7. What I show at work.
8. What I keep hidden.
9. What I show my family.
10. What I keep hidden.

The term burlesque *represents a literary, dramatic, or musical work designed for laughter. In the late seventeenth century it was applied to the works of Shakespeare and Chaucer. Not until the nineteenth century did it become a sultry striptease.*

The Two of Swords represents the parts of your psyche kept off-limits to others. The ocean and moon reflect elements fraught with emotion, revealing a card where two opposites coexist in harmony.

Parenting facts are changeable and negotiable depending on the time frame and culture you are living in. One fact remains forever true: the common essential ingredient is love.

The Sun card represents a healthy pregnancy and happy child. This card is an evocative reminder of how mothers nurture their children in utero, acting as the sun, nourishing and generating everything the baby needs.

Am I Ready for Parenthood Spread

On This Day

Today is the Roman feast day revering Jupiter, Juno, and Minerva. Jupiter was king of the gods; Juno, his wife and sister; and Minerva, Jupiter's daughter and goddess of wisdom. A sumptuous ritual feast was served and eaten in honor of this godly triad.

Summation of Spread

Are you considering becoming a parent? This celestial family is used for inspiration regarding parental readiness. While nothing prepares you for the experience of having a child and everyone moves through it in a different way, this spread examines all issues before deciding to take a leap of baby faith.

Cast Your Cards

Cast the cards delicately.

1. How do I feel about children?
2. Am I ready to put another's needs ahead of my own?
3. Am I ready to have my life radically change?
4. Am I responsible?
5. What is my financial state?
6. Do I have a support system in place?
7. What will a baby add to my life?
8. What helps me adjust?
9. What do I need to know that I don't know?
10. Why will I be an amazing parent?

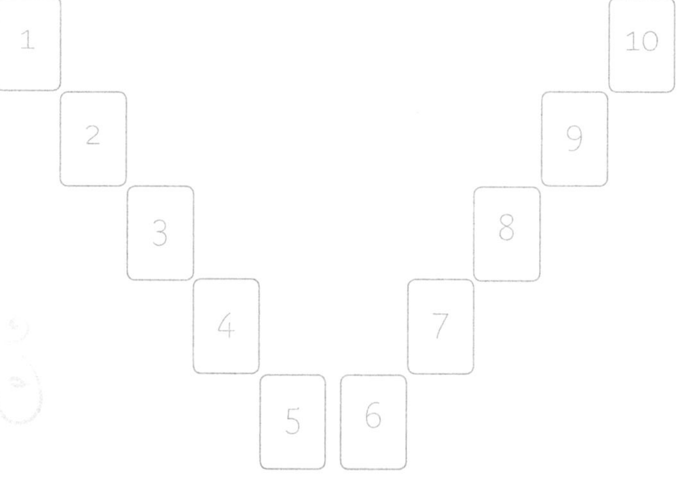

Live in the Moment Spread

On This Day

The British Empire officially adopted the Gregorian calendar on this day in 1752, skipping ahead eleven days. This solar calendar became the most widely adopted and used civil calendar in the Western world.

Though the Gregorian calendar is named after Pope Gregory XIII, it was designed by Italian astronomer and philosopher Luigi Lilio.

Summation of Spread

Are you rushing through life? Time contains strange and elusive qualities as the unit of measurement most intuitively felt and the measurement humanity arranges their entire life around. Feeling elastic and long when young, speeding quickly when older, and dragging out when bored, the optimal experience of time occurs when it disappears completely from our perception. This spread has been created to facilitate your experience of living in the moment.

The dancer on the World card moves outside human conceptions of time. She embodies living in the moment. The World card is ultimate transcendence.

Cast Your Cards

1. How do I let go of what others think of me and become unselfconscious?
2. What helps me discover the beauty of what surrounds me?
3. How do I focus only on the task at hand?
4. How can I give myself over to my senses?
5. What new activity can I select that fully engages me?
6. Can I commit to unplugging from technology?
7. What do I experience as a result of living in the moment?

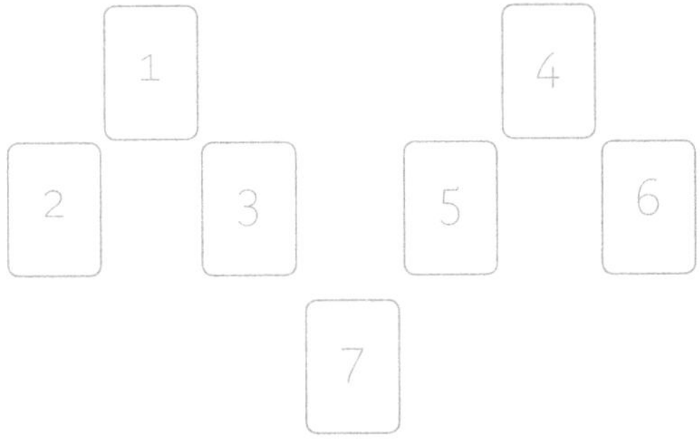

Hierophant Card Spread

In ancient Greece the Hierophant led rites, oversaw worship and sacrifice, and was the interpreter of sacred mysteries and esoteric principles. He was a mystagogue, instructing initiation and religious mystery.

While the High Priestess is the guardian of mysteries, the Hierophant is the popularizer bringing wisdom to the masses. In everyday life he is the guide, teacher, and mentor. Relating both social confirmation and the highest spiritual truths, he can represent both rigidity and tolerance.

On This Day

St. Boniface, responsible for converting the historic Pantheon building in Rome from a Pagan god–filled temple of Venus and Mars into a Christian church, began his reign as Pope Boniface IV today in 608.

Summation of Spread

Historical tarot decks include a Pope card. The Pope card was later called the Hierophant by esoteric deck makers. The Hierophant Card Spread is based on symbols found in the Hierophant card.

Cast Your Cards

Use this spread to answer any question. Format your question before casting the spread or simply let the cards answer the questions posed. Pull the Hierophant card from your deck, place it in the center of the spread, and cast your cards around it:

1. Hand Gesture: What blessings do I give to others?
2. Triple-Cross Staff: How are my fate, fortune, and destiny connected?
3. Triple Crown: Where does my authority lie?
4. Cloak: What protects me?
5. Dual Keys: What doors does my knowledge unlock?
6. Pillars: What is truth?
7. Double Clerics: Whom can I count on for support?
8. Slippers: What keeps me grounded?

New Life Spread

On This Day

The *Mayflower* set sail from Plymouth, England, on this date in 1620. The ship, symbolic of a completely new life, began early colonization of the future United States.

Summation of Spread

Are you ready to start over? Whether moving cross-country or turning over a new leaf in your own backyard, the New Life Spread asks questions to push you in new directions.

Cast Your Cards

Cast the cards in the shape of a boat:

1. What do I want out of life?
2. What do I want to experience?
3. What am I willing to change?
4. What brings meaning to my experience?
5. What empowering belief do I need to incorporate?
6. How can I work less and achieve more?
7. What is my unexpected result if I change?

Remember to be kind to yourself during the moving process. Following the death of a loved one and divorce, moving is the third most stressful event in life.

The Six of Swords depicts a journey over silent water. Ripples behind the boat reflect a challenge faced, while the water ahead is calm, suggesting better times ahead. The Six of Swords and its three figures are a reminder that this deeply emotional trip is not solitary; loved ones come along, too.

Witchy Woman Spread

In Bewitched, *almost all the female witches' character names end with the letter A, including Samantha, Endora, Esmerelda, Clara, Hagatha, Enchantra, and Tabitha.*

The High Priestess connects with the intuition of witchcraft due to her representation of all female hidden knowledge. Her flowing reserves of ancient memory are a magic repository, a basis of understanding superseding the material world. This well lies in each of us, yet we must find and cultivate this knowledge individually.

On This Day

Bewitched, the popular sitcom about a witch attempting to forsake her magical powers in order to become a housewife, airs for the first time on this day in 1964.

Summation of Spread

Are you a natural witch? The Witchy Woman Spread examines your predilection for natural witchcraft. While anyone has the ability to work magic and cast spells, the Witchy Woman Spread examines personal witchy qualities and innate powers closely.

Cast Your Cards

Cast in the shape of a broomstick:

1. What makes me a natural witch?
2. Should I cast spells?
3. How often do my intentions become reality?
4. What is my connection with nature?
5. What is the nature of my heightened awareness?
6. What do I see and sense that others don't?
7. What otherworldly planes do I have the strongest connection to?
8. How do I connect with divine energy?
9. What is my greatest magical challenge?
10. What is my greatest magical strength?

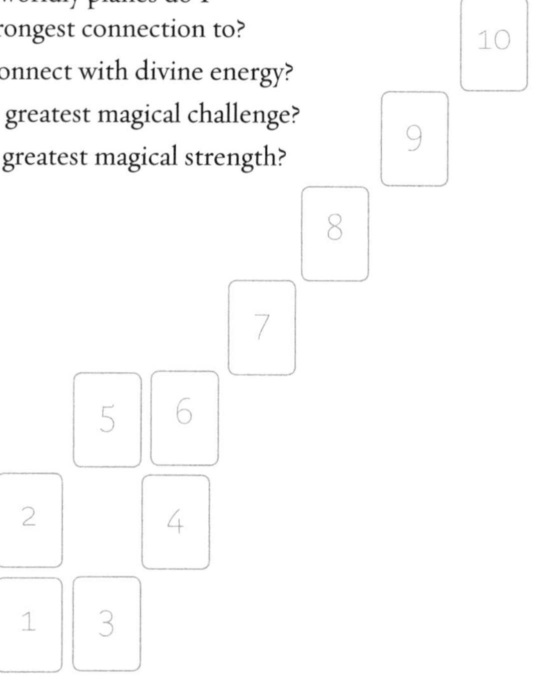

Obsession and Fatal Attraction Spread

On This Day

The psychological thriller *Fatal Attraction* was released on this day in 1987. This iconic film shows the price Michael Douglas pays for his affair with the wildly obsessed and deranged Glenn Close, ending with a bunny in a pot and a bloodstained bathroom.

Summation of Spread

Are you obsessed? Everyone falls prey to obsession from time to time. This spread has been crafted to help get ahold of obsession and steady it before things spiral out of control.

Cast Your Cards

Keep your head and cast the cards as follows:

1. Who or what is my obsession?
2. Do they know I am obsessing over them?
3. Do they return my affection?
4. What stands in the way?
5. What aids me?
6. How long will I suffer this exquisite pain?
7. Is my behavior unhealthy?
8. Will this relationship work?
9. How do I regain balance?
10. The ultimate outcome.

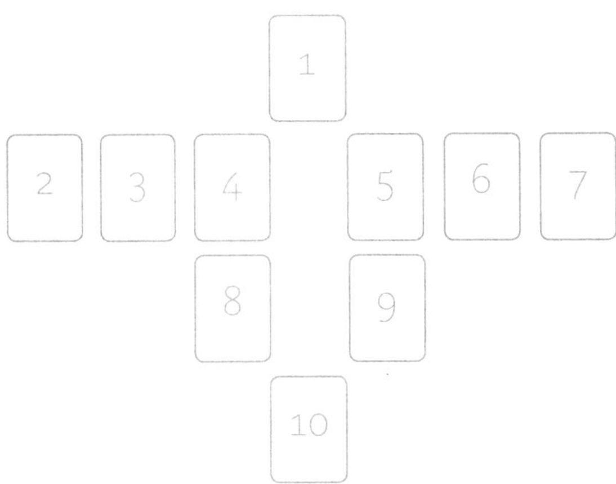

Love exerts the same stress upon the body as deep fear. Some physiological responses include pupil dilation, sweaty palms, and an increased heart rate.

The Devil card is negatively aspected by extreme obsession, stopping at nothing to satisfy itself. Representing bondage, addiction, sexuality, and materialism, this card reminds you it is time to take responsibility for your actions and ground yourself in reality.

Pirate Spread

The golden age of piracy lasted from about 1700 to 1725 as thousands of men (and a few women) turned to piracy as a way to make a living. Underpaid or cheated of wages, sailors often switched ranks, becoming pirates themselves.

The Knight of Wands represents the true pirate spirit of rushing forth to eagerly meet adventure and intrigue. Impulsive and filled with energy and enthusiasm, this knight dives headfirst into action with little thought to consequence. His motto is "act first, think later."

On This Day

Today is International Talk Like a Pirate Day, begun by two Americans who thought it would be good fun to talk like a pirate for a day.

Summation of Spread

Ready to embark upon adventure? Modern pirate and wench festivals have sprouted up everywhere as a place for like-minded individuals to gather for pirate parties. The Pirate Spread uses issues of classic pirating to discover what adventure you are embarking on today—because every day is an adventure for a pirate.

Cast Your Cards

Cast your sails, smell the sea air, feel your freedom, and cast the Pirate Spread's cards like a pirate's flag:

1. What adventure calls?
2. Where must I travel?
3. Do I have a good pirate outfit?
4. What is my weapon of choice?
5. What buried treasure awaits?
6. Where can I have a really good time?
7. How can I express wanton sexuality?
8. Do I have enough rum?
9. How can I live my life by my own rules?

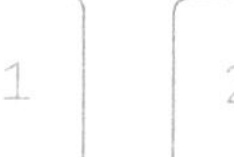

20 • September

Sophia Loren's Sensuality Spread

On This Day

Sophia Loren, eternal beauty and Italian queen of earthy sensuality, was born on this day in 1934. Sophia captures the perfect combination of alluring gorgeousness and European sensuality.

Summation of Spread

Are you ready to sex it up? Sophia Loren's smoldering gaze and commanding presence inspire this spread because sensuality has nothing to do with the outside and everything to do with how someone feels on the inside. Arrive at specific answers to each question before analyzing the entire spread.

Cast Your Cards

Light some candles and cast the cards as follows:

1. How do I put my inner judgments and critic aside?
2. What new and delicious way can I tend to myself?
3. How do I cultivate sensual awareness?
4. How can I find a new way to move my body?
5. Can I accept what really turns me on?
6. What steps can I take to get closer to my fantasy?
7. What must I indulge in?

6

Plato defines eros (erotic love) as "a passion aroused by beauty." He then uses this passion as a doorway into the transcendent—that eros catapults the soul from a physical and sexual love to the spiritual and mystical contemplation of love.

The High Priestess holds inner knowledge for those who explore the path of sensuality and sexuality. As meditation and trance bring an individual to other planes of existence, so do metaphysical worlds of vision, creativity, and transcendence open for those who understand and cultivate sensuality as a doorway or path to the occult.

Mabon Delicate Balance Spread

An ancient hunting deity, Mabon embodies male fertility and is simultaneously the youngest and oldest of souls. Stolen from his mother three days after birth, it was believed he was held captive in the otherworld. Like Persephone, he emerges in the spring as all vegetation shoots forth.

The Six of Pentacles depicts a delicate balance maintained by the scales. The figures of the card retain a triad position. Mercy, justice, and generosity are all apparent on this card. It is also a reminder to keep the scales in balance, never giving too much of yourself away to others.

On This Day

Celtic Mabon falls on this day, coinciding with the autumn equinox, when both day and night are equal. Food gathering was once communal and was maintained through seasonal harvests and slaughter. This was a festival of thanksgiving that attempted to maintain a vital spiritual and social balance.

Summation of Spread

Do you feel out of whack? Balance exists in life, whether we realize it or not. This is an opportunity to look at what and how we give and take.

Cast Your Cards

Cast in three trios:

1. What do I take from the earth?
2. What do I give back?
3. How can I honor it?
4. What do I take from my relationship?
5. What do I give back?
6. How can I honor us?
7. What do I take from myself?
8. What do I give back?
9. How can I honor it?

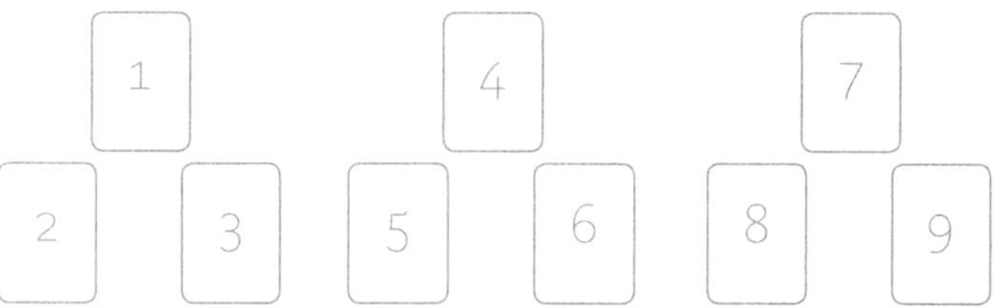

Judgement Card Spread

Joseph Smith was paid as a scryer, using his "seer stones" to locate lost items and treasure. Promoting the practice of polygamy, he took part in a long line of historical abuses, using religious dogma to subjugate, control, and repress women.

On This Day

Joseph Smith, inventor of Mormonism and the Church of Jesus Christ of Latter-Day Saints, stated that on this day in 1823 an angel directed him to a box of golden plates in the woods near his home in upstate NY, where he translated them using a "seer stone." He placed the stone at the bottom of a hat, covered his face, and read the stone. The result was the Book of Mormon, the religious text of the Mormon religion.

Summation of Spread

Self-proclaimed prophets, with their flocks of followers, usually feel their call coming from above. This "call from above" is depicted in the Judgement card. The questions of this spread are inspired by symbols found within the Judgement card.

The Judgement card represents irreversible inner transformation.

Cast Your Cards

Use this spread to answer any question. Format your question before casting the spread or simply let the cards answer the questions posed. Pull the Judgement card from your deck, place it in the center of the spread, and cast your cards around it as follows:

1. Trumpet: What is my wakeup call?
2. Angel Gabriel: Where is divine intervention?
3. Red Cross: Who is with me?
4. Flag: What am I expressing on the outside?
5. Coffins: What is stagnant?
6. Open Arms: What do I embrace?
7. Dead Rising: What is my second chance?
8. Water: What changes?

Qualities of Libra Spread

Libra is ruled by Venus, pink is the primary color, the lucky day is Friday, and the best locations for success are social activities. Libra rules the seventh house, governing marriage, partnerships, and relationships.

Justice is almost always depicted with the scales of balance, which is also the symbol of Libra. The Justice card carefully contemplates the subtle shades of right and wrong.

On This Day

Today marks the first day of the sign of Libra.

Summation of Spread

This spread is based on the essential qualities of the astrological sign of Libra: balance, easygoing, truth, beauty, perfection, and a romantic nature.

Cast Your Cards

Cast in the shape of the top half of the Libra symbol:

1. How can I healthfully balance what is going on right now?
2. How can I lighten up right now?
3. Why is truth important?
4. What is the nature of beauty?
5. Can I give up the idea of perfection?
6. Who loves me romantically?

Lawsuit Spread

On This Day

The Supreme Court of the United States was created on this day in 1789 when the Judiciary Act was passed by Congress and signed by George Washington. This tribunal is made up of six justices, who serve on the court until their death or retirement.

During the Supreme Court's first term, it made no decisions. It didn't even have a courtroom, using a committee room in the basement of the Capitol, where it remained until the Civil War.

Summation of Spread

Hopefully you will never need to cast the cards of this spread. But should you find yourself entrenched in a lawsuit, these questions can help get a firm grasp upon the situation.

Cast Your Cards

Cast in the shape of a judge's gavel:

1. Is there any way to avoid this lawsuit?
2. What is the nature of the case?
3. How can I establish a good working relationship with my attorney?
4. How do I keep my emotions in check?
5. What is in my favor?
6. What is not in my favor?
7. What helps me become victorious?
8. The ultimate outcome.

The Justice card's scales, also seen in the astrological sign of Libra, represent equality and fairness. The scales of justice were used in the Egyptian Book of the Dead. The deceased's heart was placed onto the scale in a ritual called the negative confession. This Ma'at scale is perhaps the earliest reference to the scales of justice.

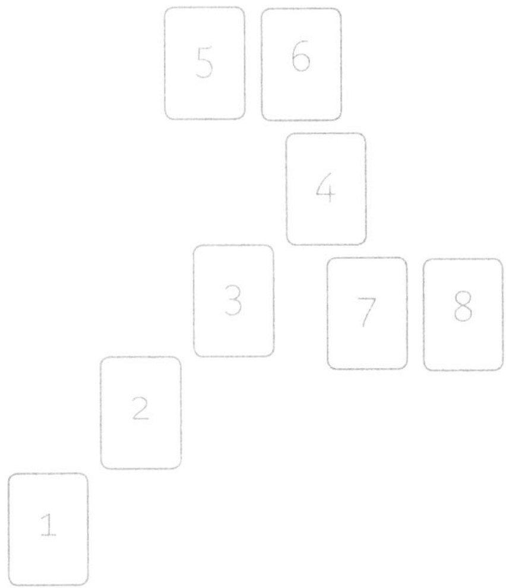

Guiding Goals Spread

Silverstein was also one of the leading cartoonists for Playboy. *Sent around the world by the magazine, he created an illustrated travel journal and collections of humorous travel vignettes.*

See how the figure on the Seven of Swords appears to sneak away with some swords? This represents the decision of what to bring with you into the future and what shall be discarded to the past. List making is a very Swordlike activity, using mental acuity and calculation.

On This Day

Beloved children's author Shel Silverstein was born on this day in 1930. A poet, songwriter, cartoonist, and screenwriter, he is best remembered for books like *Where the Sidewalk Ends* and *The Giving Tree*.

Summation of Spread

Do you need to accomplish something? Silverstein had a passion for list making, perhaps one of the reasons he was so prolific. Using a list-making technique, the Guiding Goals Spread uses tarot in conjunction with your hopes and dreams to create a concrete list. This list helps in your achievement of goals and projects.

Cast Your Cards

Cast your cards in a straight line to create prolific magic inspired by Shel Silverstein.

1. What happens when I put my goals in writing?
2. What is the biggest obstacle to achieving my goals?
3. What are the benefits to achieving my goals?
4. What do I need to learn?
5. Who can I enlist to help me?
6. What helps me visualize my goals?
7. What helps me get organized?
8. How can I reward myself for little steps taken?

Lovers Card Spread

On This Day

American musical *West Side Story* opens at the Winter Garden Theater on this day in 1957.

Summation of Spread

Inspired by *Romeo and Juliet*, this heartbreaking tale of star-crossed lovers represents the elements of opposition and attraction found in the Lovers card. The Lovers Card Spread is based on symbols found in the Lovers card.

Cast Your Cards

Use this spread to answer any question. Format your question before casting the spread or simply let the cards answer the questions posed. Pull the Lovers card from your deck, place it in the center of the spread, and cast your cards around it.

1. Nudity: In what way am I free?
2. Sun: What radiates?
3. Angel: What messages are given?
4. Snake: What am I attracted to?
5. Apple: What tempts me?
6. Fire: What am I passionate about?
7. Mountain: What do I aspire to?
8. Triangle: What is the third unknown variable?

The Rider-Waite deck uses Adam and Eve symbolism, complete with snake and apple. The card reminds us that once man and woman appear, there is a division—an opposite—and a choice must be made.

Beyond the obvious connections of love, lust, and partnership, the Lovers card signifies free will. The Lovers card suggests a rite of passage and an initiatory ordeal. With strong emotional and sexual connections, this card is sometimes love at first sight.

Star Card Spread

The Star card is the first of the series of celestial bodies in the major arcana, followed by the Moon, Sun, and World cards. Representing the heavens and universe brought down to earth, they show what is both possible and impossible, known and unknown.

The Star is a representation of love and the purest form of beauty. It is the grace that enlightens truth, a glimmer of light that illuminates the darkness. Following the tumultuousness of the Devil and the Tower, the Star is the silence following fury, the calm soothing the soul. Peace.

On This Day

Gwyneth Paltrow is born on this day in 1972. True Hollywood royalty, talented, beautiful, and charismatic, she is an ideal representation of the archetypal Hollywood star.

Summation of Spread

There are many ways that stars shine. The Star Card Spread is based on symbols found on the Star card.

Cast Your Cards

Use this spread to answer any question. Format your question before casting the spread or simply let the cards answer the questions posed. Pull the Star card from your deck, place it in the center of the spread, and cast your cards around it.

1. Posture: How can I remain open?
2. Nudity: Why is vulnerability essential?
3. Stars: How do I channel magic?
4. Jug: How do I collect wisdom?
5. Bird: What is my message from above?
6. Tree: What knowledge do I possess?
7. Mountain: What is possible?
8. Flowers: What is manifesting?

Wisdom of Confucius Spread

On This Day

Today Taiwan celebrates the Wisdom of Confucius Day, also known as Teacher's Day. Ceremonies and dancing begin as early as 6 AM, as it is believed qi (chi) energy is strongest when night ends and morning begins. The spirit of Confucius is believed to descend, filling the temples with waves of qi energy, blessing all in attendance.

Summation of Spread

The Wisdom of Confucius Spread is inspired by famous sayings attributed to the beloved philosopher.

Cast Your Cards

1. "He who knows the answers has not asked all the questions."
   What do I need to know?
2. "Choose a job you love, and you will never have to work a day in your life."
   What do I love?
3. "Everything has beauty; not everyone sees it."
   What beauty lies before me?
4. "Life is very simple; it is we who make it complicated."
   How can I streamline life?
5. "Better a diamond with a flaw than a pebble without."
   How can I accept my perceived shortcomings?
6. "The superior man is modest in speech but exceeds in actions."
   How can I stop talking and start doing?
7. "Settle one difficulty and keep a hundred at bay."
   What do I need to fix?
8. "Roads were made for journeys, not destinations."
   How do I enjoy my journey?

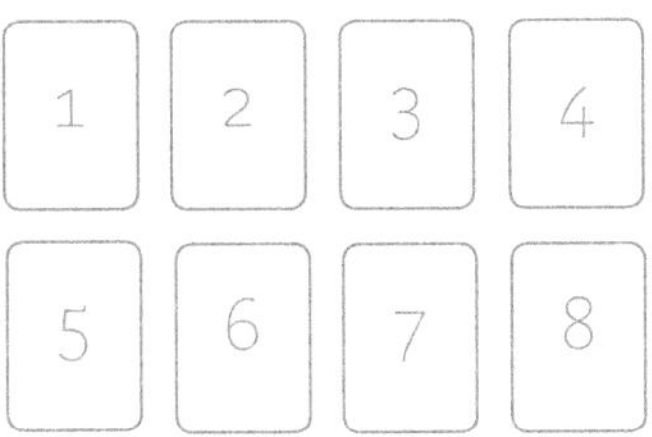

Confucius's students compiled notes of his sayings and doings after his death. Many quotes attributed to him are not direct quotes but analects (collections attributed to Confucius) based on his teachings.

The Hierophant connects to Confucius and any philosopher passing knowledge to those with ears to listen. The word *hierophant* literally translates to "the one who teaches holy things."

Seven Days of the Week Spread

It was only when the United States became aware that China and the USSR were conducting ESP research in the 1970s that they became receptive to the idea of their own psi program.

On This Day

On this day in 1995 the US government officially ended the Stargate Remote Viewing Project. Remote viewing is the ability to psychically "see" events, sites, or information from a great distance. Remote viewing research ran from the 1970s to 1995 for potential military and domestic applications.

Summation of Spread

Want a sneak peek at the week ahead? Using this controversial government program (purportedly costing over 20 million dollars while underway) as inspiration, you can remote-view yourself into the following week.

Cast Your Cards

Shuffle while thinking about the week ahead. Each card gives you the flavor of events for its day. When ready, lay one card for every day of the week, starting with whichever day you like.

1. Monday
2. Tuesday
3. Wednesday
4. Thursday
5. Friday
6. Saturday
7. Sunday

While remote viewing tends to be done under scientific and observable circumstances, any form of divination with the cards regarding information gathering of a remote place or time can be considered a form of remote viewing.

Rumi's Poetic Life Spread

On This Day

Rumi, the Persian Muslim poet, jurist, theologian, and Sufi mystic, was born on this day in 1207. His small town was in what is now known as modern Afghanistan.

Summation of Spread

Rumi's poetry transcended national, ethnic, and religious boundaries. Using beautiful Rumi quotes, this spread seeks to offer illumination and inspiration.

Cast Your Cards

Each question is formulated in the context of the given quote. Rumi's Poetic Life Spread's cards are cast in a simple single line.

1. "What you are seeking, seeks you."
   What do I seek?
2. "Don't grieve. Anything you lose comes round in another form."
   What have I lost?
3. "The wound is the place where Light enters you."
   What have I learned?
4. "Lovers don't finally meet somewhere. They're in each other all along."
   Who is my true love?
5. "Why do you stay in prison when the doors are wide open?"
   What traps me?
6. "Be like melting snow, wash yourself of yourself."
   How do I lose self-awareness?
7. "The lion is most handsome when looking for food."
   What do I feed my soul?

1 2 3 4 5 6 7

After Rumi's death, followers became Whirling Dervishes, also known as the Mevlevi Order. It is believed that Rumi, while walking, became so entranced with happiness of the Divine that he stretched out his arms and started spinning in a circle. Thus the Whirling Dervishes were born.

The suit of Cups inspires poetry, a Cups-like activity. The suit utilizes dreams, intuition, and sweeping emotion conveyed in the written word.

Films before Romero's sourced zombies from Voodoo mythology, depicting zombies as innocent creatures revived and controlled by a powerful master. Forced to do his bidding or be his work force, zombies were cheap labor for wealthy tycoons.

The Judgement Card shows the dead rising out of their coffins to the trumpet song of the angel. Traditionally, Judgement represents an awakening of the soul. Could it be a transformation into a mindless flesh eater?

Zombie Apocalypse Spread

On This Day

On this day in 1968 George Romero's black-and-white zombie film *Night of the Living Dead* premiered. It became a cult classic and a landmark zombie experience. Existential dread fills zombie movies settings where nothing—not family, love, or law—will save victims from random acts of zombie annihilation. Romero's zombies were the first depiction of a flesh-eating zombie that follows its own instinct for human meat.

Summation of Spread

Are you prepared for a zombie apocalypse? Are your survival skills up to snuff? The Zombie Apocalypse Spread reveals all.

Cast Your Cards

Cast your cards quickly, before something eats your brain:

1. Running from zombies is hard work. Am I in good cardio health?
2. What is my preferred weapon of choice?
3. Who is my zombie-killing partner?
4. Do I have enough survival experience to endure?
5. Where is the best place to hole up and defend myself?
6. What supply can I not live without?
7. My mother was bit and infected—what do I do?
8. Will I make it through alive?
9. Should I repopulate the earth?

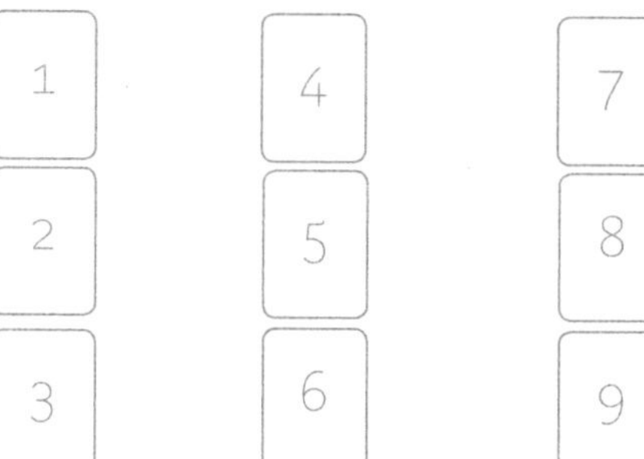

A. E. Waite's Boaz & Jachin Spread

On This Day

Arthur Edward Waite, mystic, occultist, and writer, was born today in 1857. Waite, in collaboration with Pamela Colman Smith, is responsible for the most widespread deck of tarot cards ever created, the Rider-Waite tarot, sometimes called the Waite-Smith or Rider-Waite-Smith (RWS) deck.

Summation of Spread

Waite and illustrator Pamela Colman Smith placed the symbols of Boaz and Jachin on the High Priestess card. The letters B and J stand for Boaz and Jachin, legendary pillars in King Solomon's temple. These letters have always been used to illustrate the magical concept of polarity.

Cast Your Cards

Cast in a set of pillars:

Jachin

1. Fire: Where is my passion?
2. Air: How do I think?
3. Sun: What do I do?

Boaz

4. Water: Where is my heart?
5. Earth: How do I grow?
6. Moon: What do I see?

The Rider-Waite-Smith deck was the first deck to be produced commercially in Britain. To this date it remains the world's best-selling tarot deck, setting the standard for the myriad decks to come.

The Kabbalistic Tree of Life rests on three pillars. The High Priestess figure can be understood as the middle pillar. The middle pillar represents the integration of the left and the right. The Hierophant and Justice figures also sit between two Kabalistic pillars, thus connecting tarot to the pillars of the Tree of Life.

Paul Foster Case's Mystery School Spread

Greek and Roman Mysteries were recognized public institutions in the ancient world. The two most important Western mystery schools were Dionysian, the worship of food and wine, and Eleusinian, celebrating Demeter and her daughter Persephone.

All ancient mysteries were presided over by a hierophant, an ancient Greek priest, thus connecting it to this tarot card. The Hierophant is the interpreter of sacred mysteries and arcane principles as well as the expounder of rites of worship and sacrifice.

On This Day

Paul Foster Case, occultist and author, was born on this day in 1884. Case created a modern mystery school, Builders of the Adytum (B.O.T.A.), which is still in existence to this day, offering mail-order tarot correspondence courses.

Summation of Spread

Are you ready for transformation? Mystery schools exist to provide knowledge of the nonmaterial realms. Knowledge is gained through grades, initiations, and rituals. Their symbolic structure codifies principles as well as communicates them. The lessons must be experienced in order to be understood. Mystery schools bring initiates into hidden worlds that, like dreams, can only be experienced.

Cast Your Cards

The Mystery School Spread's cards are cast in a circle, symbol of wholeness, unity, and infinity:

1. How can I transform my consciousness?
2. What specific action can I take to awaken energy in my body?
3. What dormant ability lies within me?
4. What experience do I need to have?
5. What knowledge waits for me?
6. How does my experience of life change as a result?

Gravitation Spread

On This Day

The first Earth satellite was launched into space on this day by the Soviet Union in 1957. It circled Earth every 95 minutes at almost 2,000 miles per hour, eventually falling to back to Earth three months later.

Summation of Spread

What are you drawn to? Like a satellite, you are held by the gravitational pull of certain themes repeating in your life. These themes may not be apparent early in life. Growing older, it is possible to retroactively connect the dots to see the themes emerge.

Cast Your Cards

Pay special attention to the prominent suit appearing in this spread. Cast in a circle around the first three cards, which denote your major gravitational themes.

1. First gravitational theme.
2. Second gravitational theme.
3. Third gravitational theme.
4. What places do I return to again and again?
5. What sort of friends am I attracted to?
6. What sort of romance am I attracted to?
7. What patterns make me feel comfortable?
8. Do I need to recalibrate my gravitational pull?
9. Is my gravitation leading me to authenticity?
10. What does it all add up to?

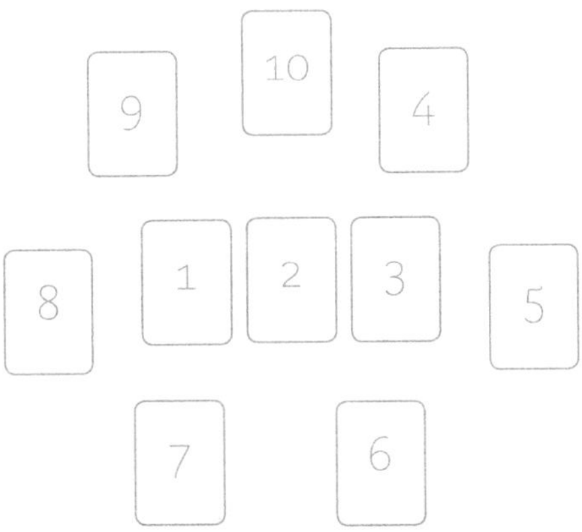

Jupiter has the heaviest gravitational pull of all the planets. A 150-pound person would weigh more than 354 pounds walking across Jupiter, while if that same person skipped across Pluto, they would weigh no more than 10 pounds.

The World card represents rotation, gravitation, and manifestation. It reminds us to pay attention to what captivates us in order to live in freedom.

Twilight's Love Triangle Spread

Meyer began writing the first draft of Twilight *upon waking from a dream of a beautiful girl and a sparkling boy lying in a meadow of flowers.*

On This Day

Twilight, the vampire novel by Stephenie Meyer, was released on this day in 2005. The story of teenage vampire love and lust ignited a generation and introduced the world to character Bella Swan. Readers divided over deciding who was the better romantic choice for Bella, vampire Edward or werewolf Jacob, and an exciting love triangle was born.

Summation of Spread

Are you tangled in a love triangle between yourself and two possible romantic choices? This spread is designed to help you make good decisions. Pulling cards, you'll reflect on the situation and uncover true feelings, followed by solid suggestions on how to proceed.

The Three of Swords represents the pain of betrayal, as in a love triangle where trust is destroyed. The Three of Pentacles depicts a working love triangle properly managed by all parties. The Three of Cups represents a love triangle with satisfied parties. The Three of Wands suggests volatile passions with no resolution in sight.

Cast Your Cards

1. Card representing myself.
2. Card representing first person.
3. Card representing second person.
4. How the first person feels about me.
5. How I feel about the first person.
6. How the second person feels about me.
7. How I feel about the second person.
8. Outcome if I choose the first person.
9. Outcome if I choose the second person.
10. Outcome if I choose neither.
11. What should I do?

Persephone's Spread

On This Day

Sundown on this day marked the Greek festival of Stenia, celebrated in honor of Demeter and Persephone. Persephone was abducted by Hades and brought to the underworld. Her mother, Demeter, refused to allow anything to grow, causing winter. Persephone was eventually released from the underworld, but not before Hades had deceived her into eating four pomegranate seeds (in some versions she willingly ate them), which ensured her return to the underworld for four months of the year.

As goddess of the underworld, Persephone speaks with ghosts and enjoys powers of necromancy. Her return to the upperworld signifies the beginning of spring.

Summation of Spread

Persephone's myth informs the questions of this spread, reflecting on the duality of her life between the upper and lower worlds.

Cast Your Cards

Cast your cards to pave a journey to the underworld and back:

1. How does my relationship with my mother inform who I am?
2. What is my greatest temptation?
3. What great lie do I believe as truth?
4. What holds me captive?
5. What sets me free?
6. How do I regenerate lost pieces of my soul?
7. How do I cultivate wisdom?
8. What do I have the power to create?
9. What am I willing to destroy?
10. How do I best maintain the balance of duality in my life?

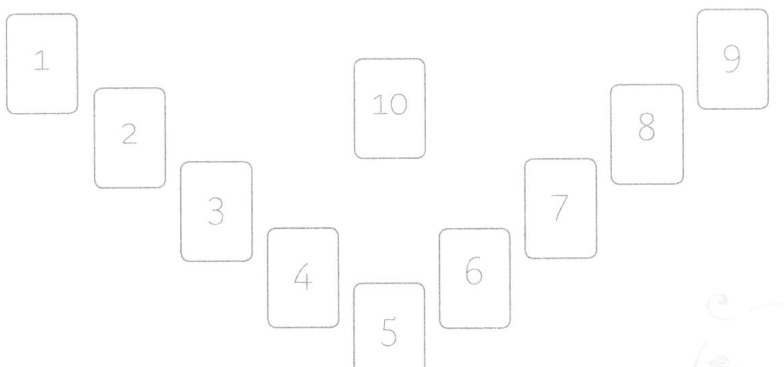

The Six of Wands depicts a celebratory parade evocative of Demeter's joy when Persephone returns as well as the general joy associated with those who've endured a long, cold winter and celebrate spring's return.

October • 7

Some scholars believe The Red Book *outlines Jung's descent into madness. Some argue he suffered a psychotic break; others argue the opposite, saying he willingly and consciously chose to embrace his unconscious.*

Jung's concept of the archetype is critical in the modern study of tarot. Understanding the major arcana as cross-cultural archetypes, it is possible to place any system of belief, dogma, or thought on top of the cards. It is a way to simultaneously understand the cards and other cultures and belief systems.

Jungian Spread

On This Day

Carl Gustav Jung's controversial ***Red Book*** was published today in 2009. ***The Red Book*** reflects a sixteen-year journey into Jung's unconscious mind. Begun in 1913, written and illustrated with psychedelic drawings, this remarkable and personal voyage of Jung's discovery finally became available for the public.

Summation of Spread

What creates the psychology of you? Jung advanced the concept of archetypes and universal ideas. He claimed each person carries five main archetypes within their unconscious. The Jungian Spread explores these concepts.

Cast Your Cards

1. Self: Who am I?
2. Shadow: What is in my dark side, the opposite of ego?
3. Anima: How do I experience the feminine?
4. Animus: How do I experience the masculine?
5. Persona: What do I present to the world?

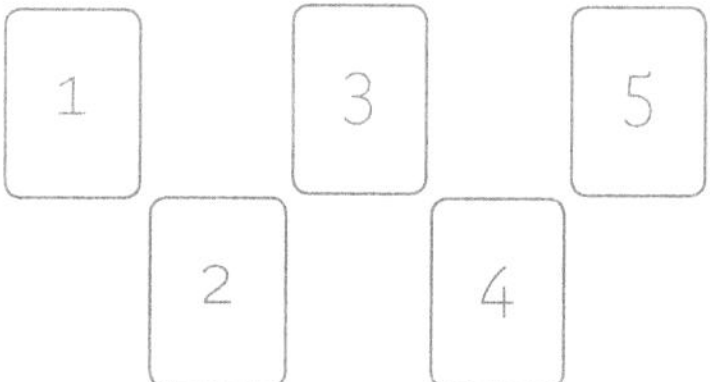

Cheiro's Lines of the Palm Spread

On This Day

Cheiro, the most famous palmist in the world, died today in 1936. Cheiro, an Irishman, devoted almost forty years to the study and practice of palmistry. Traveling through the Far East, Europe, and the United States, he perfected his knowledge of the subject.

Summation of Spread

Ready for an all-over analysis of your life? Palm reading begins with a basic examination of lines found on the palm. Size, shape, and texture are then taken into consideration. The questions of this spread come from the meanings of the lines on your palms.

Cast Your Cards

Did you know you hold the world in the palm of your hand?

1. Life Line: What is the theme of my life?
2. Head Line: Where is my mind?
3. Heart Line: What is the state of my heart?
4. Line of Mars: What is likely to happen in the near future?
5. Hepatic Line: What is my health?
6. Apollo Line: How famous and successful will I become?
7. Girdle of Venus: What is the state of my romantic relationship?

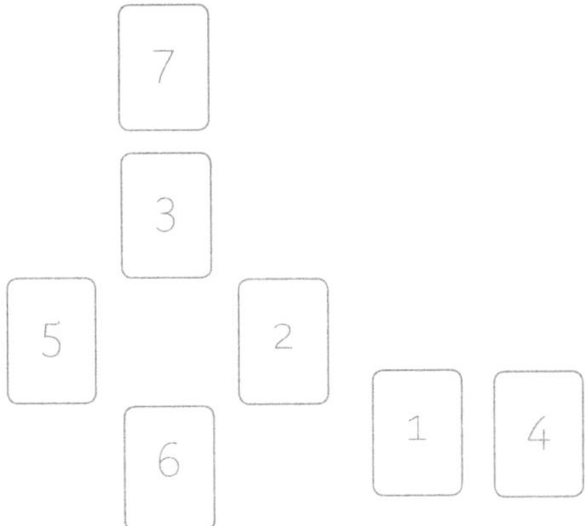

Cheiro read palms and told fortunes for many famous personalities including Mark Twain, Sarah Bernhardt, Oscar Wilde, Thomas Edison, Grover Cleveland, and the Prince of Wales.

The Ace of Pentacles relates to the art of palm reading. A pentacle rests on the palm of a hand that emerges from a mysterious cloud. Secrets and knowledge often lie in the palm of our hand. Through physical touch and examination, truths are revealed.

Supernova Spread

Supernovas aid in the formation of new stars because the shockwaves contain essential clouds of gas and heavy elements that only result from a supernova.

On This Day

The last supernova—a vast star explosion—to be seen by the naked eye was spotted on this day in northern Italy in 1604.

Summation of Spread

What in your life needs to go? An entire star is destroyed during a supernova. The questions of this spread embrace the fiery destruction of something in your life in order to facilitate new growth.

Cast Your Cards

The Supernova Spread cards are cast in a circle emanating outward from what should be destroyed.

1. What needs to end?
2. Why was it here?
3. Why must it go?
4. How do I destroy this?
5. What is a specific step to be sure I am rid of this?
6. What aids my conviction?
7. What is the final result?

The Death card echoes the lessons of galactic supernovas. The cycle of life observed on Earth repeats itself in the far reaches of outer space. The death of a star makes all life possible. Our life is made possible through the death of living things, and thus the cycle repeats through the known universe.

Depression Spread

On This Day

Ed Wood was born on this day in 1924. Best known for *Plan 9 from Outer Space*, he was the master of campy, low-budget horror movies. While battling depression, he remained incredibly prolific and obsessed with the occult till the end of his life.

Ed Wood made sexploitation and cross-genre films, but he also wrote more than eighty pulp crime, horror, and sex novels.

Summation of Spread

Does life feel hopeless? The Depression Spread takes a look at issues when feeling blue or down in the dumps. If you are ever unable to salvage yourself from depression, set the cards aside and seek professional help immediately.

Cast Your Cards

Know you are worth the time it takes to figure this out, give yourself a hug, and cast your cards:

1. How am I feeling?
2. Why am I feeling this way?
3. How can I spend more time with positive people?
4. What is one of my greatest accomplishments?
5. What am I grateful for?
6. How can I break out of my routine?
7. How can I get closer to nature?
8. What exercise do I enjoy?
9. What one single, small action I can take to feel better?

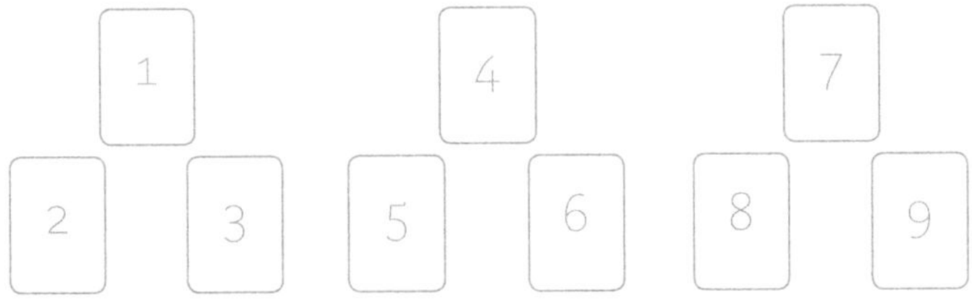

The Five of Cups can represent depression. The figure's black cloak suggests sadness, distrust, and gloomy thoughts. The overturned cups are the perception of what is lost. The background bridge is a symbol of hope, passage, and the distinct possibility of moving forward.

Make a Difference Spread

Eleanor Roosevelt advocated for women's rights long before the women's rights movement began. Remaining active in politics long after her husband's death, she was the first chair on the UN's Commission on Human Rights.

The Queen of Wands is not afraid or intimidated in standing up for her ideals and ideas of what is right. Sensing a challenge, she'll rise to the occasion. Tireless and passionate, she provokes great change in philanthropic and social arenas.

On This Day

Eleanor Roosevelt was born on this day in 1884. She was the first presidential spouse to hold press conferences, write a syndicated column, and speak at a national convention. Her outspokenness on racial issues and women's rights made her a controversial First Lady.

Summation of Spread

You have more of an effect on the world than you may realize. Roosevelt's human rights work, pedigree, and accomplishments may seem intimidating to live up to, but you can make a difference in your own backyard. Touching one life, you change a world.

Cast Your Cards

1. How do I want to make a difference?
2. How can I make the world a better place?
3. What talent or quality do I possess to help others?
4. How much time can I dedicate to a cause?
5. What is a realistic goal?
6. Where should I begin?
7. What change occurs as a result?
8. What action can I take today to make the world better?

Aleister Crowley's Reincarnation Spread

On This Day

Aleister Crowley, the world's most famous ceremonial magician and influential occultist, was born on this day in 1875.

Summation of Spread

Crowley believed himself to be the reincarnation of mystic Eliphas Levi because he was born the same day Levi died. This spread digs into your past lives to discover who you were and what you did. Repeat for as many lives as you like.

Cast Your Cards

1. Who was I in a past life?
2. Where did I live?
3. Was I happy?
4. Who was my soulmate?
5. Is it the same soulmate from this life?
6. Did I have children?
7. What did I do for a living?
8. How did I die?
9. What was my life's lesson?
10. What do I need to learn in this life?

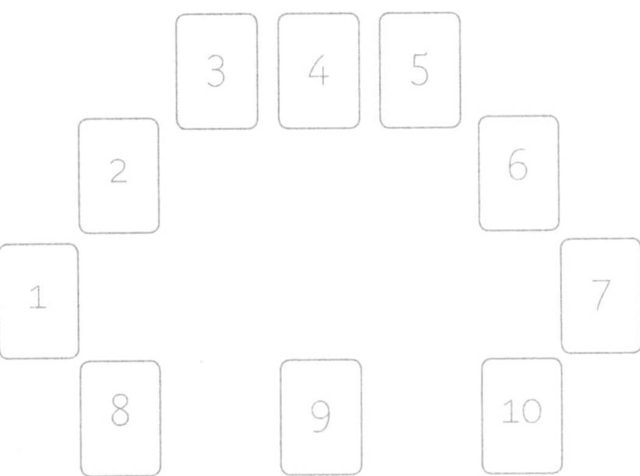

Crowley envisioned a female equivalent in his magical work, a high priestess partnership. Referring to her as a Scarlet Woman, he believed the concept of sacred prostitution had been warped and sought to restore it.

History refers to Crowley as the "wickedest man in the world." The Devil operates with no limits and no restraints. Crowley craved a world free from the obsession of fear and sin. Delighting in shocking the public, he remains to this day an infamous, fiendishly devilish historical figure.

Qualities of Mars Spread

The Egyptians called Mars Har decher, *"the red one"; Babylonians called it Nergal, "star of death"; Hebrews called it* Ma'adim, *"one who blushes"; and the Greeks called it Ares after the god of war.*

Both the Tower card and Mars are symbols of masculinity, sexuality, energy, fire, passion, and destruction. The Tower card often depicts upheaval and dramatic change. Renewal and purification come in the wake of the Tower's rumbling destruction.

On This Day

Dutch astronomer Christiaan Huygens describes and draws the bog on Mars called Sytris Major on this day in 1659. The Roman god Mars is known for sex, war, courage, passion, and strength.

Summation of Spread

This spread contains questions based on astrological associations of the planet Mars. Using these associations, questions are posed to offer greater clarity in your life.

Cast Your Cards

Cast in the shape of an upward arrow as seen in the Mars symbol:

1. Sex: What is the state of my sex life?
2. War: Am I fighting against myself?
3. Courage: What causes me to be brave?
4. Combustion: What makes me feel like exploding?
5. Progression: Where do I need to forge progress?
6. Energy: How do I best maintain my energetic resources?
7. Assertiveness: What helps me to be assertive?
8. Daring: What should I take a chance on?

Mary Greer's Breaking Barriers Spread

On This Day

Mary Greer—tarot pioneer, author, and teacher—was born this day in 1947. She has kindly offered a spread for inclusion on this day, when Chuck Yeager broke the sound barrier on October 14, 1947 (the day and year Mary was born). Launch occurred at 10:26 AM in Southern California and lasted five minutes. It marked a major milestone in the history of aeronautics, for—as PBS's *Nova* phrased it—"the sound barrier was no longer a barrier after all."

The sound a bullwhip makes when it cracks is actually a sonic boom. It was the first human invention to break the sound barrier.

Summation of Spread

This spread helps you break your own barrier. The energy you yourself create tends to get ahead of you, blocking your ability to move through to the next level of experience.

Cast Your Cards

1. What is your particular barrier?
2. What do you hope to discover or achieve by breaking through it?
3. How does this barrier get in your way?
4. What pressure or loss of control must you withstand?
5. What improvements will help you break through?
6. What's the worst that can happen?
7. What do you actually find on the other side?
8. How can this breakthrough help you in the future?

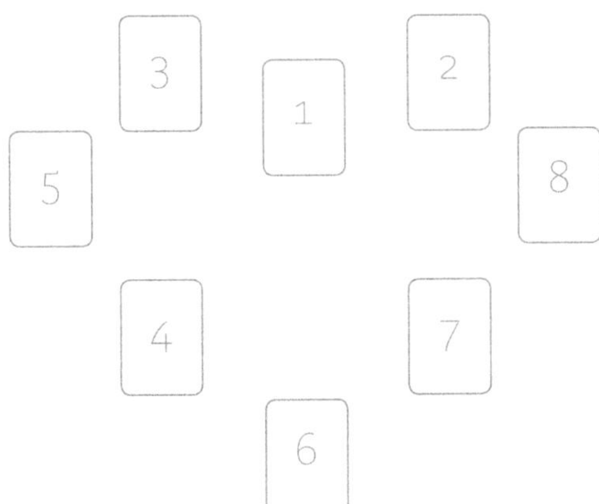

Breaking the sound barrier was a major breakthrough that set the stage for space travel: a vehicle moving through the stars. The Chariot and the Star represent human ingenuity, science, and both the vision and will to move forward despite the odds. They represent meeting challenges and achieving our highest goals.

Time Management Spread

Planning and goal setting are the most productive way to improve and use time effectively.

The Wheel of Fortune, like gray hairs or wrinkles on cheeks, is a reminder that time is a precious commodity that stops for no one. The Wheel of Fortune reminds us to use the gift of time as best we can.

On This Day

The Gregorian calendar, the universal calendar system used today, was introduced and went into effect in Roman Catholic countries on this day in 1582. The pope implemented the Gregorian calendar due to the church's desire to keep Easter near the spring equinox.

Summation of Spread

Do you have enough time or does it seem to slip through your fingers? While Pope Gregory XIII was able to reconstruct time itself, it can be hard enough to schedule daily responsibilities, let alone make time for things that really count. The Time Management Spread examines time issues.

Cast Your Cards

1. How can I work less and achieve more?
2. What do I want to spend my time doing?
3. What will I regret not doing?
4. What is my biggest time suck?
5. How can I change my behavior?
6. Should I create a new routine?
7. What will help me do so?
8. What help is available that I am overlooking?
9. What enjoyable activity makes me forget about time?

Picture of Dorian Gray Spread

On This Day

Oscar Wilde, Irish literary legend, was born on this day in 1854.

Summation of Spread

The Picture of Dorian Gray, the only published novel by Wilde, is the story of a fashionable young man who sells his soul for eternal youth and beauty. The story's themes inform this spread's questions. It asks you to consider your thoughts and opinions on art, beauty, and influence.

Cast Your Cards

Cast your cards in the shape of a magic mirror:

1. What is the purpose of art?
2. Why is beauty important?
3. Why is modern culture superficial?
4. Who is influencing me at the moment?
5. Do I flee reality with drugs or alcohol?
6. What tortures my consciousness?
7. What helps me maintain a sense of humor?

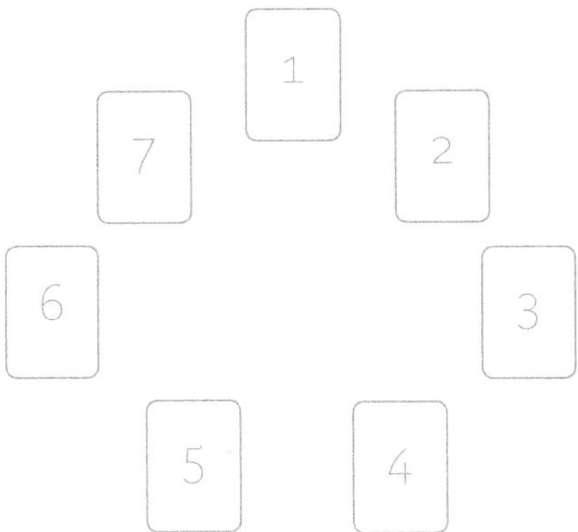

Wilde was renowned for having a razor-sharp wit. Purportedly his last words were, "My wallpaper and I are fighting a duel to the death. One or the other of us has got to go."

The Star card springs forth wells of eternal youth, represented in the flowing waters indicative of water-bearer Aquarius. The Star reminds you to stay open to inspiration and art so you are young at heart no matter your physical age.

Chartres's Sacred Labyrinth/ Higher Self Spread

The circumference of Chartres's labyrinth is 131 feet, almost the exact same size as the west rose window in the cathedral. It is also the same distance from the entrance as the west rose is from the floor. If the west wall fell, the rose would lie precisely upon the labyrinth.

The Eight of Cups is the beginning of a sacred or spiritual journey. The figure abandons all things behind him and makes his way up the mountain in search of enlightenment.

On This Day

France's world-famous Chartres Cathedral was consecrated on this day in 1260 in the presence of King Saint-Louis. Its stone floor still bears an ancient labyrinth used for walking meditations and contemplations.

Summation of Spread

Have you met your higher self? A labyrinth both creates and protects its center, allowing entry only upon certain terms. Entry is thus initiation; it is a step on the path of knowledge. This spread is inspired by elements that make up sacred labyrinths.

Cast Your Cards

Cast your cards in the shape of a winding maze:

1. Goal: What is my goal?
2. Gateway: How do I begin my journey?
3. Boundary Wall: What must I pass?
4. Branches: How should I extend myself?
5. Dead End: What gets me nowhere?
6. Fork: What decision must I make?
7. Room: What surprises meet me?
8. Outcome: What happens as a result of my journey?

Future Lover Spread

St. Luke is the patron saint of artists, students, physicians, surgeons, and butchers.

On This Day

Today is St. Luke's Day in Great Britain. Traditionally, girls gain insight into future marriage prospects today. The ritual is simple and good for the skin. Before jumping into bed, girls place a mixture of spices, honey, and vinegar onto their face, then recite the following rhyme:

St. Luke, St. Luke, be kind to me,
In dreams let me my true love see.

Summation of Spread

Who is your future love? This spread draws upon the energy of St. Luke's Day. Peek into your sensual future and discover what delicious treat of a love interest is heading your way—or who is already here.

Cast Your Cards

Get ready for the roller coaster ride and cast your cards.

1. Who is my future lover?
2. Are they already in my life?
3. How will I know when I have met them?
4. How do I draw them closer to me?
5. Will we be good for each other?
6. Will they open new worlds for me?
7. Will we be together for a long time?

The Lovers card connects to all love spreads. One of the card's main themes is choice. What choices are you making in your love life? Are you choosing the best relationship for yourself? Are your choices based on your wants, needs, and desires or those of another?

Knight's Spread

In early kingdoms, a page would become squire to a knight and would then train under them.

On This Day

Today marks the ancient Roman festival of Armilstrium, in honor of Mars, god of war. Soldiers were celebrated and their weapons ritually purified while processions moved through the streets.

Summation of Spread

Knights are the soldiers of tarot, each representing a particular type of searching, seeking, and adventuring. Each moves at the pace matching their suit. This spread makes use of their exploratory qualities by sending them out on missions for you.

Cast Your Cards

This spread is not based on a question; rather, each pair of cards plays upon a quality of the knight's suit. Remove all knights from your deck and place them in the center of your spread. Cast your randomly drawn cards face-down. Read a suggested question aloud, then flip the corresponding card for your answer.

1. Following my passion, what is in front of me?
2. What surprise awaits?
3. Following my heart, what is in front of me?
4. What surprise awaits?
5. Following my senses, what is in front of me?
6. What surprise awaits?
7. Following my curiosity, what is in front of me?
8. What surprise awaits?

Knights in readings suggest immediate action, energy, or people. They often carry messages, the subject of which is usually found in an accompanying card. Knights add a sense of urgency; when one appears, get ready for action.

Devil Card Spread

On This Day

Bela Lugosi, who immortalized the role of Dracula in the film of the same name, was born on this day in 1882.

Summation of Spread

Dracula is but one manifestation of the Devil figure in literature and popular culture. This spread is based on images found on the Devil card.

Cast Your Cards

Use this spread to answer any question. Format your question before casting the spread or simply let the cards answer the questions posed. Pull the Devil card from your deck. Place it in the center of the spread and cast your cards around it.

1. Inverted Pentagram: How am I different?
2. Hand Gesture: Where have I been misled?
3. Lovers: Whom do I dominate?
4. Nudity: Where am I most vulnerable?
5. Chains: What binds me?
6. Torch: What passion burns at my soul?
7. Bat Wings: What has gone awry?
8. Horns: Where do my animalistic instincts lead me?

The Visconti-Sforza deck, the oldest tarot deck in existence, lacks a Devil card. No one knows if he was omitted, has been lost, or was simply never thought of. The major arcana of the Visconti-Sforza cards is unnumbered; therefore, the mystery may never be solved.

The Devil represents power and control issues within oneself and in relation to the people and situations surrounding you. While the Devil can be a rip-roaring good time, it must be tempered with a dose of sanity or you may risk being carried away.

Temperance Card Spread

Temperance is one of the seven cardinal virtues. The angel depicted on the Temperance card is archangel Michael.

The Temperance card is about conscious flow. It is the effort required while sustaining, mixing, matching, and maintaining equilibrium in life. While the World denotes an effortless flow, Temperance is aware of her energy and situation. The master mixologist, Temperance is actively manipulating her magic to set herself on her true path.

On This Day

Today in 1925, the US Treasury Department announced it had fined 29,620 people for alcohol violations during Prohibition.

Summation of Spread

Prohibition, spurned by the Temperance Movement, connects to the Temperance card. This spread is based on symbols found on the Temperance card.

Cast Your Cards

Use this spread to answer any question. Format your question before casting the spread or simply let the cards answer the questions posed. Pull the Temperance card from your deck. Place it in the center of the spread and cast your cards around it.

1. Wings: What is my true potential?
2. Lilies: What is my passion?
3. Crown: What do I know?
4. Path: What direction must I go in?
5. Mountain: What is my challenge?
6. Mixing Fluid: How do I go with the flow?
7. Foot In Water: Am I connected to my unconscious?
8. Foot On Land: How do I ground myself?
9. Glowing Crown: What is attainable?

Jean-Paul Sartre's Existential Questions Spread

During World War II, Sartre worked as a meteorologist for the French army. He was captured by German troops and spent nine months as a prisoner of war.

On This Day

French philosopher, playwright, novelist, and activist Jean-Paul Sartre was awarded the Nobel Prize in Literature on this day in 1964. He declined this honor, becoming the first person in history to do so. Sartre is a brilliant mind in a long line of European existentialists.

Summation of Spread

Who are you? The word *existential* combines the words *essence, essential,* and *exist*. The word itself questions the essence of existence, which is done when performing this spread.

Cast Your Cards

Ponder the questions philosophers have asked for eons and cast this spread in the shape of an *X*:

1. What is the meaning of existence?
2. What is my true identity?
3. What is death?
4. Is there a Godhead/greater power?
5. How can I know what is right or wrong?
6. What is consciousness?
7. What is happiness?
8. What does it mean to be authentic?

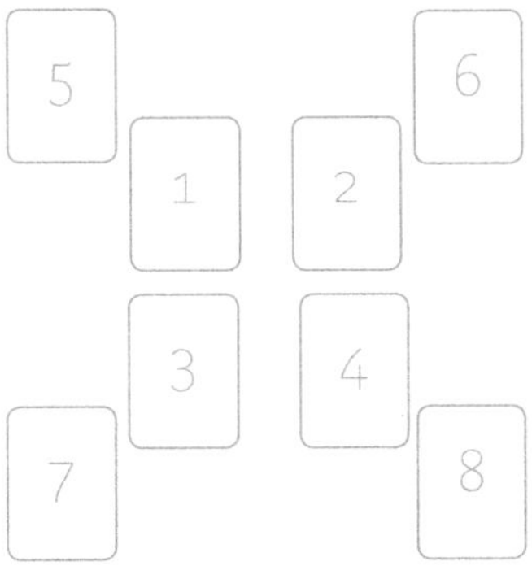

The Hanged Man is the philosopher's card due to his willingness to turn upside down, transcend consciousness, and examine life from a different point of view. He makes for an ideal contemplation of who we are and what it means to be human.

October • 23

Pluto and Mars are Scorpio's ruling planets, the primary color is red, the lucky day is Tuesday, and the best locations for success are near the water. Scorpio rules the eighth house of the zodiac, governing sex, death, joint resources, and other people's money.

Scorpio is connected to the Death card. Death represents change, intensity, and transformation—exactly what the sign of Scorpio radiates. Death clears the way so new opportunities, growth, and expansion occur.

Qualities of Scorpio Spread

On This Day

Today marks the first day of the sign of Scorpio, the scorpion.

Summation of Spread

This spread is based on essential qualities of Scorpio: powerful, emotional, determined, magnetic, sensual, and loyal.

Cast Your Cards

Cast in the shape of a scorpion's claw:

1. How do I best exert power?
2. How do my emotions serve me?
3. What can I accomplish when I am determined?
4. Who and what is attracted to me right now?
5. What makes me feel sensual?
6. What is my best quality as a friend?

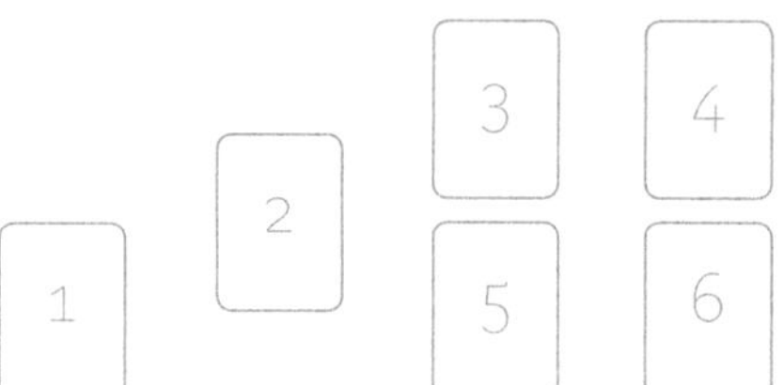

Wedding Planning Spread

On This Day

On this day in 1441, Francesco Sforza married Bianca Maria Visconti in Cremona, Italy. In honor of this wedding of Milano nobility, the Visconti-Sforza deck of tarot cards, the oldest surviving deck, was commissioned by Bianca's father as a wedding gift.

Bianca was betrothed to Francesco at the age of six; he was thirty years old at the time. Their marriage, performed when she was sixteen, was a political move to keep Sforza's power tied to Milan.

Summation of Spread

This spread uses Italian nobility as inspiration for a wedding spread. Questions address the planning of the big day to help the bride and groom make the most informed decisions.

Cast Your Cards

Cast the cards as you might throw rice or rose petals onto a happy couple:

1. What is the tone of our wedding?
2. Should we hire a wedding planner?
3. Who is our support system?
4. What helps us balance the budget?
5. What helps us get organized?
6. What will the weather be like?
7. How can we best manage conflicting personalities?
8. How can we best stay relaxed?
9. How can we make sure to enjoy the day?
10. What special aspect should we indulge in?

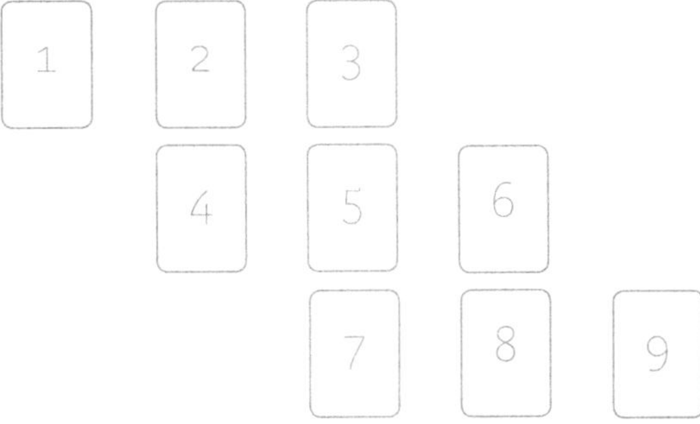

The Four of Wands represents a wedding ceremony. The draped flowers and ivy are similar to the *chuppah*, a traditional Jewish wedding canopy. The Four of Wands represents a time of fulfillment or satisfaction, but it is only momentary. There is more to come.

Pablo Picasso's Creativity Spread

Picasso was extremely superstitious. No umbrellas were to be opened in the house (thought to bring evil), no hats on the bed (fear of death within the year), and he refused to donate clothing (for fear his genius would be stolen by the wearer of his garments).

Three is the number of creativity in tarot and all mystical and occult practices. Three represents the synthesis of two opposites and the birth of something new. A three appearing in a reading—be it the Empress or the three of any suit—represents the pure creativity of that suit.

On This Day

Pablo Picasso, perhaps the most recognizable figure of twentieth-century art, was born this day in 1881. Picasso is known for defining revolutionary movements in painting, sculpture, printmaking, and ceramics. No painter before him enjoyed such a mass audience in their lifetime, and the mention of his name is synonymous with the idea of creativity.

Summation of Spread

Thinking about a new creative path or project? This spread is for you. Whether adapting a new creative practice or picking up an old art form, this spread explores avenues of thought as the creative juices start flowing.

Cast Your Cards

1. Card representing my creative activity.
2. How do I create a routine for creativity?
3. What specific daily action will I take toward my creativity?
4. How do I let go of the idea of perfectionism?
5. How do I create boundaries between my work and the opinions of others?
6. What interesting changes occur as a result of my creative path?
7. What new thing do I learn?
8. What do I create?

Find Your Voice Spread

On This Day

The Village Voice, a bohemian weekly paper, is first published on this day in 1955. Originally started in a two-bedroom apartment, its groundbreaking journalism and cultural commentary make this a classic New York paper.

Summation of Spread

Who are you? Finding your voice means exercising personal authenticity, cultivating your personal truth, and not doing things because others expect you to. It is the act of moving in the truth of what you want to do, feel, and express. While your voice evolves and changes as you grow and transform, this spread takes a look at what is unique, special, and can only be expressed through you.

Cast Your Cards

1. Who am I?
2. Why am I here?
3. What do I love?
4. What do I dislike?
5. What do I repress about myself?
6. How can I stop repressing it?
7. How can I reconnect with myself?
8. What must be expressed?
9. What do I need to do?

If there is a desire for expression but confusion on how it can be accomplished, do anything to release tension. Don't hold back. Try dancing, writing, singing, a sport, or any physical activity.

The World card stands as the shining ideal of a fully actualized and expressed human being. Completely comfortable in her skin, fulfillment and pride shine through. The World card is the ultimate confirmation of self-worth springing from inside a soul.

Volunteering Spread

Volunteers experience a "helper's high," a rush of euphoria followed by a longer-lasting period of improved emotional well-being.

On This Day

Mother Teresa was awarded the Nobel Peace Prize on this day in 1979 for her humanitarian work, particularly regarding the plight of refugees and children.

Summation of Spread

Are you looking for a way to give back? Often the desire to volunteer occurs before knowing where to donate your time. Mother Teresa inspires this spread, created to help you move in the right direction when you want to volunteer. This spread helps find the best altruistic situation for yourself.

Cast Your Cards

Cast with care and love. Any act of kindness, no matter how small, affects someone.

1. What segment of the population do I want to help?
2. What am I good at?
3. How much time do I have to dedicate?
4. Am I capable of making a commitment?
5. How can I best be of service?
6. What volunteer work am I well suited for?
7. What organization should I reach out to?

The Six of Pentacles connects to financial generosity, while the Six of Cups depicts gifts of the heart from one soul to another. The cups on the card are full of flowers. These flowers represent further growth resulting from acts of love and kindness.

School Spread

On This Day

Harvard University opened its hallowed doors on this day in 1636. The first institute of higher learning in the New World, by 1642 there were nine graduates and in other years, even less.

Summation of Spread

Are you or someone you know applying to school? From preschools to colleges, school applications and selections can be challenging and frustrating, with so much riding on the decision. The School Spread narrows your choices, highlighting good picks and pointing you in the right direction.

Cast Your Cards

Cards 1 and 4 represent choices available to the student; adjust the number of cards based on how many choices you have made. Be sure to name the school in advance of flipping the card.

1. First school choice (this card represents the school's general atmosphere and how it fits the student).
2. Chances for acceptance.
3. Student's overall experience there.
4. Second school choice(this card represents the school's general atmosphere and how it fits the student).
5. Chances for acceptance.
6. Student's overall experience there.
7. Student's strengths.
8. Student's challenges.
9. Best way to support and love the student.

Just like Hogwarts, Harvard freshmen are sorted into houses. Each of the twelve Harvard houses has its own residence hall, gym, dining, and common areas. Freshmen can choose to be sorted with up to eight friends so they won't end up with strangers.

Pages all connect to study and education. The Page of Pentacles is especially associated with studiousness and higher learning. The page's love for the physical world, natural curiosity, and concern regarding tangible change make for an ideal student.

October • 29

Feline Mystery Spread

Sir Isaac Newton, discoverer of the law of gravity, also invented the cat door—although this may be an early urban legend.

On This Day

Today is National Cat Day, created to celebrate felines, educate the public about cats needing rescue from shelters, and to honor the love and companionship the cat/owner relationship provides.

Summation of Spread

Are you catlike? Cat symbolism ranges from devilish to godly. Representing a dualistic place in human culture from their first moments of domestication, the Feline Mystery Spread uses feline qualities found inside a person to inform its questions.

Cast Your Cards

Cast in the shape of cat ears:

1. What is tame in me?
2. What is my most ferocious quality?
3. Do people find me aloof?
4. How do I locate myself in the here and now?
5. How can I be entirely self-sufficient?
6. What do I do when no one is looking?
7. Who do I want to be affectionate with?
8. What do I want to explore?

The Queen of Wands is pictured with a black cat sitting at her delicate feet. This cat is a symbol of the fierce female power coursing through this queen—a nod to her magical power and prowess belonging to the suit of Wands.

Paranoia Spread

On This Day

Orson Wells broadcasts the radio play of H. G. Wells's *War of the Worlds* on this night in 1938. Amidst the tensions and anxiety leading up to World War II, some listeners thought it was a real news broadcast, especially the ones who missed parts of it. Thinking the earth was being invaded by aliens, real-life panic ensued.

During the War of the Worlds *broadcast, some listeners poured into the streets, some headed to church, and others ran to spend their last hours with friends and family.*

Summation of Spread

Are you feeling a little nuts? This spread is not for someone suffering serious paranoia. It is crafted for those times an obsessive or randomly crazy thought becomes lodged in our head and we are convinced the worst will happen. The questions help you see your way out of it.

Cast Your Cards

1. The situation as it stands.
2. Why is this freaking me out?
3. Why do I worry the worst will happen?
4. What control do I have over the outcome?
5. What fact must I keep in mind?
6. What is the truth of the situation?
7. What helps me to stop thinking this way?
8. What positive truth can I focus on?

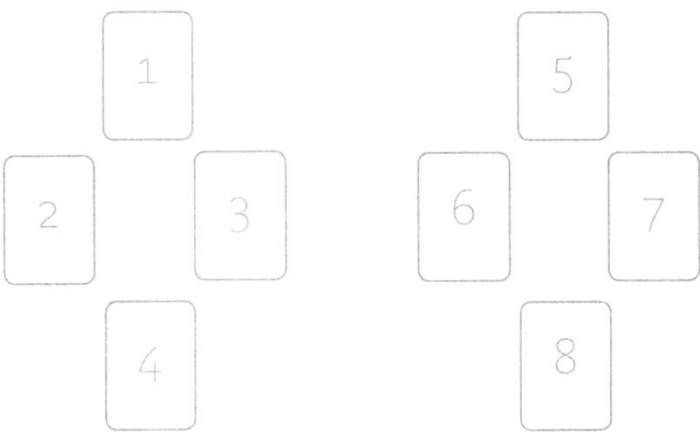

The Nine of Swords represents tortured thoughts. Fear and anxiety is created by her mind, not actual circumstance. Her blanket is covered in astrological symbols, representing myriad narratives that lie outside her mind. It is a reminder that while everyone faces fear and uncertainty, it is important not to become immobilized by it.

Halloween Year Ahead Spread

It was believed spirits roamed the earth and played tricks on this night. Treats were given to appease mischievous sprites, and hollowed jack-o'-lanterns were illuminated to scare malicious spirits away. This paved the way for modern practices.

Tarot is an intermediary device and metaphysical machine used to communicate with other worlds. Whether conversing with a ghost or spirit or speaking with the personal private psyche and inner voice, the entire deck is a testament to this wonderful holiday and all the supernatural magic filling it.

On This Day

For many, tonight is the most delicious night of the year. Tarot card readers, witches, spooks, spirits, and all manner of supernatural creatures party today. The veil between living and dead is thinnest, it is the most auspicious night for divination, chocolate and candy are doled out to offset tricks, and everyone gets a chance to pretend they are someone or something else.

Summation of Spread

What do the next twelve months have in store? Samhain, the ancient Gaelic festival, is the New Year for Witches and Pagans. Marking the end of the harvest season and the beginning of winter, the darker half of the year, it is an excellent time to take stock of what the twelve months ahead have in store for you.

Cast Your Cards

1. You
2. November
3. December
4. January
5. February
6. March
7. April
8. May
9. June
10. July
11. August
12. September
13. October
14. What should I focus on?
15. What should I reject?
16. What magic is possible?

Speak to the Dead Spread

On This Day

On this day in Mexico and in other Latin cultures the Day of the Dead is celebrated, often by building an altar to the deceased inside one's home and inviting guests. The day's rituals were born over 3,000 years ago by Aztecs and Mesoamerican civilizations. Catholic culture named today All Saints Day.

Summation of Spread

Have you ever spoken with the dead? Use tarot as a communication tool with the other side on this auspicious day. Choose to speak to a random spirit or meditate specifically on a soul you would like to speak to.

Cast Your Cards

Feel free to improvise your own questions as you see fit. Cast your cards in a spirit circle:

1. Who is here with me?
2. How did you die?
3. Why are you here?
4. What is it like to be dead?
5. What message do you want to convey?
6. What do I need to know?

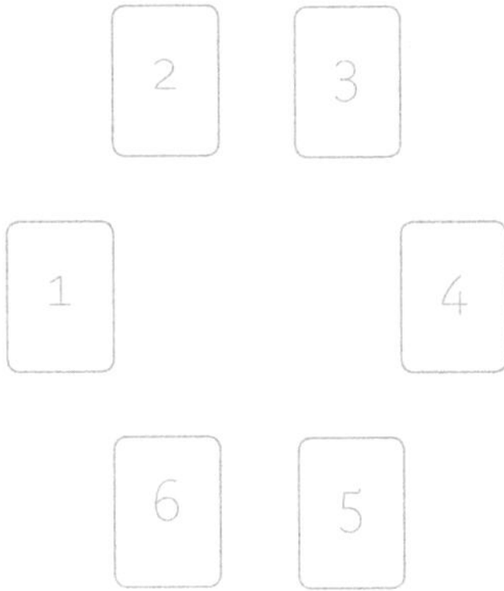

Mexican families clean the graves of their ancestors and decorate them with food, candles, and flowers. Staying up all night, they talk about the deceased; some even hire musicians to stroll through the boneyard playing their ancestors' favorite music.

The Judgement card depicts the dead rising from their graves. It is a reference to rebirth on both the highest and deepest imaginable levels. Change is sure to follow.

Break Out of a Rut Spread

Years ago, Catholics dedicated the entire month of November to praying for the souls in purgatory. Almsgiving (donating money and food to the poor) and acts of penance were said to reduce the time a soul spent in purgatory.

On This Day

The Roman Catholic Church dedicates today to all the souls currently residing in purgatory. Purgatory is generally understood as the boundary between heaven and hell; it is the temporary and often uncomfortable waiting place for those souls who need purification before entering heaven.

Summation of Spread

Do you feel stuck? In a general sense, purgatory is understood as a waiting place or waiting room before heaven. The questions of this spread are based on the idea of being stuck in earthly limbo. The questions are designed to help you break free.

The Six of Pentacles reflects almsgiving, helping others. When this card appears in a reading, discover which character you identify with. Are you the almsgiver or the figure accepting the coins?

Cast Your Cards

Cast as a lifeline up and out of a tedious waiting room:

1. What am I avoiding?
2. What am I gaining by remaining in stasis?
3. Do I blame others for my circumstance?
4. How is fear affecting my decisions?
5. What beliefs do I cling to that are no longer true?
6. How do I break out of this rut?
7. What specific opportunities should I look for?
8. How do I take a small, meaningful step forward?

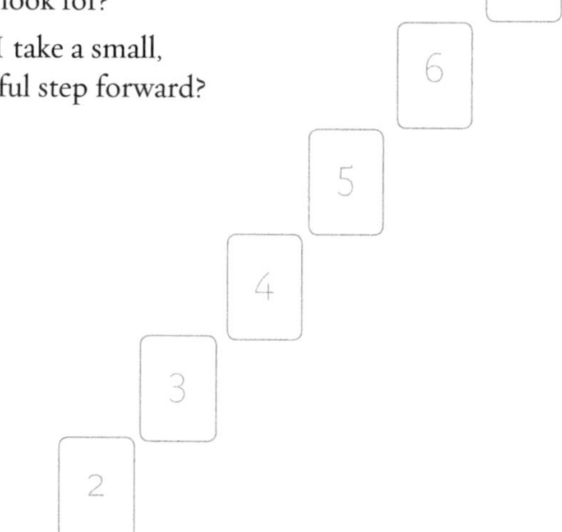

Chariot Card Spread

A careful examination of the RWS Chariot card reveals crescent moon–shaped shoulder straps supporting the profile of the human face on each of the charioteer's shoulders

On This Day

The first National Automobile Show opened in Madison Square Garden today in 1900. Thirty-one car makers put exciting new vehicles on display while men with top hats and women twirling parasols strolled among new vehicles that didn't include a horse.

Summation of Spread

Cars and all forms of vehicles are a literal translation of the Chariot card. This spread is based on symbols found in the Chariot card.

Cast Your Cards

Use this spread to answer any question. Format your question before casting the spread or simply let the cards answer the questions posed. Pull the Chariot card from your deck. Place it in the center of the spread and cast your cards around it as follows:

1. Lunar Breastplates: What is changing?
2. Crown: Where do I find dignity?
3. Laurel: Why will I be victorious?
4. Sphinxes: What are my choices?
5. Curtains: How do I connect with higher spirit?
6. Carriage Column: Where is my stability?
7. Winged Symbol: How do I fly?
8. City: What have I built?

The Chariot represents a person filled with motivation who achieves success due to personal labor and ingenuity. With its sense of forward motion, the Chariot stresses the ability to take the reins of any situation and stay firmly in the driver's seat. A sense of direction and ability is implied.

November • 4

Election Day falls on a Tuesday for travel reasons dating before the invention of the car. In the days of horse travel, a Tuesday voting day allowed for worship on Sunday, a ride to the county seat on Monday, voting on Tuesday, and then back before market day on Wednesday.

The Six of Cups represents an environment where people actively participate in civic duty. The town is protected by strong walls, representing a solid community and protection. The cups burst with flowers, a symbol that something has manifested, while warm clothing offers protection for the children, who freely give and receive love.

Civic Duty Spread

On This Day

United States' general elections for public officials fall on the first Tuesday in November, often on this date. Early November was a good fit between harvest time and brutal winter weather.

Summation of Spread

Are you an active community member? Civic duties are the social responsibility of citizens in the interest of public service. Civic duty is more than just voting, paying taxes, and serving on jury duty. The actions we take in between elections are equally, if not more, important.

Cast Your Cards

1. Do I understand how government works?
2. What do I think about political culture?
3. Can I participate in community service?
4. How do I advocate for those who need help?
5. How do I make my community a better place?
6. How can I improve the quality of life at a grassroots level?
7. What can I do for my community right now?

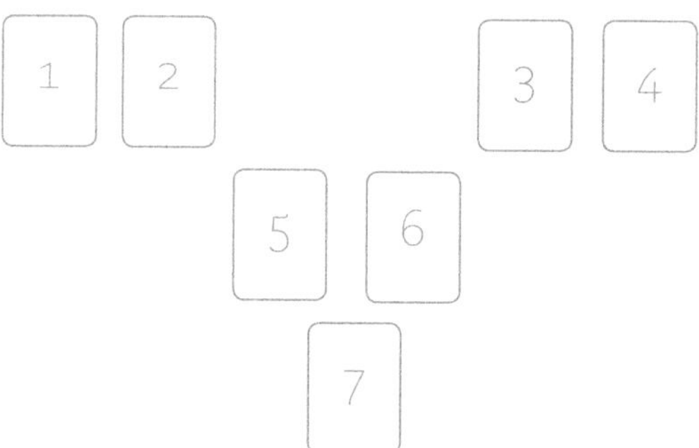

Fawkes's Change the Situation Spread

Bonfire Night is celebrated with raging bonfires, roasting marshmallows and sausages on sticks, and explosive fireworks in the cold November sky.

On This Day

Today is Guy Fawkes Day and Bonfire Night in Britain. It celebrates the infamous Gunpowder Plot of 1605 in which a group of Catholics attempted to blow up English Parliament and assassinate King James. Guy Fawkes was caught attempting to light the fuse on thirty-six barrels of gunpowder.

Summation of Spread

Are you ready to ignite an idea? This spread uses revolutionary action, albeit a failed one, to inspire a spread based on creating change. Perform this spread when ready take a grand step or make a grand gesture in the vein of changing your life.

Cast Your Cards

Anticipate your glorious outcome and cast as follows:

1. Situation as it stands.
2. Why must it change?
3. What do I want?
4. What challenges me?
5. What supports me?
6. What drastic action must I take?
7. What happens if I do nothing?
8. What will be the outcome?

The Seven of Swords connects with acts of conspiracy. The figure sneaks away from an encampment; is he creeping away forever or will he return to shake things up? When this card appears in a spread, it heralds a time of moving forward and taking only what is needed.

Hanged Man Spread

The Hanged Man and his mode of being upside down is a symbol of initiation, the transition between one state of consciousness and another. This sacrifice leads to growth, progress, and understanding.

The Hanged Man expresses a moment of difficulty, of pain and the inability to act. This is temporary, and his position is entered into voluntarily and knowingly. It is a necessary step for growth and evolution.

On This Day

Confucius's birthday is celebrated today in Vietnam. Confucius and other philosophers are prized for viewing the world through a different set of eyes than most. Alternative views align philosophers with the Hanged Man, card of artists, mystics, and seers.

Summation of Spread

This spread is based on symbols found in the Hanged Man card.

Cast Your Cards

Use this spread to answer any question. Format your question before casting the spread or simply let the cards answer the questions posed. Pull the Hanged Man card from your deck. Place it in the center of the spread and cast your cards around it as follows:

1. Gallows/Cross: What are the boundaries of my state of existence?
2. Leg Position: What crossroads am I at?
3. Arms: Over what am I powerless?
4. Halo: How am I charismatic?
5. Foliage: What am I growing?
6. Serene Face: What insight do I need to know?
7. Ropes Binding Feet: How can I give up the struggle?
8. Upside Down: What issue needs reevaluation?

Hermit Card Spread

On This Day

Albert Camus, French philosopher and author of literary classics *The Stranger*, *The Fall*, and *The Plague*, was born on this day in 1913.

Summation of Spread

The intellectual and philosophical answering of one's innermost questions is a journey that must be embarked upon alone. This process is connected with the Hermit card. The Hermit Card Spread is based on symbolism found within the Hermit card.

Cast Your Cards

Use this spread to answer any question. Format your question before casting the spread or simply let the cards answer the questions posed. Pull the Hermit card from your deck. Place it in the center of the spread and cast your cards around it as follows:

1. Cloak: Can I remain still?
2. Staff: What helps me move forward?
3. Lantern: What protects me?
4. Star: What truth do I share?
5. Mountain Top: What challenge have I overcome?
6. Mountain Range: What challenge do I face?
7. Beard: What wisdom do I possess?
8. Age: What does experience illuminate?

The Hermit's loneliness is not due to fear of the world. He uses solitude in his search for enlightenment. He listens by embracing silence and knows people by first knowing himself. Facts are not enough for the Hermit; he strives to understand and internalize everything before him.

The Hermit represents solitude, philosophy, and reflection. Seeking a retreat from distractions, he detaches from material objects, seeks a higher spirituality, and arrives at his answers by himself. He is respected as a master.

Bram Stoker wrote twelve novels, including Dracula, *which was originally titled* The Undead.

Vampire's Immortality Spread

On This Day

Bram Stoker, whose first full name was Abraham, was born in Dublin on this day in 1847. He redefined the vampire myth with his epic gothic novel *Dracula,* but during his lifetime, he was better known as the business manager of London's Lyceum Theater.

Summation of Spread

This spread is inspired by the bloodsucking myth of vampires and issues surrounding immortality. While immortality is tempting to some, it is considered a living hell to others. The question is, how would you fare as a bloodsucker?

Cast Your Cards

Summon all supernatural power and cast the cards as a creature lurking in the shadows might do:

1. Do I really want to live forever?
2. Would I feed on humans?
3. What would be my greatest strength?
4. What would be my weakness?
5. Who would I turn to be my eternal vampire companion?
6. Do they want to be turned?
7. What would I do with all that time on my hands?
8. What city would I live in?
9. At what age should I become immortal?

The Devil card represents the vampire's worst aspect. Those holding power over others in destructive, cruel ways connect with the Devil's darkness. A vampire's sensual, seductive aspect connects to the Lovers card, while immortality itself is represented in the Ace of Cups, the ever-flowing fountain of youth and Holy Grail of everlasting life.

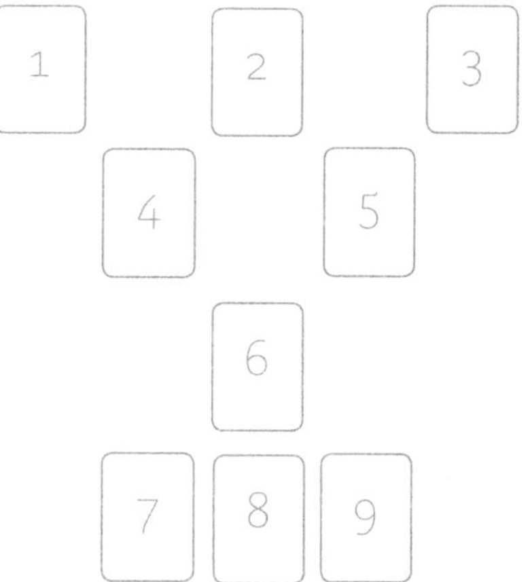

Pet Spread

On This Day

Today is the culmination of National Animal Shelter and Rescue Appreciation Week. Beginning as a campaign to acknowledge and promote the invaluable role of animal shelters, it now includes animal rescue and finding loving homes for companion animals.

Dogs have about 100 facial expressions, and most of them are made with their ears.

Summation of Spread

Do you share a strong connection with your pet? This spread, designed with your pet in mind, examines their wants and needs and helps you to strengthen your relationship.

Cast Your Cards

1. Pet's past.
2. Pet's present.
3. Pet's future.
4. How is my pet's health?
5. How is my pet feeling?
6. What does my pet want me to know?
7. What does my pet need?
8. What is the state of our relationship?
9. How can I best care for my pet?

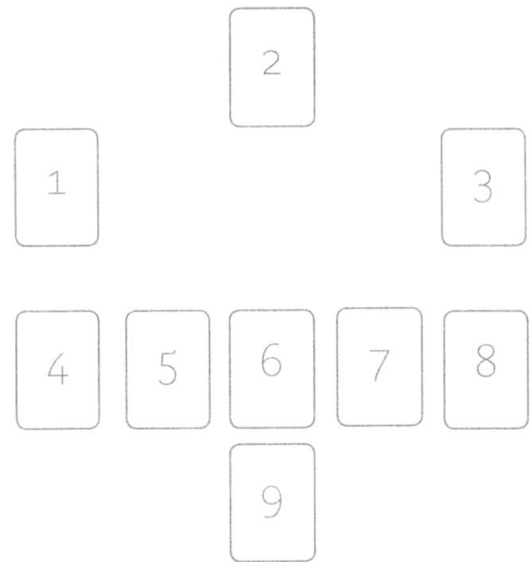

The entire suit of Cups relates to love because Cups represent emotions. *Copas* in Spain, *Coppe* in Italy, the suit derives from the playing card suit of hearts. It deals with all emotional aspects and connections reigning strong in relationships.

November • 10

Sesame Street's Inner Child Spread

Sesame Street was given its title after long discussions with the writers. Seeking a catchy name, they decided upon "sesame" due to its connection to *The Arabian Nights* and the excitement of the phrase "open sesame"!

The Six of Cups is a reference to childhood, nostalgia, and the sweetness of a walk down memory lane. Use this card to connect with your past. When the Six of Cups appears in a spread, it marks the arrival of a comforting and familiar love.

On This Day

Sesame Street aired its first episode today in 1969, and neither PBS nor children's entertainment would ever be the same. The world was introduced to Bert and Ernie, Big Bird, Oscar the Grouch, and an entire family of multicultural urban characters.

Summation of Spread

Have you spoken to your inner child lately? The inner child refers to the child still thriving within you. This term is used in popular psychology referring to who we were before the onset of puberty. In an interesting twist, repeat the spread a second time—this time, try speaking to your inner teenager.

Cast Your Cards

The point of this spread is to facilitate an actual conversation between you and your inner child. Select the age at which you are speaking to yourself. Imagine your home and your bedroom and living situation at that age.

1. What would you like to tell me?
2. What is your favorite game?
3. What is your favorite thing to do?
4. What can I do for you?
5. Do you feel ignored or left out?
6. What do you desire but aren't getting?
7. How can I provide this for you now?
8. What do you fear most?
9. How can I give you what you need?

Divorce Spread

On This Day

Today is Armistice Day, celebrating the end of World War 1. The official end of hostilities occurred at the eleventh hour of the eleventh day of November 1918. Usually this moment is marked by two minutes of silence.

Summation of Spread

History repeats bloody conflicts *ad infinitum*. With lives on the line, it is best to put down your weapons and seek peaceful resolutions requiring no one's death. This spread uses today's ceasefire date as inspiration for the Divorce Spread. It is crafted to help a person through one of the toughest of life's events.

Cast Your Cards

Cast your cards with a gentle hand and loving heart toward yourself, knowing you did everything you possibly could:

1. Am I making the best decision?
2. Is this the only solution?
3. What can be salvaged?
4. Can we remain on good terms?
5. How are my finances affected?
6. What helps me stay strong?
7. What was the great lesson?
8. How can I heal?
9. What new path opens?
10. What can I look forward to?

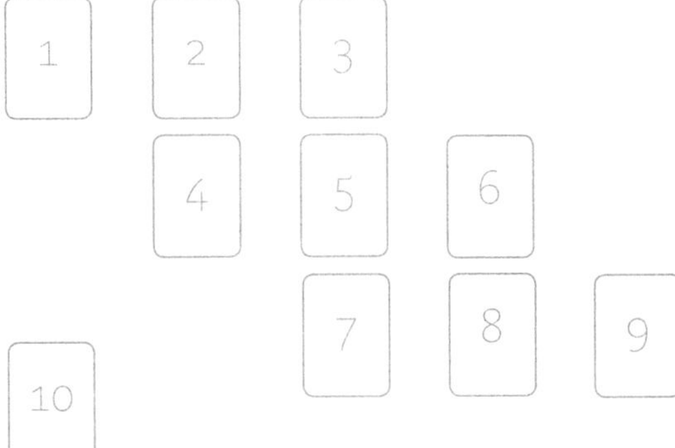

Divorce was common in ancient Rome, especially among the upper classes. A couple could divorce just by declaring their intention not to live together in front of seven witnesses.

The Four of Cups card represents a person closed off to love due to a soured relationship. The mysterious hand emerging out of the cloud reminds us that gifts of love (symbolized by the cup) are always there—one only needs to see, then accept.

Back to the Future Spread

Back to the Future *used 1.21 gigawatts and a flux capacitor to travel back in time. Despite centuries of dreams and research, time travel sadly remains beyond our reach.*

The Chariot is a card that can be used to time travel and journey into different modes of existence—consider it tarot's time machine. The only question is, where do you want to go?

On This Day

Marty McFly returns to this date in 1955 in the awesome time-traveling flick *Back to the Future*. He must make sure his high-school-aged parents unite in order to save his own existence.

Summation of Spread

Wish you could hop in a time machine? Time traveling is a fun idea, especially when we think about what we could do differently to create an alternative future outcome. It is easy to forget that our present becomes tomorrow's past. Looking at life in this way, we realize we constantly affect the future with our present actions.

Cast Your Cards

Take a moment to picture yourself ten years ago. Picture yourself now. Picture yourself ten years in the future. Cast your cards.

1. Do I make my decisions or let others make them for me?
2. What is my greatest regret?
3. What did I give up on?
4. How do I utilize my talents?
5. Am I making healthy choices?
6. What should I change right now?
7. What do I want my next chapter to contain?
8. What do I need to do right now for a better tomorrow?
9. What is my future self requesting of me?

Be Lucky on Friday the 13th Spread

On This Day

The earliest known documented reference to the bad luck surrounding Friday the 13th came on this day in 1868. The biography of Italian composer Gioachino Rossini states "like so many Italians, he regarded Fridays as an unlucky day and thirteen as an unlucky number; it is remarkable one Friday the 13th of November he died." Friday the 13th is steeped in mystery and unease.

Hotels, hospitals, and many high-rises omit marking thirteenth floors, and airports often omit the thirteenth gate.

Summation of Spread

Want to ramp up your luck factor? The Be Lucky on Friday the 13th Spread's questions are not just there to guarantee luck on Friday the 13th but to increase luck in general.

Cast Your Cards

Cast in the shape of the number 13:

1. How can I focus on staying positive all day?
2. What is my blessing?
3. Can I be adventurous?
4. How do I give more than I take?
5. What helps me expect good things?
6. How do I stay open to opportunity?
7. What helps me see serendipity everywhere?
8. Why should I believe in myself?

The Death card is the thirteenth card in the tarot deck. It reveals massive change, upheaval, and a turning point toward a new reality. Death bares all but the essential, leaving freedom in its wake. Often represented with a scythe, due to the idea of his harvesting of souls, the skeleton is the structure of our bodies, the essence of our physicality.

Monet's Unseen Opportunities Spread

The term Impressionism *was coined due to Monet's painting* Impression, Sunrise. *He was not the only Impressionist but was part of a group of artists painting in this style.*

Pages represent seeing the unseen, original insights, and outside-of-the-box thinking. Their young, fresh perspective carries with it the freedom from preconceived notions and set ideas. Borrow their enjoyable and intriguing way of looking at the world whenever you desire a fresh point of view.

On This Day

Claude Monet, the founder of the French Impressionist movement, was born on this day in 1840.

Summation of Spread

What is right under your nose? Impressionism, a style of painting adored and revered now, was seen as a radical departure in its time. Painters recorded impressions of nature that others couldn't or didn't see or understand until it was on the canvas. Artists, our modern mystics, are often first to notice what others do not. This spread makes use of the artist's device in the Unseen Opportunities Spread.

Cast Your Cards

Cast the cards face-down in the shape of an artist's canvas. Reveal the cards one by one as you move through the spread.

1. What preconceived notion must I let go of?
2. What helps me open to new opportunities?
3. How can I trust my instincts?
4. What opportunities should I look for?
5. What exists before me that I can't see?
6. How do I grab it?
7. How do I make use of it?
8. What will happen as a result?
9. What must I remember?

1	2	3
6	5	4
7	8	9

Easter Island Unanswered Question Spread

On This Day

Two Spanish ships landed on Easter Island on this day in 1770, discovering over 900 giant statues. The mysteries of how the islanders moved 86-ton monoliths or why the island was deforested remain unsolved.

Summation of Spread

What unanswered question plagues you? Easter Island is just one of a plethora of intriguing riddles abounding in the world. From famous mysteries such as who shot JFK, who was Jack the Ripper, and does Bigfoot exist to your own private enigma, this spread was created to help you unravel it. No question or unresolved mystery is off-limits.

Cast Your Cards

1. My unanswered question.
2. What is known about the situation?
3. Who carries additional information?
4. Why did it happen?
5. Do I really want the answer?
6. What is the absolute truth?

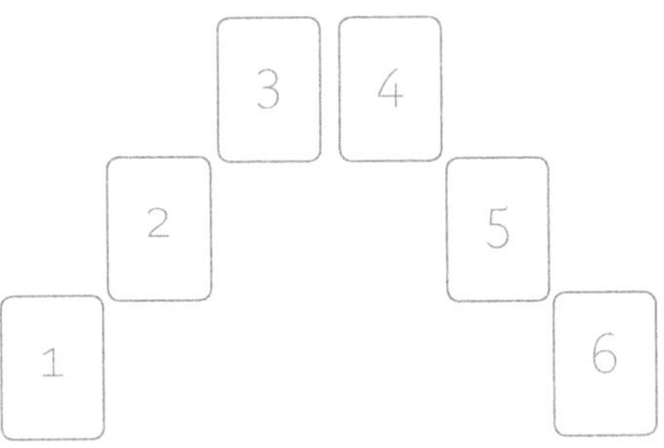

The great thing about a mystery, be it rational or spiritual, is that it keeps us questioning. Questioning leads to learning. Value mysteries because, whether you unravel them or not, they keep you moving forward.

The Page of Swords is the super spy of the tarot deck, with a keen eye for the truth and a taste for adventure mixed with the optimism of youth. This page thrives on the discovery of secrets and loves to be in control. Making excellent use of mental powers, the Page of Swords delights in the truth behind the mystery.

Hecate's Shamanic Spread

It is considered auspicious if you hear a dog's bark tonight, as Hecate allegedly roams the earth on this night with her pack of hounds.

On This Day

Tonight is Hecate's Night, an evening that honors this witch deity, once a great goddess with temples and shrines. Feasts in her honor, sacrificial offerings, and gifts left at crossroads pay tribute to this deity of magic, witchcraft, and necromancy.

Summation of Spread

Are you ready to travel between worlds? Hecate slipped easily between the realms of the living and the dead. Humans have long moved the same way using shamanic arts, the most ancient spiritual practice known to man. This spread is based upon the shaman's three worlds: lower, middle, and upper.

The Hermit and Hecate are both bearers of light—Hecate with her torch and the Hermit with his lantern. Both light the way for those who are prepared to embark on their path.

Cast Your Cards

Cast the cards in three distinct formations:

Lower World (essence of the natural world)

1. What do I need to detach from?
2. What spirit should I connect with?
3. What message does my power/totem animal have for me?

Middle World (reality as we know it)

4. What possibility exists that I don't see at the moment?
5. What is the biggest concern in my material world?

Upper World (spiritual guidance, wisdom, and true nature)

6. What is the best way to fulfill my destiny?
7. What is my purpose?
8. How do I unite with the Divine?

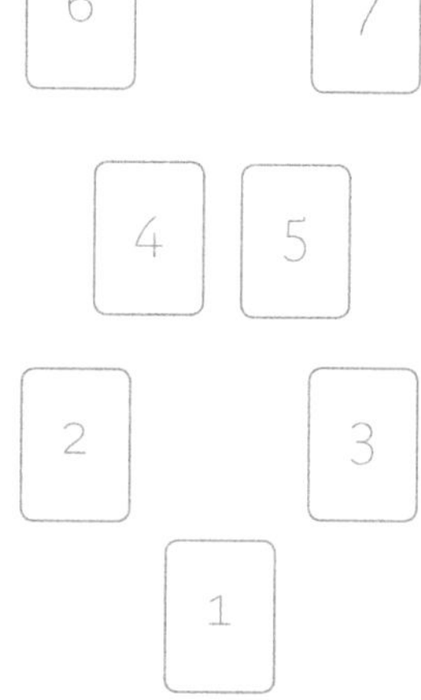

Little Mermaid Spread

On This Day

The Little Mermaid movie was released this day in 1989, and a classic was born.

Summation of Spread

What do you want to explore? Ariel is a fiercely curious heroine who desires to break boundaries and explore the unknown world beyond her aquatic home. Inspired by Ariel's tenacity, the Little Mermaid Spread asks questions to help you dive into adventure and romance.

Cast Your Cards

1. What barrier do I need to break?
2. Who or what stands in my way?
3. What gets my heart racing?
4. What new thing can I try?
5. What have I always wanted to do?
6. How do I attract new people into my life?
7. Will I find love?
8. What happens as a result of my actions?

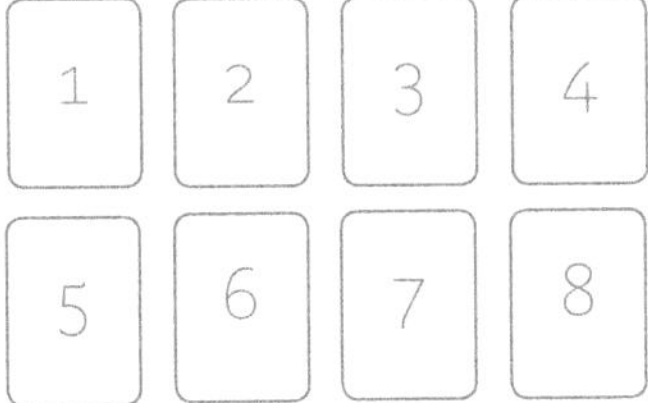

Hans Christian Andersen's version of The Little Mermaid *has a much different ending than the film version. In Andersen's version, the sea witch instructs Ariel to murder the prince. Ariel cannot bring herself to do it. Sunrise breaks over the ocean, and she throws herself into the sea and dies.*

The Fool, a spirit in search of experience, is the single most purposeful card to use when considering a new adventure. Operating outside normal rules, free and innocent, he is open to any experience coming his way. Try walking with the Fool's attitude from time to time and see what happens.

Rejection Spread

R. H. Macy had seven failed businesses before Macy's took off, Oprah was fired from a television reporting job and called "unfit for TV," and Elvis Presley was fired by a Grand Ole Opry manager and told that he "ought to go back to drivin' a truck."

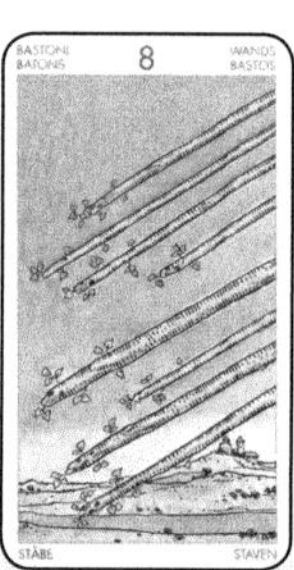

The Eight of Wands is a reminder to channel and direct your passion. The card's appearance reflects electric energy and movement. This burst of energy opens lines of communication. Do not become discouraged. Maintain patience, stock your energetic wells, do the work, and trust the Wands will land exactly where they need to go.

On This Day

On this day *Steamboat Willie*, the first animated film with sound, opened to rave reviews. It was only the beginning for Walt Disney, who had been fired by a newspaper editor who claimed Disney "lacked imagination and had no good ideas."

Summation of Spread

Have you felt the daggers of rejection? Walt Disney didn't let this rejection stop him, and neither should you. No matter whether it's romantic, professional, or any other setback, this spread takes a look at rejection and shows how it helps you bounce back bigger and better than ever.

Cast Your Cards

1. Why did this happen?
2. Why is it good this happened?
3. What will grow as a result?
4. Why is this a blessing in disguise?
5. How can I let the pain go?
6. Where should I focus my sights?
7. What helps me regroup?
8. Why should I never give up?

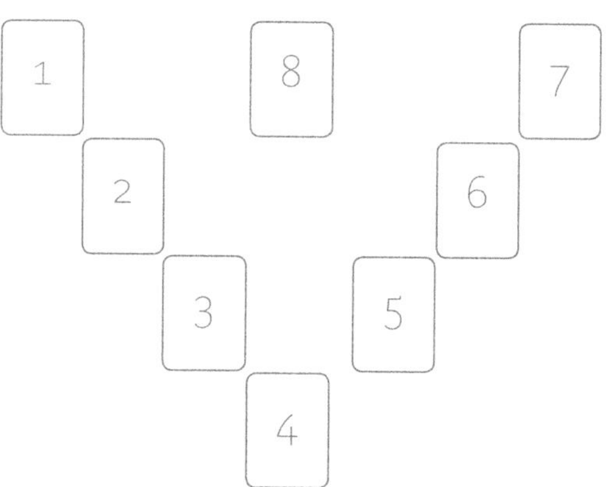

19 • November

Doom Bar Spread

On This Day

The Doom Bar, a dangerous shifting sandbar in Cornwall, England, claimed two ships on this day in 1911. Both the *Island Maid* and the *Angele* were lost within hours of one another.

Summation of Spread

Shifting sandbars operate like the lessons we keep learning and relearning in our life. Why is it others find smooth sailing while we get snagged by the same old habits, issues, and themes? This spread looks at our recurring issues and seeks to settle them once and for all.

Cast Your Cards

1. Danger I routinely run up against.
2. Why is this present in my life?
3. What is the lesson I am meant to learn?
4. Why does this persist?
5. What will dissipate this forever?
6. What will happen if I remain stuck?
7. What will happen when this is cleared from my life forever?

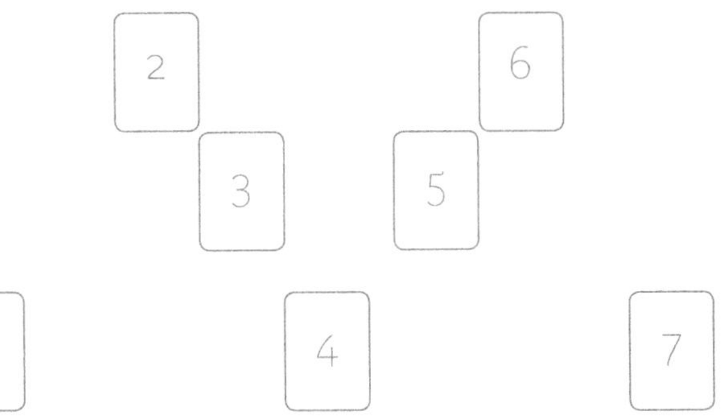

The wreck of the Island Maid *is still submerged near the Doom Bar and is a popular wreck dive destination.*

The Three of Wands is often described as a person who is waiting for their ship to come in. You can revolve this interpretation and say that the person is sending their ship out to sea. The card is numbered three, the number of creativity and vision.

Conversation with Art and Places Spread

The Metropolitan Museum of Art's collection includes over two million objects and works of art. The oldest, from Egypt, dates back to 75,000 BCE.

On This Day

The Metropolitan Museum of Art acquired its very first object on this date in 1870: a Roman sarcophagus with Cupid and Eros carved into it became the first piece in this most beguiling and haunted building of New York City.

Summation of Spread

Ready to read your cards outside of the box and take your cards outside the home? One of the most pleasurable experiences to be had with tarot is using the cards to connect with a place or a piece of art. Converse with art objects, the artists who created them, or even with the wisdom of a specific place using tarot as a communication device.

Conversation with a place requires acute listening skills. The High Priestess's subtle silence and perceptive acute hearing skills are perfectly matched for this activity.

Cast Your Cards

You must take yourself and the cards out of your home for this exercise. Select a location; it could be a museum with your favorite painting, the residence of your favorite deceased writer, or a sacred spot in nature. Create a specific list of questions or ask the ones posed below.

1. What wisdom do you offer me?
2. How does your energy fuel me?
3. What secret can you whisper to me?
4. How do I integrate this knowledge into my life?
5. Why is this place important?
6. What do I need to know?

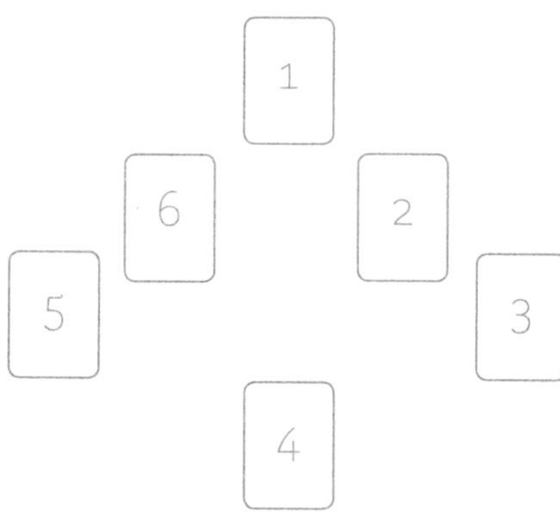

How Others See Me Venetian Mask Spread

On This Day

Venice holds Festa della Salute today. Workers lay a floating pontoon bridge over the Grand Canal. Citizens literally walk upon the water as they make their way across the bridge toward Salute Church. Once there, they give thanks to the Virgin Mary for freeing them from the sixteenth-century plague that struck this lagoon city, and they request she keeps them in good health.

Summation of Spread

What do you display to the outer world? Venice is well known for intricate carnival masks. Concealing who we truly are, masks allow us to role-play as someone or something else. This spread takes a look at the mask you put on when facing the world.

Cast Your Cards

Dart through the mist rolling across the lagoon, tiptoe down a cobblestone street, and cast your cards as follows:

1. What is the true nature of my inner self?
2. How do others interpret my truth?
3. How do I act differently when I am alone?
4. How do I behave when I think people are watching me?
5. What I think I project to the world.
6. What I actually project to the world.
7. What can I safely reveal to those around me?
8. What should I protect?

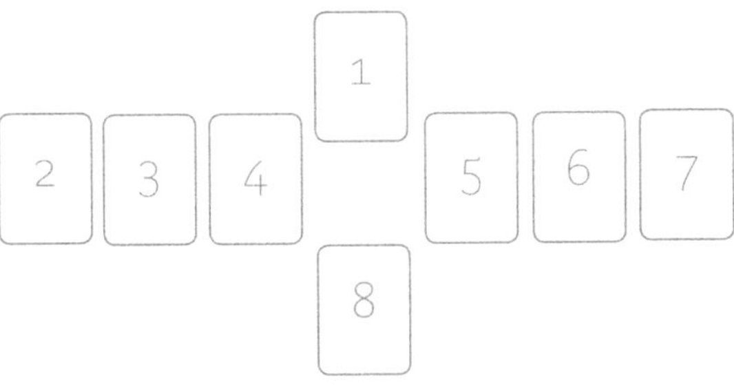

Venice enjoyed an economic boom during the Middle Ages and became a pleasure palace. During this time the popularity of masks grew as prominent society, clergy, and even servants hid their identity while engaging in immoral, unscrupulous acts of carnal pleasure.

The Fool carries the trickster energy of the deck. Indicative of hiding and playing pretend, in mythology the trickster is the creature who breaks normal rules and displays unconventional behavior. Tricksters can be cunning, foolish, or both, just like the Fool.

November • 22

Qualities of Sagittarius Spread

Sagittarius's ruling planet is Jupiter, purple is the primary color, the lucky day is Thursday, and the best location for success is anywhere outdoors. Sagittarius rules the ninth house of the zodiac, which is associated with higher education, philosophy, and long-distance travel.

The Temperance card represents the alchemical blending of elements to reach perfection, balance, and immortality. Temperance weighs and measures to discover the right combination. In the same way, Sagittarians fearlessly travel, move, and explore their world and expand their boundaries.

On This Day

Today marks the first day of the astrological sign of Sagittarius, the archer.

Summation of Spread

This spread is based on the essential qualities of Sagittarius: optimism, honesty, adventure, humor, enthusiasm, expansion, and knowledge.

Cast Your Cards

Cast your cards like Sagittarius's arrow:

1. What can I be optimistic about?
2. What should I be totally honest with myself about?
3. How do I begin my next great adventure?
4. Why is it important to have a sense of humor about myself?
5. What can I look forward to?
6. What area of my life is expanding?
7. What do I truly know?

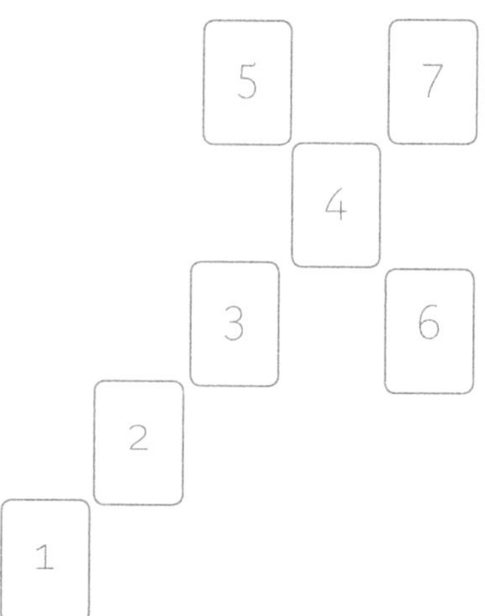

Loneliness Spread

On This Day

On this day, a German U-boat torpedoed the SS *Ben Lomond*. Steward Poon Lim went overboard and survived 133 days alone in the South Atlantic. Catching birds, fish, and even a shark, he remained alive. Years later he would say he hoped no one would ever have to break his record of the longest time at sea on a life raft.

Summation of Spread

Do you feel cut off from others? Hopefully you will never be lost at sea, but it doesn't mean you won't experience lonely periods in your life when you may feel disconnected from others. This spread looks at why you might feel this way and what you can do to break out of it.

Cast Your Cards

1. Why do I feel so alone?
2. Is this a transformational moment?
3. How can I make the most of this period in my life?
4. How is solitude a good thing?
5. Whom should I reach out to?
6. Is there an activity I can join?
7. Can I initiate new friendships?
8. Where can I take myself on a date?
9. Should I get a pet?
10. When will this pass?
11. What have I learned?

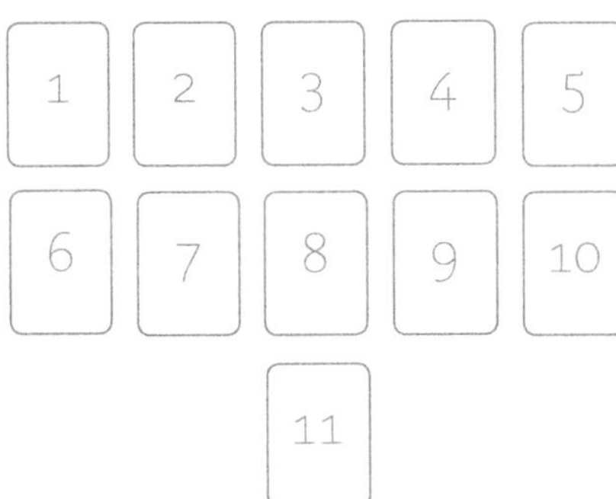

There is evidence suggesting the part of our brain that experiences physical pain also processes social separation. This means social rejection can hurt as much as physical pain. No wonder the experience of loneliness hurts so deeply.

While many cards in the deck describe a self-imposed and even enjoyable isolation, it is the painful Three of Swords that refers to the heartbreak of loneliness, isolation, and rejection. Thankfully, when the storm of this card passes, the Four of Swords awaits with restful sleep and regeneration.

Wisdom of Cups Spread

The Brumalia festival marked a break for the Roman senate. Divination was practiced to determine the city's prospects for the coming year.

Reflecting our emotional landscape, watery Cups address how and what we feel at the time we are feeling it. It is the consciousness where romanticism, fantasy, art, and imagination dwell. The cup is receptive, carrying feminine qualities.

On This Day

Today is the ancient Roman festival of Brumalia, honoring Saturn, Ceres, and Bacchus. This winter festival celebrated the long, dark nights of winter with drinking and merriment.

Summation of Spread

How are you feeling lately? You can't mention Bacchus, god of wine, without raising a cup. The suit of Cups inspires this spread. Using Cup qualities such as emotions, feelings, and love, this spread examines how you feel.

Cast Your Cards

Cast the Wisdom of Cups Spread's cards in the shape of a jewel-encrusted chalice.

1. Love: Whom do I love?
2. Feelings: Who has feelings for me?
3. Relationships: What is my most important relationship?
4. Connections: Whom do I share a deep connection with?
5. Creativity: How can I use my creativity?
6. Expression: What must I express right now?
7. Emotions: How do I feel?

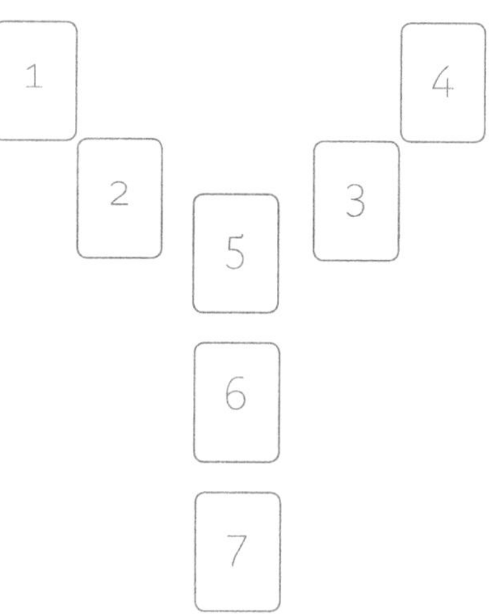

Tibetan Book of the Dead Spread

On This Day

Today in Tibet is the memorial festival of Tsongkhapa, a well-known Tibetan religious philosopher. Lamps and lanterns are lit and left on windowsills, and contained fires are lit on monastery roofs. His image is carried in processions.

Summation of Spread

Ready for enlightenment? According to the *Tibetan Book of the Dead*, the best opportunity for liberation of the soul happens as death occurs. This is when the soul encounters the five primordial expressions of ultimate cosmic energy, called the Dhyani Buddhas. These are the five principles of a fully awakened consciousness. Each principle informs a question of this spread.

Cast Your Cards

Cast the cards in a sacred circle:

1. Empty Buddha: direction and time.
   How do I slow time?
2. Immovable Buddha: wisdom.
   How do I become wise?
3. Buddha of Precious Birth: human realm, earth, fertility, and wealth.
   What am I here to do?
4. Buddha of Infinite Light: compassion.
   How can I help others?
5. Buddha of Unfailing Success: karma.
   How do I heal myself?

2

1 3

5 4

After the Chinese invasion of Tibet in 1949, over 6,000 monasteries were destroyed. It is estimated that one million Tibetans have died as a result of the brutal Chinese occupation continuing to this day.

The *Tibetan Book of the Dead*, like all books of the dead, describes the soul's journey to the afterlife. The entire major arcana could be viewed as an afterlife journey, with each card representing a lesson or challenge for the soul.

Death Card Spread

Antiquated times held the Death card as the end of all things—a veil of darkness blotting out all life, a flame extinguished, or a life ended. The Death card is commonly read by modern readers as transformation into a new state of consciousness and the beginning of something new.

If we are sensitive and allow it, the Death card is a literal metaphor that can be our greatest teacher. Reminding us of the value of life, death teaches us how to live.

On This Day

Vlad the Impaler became ruler of Walachia, a section of Romania, on this day in 1476. Rumors of his excessive cruelty spread, as did his fondness for impaling his enemies, and a few hundred years later Bram Stoker would based the character Dracula on Vlad.

Summation of Spread

The fictional Dracula and nonfictional Vlad are both symbolic of Death. This spread is based on symbols found on the Death card.

Cast Your Cards

Use this spread to answer any question. Format your question before casting the spread or simply let the cards answer the questions posed. Pull the Death card from your deck. Place it in the center of the spread and cast your cards around it as follows:

1. Skeleton: What is temporary?
2. Armor: What protects me?
3. Horse: What moves me?
4. Dead King: What is overthrown?
5. Praying Child: Who is listening?
6. Bishop: What role does religion and dogma play in my life?
7. Twin Towers: What has been built?
8. Sunrise: What new beginning awaits?

Emperor Card Spread

On This Day

Roman Emperor Marcus Aurelius gave his son Commodus the rank of Supreme Commander of the Roman Legions on this day in 176 CE.

Summation of Spread

Ancient Roman emperors are the ideal archetype for tarot's Emperor card. The Emperor Card Spread is based on symbols found in the Emperor card.

Cast Your Cards

Use this spread to answer any question. Format your question before casting the spread or simply let the cards answer the questions posed. Pull the Emperor card from your deck. Place it in the center of the spread and cast your cards around it as follows:

1. Throne: What is the stability I have created?
2. Bulls: How am I headstrong?
3. Ankh: What is eternal?
4. Ball: Where can I exercise power?
5. Crown: How do I connect with spirit?
6. River: How do I remain emotionally resilient?
7. Mountain Range: What do I leave behind?
8. Armor: How am I responsible?

The design for the Emperor has changed very little through the centuries, whereas other iconic cards such as the High Priestess and the Fool have experienced radical symbolic transformations.

The Emperor represents the idea of power, governmental authority, and male qualities of assertiveness, creative energy, directed action, and troubleshooting. Showing creative potential in action, organized and rational, his authority extends to the material realm but is lacking in the passion belonging to the Empress.

November • 28

Job for Me Spread

Time and introspection help to identify those things you love doing most. If you have the liberty, take your time figuring out your heart's desire.

The Eight of Pentacles represents happiness and pride in the work you do. It also indicates a willingness to work on the fine details to improve your life. Dedication, focus, and patience are all hallmarks of the Eight of Pentacles.

On This Day

The book *The Secret*, companion to the film, was released on this day in 2006. The book features the wildly popular Law of Attraction principle and was an instant bestseller.

Summation of Spread

Who wouldn't want to use the Law of Attraction to land a fulfilling job? Problem is, we don't always know what job we want to do. Perform this spread for guidance when you feel lost and afraid to commit to a new job or when searching out a new profession or your true calling.

Cast Your Cards

1. What do I like to do?
2. Why do I like to do it?
3. What don't I like to do?
4. Why don't I like to do it?
5. What am I naturally good at?
6. What past jobs have I found satisfying?
7. What should I avoid in my career?
8. Who is influencing my career choices?
9. Who helps me in my search?
10. What would I enjoy doing again (and again and again)?
11. What card describes the perfect job for me?

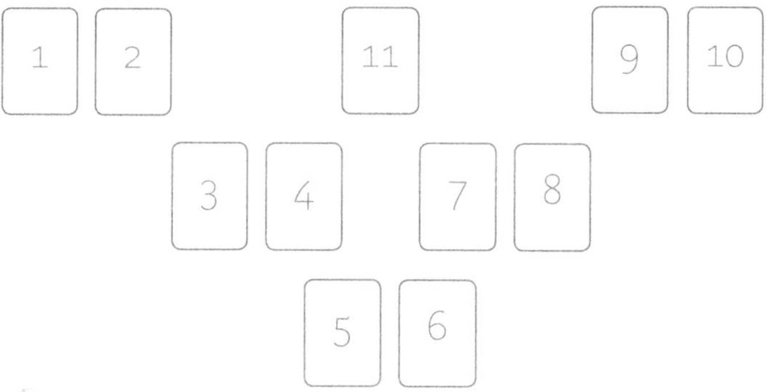

Wreath Spread

On This Day

Wreaths have been a symbol of power and strength since classical antiquity. Roman and Greek kings and emperors often wore laurel wreaths as crowns, a practice pre-dated by the Etruscans. Harvest wreaths pre-date written history as symbols of strength. Christianity adopted the natural symbol of an evergreen to represent everlasting life.

Greek and Roman kings and emperors thought their laurel wreaths connected them to Apollo, the sun god, and that the crown embodied his values.

Summation of Spread

The Wreath Spread uses the intrinsic qualities of the wreath to inform its questions. If you hang a wreath this season, ruminate over these qualities when you cast your eyes upon it.

Cast Your Cards

Cast in the shape of a wreath:

1. Strength: What strength carries me through the winter months?
2. Fortitude: What gives me power?
3. Power: What do I do with the power I have?
4. Tenacity: What must be accomplished this season?
5. Wisdom: What do I learn?
6. Hope: What is discovered?

Wreaths are found on the Six of Wands, the World, and the Seven of Cups. In each case the wreath represents elements of victory and success.

Hecate's Witch's Cabinet Spread

The chief goddess presiding over magic and spells, Hecate is often depicted as a three-figured goddess, connecting her with the Triple Goddess of Maiden, Mother, and Crone.

On This Day

Hecate, the ancient goddess of magic, witchcraft, night, the moon, ghosts, and necromancy, had two Roman days held in her honor. Today was one of them. Associated with crossroads, borders, and doorways as the overseer of the space where two realms meet, Hecate is the patron goddess of many witches.

Summation of Spread

Hecate's association with poisonous herbs and plants makes for perfect inspiration in the Witch's Cabinet Spread. The questions are based on the items you'll find on hand in any magical person's home.

Hecate often carries a torch to light the way in the underworld. Her torchlight and fierce magical attributes connect her to the Queen of Wands. This queen's wand and flower symbolize her vitality and beauty, which she does not hesitate to use as a weapon. She is encouraging and stimulates creativity around her in subtle yet highly effective ways.

Cast Your Cards

Cast the cards as you would place jars upon a dusty shelf:

1. Mugwort: What improves my clairvoyance?
2. Belladonna: What do I need to be careful of?
3. Myrtle: How do I increase my beauty?
4. Bloodroot: What deceives me?
5. Brimstone: What negativity should I repel?
6. Henbane: What helps me sleep soundly?

Rosa Parks's Defending Yourself Spread

On This Day

On this evening in 1945, Rosa Parks made history. A tiny African American woman, a humble seamstress, refused to give up her seat to a white man on a Montgomery, Alabama, bus. Her subsequent arrest and simple act of refusal started a bus boycott that kicked off the civil rights movement.

Summation of Spread

Do you need to stand your ground? This spread was created for clarity when you need to defend yourself against cruelty and unfairness.

Cast Your Cards

Believe in yourself and cast the cards as follows:

1. What helps me speak with authority?
2. How can I keep my cool while engaged with this issue?
3. Am I prepared with all the information I need?
4. Am I seeing this situation in a clear light?
5. Why is this issue so important?
6. Outcome if I do nothing.
7. Outcome if I stand up for myself.
8. What is this situation's lesson?

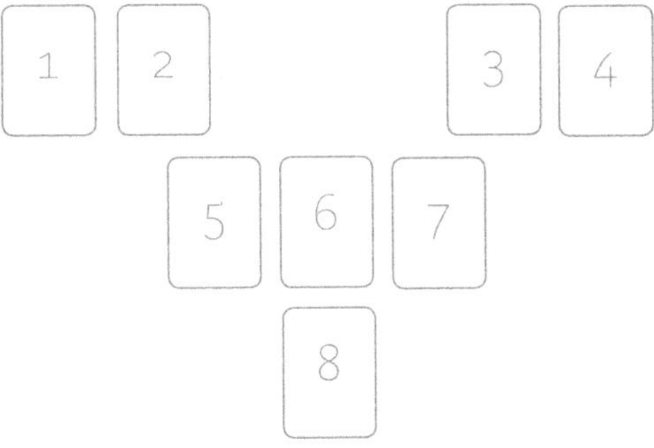

Rosa Parks sacrificed much when she unintentionally became the symbol for civil rights movements. Arrested and mistreated, she lost her job, then became a public figure. She was either looked to for inspiration or mistreated and abused by a racist public.

The Five of Swords reminds you that just because the fight is over, it does not mean the battle is finished. Just like Rosa Parks, who spent the night in jail but later became a major catalyst for change, the Five of Swords reflects only the dispute, not the repercussions.

Marquis de Sade's S & M Spread

The words sadist *and* sadism *are derived from the Marquis de Sade's name.*

On This Day

The Marquis de Sade died in his sleep on this night in 1814. French aristocrat, philosopher, and writer famous for his libertine sexuality, he rejected any moral code. Best known for his erotic works, the Marquis spent over thirty-two years of his life in insane asylums, where he would ultimately die at age seventy-four.

Summation of Spread

Inspired by the naughty French aristocrat, this spread examines eroticism and new ideas in the bedroom, especially within the framework of domination and submission.

The Eight of Swords is commonly referred to as the bondage card. The female figure is bound and blindfolded—however, once the folds are removed, she will see the world with a new set of eyes.

Cast Your Cards

Promise to be honest with yourself as you cast your cards:

1. Do I trust my partner?
2. Does my partner know what I would like to experience in the boudoir?
3. Do we communicate well on the topic?
4. How do I feel about relinquishing control?
5. Do I enjoy a feeling of power in the bedroom?
6. Do I enjoy letting go?
7. Will the experience be exciting?
8. Is this an area I should explore?
9. Will this experience bring us closer?
10. Will this satisfy me?

Bona Dea's Female Power Spread

On This Day

Today was the Roman festival of Bona Dea, associated with females, fertility, healing, and protection. Bona Dea's rites allowed women the use of wine and blood sacrifice on this night, normally off-limits in their male-centric Roman tradition.

Bona Dea's temple, near the Circus Maximus, was an important center for healing. Harmless snakes roamed the premise, and stores of valuable medicinal herbs were dispensed as needed by its priestesses.

Summation of Spread

Bona Dea's winter festival excluded men. Conducted in the home, ritually cleansed of all males—even male animals and male portraits—vines and flowers were used as decorations, and a banquet was prepared. Females gathered, female musicians performed, and all normal customs were suspended. For a male to even glimpse at this festival was punishable by blinding. This ultimate girls' night inspires the female questions in this spread.

The Queen of Cups is perhaps the most feminine queen in the deck due to her breadth of empathy. Dreamy, a sincere friend, honest, and loyal, the Queen of Cups revels in the softer aspects of womanhood.

Cast Your Cards

Cast the cards in a lemniscate, the shape of a female reclining:

1. What is the essence of womanhood?
2. What does being a woman mean to me?
3. What do female relationships mean to me?
4. What is my relationship to my mother?
5. How can I support the women I know?
6. How can I cultivate strength from the strong females in my life?
7. How can I nurture my female relationships?
8. What message do young girls need to hear?

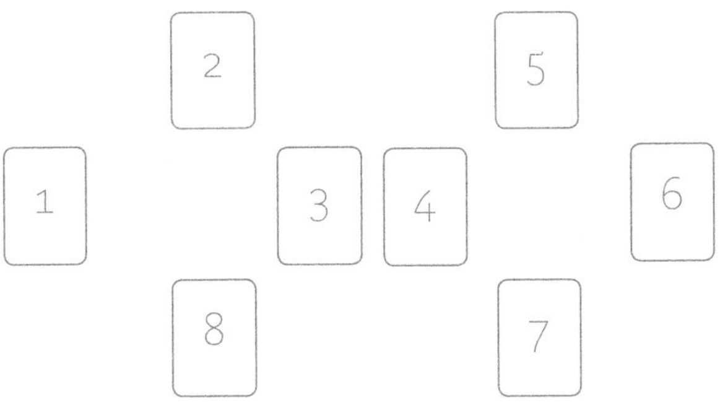

Magical Gemstones Spread

Garnets were named for the seeds of a pomegranate, amber is the softest gemstone, and in the Middle Ages women wore opals to protect their blond hair.

The suit of Pentacles is associated with gems, which are mined from the earth's soft interior. The Knight of Pentacles is often seen as a man making an offering, perhaps an engagement ring to the woman he loves.

On This Day

On this day in 2008, four robbers dressed as women entered Harry Winston's jewelry shop in Paris. They made off with over $108 million in diamonds and jewels. In 2011, twenty-five people were arrested when the missing jewels were discovered in a Paris rain sewer.

Summation of Spread

Gems are magical in their properties and have been held as talismans for centuries and bestowed as gifts for their special meanings. The Magical Gemstones Spread is based upon qualities associated with certain gems. You may never look at your jewelry the same way again.

Cast Your Cards

Cast in the shape of a gem:

1. Diamond: What is indestructible in my life?
2. Emerald: How do I encourage prosperity?
3. Ruby: How may I experience and offer unconditional love?
4. Garnet: How can I increase my health?
5. Amethyst: What addiction do I need to let go of?
6. Opal: How can I connect to my higher self and the wisdom of the ancient ones?
7. Black Obsidian: What is the best way of grounding myself and keeping away unwanted energy?
8. Lapis Lazuli: How do I increase my psychic ability?

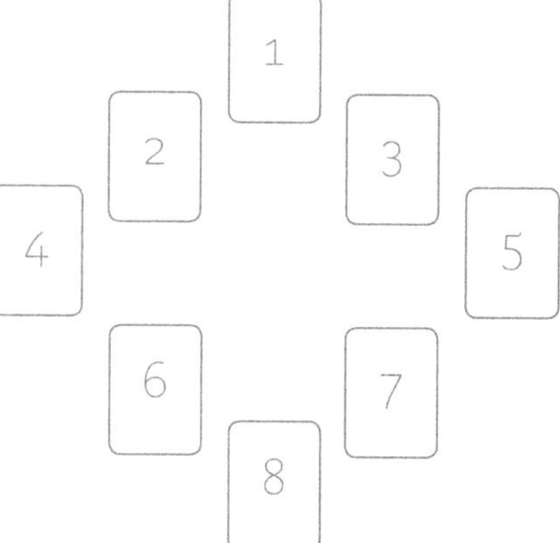

Bermuda Triangle Lost Object Spread

On This Day

A training flight of five American torpedo bombers vanished over the Bermuda Triangle on this day in 1945, one of many strange, unexplained disappearances attributed to the Bermuda Triangle. This Atlantic Ocean area, whose three vertexes are Florida, Puerto Rico, and Bermuda, is linked to extreme paranormal activity.

Summation of Spread

Lost item? Few things are more aggravating than losing a personal object. This spread aids in recovery of any misplaced object.

Cast Your Cards

This spread calls upon the magic of triangles and numbers. Occultists use the triangle as a summoning symbol. The creativity of the triangle and the wish-fulfillment power of the number 9 is used to cast the cards:

1. Where have I been recently?
2. Where is the most obvious place it would be found?
3. When did I last see it?
4. When did I last use it?
5. Should I contact anyone who might have it?
6. Is there a person who can help me look?
7. Was the item stolen?
8. Given time, will it show up on its own?
9. Where is it?

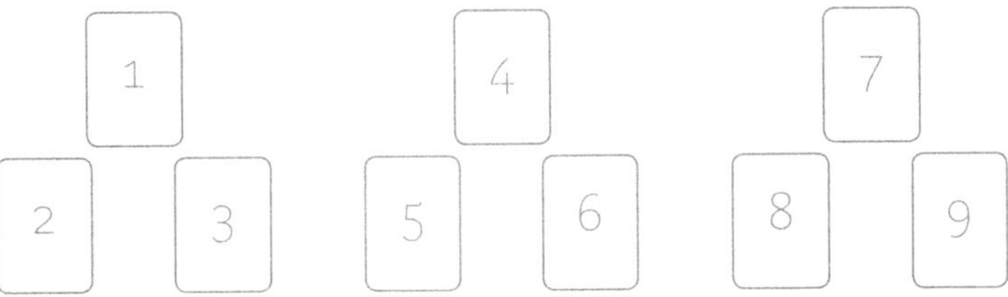

The topography of the Bermuda Triangle contains some of the world's deepest trenches. Ships and planes sinking there are likely never to be found. The area is also subject to intense, unexpected weather phenomena including water spouts, rogue waves, and underwater earthquakes.

The Bermuda Triangle and the nature of the triangle itself is viewed on the Temperance card. The angel wears a triangle within a square on her chest that represents creativity, trinity, and the power of spirit. The square represents solidity and structure. Temperance aims to balance these two qualities.

Psychic Self-Defense Spread

As a medium, Dion Fortune claimed she did not disturb the spirits of the dead by speaking with them. Rather, she channeled intelligence from a higher plane.

The Two of Swords represents the ability to bring one's attention inward, therefore forming a circle of protection, while the Eight of Swords reflects a person who is so inwardly drawn that their life becomes restrictive.

On This Day

Dion Fortune, occultist and prolific author, was born on this day in 1890. Reportedly seeing visions as young as age four, she was a Golden Dawn member who then created her own order, the Society of the Inner Light. Her novels and textbooks remain popular to this day.

Summation of Spread

In her famous book *Psychic Self-Defense*, Dion Fortune recounted how the warden at her college had conveyed a "psychic attack" on her. She reported he used yoga techniques and hypnotism, leaving her in a desperate emotional state for over three years.

Using Dion's story for inspiration, this spread aims to repel others' negativity and darkness so they do not damage the light you carry within. It's also a useful spread for removing oneself from passive-aggressive relationships.

Cast Your Cards

Imagine yourself surrounded by luminous white light and cast your cards:

1. Card representing the negative person.
2. Why are they tormented?
3. Do they wish me harm?
4. How do I spend less time near them?
5. How can I protect myself from absorbing their energy?
6. How can I remove myself from their drama?
7. How do I speed resolution of the situation?
8. What is learned?

Qualities of Jupiter Spread

On This Day

The unmanned Galileo spacecraft went into orbit around Jupiter on this day in 1995. Jupiter is the planet of luck, inspiration, and the right path. It is named for the Roman king of the gods, night sky, and thunder.

Summation of Spread

The Qualities of Jupiter Spread contains questions based on astrological associations of the planet Jupiter. Using these associations, questions are posed to offer greater clarity in life.

Cast Your Cards

Cast in the shape of a wheel. Connecting to the Wheel of Fortune card, it places your fortune at the very center.

1. Good Fortune: What is my fortune?
2. Good Health: What keeps me healthy?
3. Faith: What do I have faith in?
4. Loyalty: Who is loyal to me?
5. Justice: How am I fair?
6. Confidence: What boosts my confidence?
7. Wisdom: What gives me wisdom?
8. Philosophy: What is my philosophy?

Jupiter is the largest planet in the solar system, 318 times bigger than Earth, and contains 66 orbiting moons. Its powerful magnetic field means stepping foot upon the planet would make you weigh two and a half times what you weigh on Earth.

Like Jupiter, the Wheel of Fortune card remains in constant motion. Appearing in spreads, it represents new opportunities, possibilities, and a turning point where life as you know it begins to change.

December • 8

Jim Morrison's Addiction Spread

"The 27 Club" refers to the strange number of musicians who died at age 27, often from drug and alcohol abuse. Jim Morrison, Janis Joplin, Jimi Hendrix, Kurt Cobain, Robert Johnson, Brian Jones of the Rolling Stones, and Amy Winehouse all died at age 27.

The Five of Cups is an addiction card. The addiction was in the overturned cups. The black cloak depicts a person lost in addiction. Will they drink what is left, thereby indulging the addiction, or cross the bridge to freedom?

On This Day

Jim Morrison—Lizard King, poet, songwriter, and lead singer of The Doors—was born today in 1943. He developed a severe drug and alcohol dependency, resulting in his death in a Paris bathtub at only twenty-seven years of age.

Summation of Spread

Jim Morrison's tragic story of drug and alcohol use is an extreme example of addiction. We can be addicted to substances, thoughts, patterns, ideas, behaviors, etc. The Addiction Spread offers help and insight to break any addiction.

Cast Your Cards

Remember how strong you are and cast your cards:

1. Why is this addiction in my life?
2. How do I replace a bad habit with a good one?
3. Where is the danger zone, where I am prone to indulge in my habit?
4. How can I deal with scary emotions?
5. What must change about my lifestyle?
6. How do I create a support system for myself?
7. How can I reward myself for progress?
8. What occurs as a result of beating my addiction?

Should I Stay or Should I Go Spread

On This Day

On this day in 1992, England's Prime Minister announced that the Prince and Princess of Wales, Charles and Diana, would separate. This news sent shock waves through the world.

Princess Diana was the first commoner to marry an heir to the British throne in more than three hundred years.

Summation of Spread

Have you had enough of your relationship? This spread was created for a person deciding whether to stay in or leave a relationship.

Cast Your Cards

Call for honesty and cast your cards:

1. Is this relationship worth saving?
2. How do I feel when we are together?
3. How do I feel when we are apart?
4. Have they done something unforgivable to me?
5. Is this relationship abusive or controlling?
6. Do I feel good?
7. Am I settling for less than I deserve?
8. Can I be my true, best self with this person?
9. Do I really want this relationship?
10. Should I stay?
11. Should I go?

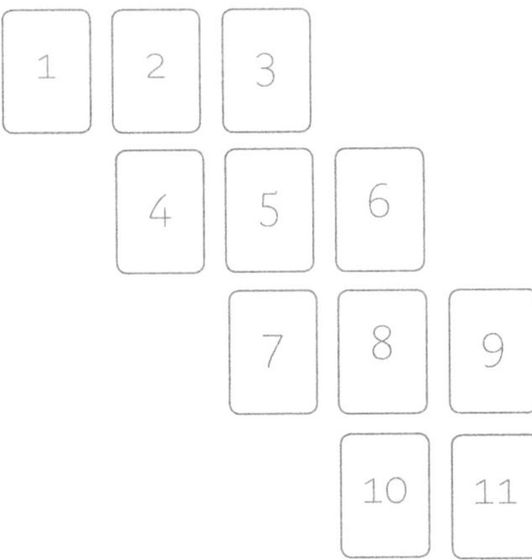

Interpreting a reversed card as the opposite of the card's traditional meaning indicates that any reversed love cards signal trouble. Action should be taken to upright the reversal. This can come in the form of communication, counseling, etc. The question always remains: is the relationship worth saving or have all possibilities already been explored?

Manage Holiday Stress Spread

Laughing lowers stress hormones and strengthens the immune system. Make sure to spend time with your favorite people who make you laugh.

On This Day

This time of year is a whirlwind of parties, shopping, family gatherings, and heightened expectations. While fun, it can also amount to a giant mountain of stress.

Summation of Spread

Are the holidays taking their toll on you? The Manage Holiday Stress Spread was created to help you keep on top of any emotions threatening to drag you down in what ideally should feel like a festive and magical time of year.

Cast Your Cards

Cast the cards lightly. There is nothing bringing you down from the twinkling white lights residing inside you.

1. What is my number-one priority this season?
2. How can I make sure I'm not doing too much?
3. How can I not overextend myself?
4. How can I not overindulge myself?
5. How can I get along better with my family?
6. What makes gift shopping fun?
7. What can I treat myself to?
8. How can I stay focused and centered?
9. What is my unexpected holiday surprise?

The Temperance card calls for balance, especially when time is of the essence. Let the angel remind you of the power of decision and boundary making. This card is also aspected by healing and health brought about by moderation in all things.

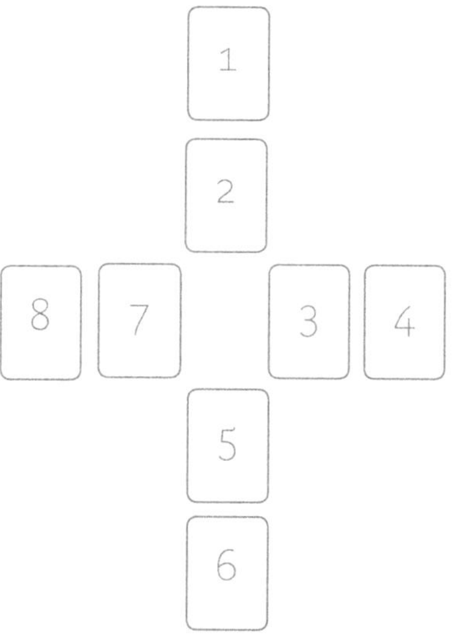

Career Advancement Spread

On This Day

The iconic film *Wall Street*, starring Charlie Sheen, opens on this day in 1987. Sheen's character rapidly advances through the ranks of Wall Street, but by the film's end he pays the ultimate price, listening to his corrupt mentor, played by Michael Douglas.

Summation of Spread

Are you ready for a promotion? *Wall Street* was about the price of shortcuts and cheating at work. This spread takes a look at how to advance in the workplace by using your assets and natural talents.

Cast Your Cards

Cast the Career Advancement Spread's cards the way you might scatter a fistful of cash:

1. What is my greatest strength at work?
2. Where do I want to go?
3. How can I make meaningful connections with someone I admire?
4. Should I ask for more work?
5. Are there classes I should be taking?
6. How can I best express myself?
7. How can I offer gratitude to my superior?
8. What is my greatest challenge?
9. How do I rise to meet this challenge?
10. What is my outcome?

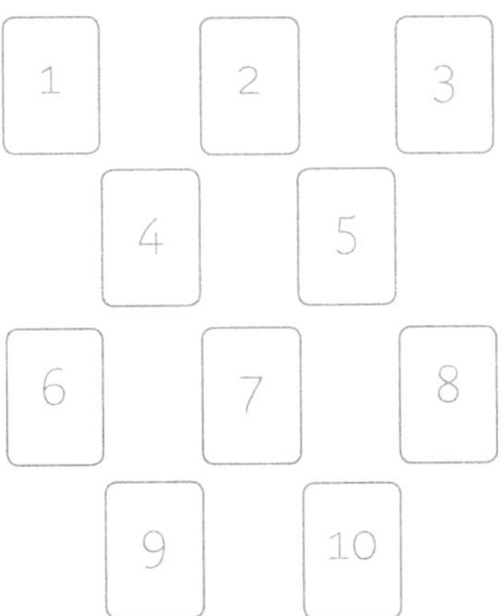

Finding a mentor is an important process of professional advancement. Offering you professional advice and guidance, they can identify obstacles and help you move over them swiftly. Find a person who is trustworthy and dependable.

The Hierophant represents the mentor connection. He passes along wisdom and knowledge to those who listen. Education, information, and revealing deeper meanings are aspected by this card. The Hierophant also identifies with groups and organizations.

Find the Perfect Gift Spread

Scientific research shows the act of giving and reciprocating gifts is evident in all cultures. It helps to strengthen and boost relationships with one another. Giving a gift with no strings attached is a simple way to let someone know you care about them.

The Six of Cups is the gift-giving card of the deck. The boy handing the girl a cup of flowers represents gifts of the soul, the number six is at the heart of the Tree of Life, and the staircase represents the ascent that follows an exchange of love.

On This Day

There are thirteen days left till Christmas. This means many people—maybe even you!—are rushing about to find the perfect gift for loved ones.

Summation of Spread

The Find the Perfect Gift Spread uses tarot cards to provoke your imagination toward an unexpected and exciting gift that will delight and surprise your friends, family, and loved ones.

Cast Your Cards

Cast in the shape of a wrapped present:

1. How much should I spend?
2. What aspect of their personality should I focus on?
3. What do their life circumstances dictate right now?
4. Is there any special hobby or interest I'm overlooking?
5. Would they prefer a gift or an experience?
6. Are they sentimental or practical?
7. Should I give a humorous or serious gift?
8. Is there something I can make for them?

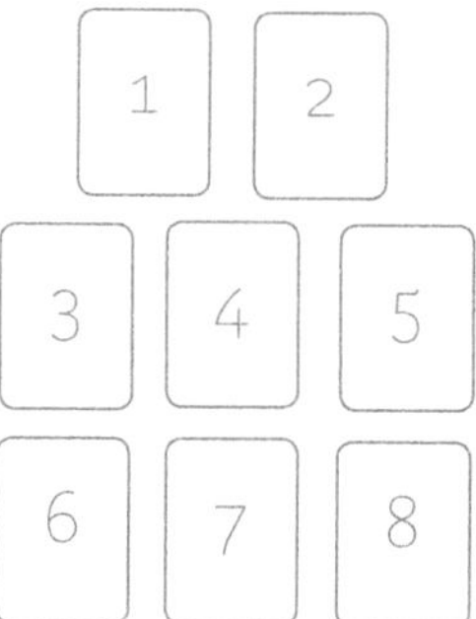

See the Light of Truth Spread

The church admits St. Lucy's backstory is built on legend and folklore.

On This Day

Before the change of calendar, today's Feast of St. Lucy was held on the winter solstice. In the Germanic world, this night is known for its surge in spirit activity. St. Lucy made a vow of chastity. Her father arranged a marriage for her anyway. Lucy decided if she removed her eyes, her groom would flee. God was so impressed, he gave her back her eyes and healed her vision. This is why Lucy is the patron saint of blindness.

Summation of Spread

This spread, inspired by the concept of blindness, looks at how a person may find light amidst perceived darkness.

Cast Your Cards

Cast your cards like a shaft of sunlight in a black pool of shadow:

1. Am I where I want to be?
2. What are my options?
3. What am I willing to change?
4. How will I feel if I do nothing?
5. What do I fear most?
6. What happens if I do not confront the fear?
7. What empowering thought must I incorporate?
8. Why do I matter?

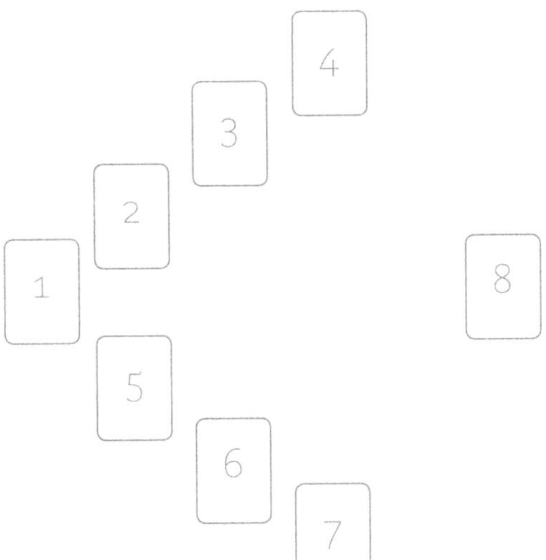

The Sun card depicts a solar influence that sheds light and truth on any situation. When the Sun card appears in a reading, it offers enlightenment and truth for the surrounding cards.

Nostradamus's Psychic Development Spread

Nostradamus also published a book about cosmetics, perfumes, and fruit preserves called The Treatise on Make-Up and Jam.

On This Day

Famous French seer Nostradamus is born on this day in 1503. Starting his career as an apothecary, famous for creating a rose pill that protected people from the plague, he eventually worked his way toward the occult. Eventually he published *Les Prophecies* (*The Prophecies*), containing over 6,338 prophesies.

Summation of Spread

Using Nostradamus as inspiration, the Psychic Development Spread discovers psychic gifts. The questions of this spread examine how you know what you know. Once a psychic gift is discovered, you can hone your talent.

Cast Your Cards

Clairvoyance (the ability to see things)

1. Have I ever seen an aura or energy field?
2. Have I ever seen a spirit?
3. Do symbols occur in my mind?
4. Do movie or book scenes appear in my mind for no reason?
5. Am I prone to visions?

Clairaudience (the ability to hear things)

6. Have I heard a voice that helped me problem-solve?
7. Do I hear music playing in my head?
8. Do I hear ringing or buzzing in my head?
9. Do I hear music, whispering, or voices when no one is there?
10. Do words pop into my head to help me solve problems?

The Page of Cups is the young psychic of the tarot deck. She trusts flashes of intuition, represented by the fish rising out of her cup.

Clairsentience (intuition as emotional, physical, or gut feelings)

11. Do I feel emotions deeply?
12. Do I feel the emotions of others in my body?
13. Do I need time alone to recharge my energetic battery?
14. Do I get tingly sensations in my body for no reason?
15. Do I know the right path by the way it feels?

Claircognizance (intuitive information popping into your head)

16. Do I get great ideas out of nowhere?
17. Am I inspired on a regular basis?
18. Do I often make subtle assumptions that turn out to be true?
19. Am I good at problem solving?
20. Do I know things without being told?

Gone with the Wind Spread

To cast the coveted role of Scarlett O'Hara, 1,400 interviews and 90 screen tests were performed before Vivian Leigh was finally selected.

On This Day

Gone with the Wind premiered today in 1939 at the Loew's Grand Theater in Atlanta, Georgia. In a three-day period of celebration, the mayor declared it a holiday and gave city workers half the day off.

Summation of Spread

Gone with the Wind is an American classic about a manipulative woman and a roguish man's turbulent love affair in the American South during the Civil War. The Gone with the Wind Spread's questions are inspired by its characters and themes.

Cast Your Cards

Fix yourself a mint julep and cast your cards:

1. Scarlett: How am I tenacious?
2. Rhett: How am I dangerous?
3. Melanie: What helps me to find graciousness?
4. Ashley: How am I gallant?
5. Survival: What makes me a survivor?
6. War: What tears me apart?
7. Land: What endures?

Land is an essential theme in *Gone with the Wind*. Scarlett closes the film, after losing everything she holds dear, realizing that "land's the only thing that matters." Land connects with the suit of Pentacles. Pentacles are what is tangible and enduring.

Tea Leaf Reading Spread

On This Day

On this day in 1773, a midnight raid known as the Boston Tea Party took place. A group of colonists disguised as Mohawk Indians boarded three British ships, dumping 342 chests of tea into the harbor in an act of protest. The history of tea leaf reading began long before this famous act of defiance and continues in parlors and kitchens across the world today.

Summation of Spread

Tea leaf readings are always performed with loose-leaf tea. The querent drinks the tea and swirls the cup. The reader, looking into the cup, spies patterns of leaves that often reveal lettered initials as well as numbers. Animal shapes appear, creating marvelous storylines. The Tea Leaf Reading Spread is based on the animal symbolism used in tea leaf reading.

Cast Your Cards

Brew a delicious cup of tea and cast your cards:

1. Snake: What role does sexuality play in my life?
2. Cat: What is the role of magic in my life?
3. Dog: How loyal am I to those I love?
4. Mouse: What element is at play that I am unaware of?
5. Horse: What will be the nature of my work for the next month?
6. Bird: What is the higher lesson I must learn?

Tea absorbs odors around it. For odors on your hands—anything from garlic to fish—simply pour some cold tea over your fingers to remove the smell.

The Ace of Cups is related to tea leaf reading due to the gorgeous chalice depicted on the card. Understood as the font of inspiration—even as the Holy Grail—when this ace appears in a reading, it signifies an outpouring of emotion. What do you think you'd see if you peered inside the Ace of Cups?

Saturnalia Relieving Stress Spread

Gift giving, from gag gifts to toys for children, played a large role in the celebration of Saturnalia and may have been the inspiration for our modern exchange of holiday gifts.

The Four of Wands is the festival and celebration card. This card reminds you to put down your work. It is time to revel in all you have accomplished. The wall implies protection, and the outdoors connect this card with nature. Homecoming is implied, and the flowers aspect beauty, joy, and growth.

On This Day

Today is Roman Saturnalia, a festival of feasting, role reversal, free speech, gift giving, and revelry. Held in honor of the deity Saturn, who ruled over a preexisting Golden Age, the revelries of Saturnalia reflected a desire to return to that once mythical age.

Summation of Spread

Are you stressed out? The key theme of Saturnalia was letting go and having fun. Of all times of the year, the holidays are the season to let loose. If stress keeps creeping in, use this spread to lighten your load and invoke some Roman revelry for yourself.

Cast Your Cards

1. How can I replace a negative thought with a positive one?
2. Where can I find release?
3. How can I attract more positive people?
4. How do I make myself a priority?
5. What makes me laugh?
6. What helps me say no?
7. How can I connect with others?
8. How can I have more fun?

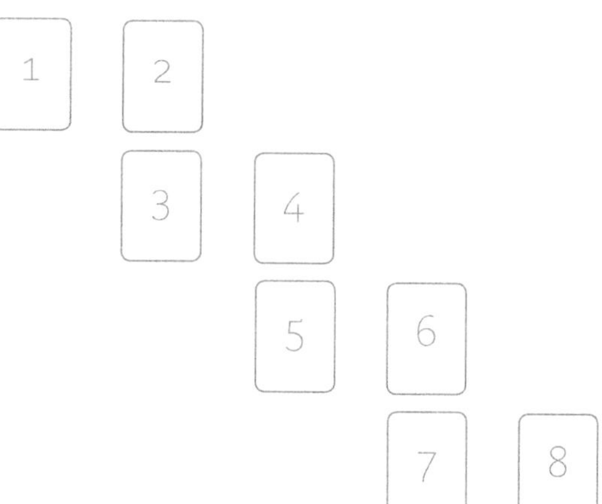

18 • December

Mistletoe Kiss Spread

On This Day

Pucker up: it is good luck to kiss under the mistletoe at this time of year. Although mistletoe is a parasitic plant that absorbs nutrients from tree trunks, it has been inspiring romance for generations across cultures.

Summation of Spread

This cheeky spread uses the holiday lore of kissing under a sprig of mistletoe to get to the bottom of who wants to kiss you and why, and whether you should agree to a liplock.

Cast Your Cards

Balm those lovely lips and cast the cards as follows:

1. Who wants to kiss me?
2. How do they act when they are close to me?
3. Is this person good for me?
4. How do they make me feel?
5. How do they really feel about me?
6. Could this be a long-term relationship?
7. Should I kiss them back?
8. Should I make the first move?

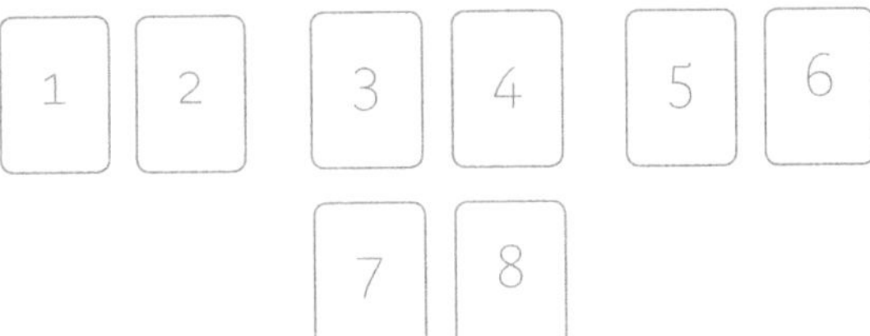

Hung around the neck, mistletoe is said to ward off evil spirits. Druids saw mistletoe as a gift fallen from heaven. The earliest documented case of mistletoe kissing was found in sixteenth-century England.

The Lovers card relates to kissing and all other acts of physical love. Make your choices well, as kissing can alter the course of your life.

December • 19

Get Rid of a Ghost Spread

Gettysburg, Pennsylvania, is considered one of the most haunted places in the United States, dripping in the blood of Civil War soldiers. New Orleans, seeped in the lore of the old South, earns another top spot in the nation's most ghostly, haunted, and unsettled locations.

In the Rider-Waite version of the Four of Cups, a hand appears like a ghostly specter reaching out to an unsuspecting fellow. All he needs to do is look up and notice the ghostly offering. The only question is, is the apparition friendly or fiendish?

On This Day

On this day in 1975, the Lutz family moved into 112 Ocean Avenue, aka the Amityville Horror house. The rest is history. *The Amityville Horror* book and film terrorized a generation.

Summation of Spread

Is something bumping in the night? Tarot can be a tool of communication, a survey of the circumstances surrounding the haunting, and can be used for suggestions on how to clear a space. This spread, inspired by one of the worst hauntings ever, aims to do that.

Cast Your Cards

Cast in the classic shape of protection, a cross:

1. What is the energy of the situation?
2. Who is haunting?
3. Why are they still here?
4. What history must I know?
5. How can I explain to the ghost they must move on?
6. How do I help them move toward the light?
7. How can I protect myself?
8. Do I need to bring in professionals?

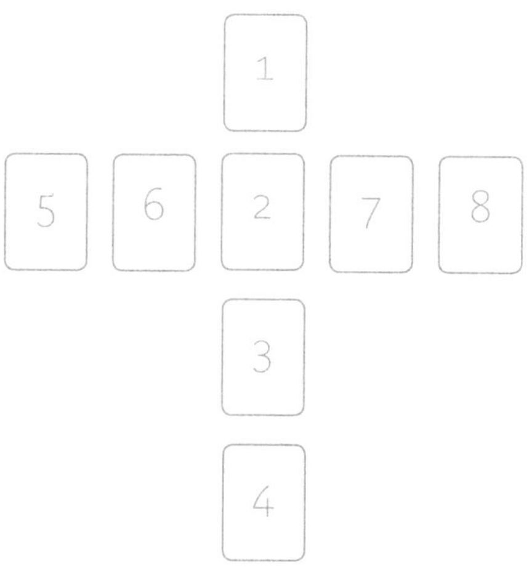

Shadow People Spread

Some paranormal investigators claim evidence points toward shadow people as being connected to extraterrestrials.

On This Day

The longest night of the year, the winter solstice, rapidly approaches. During these long, dark nights, it is the perfect time to contemplate a phenomenon you may have experienced or heard about. Shadow people, otherwise known as shadow men or shadow folk, are seen in a person's peripheral vision—sometimes just shadows quickly disappearing, some red eyed, and some report a man with a fedora-type hat.

Summation of Spread

The Shadow People Spread asks you to take a look into this phenomenon and discover what you can about these strange creatures. Then, the next time you see something out of the corner of your eye, you'll have a much better idea of what it could be.

Cast Your Cards

1. Why do they watch us?
2. What are they doing?
3. Is this my imagination?
4. Are they visitors from another dimension?
5. Should I attempt to communicate with them?
6. What do they want?
7. What do they want to tell me?

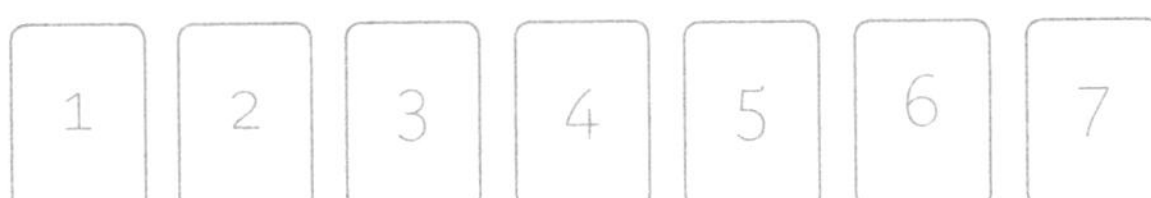

In the Seven of Cups, dreams float in the air while the figure watching may be in an altered state of consciousness. This card can also reflect illusions and false realities, a warning to carefully survey a situation.

Yule Four Sacred Directions Spread

The Yule log is burned on the eve of the solstice. Pagan goddesses were once worshiped in the log, later incorporated into fertility and protection spells. Ashes and charred bits of wood were kept until the following year.

The four cardinal directions are seen in both the Wheel of Fortune card and the World card, where creatures are depicted in the four corners.

On This Day

Yule, occurring between December 20 and 22, is a modern Wiccan sabbat falling on the winter solstice and also an alternative way to celebrate Christmas by recognizing its Pagan roots. It is also known as a Nordic Pagan festival.

Summation of Spread

Mark today's occasion by performing this special spread. It is in the dark nights of winter that we turn inward, cultivating the wisdom of the High Priestess. This spread makes use of the four sacred directions.

Cast Your Cards

Cast the cards in these directions to always know just where you stand:

East (Air/Swords)

1. What is new, fresh, and exciting in my life?
2. What is the best direction for me to take?

South (Fire/Wands)

3. What should I celebrate?
4. What can I share?

West (Water/Cups)

5. What can I let go of?
6. How do I slow down?

North (Earth/Pentacles)

7. What can my dreams teach me?
8. What do my elders want me to know?

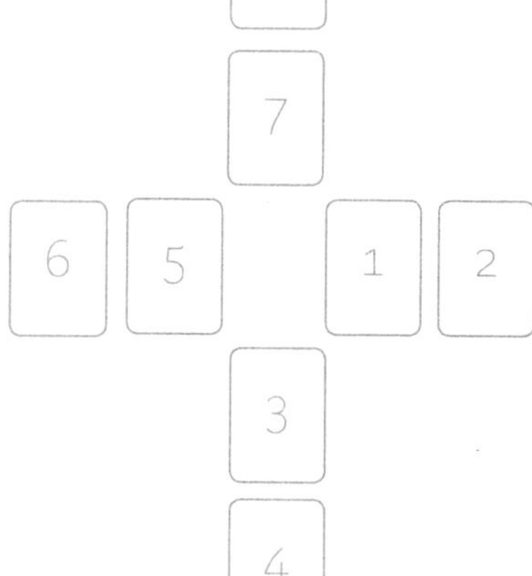

Qualities of Capricorn Spread

On This Day

Today marks the first day of the sign of Capricorn, the goat.

Summation of Spread

This spread is based on Capricorn's essential qualities: practical, ambitious, patient, humorous, determined, dominant, and successful.

Cast Your Cards

Cast in the shape of a C:

1. What do I need to be practical about?
2. What should I be ambitious about?
3. How can I cultivate more patience?
4. Where can I lighten up?
5. Where shall I place my determination?
6. In what ways am I dominant?
7. What is my definition of success?

Capricorn's ruling planet is Saturn, deep red is the primary color, the lucky day is Saturday, and the best location for success is anywhere secluded and conducive to concentration. Capricorn rules the tenth house of the zodiac, governing career and social status.

The most devious literary depictions of the Devil link him to Capricorn's preoccupation with earthly goods, wealth, and success, and would capitalize upon that quality to steal souls and enslave the greedy.

Santa's Reindeer Spread

The name Donner is German for "thunder," while the name Blitzen is German for "lightning."

On This Day

'Twas the Night Before Christmas was first published on this day in 1823 in the Troy, New York, *Sentinel* newspaper. It is largely responsible for many modern conceptions about Santa Claus and Christmas Eve.

Summation of Spread

This spread uses Santa's eight reindeer as inspiration for a fun holiday spread.

Cast Your Cards

Grab some hot chocolate and cast your cards as follows:

1. Dasher: What excites me?
2. Dancer: What makes me deliriously happy?
3. Prancer: What makes me walk tall?
4. Vixen: Who thinks I am a total sexpot?
5. Comet: How do I shine?
6. Cupid: Who loves me?
7. Donner: What must I yell from the rooftops?
8. Blitzen: What encourages my brilliance?

The Chariot connects to Santa's sleigh riding through a moonlit December night. The two sphinxes, in place of reindeer, represent the push and pull of choices we make flying along life's path.

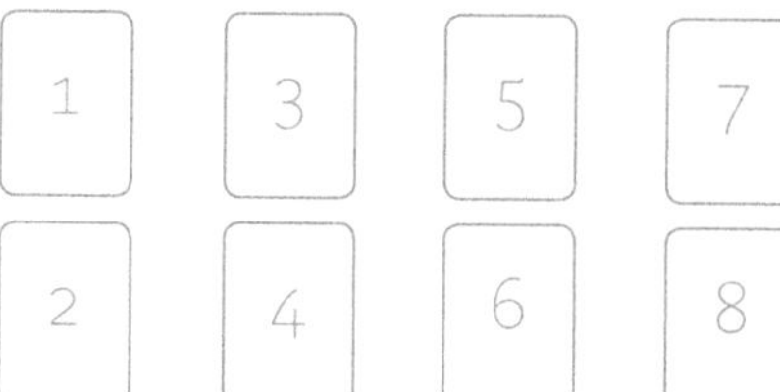

Wisdom of a Holiday Tree Spread

On This Day

Tonight St. Nick alights in his sleigh. Across the crisp night sky, he and his reindeer deliver presents to children around the world, leaving a trail of frost and glittering snow in his wake.

Summation of Spread

This evening brims with magic, hope, and belief. With no disruption and when all have deserted your room, focus on the tree. Examine its shape, color, and texture. How many shades of green does it have? Are the needles sharp or soft? Who lived in, on, or near the tree when it grew in the wild? How many wild storms and sunny days did this tree see before making its way to your home?

Cast Your Cards

After observing the tree, pull the following tarot cards to discover the spirit the tree expresses. Cast the cards like Santa doling out presents:

1. What magic do you bring to my house?
2. What do you represent as the year draws to a close?
3. What is the greatest gift I can give to those I love?
4. What can you help me bring to the new year?
5. What card is indicative of your spirit?
6. How can I honor you?

Christmas trees take an average of seven to ten years to mature. Green year-round, they are a vital sign of life and longevity and were thought to ward off evil spirits and illness.

The Queen of Pentacles is the gardener of the deck. Able to listen to the needs of animal, vegetable, and mineral and respond accordingly, all things flourish under her expert touch.

Opening a Gift Spread

The 12 days of Christmas had its origins in Christian tradition, with 12 days of religious devotion culminating with a large feast. American celebrations of these 12 days have mostly been forgotten in lieu of Santa Claus and the ever-popular New Year's Eve party.

The Six of Cups is the card of gifts from the heart and generosity to yourself and others. At times it is regarded as a walk down memory lane, especially appropriate as Christmas seems, more than any other day, a time for childhood reflections.

On This Day

Merry Christmas! Millions wake early today, tiptoeing toward decorated trees, eagerly unwrapping shiny gifts, luxuriating in the fun of toys, gifts, and delicious food. December 25 is actually the first day of the twelve days of Christmas, referenced in the popular holiday song of the same title.

Summation of Spread

This spread is an unexpected present for you. Unwrap to discover what the magic of the holiday season has in store for you all through the year.

Cast Your Cards

Take a moment to thank the tarot and honor yourself for all the soul-searching, divining, hard work, and effort you put forth this year. Make a solid promise to enjoy your day, relax, and be thankful for the goodness in your life.

Shuffle your deck. When satisfied, remove the top five cards without looking at them. Place the remaining deck in front of you. Build a house of cards—or, in this case, "wrapping" around your gift—by creating a five-card house around the deck.

When ready, begin to remove the "wrapping" of your deck, one card at a time. Contemplate each card as you remove and find the message within it. When you have removed all five cards, the deck remains in front of you.

The top card is your big gift. Turn it over to receive the gift tarot bestows upon you for the next year. This is your special card, containing a meaning just for you.

Kwanzaa Spread

On This Day

Today is the beginning of Kwanzaa, a holiday created by Maulana Karenga as the first specifically African American holiday. Its name derives from a Swahili phrase meaning "fruits of the harvest."

Summation of Spread

Kwanzaa celebrates seven principles for seven days. It is on these principles the Kwanzaa Spread is based.

Cast Your Cards

Cast your cards in the shape of Kwanzaa's seven-candle holder:

1. Unity: What binds me to my community?
2. Self-Determination: How do I define myself?
3. Collective Work and Responsibility: How well do I work with others?
4. Cooperative Economics: How can I support my community financially?
5. Purpose: What is my goal?
6. Creativity: What can I make better in my life?
7. Faith: What do I believe in?

Kwanzaa is not a religious holiday but a cultural holiday that can be practiced by anyone, and it is often celebrated alongside other holidays such as Christmas.

The Hierophant links to any brand of dogma or learning, religious or not. He stands for a shared cultural heritage and following certain disciplines. He reminds you of where to place your faith and why ritual and ceremony hold an important place in society.

Fear Spread

Bhutan remained tucked away in the eastern Himalayas, in total isolation from the rest of the world, until recently. This preserved its deep Buddhist traditions.

On This Day

Today is the Meeting of Nine Evils day in the Buddhist kingdom of Bhutan. The entire population stays home on this day. It is believed no one should venture outdoors and jobs done today would bear bad fruit, and it is the worst day to start a journey or begin a new venture. Any bad deed performed on this day multiplies negative karma.

Summation of Spread

What are you afraid of? This day has its place in Bhutanese culture and lasts only one day. It does not speak to any larger issue of fear and avoidance. The Fear Spread explores what locks you down in fear—what keeps you in stasis rather than moving forward with confidence.

The popular Celtic Cross Spread clearly shows the fear/desire connection in the 9 position of the spread. It stands as a reminder that people often fear what they desire most.

Cast Your Cards

Find a place of centeredness within before casting the cards. Performing this spread and following its direction may change your life for the better.

1. What do I want more than anything?
2. What do I stop myself from doing?
3. Why do I fear what I want?
4. Why don't I take my instincts seriously?
5. What would be the hardest thing for me to do?
6. How can I face my truth?
7. What does it mean to acknowledge my power?
8. What is my deepest fear?
9. What should I do?

28 • December

Westminster Abbey Spread

On This Day

London's Westminster Abbey opened on this day in 1065 and is the final resting place of over seventeen monarchs and the site of sixteen royal weddings. If every person laid within the abbey rose at once, it would be the greatest cocktail party the world has ever seen. Bones resting within include Geoffrey Chaucer, Charles Darwin, Isaac Newton, Charles Dickens, Thomas Hardy, Queen Elizabeth I, and Mary, Queen of Scots, among others.

Two ghosts have been reported in the abbey: a floating monk and a World War I soldier.

Summation of Spread

Ecclesiastical architecture's incredibly complex forms contain rich symbolism and meaning behind it. This spread is based on layout and architecture found within a Gothic-style building.

Cast Your Cards

Feel the power of ritual, smell the incense, and cast your cards:

1. The Nave (physical world): What does my world look like?
2. The Choir (world of the psyche, place of the soul): What does my heart look like?
3. Sanctuary (world of the spirit, splendid and brilliant): What is calling me?
4. The Altar (deity present in the sacrament): What do I worship?
5. The Rood Screen (threshold of consciousness): How do I interpret the world?
6. Aisle One (active): What am I actively engaged in?
7. Aisle Two (passive): What am I passive about?
8. Aisle Three (balanced): What is balanced?
9. What action should I take now that I know this?

6 8 7
5
4 9
3
2
1

The Hierophant, originally titled the Pope, is connected to cathedrals, abbeys, temples, and all religious architecture, as these are the dwelling and teaching places of hierophants.

December • 29

Three Witches of Macbeth Spread

On This Day

This day in 1888 marks the first performance of *Macbeth* at London's Lyceum Theater. Shakespeare may have written the witch characters to please King James, who harbored a fierce obsession with witches. The king instigated a mass witch hunt in Scotland and even wrote a book on the subject, *Daemonologie*.

Summation of Spread

The witches' prophecy sets *Macbeth*'s brutal plot in motion and inspires this spread's questions. Each witch represents a portion of life (past, present, future); she will whisper a secret in your ear to quietly keep. Do with the secret what you wish.

Cast Your Cards

Shuffle while repeating the phrase, "Double, double, boil and bubble." Cast your cards by the light of the moon, and pray you avoid the tragic fate of Macbeth:

Witch One

1. Your past.
2. Your challenge.
3. Your lesson.
4. Her secret to you.

Witch Two

5. Your present.
6. Your challenge.
7. Lesson learned.
8. Her secret to you.

Witch Three

9. Your Future.
10. Your challenge.
11. Your lesson learned.
12. Her secret to you.

Pamela Colman Smith painted sets at the Lyceum Theater, Lyceum actress Ellen Terry was the inspiration for the female on the Nine of Pentacles, and Bram Stoker was the Lyceum's business manager.

The tarot court cards thrive inside us as personality traits and potentials. Macbeth desires literal kinghood and meets a bloody end in his attempt to grasp the crown. Kings of every suit represent acting with authority, certainty, and decisive action.

Party Planning Spread

On This Day

Grab some champagne and stardust—there are more parties planned for New Year's Eve than any other day of the year. Chances are, tomorrow night you are giving or going to a party.

Summation of Spread

The Party Planning Spread was created to assist in party planning and thinking outside the box to throw a fabulous gathering. It can be performed for any occasion.

Cast Your Cards

Cast in the shape of a happy face to ensure your guests and you have a wonderful time:

1. What is the overall goal or theme of my party?
2. What food is best to serve?
3. What unique element can I add to make this extra special?
4. How can I be sure to relax and enjoy myself during the party?
5. What can I do to create a beautiful atmosphere?
6. What type of music should I select?
7. Is there anyone I forgot to invite?

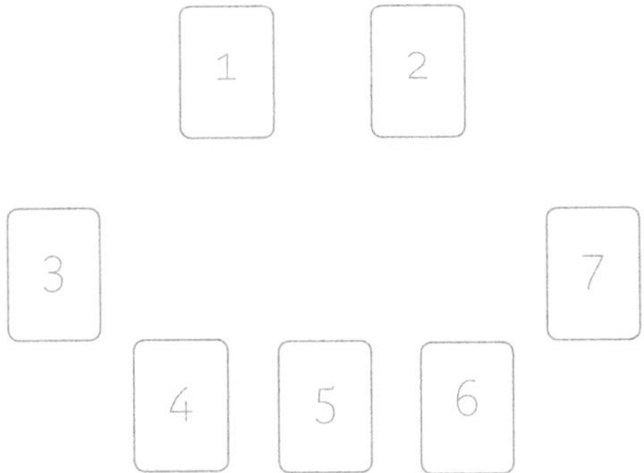

Noisemaking and fireworks on New Year's Eve are believed to have originated in ancient times, when noise and fire were believed to dispel evil spirits and attract good luck.

Emperor-like stability helps to smoothly run your gathering, as planning an excellent party comes down to good organization. This way, once it starts, the host can kick back, relax, and have fun too.

World Card Spread

In older decks, the four figures in the corner of the World card represented the four evangelists. They are also seen as the four corners of the physical world.

The World card is a direct vision of you operating at your highest possible potential. It represents an end and a beginning, completion, manifestation, success, and euphoria.

On This Day

Tonight is New Year's Eve. Beneath the champagne-and-glitter veneer, a deeper meaning exists. As the calendar changes, it is the night on which most of the world comes together to say goodbye to the old and ring in the new.

Summation of Spread

Tonight's yearly culmination is the perfect time to reflect with a spread based on the World card. This very special spread may be performed on any night of the year. Be sure to allow yourself adequate time and solitude.

Cast Your Cards

Use this spread to answer any question. Format your question before casting the spread or simply let the cards answer the questions posed. Pull the World card from your deck. Placing it in the center of the spread, cast your cards around it as follows:

1. Dancer: What can I celebrate?
2. Magic Wands: What have I conjured?
3. Wreath: What continues?
4. Androgyny: How do I find balance and expression?
5. Head (Aquarius): What am I thinking?
6. Lion (Leo): What is my passion?
7. Ox (Taurus): Where am I grounded?
8. Eagle (Scorpio): What have I changed?

Leap of Faith Spread

One Card

That's right: we're not done yet. Here's one more spread. It exists outside of calendar time and is not assigned to any day. This spread has the power to transform a life if action is taken.

But here's the thing: you are not allowed to perform this spread unless you are absolutely dedicated to acting upon the answer you receive. Think you can handle it? I know you can.

Ready?

Clear your mind.

Shuffle your deck.

Ask one simple question: *What would I do if I knew I would not fail?*

Focus directly on the card's message and do not look away until the answer has come to you.

If you want to let me know what happens after asking this or any other question, drop me a line at sashatarotdiva@gmail.com. I'm wildly curious about your journey with tarot and wish you the best of luck every single day of the year.

Happy casting!

Did you know the most succinct and helpful spreads are often ones only using a single card? One card provides laser-like focus when answering the question.

The Fool is ever ready to take a leap of faith. The Fool steps forward without fear. His results are always fresh, always new. Take his lesson to heart, leap every day, love with abandon and know that you are magic behind the cards.

Acknowledgments

Thank you...

To the ghosts of writers past, present, and future haunting the stacks of the New York Society Library. Particular thanks to the wonderful Marie Honan for graciously swinging the library's doors open.

To the electric and beautiful Edmee Cherdieu D'Alexis, Irina Peschan, Emily Naim, and Xavier Marzan for inspiring me and keeping me healthy and sane as the counterpoint to the daily physical stasis of writing and researching. Thank you for moving my body, soul, and imagination—and for shaking my ass when I'd been sitting on it all day.

To Julius Macwan, the rich velvety darkness and magic in a path.

To the lovely Barbara Moore for her encouragement and making the process easy.

To the unbelievably creative and talented Rebecca Zins, who brought this book to life.

To the wickedly fabulous J. L. Stermer.

To Rachel Pollack, Mary Greer, and Wald and Ruth Ann Amberstone for graciously offering gorgeous spreads for inclusion and for being my Hermetic beacons of tarot wisdom.

To handsome Bill and sweet Isabella: you are my everything.

Index of Spreads

Animals

Bird's-Eye View Spread JANUARY 5

Feline Mystery Spread OCTOBER 29

Horse Lovers Spread AUGUST 16

Lizard Wisdom Spread AUGUST 14

Loyalty of a Pooch Spread AUGUST 26

Pet Spread NOVEMBER 9

Snake Bite Spread FEBRUARY 10

Cinema

Back to the Future Spread NOVEMBER 12

Climb Every Mountain Spread JANUARY 26

Embrace Your Dark Side Spread SEPTEMBER 1

Evil Villain Spread JANUARY 25

Ghost-Hunting Spread JUNE 8

Gone with the Wind Spread DECEMBER 15

Indiana Jones Life's Adventure Spread JUNE 23

Little Mermaid Spread NOVEMBER 17

Mary Poppins Spread AUGUST 29

Creativity

Fairy Tales

Finance and Legal Matters

General Advice

Goddess and God

Grief, Sadness, and Moving Forward

Health and Well-Being

Holidays

Home and Family

Literary

Love and Romance

Mythical Creatures

Nature

Occult and Esoteric

Out of This World

Self-Knowledge and Personal Growth

Sensual

Spiritual

Tarot

Work and Career

To Write to the Author

If you wish to contact the author or would like more information about this book, please write to the author in care of Llewellyn Worldwide and we will forward your request. Both the author and the publisher appreciate hearing from you and learning of your enjoyment of this book and how it has helped you. Llewellyn Worldwide cannot guarantee that every letter written to the author can be answered, but all will be forwarded. Please write to:

Sasha Graham
c/o Llewellyn Worldwide
2143 Wooddale Drive
Woodbury, MN 55125-2989

Please enclose a self-addressed stamped envelope for reply or $1.00 to cover costs. If outside the USA, enclose an international postal reply coupon.

Many of Llewellyn's authors have websites with additional information and resources. For more information, please visit our website:

www.llewellyn.com